Bangladesh

Richard Plunkett
Alex Newton
Betsy Wagenhauser
Jon Murray

LONELY PLANET PUBLICATIONS
Melbourne • Oakland • London • Paris

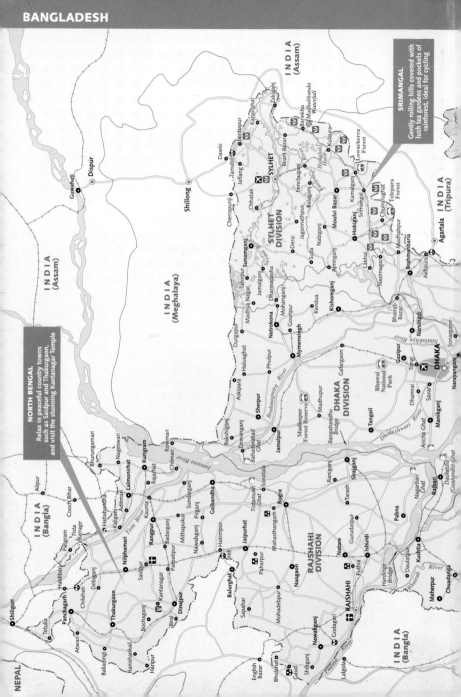

NORTH BENGAL
Relax in peaceful country towns such as Saidpur and Thakurgaon, and visit the stunning Kantanagar Temple

SRIMANGAL
Gently rolling hills covered with lush tea gardens and pockets of rainforest, ideal for cycling

INDIA
(Assam)

Guwahati
Dispur

Kamalganj
Barlekha
Madhabkunda
Waterfall
Zakiganj
Kanaighat
Tamabil
Jaintiapur
Dawki
Jaflong
Chhatak
SYLHET
Bean Bazar
Fenchuganj
Jagannathpur
Balaganj
Srimangal
Chunarughat
Lowacherra
Forest
Telepara
Forest
Moulvi Bazar
Hobiganj
Madhabpur
Brahmanbaria
Akhaura
Agartala

INDIA
(Tripura)

INDIA
(Assam)

INDIA
(Meghalaya)

Shillong

Cherrapunji

Nabiganj
Deral
Sulla
Almiganj
Lakhai
Nasimnagar
Madhabpur

SYLHET
DIVISION

Sunamganj
Tahirpur
Madhya Nagar
Jamalganj
Dharmapasha
Mohanganj
Goripur
Kendua
Kishoreganj
Narsingdi
Bharab
Bazar

Durgapur
Haluaghat
Askipara
Phulpur
Netrokona
Mymensingh

Sherpur
Dewanganj
Bahadurabad
Bakshiganj
Jamalpur

Gafargaon
Bhawal
National
Park
Gazipur
Tongi
DHAKA
Narayanganj
Sonargaon

Madhupur
Madhupur
Forest Reserve
Bangabandhu
Bridge
DHAKA
DIVISION
Dhamrai
Savar
Manikganj
Aricha
Ghat
Tangail
Dhaleswari River
Nagarbari
Ghat

Brahmaputra River

Jamuna River

Bhurungamari
Nageswari
Kurigram
Rajarhat
Rowmari
Chilmari
Sundarganj
Galbandha
Bogra
Ranjganj
Siragjanj
Tarash
Pabna
Ishurdi
Daulatdia
(Goalundo) Ghat
Rajbari

Alipur
Cooch Bihar
Patgram
Tista
Barrage
Hatibandha
Kalganj
Aditmari
Lalmonirhat
Kaunia
Rangpur
Pirganj
Mithapukur
Badargani
Pabatpur
Hakimpur
Mahasthangarh
Jaipurhat
Natore
Gurudaspur
Puthia
Kushtia
Meherpur
Chuadanga

Nilphamari
Saidpur
Kantanagar
Dinajpur
Biral
Balurghat
Paharpur
Naogaon
Mohadepur
RAJSHAHI
DIVISION
RAJSHAHI
Godagari

INDIA
(Bangla)

Shiliguri
Tetulia
Panchagarh
Chilahati
Haldibari
Debiganj
Bochaganj
Thakurgaon
Ranishankail
Haripur
Atwari
Baliadingi
Sapahar

INDIA
(Bangla)

Nawabganj
Shibganj
Gaud
English
Bazar
Bholahat
Lalgola

NEPAL

Tista River

Hardinge
Bridge
Bheramara
Daulatpur

Padma River

SRIMANGAL

Halda River

INDIA
(Mizoram)

MYANMAR
(BURMA)

CHITTAGONG HILL TRACTS

CHITTAGONG DIVISION

BARISAL DIVISION

KHULNA DIVISION

BAY OF BENGAL

Dighinala · Baghaichhari · Kasalong Forest Reserve · Khagrachhari · Langadu · Panchhari · Ramgarh · Mahalchhari · Manikchhari · Dighinala

Belaichhari · Sovalong Forest Reserve · Kaptai · Thega Forest Reserve · Ruma · Roangchhari · Thanchi · Keokradang (1230m) · Sangu Forest Reserve · Alikadam · Lama

Rangamati · Kaptai Lake · Kaptai · Bandarban · Chandanaish · Lohagara · Chakaria · Maheskhali · Ramu · Nikhyongchhari · Himachhari

Boalkhali · Anwara · Banshali · Kutubdia · Kutubdia Island · Maheskhali Island · Sonadia Island · Cox's Bazar · Ukhia · Teknaf · St Martin's Island

Parshuram · Feni · Dogarbhuiyan · Companiganj · Sitakunda · Hathazari · Fatikchhari · CHITTAGONG

Burichang · Comilla · Daudkandi · Laksam · Ramganj · Rajpur · Ramganj · Sonapur · Noakhali · Maijdi · Lakshmipur · Ramgati · Sonapur · Sandwip · Sandwip Island

Deoumari · Munshiganj · Matlab · Chandpur · Hainchar · Bhola · Hatiya

Faridpur · Magura · Jhenaidah · Madaripur · Shariatpur · Gournadi · Madhumati River · Mawa Ghat · Kaorakandi Ghat · Padma River

Tajumuddin · Manpura · Char Fasson · Mehendiganj · Bakerganj · BARISAL · Banaripara · Jhalakati · Rajpur · Bauphal · Patuakhali · Dashmina · Amtali · Barguna · Patharghata · Kalapara · Kuakata · Payra River · Patuakhali River

Narail · Jessore · Keshabpur · Kachua · Bagerhat · Mongla · Priojpur · Barna · Barisal

Benapole · Satkhira · Kalaroa · Shyamnagar · KHULNA · Dublar Island · Hiron Point · Kotka · Bhaleswari River

SUNDARBANS

Haridaspur · Hooghly River · Kolkata (Calcutta)

DHAKA–KHULNA BOAT TRIP
Cruise along rivers great and small through the lush Bangladesh heartland

SUNDARBANS
The world's greatest littoral mangrove forest, accessible by boats winding along myriad river channels

RANGAMATI
Lakeside hill station in the Chittagong Hill Tracts, capital of the Buddhist Chakma tribe

COX'S BAZAR
This bustling beach resort makes a handy base for neighbouring islands and towns

0   25   50km
0   15   30mi

ELEVATION
1500m
500m
200m
100m
0

Bangladesh
4th edition – November 2000
First published – November 1985

Published by
Lonely Planet Publications Pty Ltd ABN 36 005 607 983
90 Maribyrnong Street, Footscray, Victoria 3011, Australia

Lonely Planet Offices
Australia Locked Bag 1, Footscray, Victoria 3011
USA 150 Linden St, Oakland, CA 94607
UK 10a Spring Place, London NW5 3BH
France 1 rue du Dahomey, 75011 Paris

Photographs
All of the images in this guide are available for licensing from
Lonely Planet Images.
email: lpi@lonelyplanet.com.au

Front cover photograph
Rickshaw detail – rider's seat Dhaka (Richard I'Anson)

ISBN 0 86442 667 4

Printed by Colorcraft Ltd, Hong Kong

Contents – Text

DHAKA DIVISION 133

KHULNA DIVISION 151

BARISAL DIVISION

RAJSHAHI DIVISION 177

CHITTAGONG DIVISION 209

SYLHET DIVISION 242

LANGUAGE 258

GLOSSARY 263

INDEX 267

MAP LEGEND back page

METRIC CONVERSION inside back cover

Contents – Maps

The Authors

Richard Plunkett

Richard grew up on a farm in central Victoria. Before joining Lonely Planet he worked as a journalist for the *Age* in Melbourne, worked for several dodgy free travel rags in London and helped get the Australian edition of *The Big Issue* on its feet. Richard has worked on the LP guidebooks *India, Indian Himalaya, Delhi* and *Central Asia*; next up is *Turkey*. He used to live in Dublin but now lives out of a backpack.

Alex Newton

Raised in Madison, Georgia, Alex Newton joined the Peace Corps in the 1960s. Following almost three years' service in Guatemala as an agricultural adviser, he worked for four years on Wall St as a lawyer. He then studied development economics and French, and ended up in West Africa working on development assistance programs. Alex has also worked on LP's *West Africa* and *Central Africa* guidebooks.

He moved on to similar work in Ecuador, where he met Betsy Wagenhauser. Alex and Betsy lived and worked in Bangladesh for five years.

Betsy Wagenhauser

After eight years of teaching in Dallas, Texas, Betsy headed to Peru in 1986 and eventually ended up at the helm of the South American Explorers Club. For the next seven years, she worked extensively with independent travellers in Peru and Ecuador. She has written and photographed Insight Guides' *South America, Peru* and *Ecuador*, and co-authored two editions of *Climbing and Hiking in Ecuador* for Bradt Publications. For several years, she led trips for Wilderness Travel.

Jon Murray

Jon Murray spent time alternately travelling, and working with various publishing houses in Melbourne, Australia, before joining Lonely Planet as an editor then author. He co-authored Lonely Planet's *South Africa, Lesotho & Swaziland* and has written and updated books on destinations including West Africa, Papua New Guinea, Victoria and Hungary. He lives in country Victoria, on a bush block he shares with quite a few marsupials and a diminishing number of rabbits.

FROM THE AUTHOR

Richard Plunkett Firstly, thanks to all the people who helped me find the right bus, took me on long rickshaw rides for a pittance, threw open the doors to their houses and took my misunderstandings with good humour. Specifically I'd like to thank Runa and Yves Marre, Naimul Haq, Kazi Shamsul Haque, SM Nazrul Islam, Dr Pierre Claquin, Juliette Prodhon, Karen Middendorp, Hasan Mansur, Minhaj A Chowdhury and BICN in Dhaka; Malcolm Thetford, Kathy Walker, Craig Smith, Frunk the Punk and the Medecins sans Frontieres team in Cox's Bazar; Prasun Barua in Ramkot; David Buckley and Arinjoy Dhar in Chittagong; Eching Marma in Rangamati; Mohammed Quamrul Islam in Khulna; Mohammed Habibur Rahman in Dinajpur; Humayun Reza in Thakurgaon; Mustafa Hasan Sadik and Mohammed Hafizuddin in Bogra; the irrepressible Mr Razu in Srimangal; Basit and Shafique in Sylhet; and Mahfuzur Rahman in Comilla. Special thanks to Sajjad Hossain of Parbatipur.

Thanks to all the travellers who wrote in, but in particular to Loet Kuijpers and Gerda Hoeben, Bill Weir, Greg Bowles, Ian Lockwood, Graham Williams, Louise Jones and Chong Sau Long.

Thanks to Sharan, Adriana, Thalia, Adam and Geoff at LP, and especially to Shahara Ahmed for her help and advice. In Dublin thanks to Cameron Smith and David Wheelahan, and in London thanks to Jack Fagan.

This Book

Jose Santiago was the author of the very first edition of *Bangladesh*, way back in 1985. Jon Murray researched the second edition in 1990, Betsy Wagenhauser and Alex Newton were responsible for the third edition, researched in 1995, and this edition was researched by Richard Plunkett.

FROM THE PUBLISHER

This edition was produced in the Melbourne office of Lonely Planet. Adam Ford was the coordinating editor. Shahara Ahmed co-ordinated mapping and design. Jenny Mullaly, Brigitte Ellemor and Bethune Carmichael assisted Adam in the editing stakes, while Jody Whiteoak assisted Shahara with maps. Quentin Frayne created the language section, the cover was designed by Vicki Beale, and invaluable advice and expertise was once again provided by Sharan Kaur and Adriana Mammarella.

Thanks

Many thanks to the travellers who wrote to us and offered their helpful advice, interesting anecdotes and useful hints:

Adam ul Hoque, Aizura Hankin, Alicia Sometimes, Allison Allgaier, Ambereen Shahid, Annette Leyden, Astrid van Agthoven, BLH Ralph, Barnaby Aldrick, Ben & Suzanne Clackson, Amanda Kerley, Bob Haywood, Boydon Ralph, Cameron Kennedy, Carolyn Galbraith, Chandler Burr, Christian Loebbe, David Buckley, David Fischer, Eileen Thompson, Fabian & Julia Dilger, Geoffrey Hill, Grant Balfour, Grant Morrison, Hans de Waal, Heleen Smeyers, Ian Crowe, Imelda Almqvist-Berendsen, Ito Takumi, Jaroslaw Rudnik, Jason Cuthbert, Jasper Van Den Brink, Jennifer Denomy, Jennifer Kavanagh, John A Kerr, John Edwards, John Tracey Hemphill, John Winward, Jonathan Thomas, Josil C Gonzales, Julia Siler, Karin Crawford, Kelly Welch, Kerry Shaw, Leigh Wright, Liz Searle, Maaike Buis, Marti Joy Davidson, Martin Arker, Matthew D Rich, Mattias von Bromssen, Meyoung Cho, Michael Sauter, Nicholas Mleczko, Philip Shaw, Phillipe Cornelis, Pippa Howell, R. Buckminster Fuller, Ray Corness, Renee Weersma, Robin Upton, Sara Bennett, Scott Pegg, Sfaxi Hedi, Shahed Shuman, Shane McGrath, Steven Grimwade, Tamara Shie, Tim Walter, Tom Coates, Tomas Alonso, Tracy Odell, Trevor Sze, V Ramadass, Wouter Kersten, Yoichi Kaneko, Yvonne Briggs, Zahin Hasan, Zoe McEnally.

Foreword

ABOUT LONELY PLANET GUIDEBOOKS

The story begins with a classic travel adventure: Tony and Maureen Wheeler's 1972 journey across Europe and Asia to Australia. Useful information about the overland trail did not exist at that time, so Tony and Maureen published the first Lonely Planet guidebook to meet a growing need.

From a kitchen table, then from a tiny office in Melbourne (Australia), Lonely Planet has become the largest independent travel publisher in the world, an international company with offices in Melbourne, Oakland (USA), London (UK) and Paris (France).

Today Lonely Planet guidebooks cover the globe. There is an ever-growing list of books and there's information in a variety of forms and media. Some things haven't changed. The main aim is still to help make it possible for adventurous travellers to get out there – to explore and better understand the world.

At Lonely Planet we believe travellers can make a positive contribution to the countries they visit – if they respect their host communities and spend their money wisely. Since 1986 a percentage of the income from each book has been donated to aid projects and human rights campaigns.

Updates Lonely Planet thoroughly updates each guidebook as often as possible. This usually means there are around two years between editions, although for more unusual or more stable destinations the gap can be longer. Check the imprint page (following the colour map at the beginning of the book) for publication dates.

Between editions up-to-date information is available in two free newsletters – the paper *Planet Talk* and email *Comet* (to subscribe, contact any Lonely Planet office) – and on our Web site at www.lonelyplanet.com. The *Upgrades* section of the Web site covers a number of important and volatile destinations and is regularly updated by Lonely Planet authors. *Scoop* covers news and current affairs relevant to travellers. And, lastly, the *Thorn Tree* bulletin board and *Postcards* section of the site carry unverified, but fascinating, reports from travellers.

Correspondence The process of creating new editions begins with the letters, postcards and emails received from travellers. This correspondence often includes suggestions, criticisms and comments about the current editions. Interesting excerpts are immediately passed on via newsletters and the Web site, and everything goes to our authors to be verified when they're researching on the road. We're keen to get more feedback from organisations or individuals who represent communities visited by travellers.

> Lonely Planet gathers information for everyone who's curious about the planet – and especially for those who explore it first-hand. Through guidebooks, phrasebooks, activity guides, maps, literature, newsletters, image library, TV series and Web site we act as an information exchange for a worldwide community of travellers.

Research Authors aim to gather sufficient practical information to enable travellers to make informed choices and to make the mechanics of a journey run smoothly. They also research historical and cultural background to help enrich the travel experience and allow travellers to understand and respond appropriately to cultural and environmental issues.

Authors don't stay in every hotel because that would mean spending a couple of months in each medium-sized city and, no, they don't eat at every restaurant because that would mean stretching belts beyond capacity. They do visit hotels and restaurants to check standards and prices, but feedback based on readers' direct experiences can be very helpful.

Many of our authors work undercover, others aren't so secretive. None of them accept freebies in exchange for positive write-ups. And none of our guidebooks contain any advertising.

Production Authors submit their raw manuscripts and maps to offices in Australia, USA, UK or France. Editors and cartographers – all experienced travellers themselves – then begin the process of assembling the pieces. When the book finally hits the shops, some things are already out of date, we start getting feedback from readers and the process begins again …

WARNING & REQUEST

Things change – prices go up, schedules change, good places go bad and bad places go bankrupt – nothing stays the same. So, if you find things better or worse, recently opened or long since closed, please tell us and help make the next edition even more accurate and useful. We genuinely value all the feedback we receive. Julie Young coordinates a well-travelled team that reads and acknowledges every letter, postcard and email and ensures that every morsel of information finds its way to the appropriate authors, editors and cartographers for verification.

Everyone who writes to us will find their name in the next edition of the appropriate guidebook. They will also receive the latest issue of *Planet Talk*, our quarterly printed newsletter, or *Comet*, our monthly email newsletter. Subscriptions to both newsletters are free. The very best contributions will be rewarded with a free guidebook.

Excerpts from your correspondence may appear in new editions of Lonely Planet guidebooks, the Lonely Planet Web site, *Planet Talk* or *Comet*, so please let us know if you *don't* want your letter published or your name acknowledged.

Send all correspondence to the Lonely Planet office closest to you:

Australia: Locked Bag 1, Footscray, Victoria 3011
USA: 150 Linden St, Oakland, CA 94607
UK: 10A Spring Place, London NW5 3BH
France: 1 rue du Dahomey, 75011 Paris

Or email us at: talk2us@lonelyplanet.com.au

For news, views and updates see our Web site: www.lonelyplanet.com

HOW TO USE A LONELY PLANET GUIDEBOOK

The best way to use a Lonely Planet guidebook is any way you choose. At Lonely Planet we believe the most memorable travel experiences are often those that are unexpected, and the finest discoveries are those you make yourself. Guidebooks are not intended to be used as if they provide a detailed set of infallible instructions!

Contents All Lonely Planet guidebooks follow roughly the same format. The Facts about the Destination chapters or sections give background information ranging from history to weather. Facts for the Visitor gives practical information on issues like visas and health. Getting There & Away gives a brief starting point for researching travel to and from the destination. Getting Around gives an overview of the transport options when you arrive.

The peculiar demands of each destination determine how subsequent chapters are broken up, but some things remain constant. We always start with background, then proceed to sights, places to stay, places to eat, entertainment, getting there and away, and getting around information – in that order.

Heading Hierarchy Lonely Planet headings are used in a strict hierarchical structure that can be visualised as a set of Russian dolls. Each heading (and its following text) is encompassed by any preceding heading that is higher on the hierarchical ladder.

Entry Points We do not assume guidebooks will be read from beginning to end, but that people will dip into them. The traditional entry points are the list of contents and the index. In addition, however, some books have a complete list of maps and an index map illustrating map coverage.

There may also be a colour map that shows highlights. These highlights are dealt with in greater detail in the Facts for the Visitor chapter, along with planning questions and suggested itineraries. Each chapter covering a geographical region usually begins with a locator map and another list of highlights. Once you find something of interest in a list of highlights, turn to the index.

Maps Maps play a crucial role in Lonely Planet guidebooks and include a huge amount of information. A legend is printed on the back page. We seek to have complete consistency between maps and text, and to have every important place in the text captured on a map. Map key numbers usually start in the top left corner.

Although inclusion in a guidebook usually implies a recommendation, we cannot list every good place. Exclusion does not necessarily imply criticism. In fact there are a number of reasons why we might exclude a place – sometimes it is simply inappropriate to encourage an influx of travellers.

Introduction

Visiting Bangladesh, as one traveller put it, is not a journey – it's an experience. With 130 million people inhabiting some of the most productive land in the world, the country is as poor as it is luxuriously fertile. Bangladesh has had more than its share of misfortunes, but it doesn't deserve the image of a 'basket case'. The economy thrives on its hard-working labour force, non-government aid projects such as the Grameen Bank are models for the world, traditional arts find a place beside contemporary forms, and the resilience of the people is almost miraculous. Because it is one of the few Asian countries untouched by mass tourism, you can be sure that the hospitality of the Bangladeshi people is genuine.

Nestled snugly in the crook of the Bay of Bengal and braided by the fingers of the Ganges-Brahmaputra delta, Bangladesh offers interesting trips through the countryside on boats plying the country's innumerable rivers, reputedly the longest beach in the world, the largest littoral mangrove forest in the world, and archaeological sites of cultures dating back over 2000 years. As well, it has a fascinating architectural heritage, which includes the remains of ornately carved Hindu temples, beautiful centuries-old mosques and decaying 'Gone with the Wind' mansions of 19th century maharajas and nawabs.

In winter, when most people visit, rural Bangladesh has an atmosphere all its own, a kind of tropical Gothic; waving fields of ripening rice, eerily rustling stands of bamboo, impeccably clean villages sheltering under columns of tall palm trees, and

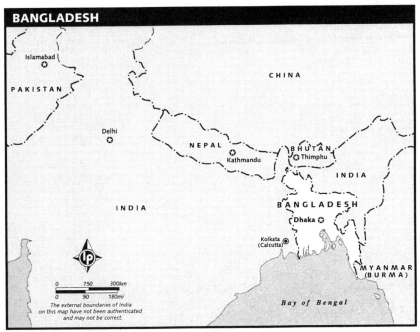

BANGLADESH

rickshaw drivers swathed in cloaks against the cool damp air.

While the country is mostly riverine plains and flat, making it fantastic for cycling, there are two major hilly areas, both of which are, relatively speaking, sparsely populated. One is around the borders of the north-east, where beautifully manicured tea estates dot the countryside. The other is the Chittagong Hill Tracts in the south-east, a surprisingly large area of rolling hills covered with verdant tropical forests and populated with colourfully dressed tribal people, only recently accessible to visitors.

In the centre of the country, just below the junction of the two major rivers of the subcontinent, the Ganges (called the Padma in Bangladesh) and the Brahmaputra (Jamuna), is the capital Dhaka. While it is undeniably messy and crowded, the vibrant markets, historic buildings, museums and a boat trip on one of the surrounding rivers make it a highlight of any visit. For the more adventurous a ride through the Old City on one of the city's 600,000-odd rickshaws is fascinating.

Travel by bus, train or aeroplane is quick, easy and amazingly cheap, with only short distances to be covered to reach markedly different environments. But for those who prefer a different kind of adventure or moving at a more leisurely pace, enjoying rural life along the way, travel by boat is the only way to go.

Travellers looking for adventure in unexplored areas are missing the point by joining the hordes in India and Nepal. While Bangladesh can't offer quite the variety of cultures and ancient monuments, life along the rivers is fascinating, the countryside of Bangladesh is lush and beautiful, and the air is by far cleaner (with the notable exception of the crowded streets of Dhaka). The backwoods villages of the hill regions await discovery. The country is also friendly – travellers crossing from India have been agreeably surprised to find border officials offering them cups of tea rather than reams of forms to fill in. Foreigners attract a fair amount of staring, but unlike India there aren't irritating touts and salesmen dogging your every step.

The National Tourist Corporation's former slogan acknowledges the country's dearth of visitors, but like them you could do worse than use it to your advantage – 'Come to Bangladesh before the tourists'.

Facts about Bangladesh

HISTORY

The history of Bangladesh has been one of extremes: turmoil and peace, prosperity and destitution. It has thrived in the glow of cultural splendour and suffered the ravages of war. Throughout its tumultuous history it has known internal warfare, suffered invasion upon invasion, witnessed the rise and fall of mighty empires and several religions, and benefited from the trade and culture brought from foreign lands.

Some medieval European geographers located paradise at the mouth of the Ganges, and although paradise was not found here, Bengal was probably the wealthiest part of the subcontinent until the 16th century.

Stretching from the lower reaches of the Ganges River on the Bay of Bengal, and north almost to the foothills of the Himalaya, the Bengal region of the subcontinent is the gateway to Myanmar (Burma) and South-East Asia, making control over it vital to successive Indian empires. Its strategic position has ensured a place in the political, cultural and religious conflicts and developments of the subcontinent through the millennia.

Early History

Perhaps the earliest mention of the region is in the 9th century BC Hindu epic the *Mahabharata*, which tells of Prince Bhima's conquest of eastern India, including Varendra, an ancient kingdom in what is now Bangladesh. References are made to several ethnic groups inhabiting the area (eg, the Pundras, Vangas and Suhmas). By the 5th and 6th centuries BC, Aryan culture had spread eastward from the Indus River in Pakistan to dominate most of northern India. Although culturally homogeneous, the Bengal region comprised small, squabbling states until the formation of the powerful kingdom of Magadha, with its capital at Patna on the Ganges.

The region's history becomes less obscure from 325 BC, when Alexander the Great set upon India after his conquest of Persia. Alerted to this formidable threat, troops from the lower Ganges, known to the Greeks as Gangaridae, united under a non-Aryan native king of the Nanda dynasty. This huge army of infantry, supported by 4000 trained war elephants and horses, was too much for Alexander's troops, who were already struggling with the oppressive heat and lack of supplies. Without giving battle Alexander retreated from India, never to return.

Chandragupta Maurya, fired by tales of the exploits of Alexander the Great, ascended the Magadhan throne and set about creating an empire, then known as Pundravardhana Bhukti. He succeeded, and it eventually spread right across northern India under his grandson, the Emperor Ashoka, one of the classic figures of Indian history. Ashoka's conversion to Buddhism in 262 BC had a long-lasting effect on the religious life of the area. Even as late as the 7th century AD, Chinese pilgrims still found Buddhism prevalent in Bengal, though it was in conflict with Hinduism.

The Mauryan empire, under Ashoka, controlled more of India than any subsequent ruler prior to the British. Following his death the empire went into a rapid decline and finally collapsed in 184 BC. It was not until the 4th century AD that northern India, including Bengal, was once again united under imperial rule, this time by the Guptas, during whose reign the arts flourished and Buddhism reached its zenith. Except for the kingdom of Sumatata, the various independent principalities in Bengal came to an end with the rise of the Gupta dynasty.

The Guptas succumbed to a wave of White Hun invasions, and in the 6th century AD Sasanaka founded the Gauda empire in Bengal. It was eventually overthrown by the warrior-king Sri Harsa, whose empire ruled the Bengal area until it was toppled into anarchy and chaos in the 8th century

AD. Buddhism was in decline and Hinduism was experiencing a resurgence; over the next couple of centuries, while northern India broke into a number of separate kingdoms, the Bengal area established a separate political identity, but was without any central authority to control the disrupting elements within the realm.

Out of the intolerably chaotic political and social conditions, a Kshatriya tribal chief who came from Varendra, Gopala, ultimately emerged as an elected leader. He introduced a settled government and became the founding figure of the Pala dynasty (8th to 12th centuries AD). The Palas were Buddhists who claimed to have descended from the sea and the sun. They continued their royal patronage of Buddhism while politically tolerating the Hindus. Dharmapala succeeded his father Gopala and established the gigantic Somapura Vihara in Varendra, known today as the ruins of Paharpur Monastery.

During the 9th century the Pala dynasty was considerably weakened by a line of imbecile kings, and in the 11th century the Hindu Senas from south India replaced the Palas as rulers in Bengal. While Bengali Hinduism did absorb Buddhist influences, such as the esoteric Tantric practices incorporated into the Kali and Vishnu cults, Buddhism was crushed by the Sena dynasty. Surviving Buddhists retreated to the Chittagong area, where a Bengali Buddhist community exists today. In less than a century the Senas themselves were swamped by the tide of Islam.

The Muslim Period

Muslim power had been creeping towards India from the Middle East for centuries before Mohammed Bakhtiar, a Khilji from the Turkistan region of Central Asia, appeared on the scene. With only 20 men, by means of a bold and clever stratagem, Bakhtiar captured Bengal in 1199 and brought the area under the rule of the sultanate of Delhi, the centre of Muslim power that already held sway over most of northern India.

For a short period the Mameluk sultanate was established in Bengal, until the Tughlaq dynasty overthrew it in 1320. The Tughlaqs extended their rule over much of the Indian Subcontinent, until their regime was exhausted by the relentless conflict of warfare. Another wave of Muslim invaders from Central Asia, this time the armies of Timur (better known in the west as Tamerlane) defeated the Tughlaqs in 1398 and their dynasty expired soon after.

The influx of Muslims from Central Asia, and of Persians from Shiraz continued, and under the Muslims Bengal entered a new era. Cities developed, palaces sprang up (as did forts, mosques, mausoleums and gardens), roads and bridges were constructed, and prosperity brought a new cultural life.

It's a puzzle why this distant corner of Muslim-ruled India became an Islamic stronghold while the heartland around Delhi stayed mostly Hindu. One reason could be that in the jungles of eastern Bengal, on the fringe of the old Hindu civilisations, the people were mostly animists or followed basic forms of Hinduism, and so were more easily converted to Islam. Another theory suggests that the slow shift eastwards by the Ganges after the Muslim conquest holds the key. As new territories fit for growing rice appeared, the Muslim rulers were able to convert the people with gifts of land. The new river trade routes also brought eastern Bengal into closer contact with Arab traders on the Bay of Bengal; many great Muslim teachers arrived by sea this way. In any case, over the centuries the area around the old mouth of the Ganges (the Hooghly, which flows through Kolkata) remained predominantly Hindu, while the area around the new delta became predominantly Muslim.

The Afghans arrived in 1520 and contributed further to the urbanisation of the land. In particular, the city of Gaud on the Indian border emerged as a cosmopolitan metropolis.

In 1526 the sultanate of Delhi was overthrown by Babur, a descendant of both Timur and Genghis Khan, and the Mughal empire under this Central Asian leader reached out to encompass most of northern India. It was not until 1576, however, that

Babur's grandson Akbar finally defeated the Bengali sultan Daud Karrani at the Battle of Tukaroi and Bengal became a province of the Mughal empire.

Gaud remained the centre of power in Bengal until it was decided to move the capital to Dhaka in 1608. Under the Mughal viceroys, urbanisation continued, art and literature flourished, overland trade expanded and Bengal was opened to world maritime trade. Intellectual and cultural life at this time was influenced mainly by the Persians, particularly by the Sufis, Muslim mystics who seek direct experience of divine love and wisdom, and who recite, or write, mystical love poetry.

Glorious at its peak, the Mughal empire ushered in another golden age in India, only to be outdone by the country's final great empire – the British Raj.

The European Period

With the growth of international maritime trade and commerce, Europeans began to establish themselves in the region. The Portuguese captured Goa in western India in 1510, and were trading in Chittagong in 1536. The Dutch followed in 1615, the British in 1651 and the French in 1674. After a few initial setbacks – the Portuguese were ousted from their foothold in 1633 by Bengali opposition, and the British failed in an attempt to capture Chittagong in 1686 – the European juggernaut rolled into Bangladesh and from then on it was unstoppable.

The four countries tussled for influence for decades, but it was the British East India Company that prevailed. This London-based trading firm had been granted a royal charter by Queen Elizabeth I in 1600, giving them a monopoly over British trade with India. The British managed to negotiate trade terms with the authorities in Bengal, and established a fortified trading post at Calcutta, dealing mainly in cotton, raw silk, yarn, sugar and saltpetre.

Following the death of Aurangzeb in 1707 Mughal power declined, and the provincial governors began to assume autonomy. In 1740 Sarfaraz Khan, the viceroy of the three provinces of Bengal, Orissa and Bihar, was overthrown by Ali Vardi Khan, a subordinate official in charge of the administration of Bihar. This heralded the rise of the independent dynasty of the nawab (Muslim prince) of Bengal, with whom the Englishman Robert Clive came in contact.

The East India Company's trading post at Calcutta was a thriving concern by now and Calcutta was fast becoming a great centre of trade and commerce. The role of Robert Clive in establishing British control over Bengal is well known. Originally a mere clerk with the East India Company, he rose to become the local head of the Company and the effective ruler of the province after a series of wars against local potentates.

In 1756 Suraj-ud-Daula, the 21-year-old nawab of Bengal, attacked the British settlement of Calcutta. The British inhabitants unlucky enough not to escape were packed into an underground cellar, where most of them suffocated during the night in the infamous 'Black Hole of Calcutta'.

A year later Clive retook Calcutta and defeated Suraj-ud-Daula in the Battle of Plassey. As a result the British became the de facto rulers of Bengal, and the East India Company governed the province through puppet nawabs, effectively exercising its raj (sovereignty) over the province. This was the start of British government intervention in Indian affairs. The company's control over Bengal aroused concern in London, leading to the passage of an act regulating its power. Following the Indian Uprising of 1857, during which Bengal had been used as a secure base for British operations, the British government took control of India from the East India Company.

British Raj

Even the Raj machine found that it didn't escape the influence of the area. The British engineers found that the rivers were sometimes beyond their taming, and the earlier British settlers in this 'backwater' came to be considered not quite *pukka* (genuine) by their more proper counterparts elsewhere in India. Quite a number of the chaps 'went native' (ie, intermarried with Bengalis and attempted closer links between the British and Bengali cultures) and they even spent their time playing a silly game they called polo.

It has been said that the British Raj ushered Bengal into another period of growth and development, but historians hotly dispute this. They consider the dictatorial agricultural policies of the British in east Bengal, and the establishment of the *zamindar* (feudal landowner) system, as being responsible for draining the country of its wealth, damaging the social fabric and directly contributing to today's desperate conditions.

Zamindars were independent rent collectors who administered areas under their jurisdiction for the Raj. Although many of them were given or adopted the title of raja (ruler or landlord), they were really entrepreneurs. In addition, they were nearly always Hindus, which grated on the predominantly Muslim peasantry of east Bengal.

The introduction of the English language and the British educational, administrative and judicial systems established an organisational and social structure unparalleled in Bengal in its breadth and dominance. There were new buildings, roads, bridges, a railway system and continued urbanisation. Calcutta became one of the most important centres of commerce, education, culture and the arts on the subcontinent.

The establishment of the British Raj was a relief to the Hindus but a catastrophe for the Muslims. Hindus cooperated with the British, entering British educational institutions and studying the English language. Muslims, on the other hand, refused to cooperate, preferring to remain landlords and farmers.

Bengal's religious dichotomy formed a significant basis for future conflict. Unlike the rest of India, the people of Bengal were predominantly Muslim. Islamic fervour against the British was strong, flaring up whenever any crop or other local product was made uneconomic by government policy.

At the end of the 19th century Bengal was an overgrown province of 78 million people, comprising Bengal, Bihar and Orissa. A massive earthquake struck the country in 1897, causing havoc over large areas of present-day Bangladesh. Many buildings and stately *rajbaris* (zamindari palaces) that caved in were never repaired; today they are decaying historical monuments. In 1905 Lord Curzon, the Viceroy of India, decided to partition Bengal for administrative purposes into East Bengal and Assam, and West Bengal, Bihar and Orissa. The new province of East Bengal and Assam, with a population of 31 million people, had its capital at Dhaka.

The Indian National Congress, which had been formed in 1885, was originally supported by both Hindus and Muslims. But the division of Bengal was seen as a religious partition, prompting the formation of the All India Muslim League in the following year. Its purpose was the protection of Muslim interests, as the Congress was increasingly being perceived as a Hindu power group.

The Brahmaputra and the Padma Rivers physically defined this first partition of Bengal. East Bengal briefly prospered, Dhaka resumed its old status as capital and Chittagong became an important sea port.

Although the partition of Bengal was initially opposed by Muslims and Hindus alike, when the divided province was reunited in 1912, opinions among Muslims had shifted. They feared a return to social, economic and political dominance by Hindus, and pressed for Muslim autonomy.

At the same time the imperial capital of the British Raj was moved to Delhi, and although Calcutta remained an important commercial, cultural and political centre, the rest of Bengal was neglected. Political agitation increased over the next few decades as did the violent enmity between Muslims and Hindus. Although there was a movement in favour of a united Bengal, most Muslims supported repartition and the formation of a Muslim state separate from India.

Bengal's lowest point came in 1943, when five million people starved to death in the Great Bengal Famine. As is usually the case, natural disaster was only part of the problem. The crops had failed due to drought for two seasons, but the Raj authorities were still buying up all the food grain for the Allied forces fighting in WWII. The railway rolling stock had been taken over by the army, and river freighters had been sunk to prevent them being captured by the Japanese. The cities were overwhelmed with starving refugees, Bengal's reputation for dire poverty became fixed and the last shreds of respect for the British administration disappeared.

Independence

As the Indian National Congress continued to press for self-rule for India, the British began to map out a path to independence. At the close of WWII it was clear that European colonialism had run its course and Indian independence was inevitable. Moreover, the UK no longer had the desire or the power to maintain its vast empire, and a major problem had developed within India itself.

The large Muslim minority realised that an independent India would be a nation dominated by Hindus and that despite Mahatma Gandhi's even-handed approach, other Hindu politicians would not be so accommodating or tolerant. The country was divided on purely religious grounds with the Muslim League headed by Mohammed Ali Jinnah representing the majority of Muslims, and the Indian Congress Party, led by Jawaharlal Nehru, commanding the Hindu population.

India and Pakistan achieved independence in 1947 but the struggle after the war had been bitter, especially in Bengal where the fight for self-government was complicated by the conflict between Hindus and Muslims. The British realised that any agreement between the Muslim League and the Indian National Congress was impossible, so the viceroy, Lord Mountbatten, seeing no other option, decided to partition the subcontinent. The Muslim League hoped that East Pakistan would have been much larger, incorporating what is now northeastern India and the state of Bangla (West Bengal). When the Boundary Commission made its decisions public, Jinnah described the territory that was allocated to Pakistan as 'moth-eaten'.

East Pakistan

The two overwhelmingly Muslim regions of pre-partition India were on the exact opposite sides of the subcontinent, in Bengal and the Punjab. In Bengal the situation was complicated by Calcutta, with its Hindu majority. There, jute mills and a developed port contrasted with Muslim-dominated East Bengal, also a major jute producer, but with virtually no manufacturing or port facilities.

The Muslim League's demand for an independent Muslim home state was realised with the creation of Pakistan in 1947. This was achieved by establishing two separate regions, East and West, on opposite sides of Indian territory. For months, a huge and bloody exodus took place as Hindus moved to India and Muslims moved to East or West Pakistan.

But despite the fact that support for the creation of Pakistan was based on Islamic solidarity, the two halves of the new state had little else in common. The instability of the arrangement was obvious, not only in the geographical sense, but for economic, political and social reasons as well.

The people living in East Pakistan spoke Bangla, while the West Pakistanis spoke Urdu, Pushtu, Punjabi and Sindhi; the East Pakistani diet was mainly fish and rice while that of the West Pakistanis was meat and wheat.

The country was administered from West Pakistan, which tended to direct foreign aid and other revenues to itself, even though East Pakistan had more people and produced most of the cash crops. From early on these differences and inequalities stirred up a sense of Bengali nationalism that had not been reckoned with in the struggle for Muslim independence.

The Bengalis of East Pakistan had no desire to play a subordinate role to the West Pakistanis. The resentment was exacerbated by the fact that when the British left, most of the Hindus in the administrative service fled en masse to India, leaving a vacuum that could only be filled by trained West Pakistanis and not by the local Muslims. Nor did West Pakistanis show a great deal of respect for Bengalis – the president of

Pakistan, a West Pakistani, reportedly said that Bengalis 'have all the inhibitions of downtrodden races and have not yet found it possible to adjust... to freedom'. There was dissatisfaction in all spheres of Bengali life.

When the Pakistani government declared that 'Urdu and only Urdu' would be the national language, a language that virtually no-one in East Bengal knew, the Bengalis decided that this was the last straw. The primacy given to Urdu resulted in the creation of the Bangla Language Movement, which rapidly became a Bengali national movement and the real beginning of the move towards independence. There were riots in Dhaka, and on 21 February 1952, 12 students were killed by the Pakistani army (see the boxed text 'Politics & Students' later in this chapter for more information). Pakistan's fledgling democracy gave way to military government and martial law.

The Awami League, led by Sheikh (pronounced 'shake') Mujibur Rahman, emerged as the national political party in East Pakistan, and the Language Movement became its ideological underpinning. During the 1960s the Awami League grew more powerful and instigated numerous protests against domination by West Pakistan.

The catastrophic cyclone of 1970 devastated East Pakistan, killing some half a million people, and while foreign aid poured in, the Pakistani government appeared to do little. Support for the Awami League peaked and in the 1971 national elections it won 167 of the 313 seats, a clear majority. In East Pakistan it won all the seats except one (which was held by Tridiv Roy, the raja of the Buddhist Chakma tribe of the Chittagong Hill Tracts). Constitutionally the Awami League should have formed the government of all Pakistan, but the president, faced with this unacceptable result, postponed the opening of the National Assembly.

Riots and *hartals* (strikes) broke out in East Pakistan. At Chittagong, a clash between civilians and soldiers left 55 Bengalis dead. When President Khan secretly returned to West Pakistan in March 1971 after talks with Sheikh Mujib had failed,

Sheikh Mujib was arrested and Pakistani troops went on the rampage throughout East Pakistan, burning down villages, looting shops and homes, and indiscriminately slaughtering civilians.

The Liberation War

At the Race Course rally of 7 March 1971 in Dhaka (at what is now Ramna Park), Sheikh Mujib stopped just short of declaring East Pakistan independent. In reality, however, Bangladesh (land of the Bangla speakers) was born on this day. Sheikh Mujib was arrested on 26 March, taken to West Pakistan and thrown into jail. This ignited the smouldering rebellion in East Pakistan.

When the Mukti Bahini (Bangladesh Freedom Fighters) captured the Chittagong radio station, Ziaur Rahman announced the birth of the new country and called upon its people to resist the Pakistani army. President Khan responded by sending more troops to quell the rebellion. In a classic piece of misjudgment, he had made earlier claims that 'the autonomy issue has been created by a few intellectuals. A few thousand dead in Dhaka and East Pakistan will be quiet soon'.

The ensuing war was a short but bloody one. General Tikka Khan, 'the Butcher of Baluchistan', was instructed to rid the country of Sheikh Mujib's supporters and his troops began the systematic slaughter of the Mukti Bahini and other 'subversive' elements such as intellectuals and Hindus.

A few army units made up of East Pakistanis rebelled in time to avoid capture, but they were heavily outnumbered and without supplies. By June the struggle became a guerrilla war, with more and more civilians joining the Mukti Bahini. With the whole countryside against them, the Pakistani army's tactics became more brutal. Napalm was used against villages.

West Pakistan had taken Dhaka and secured other major cities, and by November 1971 the whole country suffered the burden of the occupying army. The searches, looting, rape and slaughter of civilians continued, and during the nine months from the end of March 1971, 10 million people fled

The Slaughter of the Intellectuals

Immediately following Sheikh Mujib's arrest on March 26 1971, all hell broke out. Blaming the Hindu intellectuals for fomenting the rebellion, the generals immediately sent their tanks to Dhaka University and began firing into the halls, killing students. This was followed by the shelling of Hindu neighbourhoods and a selective search for intellectuals, business people and other alleged subversive elements. One by one they were captured, hauled outside the city and shot in cold blood. Over the ensuing months, the Pakistani soldiers took their vicious search for subversives to every village. By then, if there had ever been a distinction made between intellectuals and Hindus, it was gone. When captured, men were forced to lift their lungis to reveal if they were circumcised; if not, they were slaughtered.

While estimates vary widely, probably close to a million people died in the conflict. Years later, General Tikka Khan, who was initially in command during the Savar slaughter, admitted to murdering 'only' 35,000 intellectuals. And the murderers were never punished; indeed today they are heroes. Tikka, for example, retired in comfort and years later, in 1989, this 'grand old man' of the Pakistani army, as he was affectionately called, became the Governor-General of Punjab Province.

to refugee camps in India. Rape was so widespread and systematic that it appeared to be an attempt to change the racial makeup of the country. Clouds of vultures cast ghastly shadows all over the country.

Border clashes between Pakistan and India became more frequent as the Mukti Bahini, whose forces were being trained and equipped by India, were using the border as a pressure valve against Pakistan's onslaught. Finally, the Pakistani air force made a pre-emptive attack on Indian forces on 3 December 1971 and it was open warfare. The end came quickly. Indian troops crossed the border, liberated Jessore on 7 December and prepared to take Dhaka. The West Pakistani army was being attacked from the west by the Indian army, from the north and east by the Mukti Bahini and from all quarters by the civilian population.

It's a chilling insight into the military mentality that, during a particularly savage war, the Indian commander's surrender demand to his old school chum commanding the Pakistani army should be: 'My dear Abdullah, I am here. The game is up. I suggest that you give yourself up to me'.

By 14 December the Indian victory was complete, and Pakistan's General Niazi signed the surrender agreement on 16 December. Some Bangladeshi historians think that this was in the nick of time, as the US navy's 7th Fleet was steaming up the Bay of Bengal. They were coming ostensibly to evacuate Americans from Dhaka but it was feared that the real purpose was to aid their Pakistani allies.

On his release from jail, Sheikh Mujib took over the reins of government, announcing the establishment of the world's 139th country.

Bangladesh

The People's Republic of Bangladesh was a country born into chaos; shattered by war, with a ruined economy and a totally disrupted communications system, the country seemed fated to continuing disaster. Pakistan's infamous pogrom against intellectuals had almost destroyed the new country's educated class and it appeared that Sheikh Mujib, though a skilful leader in wartime, did not have the peacetime ability to heal the wounds.

The famine of 1973–74 set the war-ravaged land and its people back even more. A state of emergency was declared in 1974 and Sheikh Mujib proclaimed himself president. The abuses and corrupt practices of politicians and their relatives, however, prompted a military coup on 15 August 1975. Sheikh Mujib and his entire household were slaughtered. Only two daughters who were out of the country at the time survived. One was Sheikh Hasina, who later became prime minister.

Khandakar Mushtaq Ahmed became president, declared martial law and banned all political activities. A counter-coup four months later brought Brigadier Khalid Musharaf into power – for four days. He was overthrown and killed, and power was assumed by a military triumvirate led by Abusadet Mohammed Sayem, the Chief Justice of the Supreme Court. As president and chief martial law administrator, he governed for nearly two years, with the heads of the armed services as his deputies.

In late 1976 the head of the army General Ziaur Rahman, who had led the Mukti Bahini during the Liberation War, took over as martial law administrator and, following the resignation of President Sayem in April 1977, assumed the presidency.

The overwhelming victory of President Zia (as Ziaur Rahman was popularly known) in the 1978 presidential poll was further consolidated when his party, the newly formed Bangladesh Nationalist Party (BNP) won two-thirds of the seats in the parliamentary elections of 1979. Martial law was lifted and democracy and stability returned to Bangladesh. Zia, who proved to be a competent politician and statesman, turned more and more to the west and the oil-rich Islamic countries. Assistance began pouring in and over the next five years the economy went from strength to strength.

During a military coup attempt in May 1981, President Zia was assassinated. There was no obvious successor, so Justice Abdul Sattar was appointed as acting president. Faced with a population in a political frenzy, a general election was held in which Sattar, as candidate for the BNP, won 66% of the vote. He formed a cabinet and the country appeared ready to settle down. The population's peaceful return to the rule of law was a reflection of the stability that Zia had created.

However, there was increasing concern over government methods and on 24 March 1982 General Hossain Mohammed Ershad seized power in a bloodless coup, becoming the country's 7th head of state since inde-

pendence just 11 years earlier. Once again Bangladesh was placed under martial law. Ershad announced a mixed cabinet of politicians and army officers, and pledged a return to parliamentary rule within two years. As Zia had done, he formed his own political party, the Jatiya Party, and then solidified his power by handing out highly valuable plots of land in the Dhaka enclave of Baridhara to various generals.

The pledge to hold elections was never honoured. The general election scheduled for 1985 was cancelled and in its place Ershad held a referendum in an attempt to pacify his critics. The opposition parties dismissed this as a farce, and many refused to take further part in the political process.

Despite Ershad's disregard for both the pledge and the spirit of democracy, the country progressed economically during the late 1980s. In early 1990, however, the economy began to unravel and by the summer massive rallies and hartals were being held in the streets.

Zia's wife, Begum Khaleda Zia, with no political experience, was put forward as the head of the BNP. Her steadfast call for Ershad's resignation created a favourable image. As military support waned, Ershad had no choice but to resign. Shortly thereafter he was thrown in jail to await trial on charges of corruption. A neutral caretaker government was appointed to oversee parliamentary elections in early 1991, and democracy was restored.

The ensuing campaign was reasonably free and open. Sure of victory, the Awami League, headed by Sheikh Hasina and supported by the older generation involved in the struggle for independence, waged an uninspired campaign. When the votes were counted, they had about 33% of the vote compared to the BNP's 31%, but the BNP won about 35 more seats in parliament. The BNP further liberalised the economy and took a more outward approach to foreign policy by contributing troops to international peacekeeping missions. Besides raising the country's profile, this strategy also kept the army busy with matters other than domestic politics.

The Awami League never fully accepted the election result and began to agitate against the BNP. A long and economically ruinous program of hartals eventually served to bring down the BNP government in June 1996, and the Awami League took power. The BNP has since returned the favour by holding hartals against the Awami League. The conflict between Sheikh Hasina and Begum Khaleda, sometimes called the 'Battle of the Begums', is bitter and personal, and shows no sign of abating. It may be democracy but the endless hartals, strikes and demonstrations have been hugely costly, and have prevented the country from achieving the sort of economic growth rates needed to reduce poverty and allow Bangladesh to join the ranks of the Asian tiger economies.

GEOGRAPHY

Although some geographers have divided Bangladesh into as many as 54 distinct geographical regions, the country's most obvious features are that it's very, very flat and the rivers are correspondingly vast. The two hilly areas are the hills of sedimentary rock around Sylhet, which mark the beginnings of the hills of Assam, and the steep parallel ridges of the Chittagong Hill Tracts, which run along the Myanmar border.

Bangladesh has a total area of 143,998 sq km, roughly the same size as Wisconsin, or England and Wales combined. It is surrounded to the west, north-west and east by India, and shares a south-eastern border with Myanmar for 283km. To the south is the Bay of Bengal.

The topography is characterised by alluvial plains, bound to the north of Bangladesh by the submontane regions of the Himalaya; the piedmont areas in the north-east andthe eastern fringes adjacent to Assam, Tripura and Myanmar are broken by the forested hills of Mymensingh, Sylhet, and Chittagong. The great Himalayan rivers, the Ganges and the Brahmaputra, divide the land into six major regions, which correspond to the six governmental divisions: north-west (Rajshahi), south-west (Khulna), south central (Barisal), central (Dhaka), north-east (Sylhet) and south-east (Chittagong).

The alluvial river plains, which dominate 90% of the country, are very flat and never rise more than 10m above sea level. The only relief from these plains occurs in the north-east and south-east corners of the country, where the hills rise to an average of 240m and 600m respectively. These hills follow a north-south direction. The highest peak in Bangladesh is Keokradang (1230m), which is about 80km south-west of Chittagong in the Hill Tracts.

Overall, Bangladesh has no great mountains or deserts, and is characterised more by wooded marshlands and jungles, with forest regions in Sylhet, Mymensingh, the Sundarbans, the Chittagong Hill Tracts, and Tangail in Dhaka Division. These forest regions constitute 15% of the total land area.

Almost all of Bangladesh's coastline forms the Mouths of the Ganges, the final destination of the Ganges River, and the largest estuarine delta in the world. The coastal strip from the western border to Chittagong is one great patchwork of shifting river courses and little islands. Over the whole delta area, which extends into India, the rivers make up 6.5% of the total area.

The south-eastern coast, south from the city of Chittagong, is backed by the wooded Arakan Hills which overlook a sandy coast for about 120km through to the town of Teknaf at the southernmost point.

In all of Bangladesh the only place that has any stone is a quarry in the far north-western corner of Sylhet division bordering India. That's one reason you'll see bricks being hammered into pieces all over the country: the brick fragments are substituted for stones when making concrete.

Rivers

Rivers are the most important geographical feature in Bangladesh, and it is rivers that created the vast alluvial delta. The outflow of water from Bangladesh is the third highest in the world, after the Amazon and the Congo systems. As much water flows through the country as through all of Europe, and it's only barely the size of Greece.

Bangladesh's rivers have been described as 'young and migratory', and even in the last 100 years there have been massive changes of course. This is not new. In 1787 the Jamuna realigned itself during a massive flood that killed a third of the population, shifting from its old route past Mymensingh and east of Dhaka to its current channel, running directly south from the Indian border to meet the Padma approximately 70km due west of Dhaka.

The history of the country is full of important cities becoming ghost towns because the rivers they were built on silted up or changed course; the earliest inscription found in the country exhorts people to store grain in expectation of future floods. Many of the little lakes and ponds scattered around the country are the equivalent of the Australian billabongs – lagoons created when branches of meandering rivers are cut off.

Annual flooding during the monsoon season is part of life in Bangladesh. Some experts speculate whether the flooding is getting worse and whether deforestation in India and especially Nepal, which causes increased runoff, may be the reason. Another theory holds that the riverbeds have become choked with silt from once-forested land, making flooding more severe. Other experts are not so sure there has been a change. Regardless, there has been increased pressure to 'do something' and find a 'permanent solution'. Part of the problem of doing anything, however, is that the country depends for its fertility on regular flooding, and simply building massive dikes along riverbanks could be disastrous for agricultural output.

The Jamuna (Brahmaputra) and the lower Meghna are the widest rivers, with the latter expanding to around 8km across in the wet season, and much more when it is in flood.

The Ganges, which begins in the Indian state of Uttar Pradesh, enters Bangladesh from the north-west. It joins the Brahmaputra in the centre of the country, northwest of the capital, Dhaka. The Ganges and the Brahmaputra Rivers both receive new names once they pass into Bangladesh: the Ganges becomes the Padma, while the

Brahmaputra is known as the Jamuna. It is these great rivers and their countless distributaries that have the most apparent effect on the landform – constant erosion and flooding over the alluvial plains change the course of rivers, landscapes and agriculture. The Jamuna alone is estimated to carry 900 million tonnes of silt each year. Islands of rich silt called *chars* appear and disappear in the wide riverbeds and at the mouths of the rivers almost annually. Char islands are impossible to protect from flooding or erosion, but as they are some of the richest farmland (being pure silt) it's futile to try and stop people settling on them.

CLIMATE

The climate of Bangladesh is subtropical and tropical with temperatures ranging from an average daytime low of 21°C in the cold

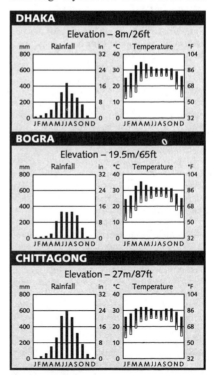

season to a top of 35°C in the hot season. Annual rainfall varies from 1000mm in the west to 2500mm in the south-east and up to 5000mm in the north near the hills of Assam.

Three-quarters of the annual rainfall occurs between June and September. The 90% to 95% humidity in this season is almost unbearable for some travellers. The humidity remains high all year round, producing thick fogs in winter, and making chilly nights in the north feel much colder than they are.

Bangladesh has three main seasons: the monsoon or wet season from late May to early October; the cold season from mid-October to the end of February; and the hot season from mid-March to mid-May. There are two cyclone seasons – May to June and October to November.

Rajshahi division shares some of neighbouring north India's extremes of climate. It is the hottest region in the country in summer, and between the end of March and the end of April the *pashi*, a blistering wind, blows through the day. In winter it can get quite cold at night, down to 3°C some years, when freezing fogs bring normal life to a standstill and many poor people die.

In the cold season the weather is drier and fresh, and the days are usually sunny with clear blue skies. Temperatures range from 5°C overnight in the far north to 22°C during the day. Rainfall is negligible, although even in winter a brief thunder shower may come along.

Early March is still reasonably pleasant with tolerable humidity, warm days and nights, and clear skies. But by April, as the monsoon approaches, the temperature rises to around 40°C during the day and 29°C overnight. With increasing humidity, this time of the year can be almost intolerable. Lethal hail storms are also quite common, with reports of some hail stones weighing half a kilogram. The winds that provide this unusual weather whirl up from the Bay of Bengal, then U-turn at the Himalaya and carry their icy cargo back to Bangladesh. They are known as *guarni jour*.

The Cyclone Zone

Every few years it seems Bangladesh is hit by another disaster. While there are periodic floods and droughts, the most catastrophic by far in terms of human life are cyclones.

Bangladesh is in the world's worst area for cyclones due to a unique combination of factors: a large tide (5m near Sandwip Island), a funnelling coast configuration that increases the height of waves, low flat terrain, and frequent severe tropical storms. There is one major cyclone every three years on average. The worst seasons are May to June and October to November, and the area where damage tends to occur most frequently is in the east around Chittagong and Cox's Bazar.

People still talk about the 1970 cyclone, when between 300,000 and 500,000 people died. The 1991 cyclone, which occurred during peak high tide, was stronger, affected over twice as many people and destroyed four times as many houses. However, the death toll of between 140,000 and 200,000 was less than half that of 1970.

A major reason for the reduction of fatalities was the presence of storm shelters, a number of which had been constructed since 1970. If you travel around the Cox's Bazar area you'll definitely see a few. Some are multi-functional, serving as schools too.

The usual starting date for the monsoon is somewhere between late May and mid-June. It doesn't rain solidly all day every day – there tends to be an initial downpour, which is fairly soon followed by clear skies. The air feels cleaner and sweeter-smelling and the rain is a great help in countering the oppressive heat prevalent during the hot season.

Although there are only three observable seasons in Bangladesh, the locals commonly refer to six:

•	**Basanto** (spring)	February to April
•	**Grishma** (summer)	April to June
•	**Barsha** (rainy)	June to August
•	**Sharat** (autumn)	August to October
•	**Hemanto** (misty)	October to December
•	**Sheet** (winter)	December to February

Seasonal Floods

If you arrive here by air during the monsoon season, you'll be astounded by how much of the country appears to be under water – around 70%. And this will probably be just the normal flooding that occurs. Imagine what it must be like when there's a real flood! Many first-time visitors to Bangladesh assume that the flooding is due to heavy rainfall in the country during that time of year. In fact, local rainfall is only partly responsible – most of the water comes from the Padma (known as the Ganges upstream in India), the Meghna and the Jamuna (Brahmaputra) Rivers.

For Bangladeshis, annual flooding is a fact of life. Wading through waist-high water to the nearest tube well for potable water is just part of living in difficult circumstances. Much of the flooding, which affects about a third of the country, is regarded by farmers as beneficial, replenishing worn soils with nutrients. It's when the rivers rise above their normal limits that problems arise.

The last great flood was in 1998, when all three of the country's major rivers reached flood levels at the same time. Some 16 million people were made homeless. In Dhaka, even houses on fairly high ground were inundated, and Zia airport was covered with water and had to be shut down.

ECOLOGY & ENVIRONMENT

Preserving the environment is not as much of a priority as human survival in Bangladesh. The ever-swelling population and the growing scarcity of land forces landless peasants onto marginal forest lands and temporary river islands, farmland soils are being damaged by overuse, and the rivers are being polluted by chemical pesticides used to boost crop yields. The water table is under threat as deep tube wells extract clean water for drinking, while in certain areas these wells are affected by arsenic leaching into the water table from the underlying bedrock.

With the continuance of global warming, believed by many scientists to be caused by the greenhouse effect, Bangladesh, as one of the 10 countries in the world most vulnerable to a rise in sea level, will be drastically affected. Present predictions indicate the sea will rise by 8cm to 30cm by 2030, and 30cm to 110cm by 2100. A 1m rise in the Bay of Bengal would result in a loss of 12% to 18% of the country's land area.

Loss of land is just one consequence – severe flooding and reduced agricultural potential are almost inevitable. Seasonal flooding will become wider, deeper and more prolonged because a higher sea level will retard drainage. This will increase the salinity of ground water. Tidal waves during cyclones are likely to be more severe as well.

This is indeed a cruel twist of fate, since Bangladesh, as a poor, agricultural society, has contributed very little to global warming. Even with assistance from the Dutch, who are helping to devise a strategy to cope with rising water levels, the question remains whether Bangladesh will have the capacity to develop and apply the appropriate technology.

FLORA & FAUNA

Like most of the northern flatlands of the subcontinent, Bangladesh is both subtropical and tropical. This has given rise to a great variety of flora and fauna.

Flora

About 10% of Bangladesh is still forested. Half of the remaining forest is in the Chittagong Hill Tracts and a further quarter in the Sundarbans, with the rest scattered in small pockets throughout the country.

The forests fall into three distinct regional varieties: the forests of the tidal zones along the coast, often mangrove but sometimes hardwood, in much of the Sundarbans; the forests of *sal* (hardwood) trees around Dhaka, Tangail and Mymensingh; and the upland forests of tropical and subtropical evergreens in the Chittagong Hill Tracts and parts of Sylhet.

Even away from the forests, Bangladesh is a land of trees. Lining the old Trunk Road in the west are huge rain trees, and every village is an arboreal oasis, often with spectacular banyan or *oshot* trees. The red silk-cotton or kapok tree is easily spotted throughout the countryside in February and March, when it loses its leaves and sprouts a myriad of red blossoms. Teak was introduced into the Hill Tracts last century, and the quality approaches that of Myanmar; it's much better than Indian teak.

Given that half the country is located in the tropics, flowering plants are an integral part of the beauty of Bangladesh. Each season produces its special variety of flowers. Among them is the prolific water hyacinth. Its carpet of thick green leaves and blue flowers gives the impression that solid ground lies underneath. Other decorative plants that grow easily are jasmine, water lily, rose, hibiscus, bougainvillea, magnolia, and an incredible diversity of wild orchids in the forested areas.

Fauna

Bangladesh is home to the royal Bengal tiger and other members of the cat family such as leopards and the smaller jungle cat. Tigers are almost exclusively confined to the Sundarbans, but their smaller relations prey on domestic animals all over the country. There are three varieties of civet, including the large Indian civet, which is now listed as an endangered species. Other large animals include Asiatic elephants (mostly migratory herds from Bihar), a few black bears in Chittagong Division, wild pigs and deer. Monkeys, langurs, gibbons (the only ape on the subcontinent), otters and mongooses are some of the smaller animals. There were once wild buffalo and rhinoceros, but all became extinct this century.

Reptiles include the sea tortoise, mud turtle, river tortoise, pythons, crocodiles and a variety of poisonous snakes. The voluble gecko lizard is, appropriately, known as *tik-tiki*. Marine life includes a wide variety of both freshwater and marine fish.

Bird-Watching

Between the natural and human problems of Bangladesh, it's difficult to imagine that the country can boast being the habitat of more than 650 species of birds, almost half of those found on the entire subcontinent.

The brown wood owl is one of many species of owl that are native to Bangladesh.

Tucked between the Indian subcontinent and the Malayan peninsulas, Bangladesh attracts both the Indian species in the west and north of the country, and the Malayan species in the east and south-east. It is also conveniently located for migrants heading south towards Malaysia and Indonesia, and those moving south-west to India and Sri Lanka. In addition, there are a number of Himalayan and Burmese hill species that move into the lowlands during the winter. Despite the fact that many of these species are rare or localised and that the overall number of birds has declined in the past two decades, bird-watching in Bangladesh can be rewarding.

Within Dhaka division, the Madhupur Forest, south-west of Mymensingh, is an extremely important habitat worthy of national protection. This area is great for a variety of owls, including the popular and rare brown wood owl, wintering thrushes and a number of raptors, to mention a few. The Jamuna River floods regularly, and from December to February provides winter habitats for waterfowl, waders and the occasional black stork.

Sylhet division has extensive natural *haors* (pronounced 'HOW-ars', wetlands) in this low-lying basin, and during the winter season it is home to huge flocks of wildfowl. Outstanding species include the rare Baer's pochard and Pallas' fishing eagle, along with a great number of ducks and skulkers. The remaining fragments of evergreen and teak forests are also important habitats, especially along the Indian border near the Srimangal area. The blue-bearded bee-eater, red-breasted trogon and a wide variety of forest birds, including rare visitors, are regularly seen in these forests. Preservation of these forests and haors is critical for sustaining this variety of rare wildlife.

One of two important coastal zones is the Noakhali region, particularly the islands near Hatiya, where migratory species and a variety of wintering waders find suitable refuges. These include large numbers of the rare spoonbilled sandpiper, Nordman's greenshank and flocks of Indian skimmers.

The Sundarbans, the second important coastal zone, is the richest for all kinds of wildlife, and the most difficult to penetrate. With its miles of marshy shorelines and brackish creeks, it supports a great number of wetland and forest species, along with large populations of gulls and terns along the south coast. Eight varieties of kingfisher have been recorded here, including the brown-winged, white-collared, black-capped and the rare ruddy kingfisher.

Overall the most exciting time of year for bird-watching is during the winter from November to March. See the Books section in the Facts for the Visitor chapter for a list of field guides.

Endangered Species

It is well known that the royal Bengal tiger is an endangered species. The government recently set aside three specific areas within the Sundarbans as tiger reserves, but numbers are low. See the Sundarbans National Park section of the Khulna Division chapter for more information.

Other species that are rare or under threat include Indian elephants, hoolock gibbons, black bears and the Ganges River dolphin. Reptilian species under threat include the Indian python, the crocodile and various turtles.

Many of the diverse bird species are prolific, but some are vulnerable, including Pallas' fishing eagle and Baer's pochard.

National Parks & Reserves

There is a dismal lack of designated national parks, reserves and conservation areas in Bangladesh overall. With millions of people to feed, perhaps it's asking too much to make good agricultural land off-limits. However, the situation is a Gordian knot, since in many ways survival depends on intact natural areas. Unfortunately, due to intense human pressure, these are disappearing fast. To make matters worse, designated parks and reserves are not strictly controlled and blatant misuse, even by those who are paid to protect them, is an everyday occurrence.

Bhawal National Park Also known as Rajendrapur National Park, it is located in Dhaka division, about 38km north of Dhaka city. The area mostly comprises regrowth sal forest and open picnic spots. There are a few walking trails.

Sundarbans Reserve This is the finest natural area in the entire country, mostly due to its impenetrable jungle forests and maze of rivers. Located in the southern half of the Khulna division, it's part of the world's largest mangrove forest and home to the Bengal tiger.

Madhupur Forest Reserve This is a degraded sal and mixed forest with some remaining old growth; it's roughly 130km north-west of Dhaka (three hours by car) on the road between Mymensingh and Tangail. Over the past 20 years its size has been cut in half, but it continues to be a very interesting forest rich with wildlife.

Lowacherra Forest Reserve Some 8km east of Srimangal in the greater Sylhet area, this hilly sal forest is similar in size to Madhupur Forest, though the species of wildlife varies slightly.

Telepara/Satcheri Forest Reserve This mixed evergreen/teak forest is about 60km south-west of Srimangal. Within its boundaries is a sandy basin that is excellent for bird-watching.

Singra Forest Reserve In the Rajshahi division, well north of Dinajpur, this reserve is a fairly uniform sal forest with mixed woodland on the boundary.

GOVERNMENT & POLITICS

Bangladesh is a constitutional republic with a multiparty parliamentary democracy in which elections by secret ballot are held on the basis of universal suffrage. The theoretical head of state is the president. The president is elected by parliamentarians for a five-year term and can hold office for no more than two terms, whether or not these terms are consecutive. Although the president appoints the prime minister, the real executive power rests with the prime minister. The present prime minister is Sheikh Hasina Wajed (daughter of Sheikh Mujibur Rahman) of the Awami League, appointed in June 1996.

As in the UK, the prime minister must call elections at least every five years. In the 1991 elections, the BNP won a majority of the 300 seats up for election, and in the June 1996 elections the Awami League won. However, it needed the support of the Jatiya Party, the party of former President Ershad (see Bangladesh under History earlier in this chapter), to form a majority. Sheikh Hasina immediately released Ershad from jail.

An additional 30 seats are reserved for women and, since they are allocated by parliament, this effectively rewards the majority party with 30 more seats. Women can contest any elected seat in parliament, and have won seats in the past two elections. While the presence of women in parliament and as leaders of the two main parties is said to demonstrate the country's commitment to women's participation in the government, opponents claim it's only for show because at the cabinet and sub-cabinet levels, women are conspicuously absent.

Politics & Students

Probably nowhere in the world do students play such a pivotal role in politics as in Bangladesh. There's always news about another gun-toting student riot at Dhaka University. Dormitory bombings and assassinations of student leaders are common everyday occurrences. Since independence some 55 people have been killed due to student riots on campus, many killings occurring as a result of inter-faction disagreements.

Students today are empowered by recent tradition, stemming largely from the key role they played in the Liberation War. When the war started it was no mistake that the Pakistanis aimed their tanks first at Dhaka University. Many students were among the intellectuals targeted for massacre.

Today the main political parties view students' support as crucial and court their allegiance by supporting student activists. Most of these 'permanent students', who live on campus for years, are paid political activists. Most of the followers have an inkling that if they don't support one of the major parties and do their bit to get it into power, they have little chance of getting a government job.

As a result, many of the state universities have become the scene for ongoing clashes between the major parties. After every bloody clash the universities close down, sometimes for weeks. This pattern constantly repeats itself, followed by the invariable public outcry for the government to 'do something' – which it rarely does. None of the major parties want to lose such an important source of street muscle. Under these conditions it's quite normal for students to take eight or 10 years to complete what would under normal circumstances be a three-year degree.

The indigenous tribal people who, as in the Indian constitution, are referred to in the Bangladesh constitution as the 'backward section of citizens', have no seats specifically reserved for them, but some members from minority groups are in the Awami League government. The tribal people of the Chittagong Hill Tracts enjoy a fair degree of autonomy.

The opposition is led by Begum Khaleda Zia and the BNP. The BNP has generally held a more strongly nationalist and anti-India stance than the Awami League. While there are other parties, most of which are more about personalities than policies, the most significant one is the Jamaat-e-Islami, an Islamic fundamentalist party that is said to be the best organised in the country.

Although 89% of the population is Muslim, Bangladesh is constitutionally defined as a secular democracy. Unlike in many Islamic countries, the Muslim clergy don't hold sway in national politics.

Administratively, the country is divided into six divisions: Dhaka, Khulna, Barisal, Rajshahi, Chittagong and Sylhet. Each division is in turn divided into districts, and districts into *thanas*. It is at these lower levels that the government has the most impact on people's daily lives. But while elections are held for lower-level positions, local governments have only a democratic veneer because elections are held infrequently and elected officials, once in office, are not very responsive to the public.

Relations with India

On the international front, Bangladesh is on good terms with the western world and has sent troops around the world to help out in hot spots including the Gulf War, the invasion of Haiti and the war in Bosnia. But when it comes to neighbouring India, Bangladesh won't lift a finger.

Basically, the two countries are at political odds with one another. Religious conflicts over the centuries between Hindus and Muslims are an underlying reason. During the Raj era, Hindus were favoured by the British, adding fuel to Muslim resentment against the wealthier Hindus.

While Bangladeshis have a close affinity with West Bengalis because of their common language, relations with the Indian government are on a very different footing. When Nehru agreed to bind the area of Bangladesh with Pakistan at the time of Indian independence, the Bengalis felt they had been used. And the Indian army's assistance years later in bringing the Pakistani army to its knees during the Liberation War was viewed, quite rightly, more as a matter of self-interest.

The most contentious issue is emigration from Bangladesh to India. Precise figures are impossible to come by, but perhaps as many as 150,000 Bangladeshis illegally enter India every year. There is considerable tension in neighbouring Indian states such as Assam and Meghalaya between locals and Bangladeshis, which frequently turns violent. Indian border guards regularly shoot at people who stray near the border. In Rajshahi division there remains the issue of enclaves of territory on either side of the border. Other contentious issues include smuggling, which runs strongly in India's favour, and a dispute over an island in the Bay of Bengal, known as New Talpatty in Bangladesh and New Moore Island in India.

For many years the distribution of water from the Ganges River, which becomes the Padma River when it enters Bangladesh, was a major source of conflict between the two countries. The Farakka Barrage, just upstream from the Bangladeshi border, channelled water away from Bangladesh into the Hooghly River, which runs through Bangla (West Bengal). During the dry season only a tiny share of precious water reached Bangladesh, and so in a country subject to flooding there was the bitter irony of large regions suffering an artificial drought. A treaty signed in 1996 seems to have solved the issue equitably.

National Flag

First flown 'officially' from the roof of the rebel Bangladeshi embassy in Calcutta when the Liberation War began, the Bangladeshi flag is green for the lush country (not for Islam, as some fundamentalists

Grameen Bank

Founded in 1976, the Grameen Bank now operates in half the country's 68,000 villages and has more than US$500 million in assets. It is as much a cult as a business, and founder Mohammed Yunus is its 'guru'.

Yunus opposes the traditional concept that a borrower must be educated to be risk-worthy and that micro-loans can't be profitable. He feels that if financial resources are available to poor landless people at existing commercial terms, millions of small families with millions of small pursuits can create a development wonder.

Grameen Bank targets destitute women and under its lending formula, prospective borrowers form groups of five neighbours who vet each others' loan requests and ensure weekly paybacks. If one member fails to pay, the group receives no further loans; peer pressure tends to keep things straight. Interest rates are 20%. Loans can vary from US$65 to around US$1000, but the average is US$120, typically enough to purchase a cow, a sewing machine or a silkworm shed. Most loans (91%) go to women because Yunus believes they are more reliable; women tend to plough money into the needs of the family while men more often spend it on themselves. By the bank's statistics, the default rate is around 2% and it claims that about a third of the borrowers have crossed the poverty line.

The program is not without its sceptics. The bank's claims are difficult to verify because of slow reporting. Its default rate calculation may be suspect; some say that by normal banking standards the rate would be much higher. With so much foreign money pouring into the bank, it's not clear whether the bank is a sustainable institution and thus a viable model for other countries and institutions lacking such resources.

Repayment of loans begins after the first week; many borrowers complain that this is too limiting. Some don't know how they'll use the loan, but because the money is there and they're eligible, they accept it. Reportedly, some borrowers lie about the purpose of the loan and use it for personal reasons such as dowry demands.

Regardless of the unresolved issues, Grameen Bank is politically popular, highly visible, and has made an impact. Similar programs have emerged; BRAC (the Bangladesh Rural Advancement Committee) has one that is almost identical, with similar default rates and slightly more flexible repayment schedules. The benefits to women borrowers are immeasurable. Through working collectively and with the growth of self-esteem, they can improve their deplorably low status in Bangladesh.

would prefer) with a red circle for the bloodshed at the country's creation.

ECONOMY

Bangladesh is quite poor, with the average per capita income at around US$225 by the GDP standard, or US$1370 by the purchasing power standard. The country's gross domestic product is US$35 billion. On the United Nations Human Development Index, a development scale based on a combination of gross national product, literacy and life expectancy, Bangladesh is ranked 146th out of 173 – ahead of 27 other countries and neck and neck with Nepal. Approximately US$1.5 billion per annum in

aid has been pumped into the country over the past decade or more.

Still unable to shed its 'basket case' image, the country continues to attract foreign aid from a large number of organisations from around the globe including aid agencies such as Unicef, UNDP, Unesco, WHO, USAID, GTZ and Danida. Much of it has gone into the family planning sector; the country's declining birth rates are the result. For years foreign aid has provided over 50% of the government's development budget, but the figure is now less than 30% and declining rapidly. The Bangladeshi government maintains that as long as foreign donors increase access to their markets (especially the garment market) to offset the decreased aid levels, it won't complain. To some extent, this has been happening.

Every year thousands of Bangladeshis leave to work in the Middle East and Asia, especially Saudi Arabia, the UAE and Malaysia. Undoubtedly many more work illegally in India. Many send money back to their families in Bangladesh. The amount of remittances now totals US$1.5 billion plus another half billion or so thought to come in through unofficial channels. However, for the workers abroad, it's a trade-off; for substantially higher pay they endure a fairly pathetic life, alone in a strange country and often receiving little respect. While many return after just a few years, others remain and prosper.

On the macroeconomic level, Bangladesh has a liberalised market-oriented economy and none of the major political parties seem to question this overall policy, only its implementation. Investors complain that decisions made to open up the economy are only gradually implemented, if at all, and that corrupt politicians and bureaucrats impede them at every step.

The annual growth in the economy remains around 5%, which is actually lower than in the early 1980s, when economic reforms began. Due to pressure from trade unionists, the government has been moving slowly towards privatising state enterprises, and these enterprises continue to drain the state coffers. Although the country is now close to self-sufficiency in rice, agricultural production has been stagnant since 1991. Excluding garments, the manufacturing sector's annual growth is only fair at just 4.5%. The only growth sectors are fisheries and livestock, which are of relatively minor importance.

The main reason, however, for the country's mediocre growth rate is that Bangladesh is failing to attract investment. Foreign investors are staying away because of the volatile political situation.

One bright spot, however, is the ready-made garment industry. Incredibly low wages (between US$20 and US$30 a month) and a relatively disciplined workforce are Bangladesh's drawing cards. Most of the garment factories are in and around Dhaka and Chittagong, and women, mostly from poor families, hold nearly 90% of the more than one million jobs. Bangladesh is now the largest supplier of T-shirts to Europe and it's the seventh largest apparel supplier to the US. Entrance into the brand-name market seems to be the next step.

In the 19th century Bengal was known for its production of jute, the 'golden fibre'. The humid climate is perfect for growing jute and jute sacks were in demand worldwide. Today, polythene has nearly destroyed the industry – even the grain that is donated from abroad arrives in plastic bags. Although Bangladesh still produces 80% of the world's jute, the industry is in rapid decline. It now accounts for just a fraction of total exports, down from 62% in 1982. Cheap jute carpets and jute handicrafts for export are helping the industry to survive, but whether this natural fibre makes a comeback remains to be seen.

Child Labour

Use of child labour (children under 14 years of age) in garment factories is a vexed issue. US unions have lobbied their government to prohibit Bangladeshi textiles from entering the US, which is the largest market for such garments. The issue is complex because in Bangladesh the children (estimated at between 50,000 and 100,000) barred from working in export industries will not go to school; they'll probably end up with worse jobs, such as brick-breaking, begging, or prostitution. Many of the children come from families with no fathers and many young siblings; they have no choice but to work. With an income families can afford to educate some of their children. There have been demonstrations in Dhaka by child labourer organisations against the threatened ban. They argue that rather than caring about the welfare of the child workers, the powerful US unions simply want to protect jobs at home.

The discovery of large reserves of natural gas in Chittagong division would seem like the perfect opportunity to boost the economy's development, but again the exploitation of the potentially valuable reserves has become bogged down in politics. A plan to construct gas-powered electricity generators and sell energy to India has come unstuck because of the fierce opposition of the BNP. Somehow the BNP reasons that selling electricity to India would be a loss for Bangladesh. There is also opposition to giving multinational companies concessions to run the gas fields.

POPULATION

The population of Bangladesh is around 130 million, making it the most densely populated country in the world, with the exception of several city-states (Singapore and Malta). On a per sq km basis, it is three times more populated than India and seven times more populated than China. Nevertheless, what is not well known is that there are several other sizeable areas in the world that are just as crowded – Java (Indonesia's principal island), for example, has a population density equal to Bangladesh's. The population is growing by about 2 million people every year.

Despite the density of its population, rural Bangladesh (which is where most of the people live) is only just beginning to feel crowded. There aren't endless sprawls of depressing slums and industrial wastelands, mainly because land is far too precious to sprawl over and industrial development is still fairly low. The countryside is green and lovely and the air outside Dhaka is still clean. Anyone flying in from Kathmandu or Delhi will see a marked visual difference in the air quality.

The country's family planning program has been remarkably successful. The average number of children per woman has fallen from 6.3 in 1975 to 2.9 in 1999. The average desired family size is now less than three children. The population growth rate was down to 1.6% in 1998 and was well below the economic growth rate. Despite this successful decline in popula-

Poverty

Despite an economic growth rate that exceeds the population growth rate, the situation for the country's poor – about half the population – is dire, despite signs of marginal improvements. The benefits of growth need to 'trickle down' more. Statistics show, for instance, that while the population with virtually no land (one-fifth of a hectare or less) remains constant at 47%, the proportion of absolute landless (19%) is increasing. The landless make up the bulk of the 'floating people', the poorest of the poor who sleep, eat and die on railway platforms, street corners and other public places. By some estimates the amount of cultivable land already taken up by housing exceeds 10%, and over the next 50 years up to a third of the land will be taken up by housing.

Other statistics show, startlingly, that the people may be physically shrinking. A recent study showed that children aged 11 years have lost height and weight between 1937 and 1982. The study may be flawed but no one would dispute that the huge percentage of children who are malnourished is not declining. Because of these dire statistics, the World Bank has altered course slightly and now has nutrition projects targeting children under age five.

tion growth, the country's population is expected to double in another 35 to 40 years, eventually levelling off between 230 and 280 million people.

PEOPLE

Perhaps because of their country's bloody birth, the proud nationalism of Bangladeshis extends to their concept of themselves as a people. It seems a bit forced, but some academics here argue that Bangladeshis have always been a separate cultural and even racial unit on the subcontinent. This is somewhat fancifully stretched to include the tribes of the Chittagong Hill Tracts, and is used as a justification for their forced integration into the mainstream culture.

It took the Aryan invaders 1000 years to tame the jungles of the Gangetic plain and reach Bengal, and on the way the meat-eating warriors evolved into contemplative Hindus. It is claimed that the region's original Dravidian tribe, the Bangs, were pushed into the jungles of the delta by the Aryan invaders, but were not initially conquered. Here, their culture developed and, as one author put it, 'unlike many other Dravidian tribes the Bangs...were intelligent, imaginative and nomadic'. The late arrival of the (by now) much less aggressive Brahmin culture resulted in integration with the locals, rather than conquest and outcast status as happened to other aboriginal tribes on the subcontinent.

The Bangladeshi pride in ancestry is balanced by the Islamic slant of intellectual life, which tends to deny the achievements of the preceding Buddhist and Hindu cultures. The antipathy to Hinduism isn't just religiously inspired – it was the Hindu zamindars who grew rich on the toil of the Muslim peasantry under the Raj. The zamindars' lifestyle of 'wine and women' isn't approved of (nor is song in some fundamentalist circles), and the Tantric overtones of Buddhism are regarded as depraved.

Bangladesh has been a melting pot of peoples and cultures for a very long time. Peoples from Myanmar and the Himalaya, Dravidians (the original inhabitants of the subcontinent), and the invading Aryans made up the first blend of people here. With the arrival of the Mughals, people from all over the Islamic world began settling in Bangladesh.

The Dravidians, with their racial origins in the Deccan Plateau, are mainly Hindus and constitute about 12% of the population. The Muslims, who constitute 87%, are of mostly Dravido-Aryan origin. The original tribal people still exist, mainly in the Chittagong Hill Tracts, though they now number less than 1% of the total population. Many of the tribes have been converted to Christianity, although animism still strongly influences their beliefs and practices. The Tibeto-Burmese inhabitants are mainly Buddhists and less than 1% of the

population is Christian. There is also a small community of Bengali Buddhists who live outside Chittagong.

The Muslims and Hindus have a cultural affinity with Bangla (West Bengal) and speak Bangla themselves, while the Buddhists have their own distinct culture and dialects related mainly to Burma and the tribal culture of eastern India. Apart from the tribal people, the Christian people here mostly have Portuguese names and are usually English-speakers.

Families stick together, even in the more westernised middle classes. Most people have a 'home village' to which they return on weekends or holidays. This is so pervasive that an unquestionable excuse for your laundry not being returned on time is 'the room boy has gone to his home village'.

The vast majority of Bangladeshis are tied to the land, either as farmers or as agricultural labourers. In much of the country lifestyles have remained largely unchanged for millenia. The small urban middle class (in the sense of a class of people who live something like the western consumer lifestyle) live much like their western counterparts. Younger people from richer families are under great pressure to get a good education at a prestigious university or college, so student life tends to be subdued. Leisure time for the upper classes is usually spent at home with the TV or maybe a computer, as the cities have relatively few entertainment options besides cinemas and video lounges.

Tribal People
The tribal population of Bangladesh numbers almost one million. They generally live in the hilly regions north of Mymensingh, the Sylhet area, and more than half a million are concentrated in the wooded Chittagong Hill Tracts. Others live in urban areas such as Chittagong and Cox's Bazar.

The tribes living in the Chittagong Hill Tracts include the Chakma, Mogh, Mru, Murung, Mizo, Kuki, Bam, Tripura, Sak, Tangchangya, Shandu, Banjugi and the Pankhar. The Chakmas constitute the major tribe here, and next to them are the Moghs, who are also found in Cox's Bazar and the Khepupara region near Kuakata in Barisal division. These tribes are sometimes collectively known as Jhumias, from *jhum*, their method of slash-and-burn agriculture. Because vast areas of their territory now lie under the waters of Kaptai Lake, and because of land appropriation by settlers, their sustainable 10-year rotation of cultivation has been cut to three, which doesn't give the forest time to regenerate properly.

The tribes that live in the Sylhet Hills – the Khashias, Pangous and the Manipuris – usually have their settlements on the hilly frontier areas. Some of them have become businesspeople and jewellers in Sylhet.

The Garos (or Mandi, as they call themselves), Hanjongis, Hadis, Dahuis, Palais and the Bunas live in the hilly regions north of Mymensingh in Haluaghat, Sreebardi, Kalmakanda and the Garo Hills, and some live west of Mymensingh around the Madhupur Forest.

Many of the workers on the tea gardens and estates are Santal and Oraon tribals, brought here by the British from the hills of eastern and central India. They are sometimes referred to as the 'tea tribes'. Their religion is a mixture of animism and simple forms of Hinduism.

Other tribal groups, such as the Kochis, Hus, Mundus and Rajbansis, are scattered in urban settlements in Rangpur, Dinajpur, Bogra, Rajshahi, Noakhali, Comilla and Bakerganj.

The tribes in the Mymensingh Hills were originally nomads from the eastern states of India and those in the Chittagong Hill Tracts originate from Myanmar. The tribal groups have their own distinct cultures, art, religious beliefs, superstitions, farming methods and attire. Many of the tribes are Buddhist, though some still retain their animist religion which, to some extent, has been influenced by Hinduism. Centuries ago, the offering of human sacrifices was part of the ritual of some tribes who believed that slaying another man endowed the slayer with the victim's attributes.

Rice and wine are the staple food of these hill people, but included in the tribal menu

MARTIN HARRIS

The Manipuri people from the hills in Sylhet division are famous for their dances.

are snakes, beetles, fish, snails, pigs, dogs, buffaloes, deer, ants and chickens. Many of the tribes influenced by Hinduism, along with the Chakmas, Moghs and Marmas who are Buddhist, cremate their dead. Others, such as the Khashias, bury their dead and place headstones on their graves.

The dwellings of the hill people are usually bamboo huts, either on stilts or flat on the ground, and their farming methods are ancient.

Many of the tribes still have very little contact with the outside world, but as modern civilisation begins to encroach on their territories, more and more of the younger villagers are moving to the urban areas for employment. The Chakmas, for instance, now make saris and tribal jewellery and have established or joined weaving industries. They have begun to accept western education and clothing, and even use western medicine in lieu of herbs and mantras. Many of the smaller tribal languages are dying out.

Found within the broad racial group of the plains people who make up the vast majority of Bangladeshis are subgroups who, although apparently integrated into the culture, continue to pursue strikingly different lives. The Bauls, for example, are wandering beggar-minstrels whose sexual freedom and fondness for bhang (marijuana) are abhorred by the mainstream, but they are good musicians and are welcomed at weddings and parties.

River Gypsies

Bangladesh's river gypsies, the Badhi or Badhja, make up about 50% of the riverboat people of the country and are mainly low-caste Hindus. They move as a clan from one river to another, selling herbal medicine and jewellery which includes the pink pearls they gather from river oysters. During the monsoon, when the rivers swell and streams extend to outlying villages, the Badhi scatter far and wide to trade; but in winter they move back to their usual havens such as Mirpur, Savar and the Dhakeswari River.

Their houseboats are very tidy, neat and clean with shelves for garments, bedding, pots and pans. Each houseboat holds a family, generally with just two or three children. There seem to be few elderly river gypsies. The gypsies live their whole lives afloat but development, even in Bangladesh, is starting to number their days. Motorised vessels, manufactured jewellery and modern medicine have made inroads and some gypsies now send their children to school. Still, modernisation is a slow process in Bangladesh, and it's likely to be a long, long time before the houseboats disappear.

EDUCATION

Primary education was declared compulsory in 1991, but due to inadequate government support there is an abysmal lack of classrooms and teachers. Political conflict extends even to the appointment of primary school teachers – newspapers report riots in villages where a teacher aligned with the BNP competes with an Awami League candidate. The attendance record of teachers who owe their jobs to political patronage is notoriously bad. The facilities that do exist are overcrowded and suffer from a shortage of textbooks and other resources.

Extreme poverty compounds things, and many children have to work or care for younger siblings out of necessity. Most parents, facing tons of work and seeing little relevance in what their children learn at school, take them out after a year or two. As a result, 62% of the population is illiterate (for women the figure is 74%). There is a bold program to achieve universal literacy by 2006, but it is yet to be seen if the government has the will or resources to achieve it.

Secondary education covers classes six to 10, culminating with the first national examination at the end of 10 years of study – the Secondary School Certificate. Secondary education is not free; tuition, textbooks and supplies must be paid for by the student. In some areas there are separate schools for girls and boys, though the quality of the buildings and facilities varies. Private schools, ranging in tuition from US$10 to US$200 a month, offer the best alternative for those who can afford it.

ARTS

The people of the Bengal region share a similarity of language, dress, music and literature across the national boundaries. Certainly the Bengali passion for both politics and poetry seems to spill across the border between Bangla (West Bengal) and Bangladesh. The region also has a multifaceted folk heritage, provided by its ancient animist, Buddhist, Hindu, and Muslim roots. Weaving, pottery and terracotta sculpture are some of the earliest forms of artistic expression. During the Hindu and Buddhist periods, the historic legends and religious deities were depicted in terracotta. The necessities of clothing and utensils for cooking provided another medium for aesthetic creation.

Literature, too, had a place early on. Oral traditions of verse, in the forms of Hindu and Buddhist translations and local mytho-

Bangladesh Rural Advancement Committee (BRAC)

The world's biggest non-government organisation (NGO), BRAC was founded in the early 1970s as a relief organisation during the Liberation War. BRAC later expanded its activities into development work, including rural credit, skill development and health care. BRAC is best known, however, for its non-formal primary education program. This program supplements the government primary education system by catching those in the rural areas, particularly girls, who never enter grade one or who drop out within a year.

BRAC targets children of illiterate destitute people, particularly the landless. Today, it's renowned as an innovator in the field of education. Class hours are flexible and scheduled around work demands on children's time, and at least 70% of the students (ages eight to 16) are girls.

The curriculum focuses on just a few subjects that are relevant and useful for the pupils and their families – Bangla, English, arithmetic, and social studies (which includes training in health, hygiene, nutrition, horticulture, safety and the community). Teachers, 80% of whom are women, are usually married with at least nine years of schooling and receive 13 days training and a nominal monthly allowance from BRAC. The teaching method is participatory, with students divided into groups of six. Students in each group learn from each other, with the teacher acting as a facilitator, and while there are periodic informal tests, there are no formal annual exams.

Today there are over 30,000 schools in operation covering over 70% of the country's district-level thanas. Student enrolment is now close to one million and drop-outs, the government system's biggest problem, are few. A good number of graduates who follow the standard three years of schooling enter public schools at an advanced level.

However, not everyone is happy with BRAC. Some conservative Muslim clerics have accused the program of being Christian and have even instigated the tearing down of schools; their real gripe seems to be that BRAC is educating women. Despite this, the program's success has drawn such international attention that BRAC is now branching out to help organisations in other developing countries, especially Africa, to do the same.

---

logy, were preceded by itinerant theatre performing groups, whose rural wanderings date back 2000 years. Even today poetry is taken seriously by the Bangladeshis, who consider themselves, at heart, to have the depth of passion and sensitivity of a poet.

Architecture

For details about Bangladeshi architecture, see the 'Architecture of Bangladesh' special section later in this book.

Folk Art

Most of the traditional culture is folk culture although, except for the revival in weaving and dyeing, about the only places you'll see concrete examples of it are museums.

Weaving has always held a special place in the artistic expression of the country. In the 7th century, the textiles of Dhaka weavers were finding their way to Europe, where they were regarded as *textiles ventalis*, fabrics woven of air. These fine cotton muslins, woven centuries ago in the old capital of Sonargaon, are still plied by traditional weavers in Tangail, though the exquisite fine thread is no longer available. The most artistic and expensive ornamental fabric is the *jamdani*, or loom-embroidered muslin or silk, exclusively woven for the imperial household centuries ago. Evolving as an art form under the influence of Persian design, the jamdani gained a unique position in the world of weaving. Floral, geometric and animal designs are used in these fabrics.

Needlework has become a cottage industry. Most well-known are the *nakshi kantha*, embroidered, quilted patchwork cloths produced by village women, which hold an important place in village life. They are used as trousseaux, and the embroidery depicts

National Anthem

MARTIN HARRIS

Rabindranath Tagore

My Bengal of gold, I love you
Forever your skies, your air sets my heart in tune
As if it were a flute
In spring, oh mother mine, the fragrance from
 your mango groves makes me wild with joy
Ah, what a thrill!
In autumn, oh mother mine,
In the full-blossomed paddy fields
I have seen spread all over – sweet smiles!
Ah, what a beauty, what shades, what an affection
And what a tenderness!
What a quilt have you spread at the feet of
 banyan trees and along the banks of rivers!
Oh mother mine, words from your lips are like
Nectar to my ears!
Ah, what a thrill!
If sadness, oh mother mine, casts a gloom on your face
My eyes are filled with tears!

Original in Bangla by Rabindranath Tagore

and keeps alive local history and myth. There are women's cooperatives that now produce the kantha commercially, and examples can be found in handicraft stores in the major cities. For more information, see the special section, 'Nakshi Kantha' later in this book.

The most pervasive form of popular culture, the paintings on rickshaws and trucks, also upholds local history and myth. Many paintings are just rehashes of film posters, but some, especially those on trucks, are very fine examples of naive art. Make an effort to look at some before you get overwhelmed by the sheer quantity. One recurrent motif is a winged creature with a woman's head.

Folk Theatre

Jatra, or folk theatre, is common at the village level, and usually takes place during harvest time or at *melas*, village fairs. The performances, conducted with much music and dance, were traditionally based on religious, folk, or historic themes that served to preserve the lore of the village. Today's dramas mainly centre on social or political themes, and have become an effective means of communication. *Kabigan* is a form of folk debate conducted in verse, commonly performed during festivals.

Literature

Best known in the literature of Bangladesh are the works of the great Bengali poets Rabindranath Tagore and Nazrul Islam, whose photos are – somewhat curiously – displayed in restaurants and barber shops. Tagore received international acclaim in 1913, when he was awarded the Nobel Prize for Literature for his book, *Gitanjali,* though he had always been close to the Bangladeshi heart. Despite his Hindu upbringing, Tagore wrote from a strong cultural perspective that transcended any particular religion. He celebrated 'humble lives and their miseries' and supported the concept of Hindu-Muslim unity. His love for the land of Bengal is reflected in many of his works, and a portion of the lyrics in one of his poems was adopted as the national anthem (see the boxed text).

The 'rebel poet' and composer Nazrul Islam is considered the national poet of Bangladesh. During the time the country was suffering under colonial rule, Islam employed poetry to challenge intellectual complacency and spark feelings of nationalism.

Music & Dance
Traditional Bengali music is gradually being subsumed by the cultural dominance of Indian music. Classical music, *uchango*, is similar to Indian classical music, but tends to be more simple and wistful than vigorous. Village songs, *polligiti*, are more lively, but the themes of love and loss continue. Popular music is likewise sentimental and is usually played on acoustic instruments, a great relief after Indian film music. A popular singer of modern songs is Shumana Huq; her cassettes are available everywhere. The bamboo flute is a folk instrument with a haunting tone, and even on Dhaka's noisy streets you'll occasionally hear one.

There are many folk dances, but classical dance is largely borrowed from Indian models and is frowned upon by the more severe religious leaders.

SOCIETY & CONDUCT
Apart from the obvious religious differences, Bangladesh does not differ markedly from the culture found in the Indian state of Bangla (West Bengal). Centuries of isolation, even when foreign powers ruled, have produced people, customs and values that are typically Bengali in nature. On the surface, Bangladeshis may seem abrupt and unsophisticated. At the heart of things, they are warm, hospitable and exceedingly helpful. If you find yourself in a jam, don't be surprised by the Bangladeshis who will go out of their way to help you; as one traveller commented, you're not just a tourist but an honoured guest. Many people see it as a duty to assist a visitor to their country.

Traditional Culture
Family More than 80% of the population live in rural villages. Even for the city dwellers, there is a strong connection to the 'home village'. Most earn their living from the land, either by farming their own, which is becoming less common as the population increases, or by working for someone else. Rural lives are bounded by dependency: on the elders of the family, on the employer or village patron, or on some other authority figure. Loyalty to the group is an essential cultural value in Bangladesh, one that carries over to urban life.

At the core of this group is the extended family, which forms the basis of social and economic life in Bangladesh and remains a cornerstone despite the recent shift towards nuclear families. The head of the household assumes much of the responsibility and provides for parents, children and other relatives. They all may occupy one house or compound area, and establish separate kitchens as the family grows and more independence is sought. When a son marries, his wife is brought to the family home and assumes the duties outlined by her mother-in-law. The family is a tightly knit group, not only for economic and protective reasons, but as a major centre of both recreational and social activities.

Clothing The most common form of dress for men is a *lungi* and an ordinary shirt. Trousers and other western clothing are popular among the younger generation and businesspeople, though once they are at home almost everyone reverts to traditional dress. The lungi is a cylindrical, skirt-like garment that is wrapped and tied at the waist. A T-shirt or button-down shirt is worn over it. The Indian-style Punjabi suit, an open-collared tunic worn over loose-fitting pants, is also a popular style of dress.

The majority of women wear a sari, a six-foot length of material wrapped in a complicated fashion around their bodies. Worn under this is a short blouse and a plain cotton skirt. A *salwar kameez*, a long dress-like tunic worn over baggy trousers, is the modern woman's alternative to the sari. A long scarf called a *dupatta* or *orna* is draped backwards over the shoulders to cover the chest. One end of the scarf can be used to cover the head for a more modest appearance.

Travellers find themselves the focus of
everyone's attention in Bangladesh.

Staring The western concept of privacy is
not a part of the culture in Bangladesh and
you will probably see this exemplified most
in the Bangladeshi habit of staring at the
unusual – be it an activity, event or person.
Foreigners especially can draw a crowd by
merely stepping out onto the street. Depending on the circumstances and locale, a
group of 30 tightly knit spectators crowding
in to get a look is not unusual. Even better
are the 'saviours' who come to the rescue,
knock back the closest of the crowd, only to
stand there and stare for themselves. For
most westerners, this is an extremely uncomfortable custom, if not downright an-
noying. And it only gets worse because it's
never-ending.

The only solution is to understand plainly
that the prohibition against staring is essentially a western one, and it has no place in
Bangladeshi tradition, and that absolutely
no harm is meant. To be fair, the person
being stared at is probably the most interesting thing that has happened to the starer
all week. Given this, it is still sometimes
difficult to keep the right perspective. When

a little respite is needed to save the sanity,
try ducking into a nearby shop. In most
cases the proprietor will courteously offer
you a seat, chase away the lingerers, and
send the shop assistant off to fetch you a
cup of tea.

Nonverbal Communication The subcontinental head-waggle is a ubiquitous
form of non-verbal communication. Wag-
ging the head from side to side in response
to a question may mean 'no', or 'not sure',
while a single tilt to one side is a sign of
assent or agreement.

Women

Poorer Bangladeshi women bear the brunt
of many of the country's problems. Numerous pregnancies, hard work and a poor diet
mean that many women suffer ill health.

One thing that the visitor may notice
quite quickly is the absence of women on
the streets and in the marketplaces. All the
shopkeepers, produce sellers and hawkers
are men; the outright majority of those
doing the buying, the tea-sipping, and the
standing around are men.

Strict purdah, the practice of keeping
women in seclusion in keeping with the
Quranic injunction to guard women's modesty and purity, is not widely observed in
Bangladesh. It is sometimes found in the
middle to lower-class families, who tend
to be the most conservative element of
society, but most of the poorer segment cannot afford the luxury of idle females. The
generally progressive upper-class, with the
benefit of an urban education, consider
themselves too sophisticated to put up with
it. Even in the absence of purdah, however,
cultural tradition and religious custom serve
to keep women 'under wraps', and relationships between men and women outside
of the family are very formal.

The birth of a daughter is met with less
fanfare than that of a son. The sum of a
girl's training is usually directed towards
the family, home, and eventually mother-
hood. Formal education is not a given, especially if there are sons who require the
family's financial resources in order to be

schooled. In rural areas, only 25% of primary school students are female; a big percentage of girls are not enrolled at all. The overall illiteracy rate for women rises above 80%. Most marriages are arranged by the parents, and in rural villages the general marriageable age for girls is well below the legal minimum of 18 years.

There are a number of development projects that are directed at women's concerns. These focus on training programs regarding health care and legal representation and are intended to foster independence and self-sufficiency. Grameen Bank has become an international success story by lending small amounts of money to individual rural women. See the Grameen Bank boxed text earlier in this chapter for more information.

An alternative development model proposed by the organiastion known as UBINIG (Unnayan Bikalper Nitinirdharoni Gobeshona, which means 'Policy Research for Development Alternatives'), a private organisation concerned with social research and policy critique, involves improving Bangladesh's economic position and raising the economic and social status of women through village-based industries. See the Work section in the Facts for the Visitor chapter for more information about this organisation. Among the wealthier classes many women go to university and there are many professional women.

Dos & Don'ts

Within the Bangladeshi culture, there are a number of social conventions that stem from Islamic and other much older customs. Being sensitive to local custom will make travelling easier and provide a broader perspective on the people and their lifestyle.

Quranic injunctions make it clear that men and women cannot safely form friendships or interact beyond the most formal level. If they do, the worst will happen – the woman will be deprived of her purity and be ruined for life. This tradition fits in with Hindu culture as well. Among the educated upper-class, there is less regard for strict adherence to the social norms, but among the general population the roles are clearly defined. Public physical contact between men and women – between travelling companions, even married ones, or with Bangladeshis – is unacceptable.

On the other hand, physical contact between men is quite common. There's nothing out of the ordinary for two men to walk down the street holding hands and in no way does this indicate homosexuality; it's just the custom. Village boys always seem to want to get in on the act by shaking hands with foreigners, and teenage boys sometimes aim especially for women, but if this gets out of hand you can gracefully refuse.

Modesty in dress, more so for women, is extremely important. Sleeveless shirts and shorts or short skirts are definitely out. For details, see What to Wear in the Women Travellers section of the Facts for the Visitor chapter. Bangladeshi men don't normally wear shorts or sleeveless shirts; a man dressed this way would not necessarily offend, but would certainly attract even more attention.

The left hand is considered unclean, as it is used for toilet purposes. It is courteous to receive or give anything using only the right hand, but it is especially important when offering or receiving food. You may see bread being torn using both hands, but the food that goes into the mouth will be in the right hand. Likewise, water may be drunk from a glass with the left hand because it is not being directly touched. Bangladeshis eat with their hands, and in the smaller towns and villages you may be hard pressed to find an eating utensil.

Feet are also considered unclean, and shoes are generally removed before entering a home. Sitting with a foot pointing toward another person is discourteous, as is stepping over part of someone's body. The thumbs up signal is considered rude.

If a non-muslim wishes to enter a mosque they should first get the approval of the guardian at the door. Women are not usually allowed inside, unless there is a special women's gallery. Take off your shoes and leave them at the door (there's usually a rack for storing them). Walking around in dirty socks or with dirty feet is just as bad as keeping your shoes on, so make sure they're fairly clean. Only visit outside of prayer times, and if anyone is praying in the mosque don't walk in front of them.

RELIGION

Only Indonesia, Pakistan and perhaps India have a larger Muslim population than Bangladesh. A century ago Hinduism represented a third of the country, but now only 10% of the people are Hindus. Some Buddhism and Christianity also exists.

Islam

Bangladesh's Muslim majority is almost entirely Sunni. Although there is a vocal fundamentalist minority, the Liberation War affected the attitude to fundamentalist Islam. This is because some fanatics collaborated with the Pakistanis because of their belief that rebelling against Pakistan, the 'land of the pure', was a crime against Islam.

Islam's founder, the Prophet Mohammed, was born in 570 AD in Mecca, in modern-day Saudi Arabia. The revelations he received from Allah (God) were compiled into the Muslim holy book, the Quran. As his purpose in life was revealed to him, Mohammed began to preach against the idolatry of which Mecca was then a centre. Muslims are strictly monotheistic and believe that the worship of idols is a sin – a view that is diametrically opposed to Hinduism. Muslim teachings correspond closely with the Old Testament of the Christian Bible. Mohammed is the last in the line of prophets, which includes Moses and Jesus, although Jesus is not considered the son of God.

Eventually Mohammed's attacks on local business caused him and his followers to be run out of town in 622 AD. They fled to Medina, the 'city of the prophet', and by 630 AD were strong enough to march back into Mecca and take over. Although Mohammed died in 632 AD, most of Arabia had been converted to the new faith within 20 years.

At an early stage, Islam suffered a schism that continues to this day. The third caliph, successor to Mohammed, was murdered and followed by Ali, the prophet's son-in-law, in 656. Ali was assassinated in 661 by the governor of Syria, who set himself up as caliph in preference to the descendants of Ali. Most Muslims today are Sunnites (or Sunni), followers of the succession from the former governor of Syria, while the others are Shias (or Shi'ites), who follow the descendants of Ali. Bangladesh's small Shia community is mostly descended from Iranian traders, who mainly live in Dhaka and Chittagong.

In the Indian subcontinent Islam was mostly spread by Sufis, followers of a branch of Islam from Central Asia. Sufism is a philosophy that holds that abstinence, self-denial and tolerance – even of other religions – are the route to union with God. Sufi missionaries were able to convert Hindus in Bangladesh with beliefs that have similarities to some branches of Hinduism. Major Sufi sects in Bangladesh include the Naqshbandhis, originally from Central Asia, and the Chishtis, who were founded in Ajmer, India. The Chishtis are best known for championing *qawwali* music, a form that was made popular in the west by the late singer Nusrat Fateh Ali Khan.

Pirs are Sufi religious leaders whose status is something like a cross between that of a bishop and a sage. In much the same way that people maintain their clan roots in a home village or district, many people have a pir to whom their family or village looks for spiritual (and sometimes political) leadership. The largest Sufi centre in Bangladesh is Dewanbag Pak Darbar Sharif, 2km east of Kanchur Bridge on the Dhaka-Chittagong highway.

The annual Biswa Ijtema, an international Muslim gathering second in size only to the hajj (pilgrimage) to Mecca, is held on the outskirts of Dhaka, usually in January.

During the month-long observance of Ramadan, Muslims are prohibited from eating between sunrise and sunset – this might affect your eating habits too.

Hinduism

Hinduism in Bangladesh lacks the pomp and awe of the religion in India, but because of that it's possible to understand it here more easily – people are very willing for you to watch and even participate in Hindu ceremonies. It's always worth checking out any Hindu temple you come across in case something is happening, or just to meet people whose colourful cosmos is such a contrast from the austere Muslim majority's. In many larger towns there is a Ramakrishna Mission that might have information on festivals.

The Hindu minority was persecuted during the Pakistani era, and targeted by the murderous Pakistani army during the Liberation War. As a result many fled to India. Since 1971, relations between Hindus and Muslims have been by and large peaceful with respect to the sufferings of Hindu Bangladeshis during the struggle for independence. One notable exception was in 1992, when the destruction of the Babri mosque in India by Hindu fanatics unleashed a wave of violence against Bangladeshi Hindus, an event captured in Taslima Nasrin's book *Shame* (see Books in the Facts for the Visitor chapter for more information). Many Hindus have emigrated to India in the decades since Partition in 1947. The Indian state of Tripura, tucked between Sylhet and Chittagong divisions was once predominantly tribal, but now has a majority of Bengali Hindus.

Buddhism

Buddhists today are a tiny minority of the population and are mostly tribal people in the Chittagong Hill Tracts. A small ethnic Bengali community also exists. The Buddhist culture that once flourished here and made Bangladesh a major pilgrimage centre had faded under pressure from Hinduism before the arrival of Islam, but its influence lingered in the styles of sculpture and the generally relaxed way of life. Some scholars claim that Tantric Buddhism, now largely confined to Himalayan countries, began here. Most of the temples and monasteries in Chittagong division reflect the influence of neighbouring Myanmar (Burma) rather than Bangladesh's Buddhist past.

Christianity

Although there is a very small Christian population here, mostly comprising descendants of Portuguese traders, there is quite a strong Christian presence courtesy of the foreign aid organisations. There are also a number of missionary groups that have found their footing in rural areas through the operation of development projects and health care programs. Since overt proselytising is forbidden by the Muslim government, these groups focus on providing aid to the needy and serving Christians in the community rather than attempting to make converts. For this reason, missionaries in Bangladesh tend to be a bit more relaxed overall about religious matters.

Facts for the Visitor

HIGHLIGHTS

Bangladesh doesn't have a lot of conventional tourist 'sights'. The fascination of the country lies more in observing life going on around you than in taking souvenir snaps of a Taj Mahal or an alpine vista. The most enjoyable aspects of your stay could be a rickshaw ride, a boat trip, visiting a village, even walking the teeming streets of Dhaka.

That said, there are a few sights that make a worthwhile excursion. On the eastern side of the country these include the tea gardens (especially around Srimangal), the fascinating Rangamati and Bandarban in the Chittagong Hill Tracts, the beach stretching from Cox's Bazar to the southernmost tip of the country, and the Buddhist temples in the Cox's Bazar and Hill Tracts areas. A more off-beat sight in this region is the ship-breaking yards on the coast just north of Chittagong.

In the west, highlights include the vast watery forests of the Sundarbans National Park, the mosques at Bagerhat, the palace at Natore, the Hindu temples of Puthia, the country's best archaeological site at Paharpur, and the stunning Kantanagar Temple.

For sheer urban mayhem you can't beat Dhaka, in the centre of the country. A boat trip to or from here to one of the southern cities is a highlight. To the north of Dhaka the Madhupur Forest and the tribal villages of the Mandi people are worth a visit, and some say the city of Mymensingh has the country's most lavishly decorated rickshaws.

The unpleasant aspects of Bangladesh include the following: Dhaka's air pollution, kamikaze traffic, cramped buses, loud hawking and spitting, drab hotel rooms, stomach bugs, injured and disabled beggars, and the sense that you couldn't attract more staring if you were a 10m-high Martian.

SUGGESTED ITINERARIES

If time is limited to only a couple of days, the best way to get a taste of the country would be to take a boat cruise with one of the tour operators listed in the Dhaka chapter. A half-day cruise on the rivers around Dhaka could also include some sightseeing around the city. In three days you could take a boat cruise, visit the old capital at Sonargaon and visit the markets of Dhaka.

There are too few tourists to Bangladesh for a 'backpacker trail' to have evolved at this stage, but for travellers planning on travelling overland from India an itinerary might go like this:

- After crossing the border at Benapole stay overnight in Jessore, then head down to Khulna and Mongla and take a boat trip into the northern fringes of the Sundarbans.
- From Khulna or Mongla you could take a boat to Barisal, and then go by road or boat down to the beach at Kuakata. Alternatively, from Khulna or Mongla you could take the ferry to Dhaka. A couple of days in the capital will probably suffice, and you could then head to Srimangal and spend a few days cycling around the tea gardens.
- You could then cross back into India at Tamabil north-east of Sylhet, or head south to Chittagong. From this port city it is easy to head into the tribal lands of the Chittagong Hill Tracts, or head south to Cox's Bazar. The temples and islands found around Cox's Bazar are worth visiting, and you have a decent chance of meeting other travellers here. From Cox's Bazar you could make your way back to Dhaka, and then head north.
- Mymensingh and the Madhupur Forest are easy to reach from the capital, and from here you could head into Rajshahi division across the Bangabandhu Bridge. The Hindu temples at Puthia are worth a look, but Paharpur and Kantanagar Temple, further north, are highly recommended – they are definitely highlights. The town of Thakurgaon is a nice way to get a taste of rural life, and it's fairly easy to head north, cross the border at Chilahati and head for Sikkim or Darjeeling.

For specific information and advice about travelling between destinations, see the Getting Around chapter and the Getting There & Away entries in the relevant sections throughout this book.

Travellers' Impressions

Whether their visit was weeks, years or centuries ago, travellers' interests seem to be the same – the prices, the climate, the people, the curiosities and so on. Some impressions of Bangladesh:

Fa Xien

A 5th-century Chinese Buddhist pilgrim, Fa Xien came here via the Karakoram where the Gupta imperial power held sway. He visited Buddhist pilgrimage centres in northern India and was impressed all the way through by the great structures and the prosperity of the land.

Xuan Zhang

Xuan Zhang was another Chinese Buddhist traveller, who came via the Karakoram two centuries later. He was similarly amazed by the temples, stupas and monasteries where thousands of *bhikkus* (monks) lived, which he described as 'ornaments of the earth, as high as mountain peaks, obstructing the very course of the sun with their lofty and imposing towers'. He probably exaggerated a little.

Marco Polo

Travelling as an emissary of Kublai Khan in the 14th century, the famed Venetian traveller came close to the southern borders of China, but may never have actually visited Bangala. Hence, his information certainly does not sound first-hand. He described Bangala as a province of southern China close to India, populated by wretched idolaters with a peculiar language.

Ibn Battuta

A Moroccan from Tangier, this 14th-century visitor noted how inexpensive Bangala was. He stocked up on female slaves, who seem to have been available at bargain-basement prices that century. Of Bangala he wrote: 'There are innumerable vessels on the rivers and each vessel carries a drum and when vessels meet each of them beats a drum and they salute one another'. He visited Sylhet to see a famous Persian saint who lived in a cave and fasted for 10 days and drank cow's milk on the 11th. 'He would then remain standing all night in prayer.' The saint apparently said his prayers in Mecca each morning but was present in his cave the rest of the day. He also paid a special visit to Mecca each year on the occasion of the Id festival.

'We travelled down the river for 15 days (from Sylhet to Sonargaon),' he wrote, 'between villages and orchards just as if we were going through a bazaar. On the banks are waterwheels, orchards, villages to the right and left like those on the Nile River'. He met religious mendicants, Sufis and fakirs and described the land as scenic and luxuriant. In summer, he reported, the creeks and inlets steamed up and as one went through them one had a 'vapour bath'. The people in the west, he continued, were oppressed and called the land Dazaki-i-pur Niamat – 'a hell crammed with blessings'.

Mu Huang

This Chinese traveller visited Sonargaon in the 15th century, probably as a seaman. He described foreign vessels arriving and lying at anchor in estuaries while small boats ferried them to the inland river port. He was similarly impressed by the general prosperity of the land and its wealthy cities with their palaces, temples and gardens. Like Ibn Battuta he noted that there were many Sufis and fakirs.

Zaheed Beg

In the 17th century this Mughal visitor observed that no one liked the country. Mughal officials and military officers stationed here demanded increased salaries, higher ranks and payment in cash. It was an unhealthy land and Zaheed Beg, on being nominated as viceroy of Bangala, exclaimed: 'Ah... your majesty could find no better place to kill me than Bangala.'

PLANNING
When to Go

Tropical Bangladesh can be visited year round, but there's no doubt that the most pleasant time is in winter. It's hottest during the pre-monsoon spring from April to mid-June, when both temperature and humidity climb steadily to very uncomfortable levels. By mid-June the monsoon begins and things cool off slightly, though it remains extremely muggy. The whole country begins to fill up with water, the bulk of it coming down the rivers from the Himalaya. It's a fascinating time to visit but the humidity, the difficulties of travel and a higher risk of getting sick are serious deterrents.

It begins to cool off and dry up by October, and between November and February the weather is at its best. The evenings can get quite chilly in December and January.

Maps

Lonely Planet's *India & Bangladesh* travel atlas is a useful resource for travellers. For a reasonably good sheet map of the country, purchase the *Bangladesh Guide Map* by The Mappa. The Mappa also publishes a good Dhaka map – *Dhaka City Guide Map*. You'll find the latter two in Dhaka at Boi Bichitra on Gulshan Ave, at the bookshops at the Sonargaon and Sheraton hotels, at The Mappa offices (☎ 811 7260) in the city centre at 112 Green Rd, and possibly at the New Market (the south-eastern corner). The Bangladesh Guide Map definitely has errors, but it's far better than the many older, locally produced maps on the market, which are terrible. The older Dhaka city maps are just as bad, except for the Parjatan *Dhaka Tourist Map*, which is a vast improvement over past editions.

Another excellent map company is Graphosman (☎ 955 2394), which has maps of each division of the country and a detailed map of the Chittagong Hill Tracts. Its office is in Karim Mansion, North-South Rd, in central Dhaka. You may find street vendors selling these and other maps as well.

What to Bring

The weather is warm year-round, so you don't need to bring much clothing. Light,

cotton clothing for wearing in summer, a rainproof jacket for the monsoon (or buy a sturdy cloth umbrella here), and a woollen pullover or light jacket for chilly winter nights, especially in the north. Shorts are unacceptable in public for women. Men can wear shorts in public, but it is not advisable when you're in traditional areas as it will only make you stand out more, thus increasing the amount of staring that you will have to endure.

Steep gangplanks and slippery decks are a major part of travel here, so bring shoes with a good grip. Rubber thongs (flip-flops) can be bought here – they are also good for lounging around the hotel and protecting your feet from fungal infections in the shower.

Bearing in mind the strength of the tropical sun, it would be a good idea to bring a hat, sun cream and sunglasses. To keep mosquitoes away, bring some roll-on repellent. Coils for your room at night are available everywhere.

In rural areas where electricity is unreliable and many streets are unlit, a torch is essential. Batteries can be bought locally and inexpensively, but they don't last as long as those brought from home. A lock for the occasional dodgy hotel door would be handy, and a universal sink plug may also prove to be useful.

A complete range of western toiletries is available in Dhaka, and to a lesser extent in the major cities. They tend to be more expensive than what you'd normally pay when you're at home.

RESPONSIBLE TOURISM

Bangladesh's foreign tourist industry is tiny compared to the domestic one, but travellers should be sensitive to their impact on the local environment and society, and try to spend their money in ways that benefit local communities. The tour operators listed in this book are all locally owned, but if you plan to visit Bangladesh or part of Bangladesh on an organised tour, ask how the money is spent. Companies should employ local guides and staff.

The tribal people of Bangladesh are quite vulnerable, not only to encroachment on their land but to the undermining of their culture and social systems by insensitive visitors. Visitors should be careful to get the permission of local chiefs and elders to stay overnight in tribal villages, ask permission to take photographs, and pay fair prices for handicrafts.

The Sundarbans is a sensitive environmental region. Don't dispose of non-biodegradable waste by simply throwing it overboard, and try to ascertain in advance how the tour operator plans to deal with rubbish.

Sex tourism does exist in Bangladesh, and it is said that most customers come from wealthy Arab countries. Prostitution is quite common in the areas of Dhaka frequented by foreigners and the local elite, and because it is illegal it is entirely unsupervised by health authorities. Be warned that besides the health risks, the racket is controlled by the mafia and if you get robbed no-one is going to feel sorry for you. Child prostitution also exists.

Many countries now have extraterritorial child sexual abuse laws. This means that sex offenders can be prosecuted in their home country for crimes against children committed in other countries. At the same time countries that have traditionally attracted sex tourists are now prosecuting foreigners for abusing children.

If you suspect that child sex offences are being committed by someone you should act immediately. This could prevent further abuse. ECPAT (End Child Prostitution and Trafficking) recommends the following steps:

• Report it to the local police.
• Report it to the consul at the embassy of the alleged perpetrator, if the perpetrator is a foreigner.
• If the nationality of the perpetrator is unknown report it to your own consul/embassy.
• If offences are committed within a hotel/guesthouse report it to the management.
• Report it the relevant authorities when you return home (if the perpetrator is a foreigner).

Additionally, if you wish to, you can report the offence to ECPAT groups in your country. Their Web site can be found at http://www.ecpat.net/

A few tourist-oriented shops still sell products from endangered animals, such as ivory. Think of how this item will be replaced if you buy it. In any case souvenirs made of tortoise shell, ivory and animal pelts will be confiscated by customs in your home country and it is possible you could be fined or even jailed.

There has long been an illegal trade in exported antiquities from the country, in particular relics from the Hindu or Buddhist eras. Certain antique dealers in Dhaka operate with little fear of the police, but again think of how these items will be replaced – by looting more of the country's heritage.

TOURIST OFFICES

The Bangladesh Parjatan Corporation is the national tourist office. Theoretically it provides tourist information, runs tours from Dhaka and has four tourist offices in that city. In practice it has one mildly useful tourist office and runs a chain of relatively expensive hotels/motels. The best place for information is the main Parjatan office on Old Airport Rd, Tejgaon (☎ 02-317836, 817855/9, fax 817235). It also has offices at the Dhaka Sheraton Hotel (☎ 02-509479), the Sonargaon Hotel (☎ 02-811641, 814937) and Zia International Airport (☎ 02-894416). Usually these offices have little to offer except a batch of brochures.

Parjatan also advertises that you can get tourist information at its hotels outside Dhaka, but in fact they can do little more than help you find a rental car. These hotels are in Bogra, Chittagong, Cox's Bazar, Dinajpur, Kuakata, Rajshahi, Rangamati, Rangpur and Sylhet. See the individual city sections in the relevant chapters for details.

VISAS & DOCUMENTS
Passport

Your passport should be valid for at least six months beyond the duration of your stay. You'll need your passport to register at hotels, but if you're staying long-term then it isn't strictly necessary to carry it with you at all times. Police are usually very helpful and rarely hassle foreigners. If it's back at the hotel, you should have no worry (if it's in a security box). Incidentally, it is said to be possible to acquire a Bangladeshi passport for US$100 or so, if you know the right people.

Visas for Bangladesh

Visas are required for citizens of all countries except Japan and South Korea, who can stay for 90 days visa-free, and Sri Lankans, who can stay 30 days without a visa.

Theoretically everyone else can purchase a visa at Dhaka's Zia International Airport, but in practice this is not a good idea. Visitors are vulnerable to officials trying to rip them off, and sometimes airport officials won't give any visas (when foreign leaders are visiting the country and security is tight, for example). You can get visas from all neighbouring countries and generally the process is simple and straightforward. The fee varies according to nationality: US$21 for Americans and Australians, US$13 for Germans, US$37 for Canadians, US$41 for the French and UK£40 for Britons. If you later decide to extend your stay, extensions can be obtained, though this requires tangling with Bangladeshi bureaucracy.

In Washington, the Bangladeshi embassy requires two photos and payment by money order (include a self-addressed envelope with applications made by mail). Applications in person are received from 9 am to noon and passports can be collected the following day from noon. The process at the high commission in London is similar, except that the applicant is asked to provide the names and addresses of two contacts in Bangladesh; listing two hotels seems to satisfy this requirement.

Bangladesh has embassies in many countries in the region. While the consulate in Kolkata (Calcutta) can be unpredictable, the consulate in Agartala in Tripura issues visas without fuss. The Bangkok embassy gets good reports. The embassy in Kathmandu reportedly only issues visas to Nepali citizens.

The Bangladeshi embassy in Delhi accepts applications on weekdays between 10 am and noon; you can pick up your passport in the afternoon. Fees in Delhi and Kathmandu are in line with what they cost at Dhaka airport. See Bangladesh High Commissions & Embassies Abroad under Embassies & Consulates later in this chapter for contact details. If you can't get a visa in your home country, getting a visa in India or Thailand shouldn't be a hassle.

Visas valid for six months from the date of issue and good for stays of three months are the norm. However, if you don't request a three-month visa you may end up with a visa valid for only one month. There's no difference in price.

Requests for visas for stays longer than three months are usually denied. However, if you're persistent, requests based on the demands of a job are more likely to be successful and you might be one of the lucky few who get a visa valid for a six-month stay. The cost is often slightly more (eg, UK£52 for Britons in London).

Visa Extensions Apply for visa extensions in Dhaka at the Immigration & Passport Office (☎ 955 6020), at 127 New Eskaton Rd, Mogh Bazar. Bring one photo. Extensions up to a total stay of three months are generally easy to obtain. If you received a 15-day visa at the airport, you should have the extension the same day if you apply before 11 am. If you've been there three months and wish to extend beyond that, the process will often take up to a week or more, and there is no assurance that you'll receive an extension. The better the reason you have for needing the extension and the more convincing you are, the better your chances are.

Try not to overstay your visa – there is a charge of Tk 500 per day for each day extra! In some cases travellers have been charged even more, given no receipt and the extra charge has not been explained. Corruption is rampant in cases of requests to extend stays longer than three months, so start the process early – at least a week before the expiration date if you've already been there three months.

The office is open Saturday to Thursday from 10 am to noon for receiving applications (in triplicate). Routine extensions can usually be collected after 2.30 pm, although a wait of a day is not unusual. Fees for three-month visa extensions vary according to nationality, eg, US$45 for Americans, US$65 for Britons, US$41 for French people, US$21 for Australians, US$13 for Germans. Some Britons, however, have been charged as much as Tk 2600. If you can't get an extension, it's fairly easy to leave and get another three-month visa in Nepal or India, but the consulate in Kolkata may refuse if they see you've just completed a three-month stay.

Visas for Neighbouring Countries

For addresses of embassies within Bangladesh, see Embassies later in this chapter.

Bhutan Bhutanese visas are only issued at Paro airport or at the border post of Phuentsholing. For a tourist visa you must apply through a tour operator who can sponsor your visa. For information on reputable tour operators and travel in Bhutan, see Lonely Planet's *Bhutan*.

India Six-month multiple-entry visas are now issued to most nationalities whether or not you intend staying that long or re-entering the country. You need two passport photos and must pay a fee, which varies with nationality. For Australians the fee is A$55, for Britons £19, for Americans it costs US$65 and for French people 200FF; it is payable in taka. The Indian High Commission in Dhaka is open Saturday to Thursday from 9 am to 4.30 pm; visa applications are accepted from 9 am to 11.30 am.

There is a Tk 230 fee for a telex or fax to your home country to check if you're a criminal. Bring plenty of change because they never seem to have any. Visas usually take five days to a week to be issued. A special permit is needed to enter the northeastern states of Mizoram, Manipur, Nagaland and Arunachal Pradesh, and these are never granted by embassies.

Myanmar The embassy receives visa applications between 9.30 am and 12.30 pm Sunday to Thursday. The application form is very simple. Four-week visas are issued

routinely in 24 hours. The cost is US$20 in taka for all nationalities.

Nepal The Nepali embassy faces the US embassy. The visa office takes applications between 10 am and noon Sunday to Thursday and visas are issued within 24 hours. Bring one passport photo. The fee, which is the same for everyone, is US$15 for visas valid for stays of 15 days, US$25 for 30 days, and US$30 for 60 days. Since obtaining a visa at the airport in Kathmandu requires no photo and costs the same, most people get them there.

Thailand Most nationalities get a 30-day visa on arrival in Thailand. This visa can't be extended. Two-month visas issued by the Thai embassy cost US$12 in taka, and can be extended for one more month in Thailand. The visa office takes applications between 9 am and noon Sunday to Thursday. Applications made early in the morning can be processed in 24 hours.

Travel Permits

Permits are required if you wish to visit the Sundarbans during your stay. You will also need a permit if you wish to go to India by road and you arrived by air. Permits are no longer required to visit the Chittagong Hill Tracts.

The District Forestry Office (☎ 041-720665, 721173) in Khulna issues permits to the Sundarbans. Permits are issued on the spot and cost only Tk 4 per person per day. See Travel Permits to the Sundarbans in the Khulna section of the Khulna Division chapter for more information.

If, having entered by air, you leave Bangladesh via a land border crossing, a road permit is required. See the Land section in the Getting There & Away chapter for details.

Travel Insurance

A travel insurance policy for medical emergencies is necessary for Bangladesh. Your policy should cover an emergency flight home. There is a wide variety of policies available, so check the small print.

Some policies specifically exclude 'dangerous activities', which can include motorcycling and even trekking. A locally acquired motorcycle licence is not valid under some policies.

For theft and loss you will require documentation from the Bangladeshi police; getting these documents is a hassle, often requires a 'fee', and even then your insurance company may not honour it.

Driving Licence
A driver's licence might conceivably be useful as a second identification document in some instances but unless you're brave enough to be driving in Bangladesh, a licence is of no use because there are no self-drive car rentals.

If you are driving to Bangladesh you will need an International Driver's Licence, a *carnet de passage en douane* (a document from the motoring organisation in the country of registration of the vehicle, which says that you will not sell the vehicle abroad without paying import duties), and preferably an entry permit from the Bangladeshi consulate in Kolkata or the high commission in Delhi. See Bangladeshi Embassies & Consulates under Embassies & Consulates later in this chapter for contact details.

Vaccination Certificates
It is a good idea to have copies of all of your vaccination certificates with you when you enter Bangladesh, especially yellow fever if you are coming from a high-risk area. An International Health Certificate is theoretically also required, but foreigners are not asked to show it. For details of vaccinations advised, see the Health section later in this chapter.

Business Cards
You'll find business cards extremely useful. In the business world you are nobody without one, and in social settings one of the first things people often do is to exchange them. They're also handy if you want to stay at a government rest house. Getting 100 business cards made up in Dhaka costs from Tk 100.

Copies
All important documents (passport data page and visa page, credit cards, travel insurance policy, air/bus/train tickets, driving licence etc) should be photocopied before you leave home. Leave one copy with someone at home and keep another with you, separate from the originals.

It's also a good idea to store details of your vital travel documents in Lonely Planet's free online Travel Vault in case you lose the photocopies or can't be bothered with them. Your password-protected Travel Vault is accessible online anywhere in the world – you can create it at www.ekno.lonelyplanet.com.

EMBASSIES & CONSULATES
Bangladeshi Embassies & Consulates

Australia (☎ 02-6295 3328, fax 6295 3351) 35 Endeavour St, Red Hill, Canberra, ACT 2603 Web site: www.users.cyberone.com.au /bdeshact

Belgium (☎ 02-640 5500, fax 646 5998) 29-31 Rue Jacques Jordaens, 1050, Brussels

Bhutan (☎ 2539, fax 22697) Plot No IIIG-3, Upper Chubachu, Thimpu

Brazil (☎ 61-248 4905, fax 248 4609) SHIS, QL-10, Conj. 01 Casa 17, Brasilia-DF

Canada (☎ 613-236 0138, fax 567 3213) 275 Bank St, Suite 302, Ottawa, Ontario K2P 2I6 Web site: www.iosphere.net/~bhc

China (☎ 10-532 3706, fax 532 4346) 42, Guang Hua Lu, Beijing

France (☎ 1-45 53 41 20, fax 47 04 72 41) 5 Square Petrarque, 75016 Paris

Germany (☎/fax 30-398975) Dovestrasse 1, 10557 Berlin

Hong Kong (☎ 2827 4278/9, fax 2827 1916) Room 3807, China Resources Bldg, 26 Harbour Rd, Wanchai

India (☎ 11-683 9209, fax 683 9237) 56 Ring Rd, Lajpat Nagar 111, New Delhi
Consulate in Kolkata: (☎ 33-247 5203, fax 247 0941) 9 Circus Ave, 700 017
Consulate in Agartala: (☎ 0381-224807) Kunjaban Rd, 799 006

Indonesia (☎ 21-525 1986, fax 526 1807) 12 Jalan Situbondo, Menteng, Jakarta

Italy (☎ 6-807 8541, fax 808 4853) Via Antonio Bertoloni 14, Rome 00197

Japan (☎ 03-3442 1501, fax 3447 3676) 7-45 Shirogane, 2 Chome, Minato-ku, Tokyo 108

Malaysia (☎ 3-242 3271, fax 241 3381) 204-1
Jalan Ampang, 50450, Kuala Lumpur
Myanmar (Burma) (☎ 01-51174, fax 38745)
56 Kaba Aye Pagoda Rd, Yangon (Rangoon)
Consulate in Sittwe: (☎ 043-21126) Main Rd,
South Lanmadaw Quarters
Nepal (☎ 1-414943) Maharajganj, Ring Rd,
Ward 22 Shanti Ashram, Kitta No 9, Kathmandu
Pakistan (☎ 51-213885, fax 213883) House 24,
St No 28, F-6/1 Islamabad
Consulate in Karachi: (☎ 21-516 597, fax 568
2303) 9 Choudhury Khaliquzzaman Rd, 0401
Philippines (☎ 2-817 5001, fax 816 4941) 2nd
floor, Universal Re Bldg, 106 Paseo De
Roxas, Makati, Metro Manila
Russia (☎ 95-246 7900, fax 248 3185) 6
Zemledelcheski Perculok, Moscow
Singapore (☎ 225 0075, fax 255 1824) 06-07
United Sq, 101 Thompson Rd, Singapore 1130
South Africa (☎ 12-45 3366, fax 45 3330) 133
Ouderberg Rd, Waterkloof Heights, Pretoria
South Korea (☎ 2-796 4065, fax 790 5313) 35-
5 Hannam 1-Dong, Yongsan-Ku, Seoul
Sri Lanka (☎ 1-502 198, fax 508 123) 286
Bauddhaloka Mawatha, Colombo 7
Sweden (☎ 08-679 9555, fax 611 9817) 1st
floor, Anderstorpvagen 12, 17154 Stockholm
Switzerland (☎ 22-449 340/9, fax 738 4616) 65
rue de Lausanne, 1202 Geneva
Thailand (☎ 2-392 9437, fax 391 8070) House
No 727, Thonglor, Soi-55, Sukhumvit Rd,
Bangkok, 10110
UK (☎ 020-7584 0081, fax 225 2130) 28
Queen's Gate, London SW7 5JA
Consulate in Birmingham: (☎ 0121-643 2386,
fax 643 9004) 31-33 Guildhall Bldg, 12
Navigation St, Birmingham, 42 4NT
Consulate in Manchester: (☎ 161-236 4853,
fax 236 1064) 3rd floor, 28-32 Princess St,
Manchester, MI 4LB
USA (☎ 202-342 8373, fax 333 4971) 2201
Wisconsin Ave NW, Suite 300, Washington
DC 20007
Web site: members.aol.com/banglaemb
Consulate in Los Angeles: (☎ 310-441 9399,
fax 441 4458) 10850 Wilshire Blvd, Suite
1250, CA 90024
Consulate in New York: (☎ 212-599 6767, fax
682 9211) 211 E 43rd St, Suite 502, NY 10017

Your Own Embassy

It's important to know what your own
embassy – the embassy of the country of
which you are a citizen – can do to help you
if you get into trouble. Generally it won't be
much help in emergencies if the trouble

you're in is remotely your own fault. Remember that you are bound by the laws of the country you are in. Your embassy will not be sympathetic if you end up in jail after committing a crime locally, even if such actions are legal in your own country.

In genuine emergencies you might get some assistance, but only if other channels have been exhausted. For example, if you need to get home urgently, a free ticket home is exceedingly unlikely – the embassy would expect you to have insurance. If you have all your money and documents stolen, it might assist with getting a new passport, but a loan for onward travel is out of the question.

Some embassies used to keep letters for travellers or have a small reading room with home newspapers, but these days the mail-holding service has usually been stopped and even newspapers tend to be out of date.

Embassies & Consulates in Bangladesh

If you are going to spend a considerable length of time in a remote area, it is probably a good idea to register with your embassy.

Australia (☎ 600091/5) 184 Gulshan Ave,
Gulshan
Belgium (☎ 600138) 22 Gulshan Ave, Gulshan
Bhutan (☎ 818 6863) House 5/E, Gulshan Ave,
Gulshan
Canada (☎ 818 3639) House 16/A, Rd 48,
Gulshan
Denmark (☎ 818 1799) House 1, Rd 51, Gulshan
France (☎ 601049) House 18, Rd 108, Gulshan
Germany (☎ 818 4735/7) 178 Gulshan Ave,
Gulshan
India (☎ 506346) House 120, Rd 2, Dhanmondi
Italy (☎ 818 2781/3) corner of Rds 74 & 79,
Gulshan
Japan (☎ 817 0087) Dutabash Rd, Baridhara
Malaysia (☎ 818 7759/60) House 4, Rd 118,
Gulshan
Myanmar (Burma) (☎ 601461) 106 Gulshan
Ave, Gulshan
Nepal (☎ 601890) corner of UN Rd and Rd 2,
Baridhara
Netherlands (☎ 818 2715/8) House 49, Rd 90,
Gulshan

Norway (☎ 818 3880) House 9, Rd 111, Gulshan
Pakistan (☎ 818 5388/9) House 2, Rd 71, Gulshan
Russia (☎ 818 8147) House 9, Rd 79, Gulshan
Sweden (☎ 818 4761/4) House 1, Rd 51, Gulshan
Switzerland (☎ 817 2874/6) House 31/B, Rd 18, Banani
Thailand (☎ 817 3261) House 19, Rd 62, Gulshan
UK (☎ 818 2705/9) 13 UN Rd at Dutabash Rd, Baridhara
USA (☎ 813 1891/2) 9 Park Rd at Madani Ave, Baridhara

CUSTOMS

The usual '200 cigarettes, one litre of alcohol' rule applies. Foreigners will be permitted to bring in US$5000 and Tk 300 without any need for declaration. For Bangladeshis the amounts are US$2500 and Tk 300. Don't be surprised if even the border officials themselves don't know the exact amounts.

On departure tourists are allowed to reconvert 25% of the total foreign currency encashed in the country. This is only possible at the airport in Dhaka, and you will need to have you encashment slips with you to use as proof.

The rules are a little vague. Don't arrive at the airport with a lot of taka for conversion, especially if you're leaving in the middle of the night – the bank might be 'closed' or they might claim that it has insufficient dollars, and the staff who happen to be hanging around will change your money at rip-off rates.

MONEY
Currency

The principal unit of money is the taka (Tk, pronounced 'tahka'), which is further divided into 100 paisas. There are 10, 20 and 50 paisa, and Tk 1, Tk 2 and Tk 5 coins. There are notes in denominations of Tk 1, Tk 2, Tk 5, Tk 10, Tk 20, Tk 50, Tk 100 and Tk 500.

Torn-note phobia isn't as bad here as it is in India, but you do sometimes find that a tear means that a note will be refused by merchants. Most banks will usually exchange torn notes for more acceptable untorn ones.

Exchange Rates

Exchange rates have been stable in recent years, with a slight annual devaluation.

country	unit		taka
Australia	A$1	=	Tk 32
Canada	C$1	=	Tk 35
euro	€1	=	Tk 50
France	10FF	=	Tk 77
Germany	DM1	=	Tk 26
India	Rs 100	=	Tk 117
Japan	¥100	=	Tk 47
New Zealand	NZ$1	=	Tk 25
Thailand	100B	=	Tk 135
UK	UK£1	=	Tk 82
USA	US$1	=	Tk 51

Exchanging Money

US dollars is the preferred currency, with British pounds running a distant second. American Express, ANZ Grindlays, HSBC and Standard Chartered Bank have branches in Dhaka and Chittagong; ANZ Grindlays has branches in other major cities such as Khulna and Sylhet. The government-owned Sonali and Janata banks usually change money, although some rural branches won't. Uttara, Agrani and Pubali will often change money; other private commercial banks include Al Baraka Bank, Arab Bangladesh Bank, National Bank and The City Bank.

Cash It helps to have some US dollars with you when you can't change travellers cheques or use a credit card. Changing cash into taka is no problem; there are many authorised moneychangers in the cities that legally convert cash on the spot at good rates. Better still, they're open all hours and they can convert taka into US dollars as well. With the liberalisation of the economy, there is essentially no black market.

Travellers Cheques Standard Chartered Bank and ANZ Grindlays are best if you have British travellers cheques, including those from Thomas Cook. However, ANZ Grindlays' commissions at Tk 350 per cheque are ridiculously high compared with Standard Chartered's at Tk 65/90 for each US$50/100 travellers cheque.

Many banks will not cash travellers cheques if you don't have the receipt showing proof of purchase, so be sure to bring it along. There usually isn't a fee if you cash travellers cheques at branches of the issuing bank.

ATMs Dhaka and Chittagong have a handful of ATMs (a grand total of 10), and it is possible that an ATM will be set up in Khulna. Any card with a Plus or Cirrus logo is accepted at ANZ Grindlays and HSBC ATMs; Standard Chartered ATMs are only accessible to local account holders.

Credit Cards Credit cards, especially Visa, MasterCard and American Express, are widely accepted at major hotels, guesthouses and restaurants in both Dhaka and Chittagong, but virtually nowhere else. American Express cardholders can obtain cash or travellers cheques with their cards. Cash advances on credit cards can be made at ANZ Grindlays and HSBC banks.

International Transfers If you need money transferred to you in Bangladesh, it can be done via American Express or Western Union: have someone at home go to an American Express office and ask them to credit it to you (full name and passport number required) in Dhaka. One traveller reported having cash in hand within 12 hours of the call. Another traveller reported waiting only three days for the money, including the time it took for his telegram to get to the UK.

Security
Petty theft in Bangladesh is rare but on the rise. It's a good idea to use a money belt when you're going about town, especially in Dhaka, and to make use of safe deposit boxes if you're staying at a top-end hotel.

Costs
Bangladesh is a very cheap country to travel in if you're prepared to travel on a budget, even cheaper than India – but the quality of budget food, accommodation and travel is low. It is possible to travel on Tk 200 (US$4) a day by travelling 2nd class on trains and on local buses, staying at hotels

for around Tk 60 (typically tiny rooms with fans plus a bathroom which may or may not be attached), and eating at the cheapest restaurants (Tk 20 a meal).

Travelling at this level does not mean you'll have a buggy room every night; a good percentage of cheap hotels are quite decent. However, if you want to escape nerve-shattering buses and avoid stomach bugs, you'll have to move up a notch, although it's still quite inexpensive (US$10 to US$15 a day).

Tipping
Baksheesh (pronounced 'BOHK-sheesh'), in the sense of a tip or gift rather than a bribe (an admittedly fine line), is part of life in Bangladesh. Don't see it as begging; it's part of Islamic morality that rich people give part of their income to those less fortunate. There are some peculiarities to this system though; one expat reports that he has to pay baksheesh to have the phone bill delivered, or else it never arrives and the phone is disconnected without any warning. If you're going to be repeatedly using a service, an initial tip ensures that decent standards will be kept up.

In expensive restaurants in Dhaka that are mostly frequented by foreigners, waiters often expect a small tip, typically in the 5% range.

Bargaining
Many transactions require bargaining. This can be fun and is a normal part of life, not an attempt to rip you off. The perfect deal is one in which both parties are satisfied, so always leave room to manoeuvre. It often takes only a very small increase in your offer for the vendor to feel that honour has been satisfied. A rule of thumb is to offer about half of the original price and work up from there.

For those who absolutely detest the bargaining ritual, decide ahead of time what the item is worth to you. If the vendor's price is lower, you've come out ahead. If it's higher, state your price and be willing to leave it if it's not accepted. In most cases, vendors know when you mean business, and if your offer is a fair one, they won't let you get too far away before they decide to agree to it.

Bear in mind that most vendors live hand-to-mouth and a few extra taka are going to help them more than it's going to hurt you.

POST & COMMUNICATIONS
Sending Mail
The postal system in Bangladesh works surprisingly well, despite the impression you get upon entering most post offices. Inside, it's dark and gloomy and you have to wait around for an attendant to show up, and then they won't know how much postage to put on your letter back home. You start wondering whether, if you leave it there, it will make it past the first rubbish bin. The answer is 'yes', and it will take about 10 to 15 days to get there.

Receiving Mail
If you're going to be in the country long enough to receive a package, or if you think luck is on your side, you'll eventually find the one person at the GPO who admits he knows the procedure. Make sure you don't lose the scrap of paper that appeared at poste restante to notify you of the package's arrival. Postal hours are 9 am to 3 pm Saturday to Thursday.

The poste restante service in Dhaka is at the main GPO on Abdul Gani Rd; it's the first door on your right upon entering the main hall. Service is not the best and the person responsible for keeping the box sometimes decides to leave early. When looking for letters, be sure to ask to see the 'second' box after going through the main stack. For mysterious reasons, the policy is to store some letters in a completely different place.

Telephone & Fax
International calls are very easy to make. Many phones have direct dial service via satellite. Rates are 25% lower all day Friday and on other days from 11 pm to 8 am. Local calls present no problems, but between cities it is often difficult to hear the other end. The only way to make a 'public' phone call is to use the telephone and fax services available at numerous small business centres in Dhaka, Chittagong and even some smaller towns; they're usually well marked. Charges are about double the actual telephone rate, eg, Tk 120/130/140 a minute to Australia/Europe/America. If you use one of the major hotels instead of the small business centres you'll pay two or three times as much. The numbers for long-distance information are 103 (domestic) and 162 (foreign). International operators speak English; many other operators do not.

Internet
Access is limited in Bangladesh, but there are some Internet cafes in Dhaka, and some top-end hotels in Khulna may be able to help. Some computer shops in Chittagong might let you send emails. See the relevant chapters for more information.

INTERNET RESOURCES
The World Wide Web is a rich resource for travellers. You can research your trip, hunt down bargain air fares, book hotels, check on weather conditions or chat with locals and other travellers about the best places to visit.

There's no better place to start than by visiting Lonely Planet's very own Web site (www.lonelyplanet.com). Here you'll find summaries on travelling to Bangladesh and just about every other place on earth, postcards from other travellers, and the Thorn Tree bulletin board, where you can ask questions before you go or give advice when you get back. You can also find travel news and updates to many of our guidebooks, and the subWWWay section links to useful travel resources elsewhere on the Web.

The most comprehensive Web site on Bangladesh is at www.virtualbangladesh .com, with news, a 'frequently asked questions' section, information on tourist sites and comprehensive links. Several Bangladeshi English-language newspapers and magazines have Web sites, including the *Daily Star* (www.dailystarnews.com), the *New Nation* (www.nation-online.com) and the *Independent* (www.independent-bangladesh.com).

For expatriates working in Bangladesh, the Bangladesh International Community News has an email newsletter, free personal-want ads and listings of international community events. The site (www .bicn.com) is updated weekly between August and May.

For images of Bangladesh one excellent site is www.drik.net, run by the Drik photography agency. There is also an interesting site dedicated to rickshaws and rickshaw art by an American academic at netnow.micron.net/~ricksha.

The official government Web site is at www.bangladeshgov.org. It has contact details for all the ministries as well as potted biographies of the prime minister, president and the 'Father of the Nation', Sheikh Mujibur Rahman.

BOOKS
There's remarkably little published in the west about Bangladesh, and while there's quite a lot of English-language publishing going on in the country, it's mostly by small companies. University Press Ltd (UPL) is a Dhaka publishing company with an impressive list of current titles covering a wide range of topics of interest to the traveller. See the Bookshops section in the Dhaka chapter for more information.

Most books are published in different editions by different publishers in different countries. As a result, a book might be a hardcover rarity in one country while it's readily available in paperback in another. Fortunately, bookshops and libraries search by title or author, so your local bookshop or library is best placed to advise you on the availability of these recommendations.

Lonely Planet
Lonely Planet publishes the *India & Bangladesh* travel atlas, as well as guides to all neighbouring countries including India, Nepal and Myanmar (Burma). You'll find the *Bengali phrasebook* is extremely useful.

Read This First: Asia & India is essential reading if you're tackling Bangladesh for the first time. Lonely Planet has also published *Chasing Rickshaws*, a tribute to cycle-powered vehicles and their drivers by Tony Wheeler and photographer Richard I'Anson.

Guidebooks & Travel
There are no other guidebooks to the country currently available. *A Handbook for Travellers in India, Nepal, Pakistan, Bangladesh & Sri Lanka,* with a short and fairly useless section on Bangladesh, is sadly out of print. This solemn guidebook was first published in the 19th century; if you spot a second-hand copy, grab it. *On the Brink in Bengal* by Francis Rolt is the only travelogue written about the country, with a strong focus on encounters with the minority tribal populations. This, too, is out of print, but worth reading if you can get a copy. *Bangladesh* by BL Johnson is one of the few general books on the country published in the west.

History & Politics
Most histories of Bangladesh or the Bengal region are usually published either in Dhaka or Kolkata. Titles include *Bangladesh: Emergence of a Nation* by AMA Muhith; *Bangladesh: From Mujib to Ershad* by Lawrence Ziring; *The Separation of East Pakistan* by Hasan Zaheer; and *Pakistan – Failure in National Integration* by Rounaq Jahan. Other titles available in Dhaka (or possibly Kolkata) include:

Arguing with the Crocodile; Gender and Class in Bangladesh by Sarah C White raises key issues concerning class relationships and women's impact on social policy within the community.

The Fifty Percent by Salma Khan reveals the exclusion of women from development activities and focuses on the important need for investment in women in order to help generate surplus economy.

Francis Buchanan in Southeast Bengal (ed Willem van Schendel), an 18th-century chronicle providing some of the earliest detailed information about rural Bangladesh.

In Quest of Empowerment by Ainon Nahar Mizan documents the impact of the Grameen Bank on women's power and status.

No Better Opinion? by Hameeda Hossain, Roushan Jahan and Salma Sobhan examines the role of women as cheap labour in industry.

Of Blood & Fire: The Untold Story of Bangladesh's War of Independence by Jahanara Imam is the acclaimed story of the war from the perspective of a Dhaka housewife. Written in diary form, the author writes movingly of the events of 1971 and the impact on her family, including the death of one of her sons. There is an English translation by Mustafizar Rahman.

A Tale of Millions by Rafiqul Islam is the story of the Liberation War told by a senior army officer who was one of the first to rebel. It goes into great detail about his engagements and is a bit sketchy on everything else, but it's a reasonable read.

The following recommended books are all available internationally:

Art and Life in Bangladesh by Henry Glassie is the very best sort of coffee-table book. It explores how art, craft and everyday life meld together in the work of ordinary potters, rickshaw painters, weavers and metal workers. The author interviewed hundreds of people and his fascination and enthusiasm shows in the text.

Heroes by John Pilger, the left-wing journalist, includes an incisive analysis of the 1970 floods and the ensuing war.

Lajja (Shame) by Taslima Nasrin. The Bangladeshi counterpart to Rushdie, Nasrin made international waves and became a 'persona non grata' in Bangladesh, where her novel was banned. Set during the 1992 Muslim-Hindu clash over the destruction of the Babri Masjid at Ayodhya in India, her fictional Hindu family, loyal Bangladeshis, become targets for the violence provoked by Muslim fundamentalists. See the boxed text 'Taslima Nasrin and the Politics of Shame' in this chapter for more information.

Midnight's Children by Salman Rushdie contains a graphic, almost surreal account of the 1971 war which is hard to beat.

The Price of a Dream: The Story of the Grameen Bank by journalist David Bornstein gives an even-handed account of the work of Mohammed Yunus and the Grameen Bank. For a book about economic development it's a surprisingly easy and pacy read, with plenty of insight into the character of Professor Yunus and his country. This is just one of a growing number of books about the Grameen Bank, but it is one of the best.

Architectural history is well covered in three locally produced, illustrated volumes by Dr Nazimuddin Ahmed: *Discover the Monuments of Bangladesh, Buildings of the*

British Raj in Bangladesh and *Epic Stories in Terracotta.* Several titles that focus on history in legend and myth include *Folk Tales of Bengal* by Lal Behari Dey, *The Myths of Bangladesh* by Anwarul Karim, and *Princess Kalaboti and Other Tales* by Niaz Zaman.

General

A few titles have emerged that examine Bangladesh from a variety of perspectives:

The Art of Kantha Embroidery by Naiz Zaman, illustrated by line drawings and photographs, examines the technique of kantha embroidery and the rural women involved in its production (see the 'Nakshi Kantha' colour section, between pages 128 and 129 for information on this art).

Bangladesh: Reflections on the Water by James J Novak is the best introduction to the country and gives a personal and penetrating overview of the land and its people.

Bangladesh: the Guide by Elaine Bigalow provides useful insights for a greater understanding of the culture.

A Quiet Violence by Betsy Hartmann and James Boyce is the account of two Americans who lived for nine months in a small rural village.

The Rickshaws of Bangladesh by Robert Gallagher is a study of the ubiquitous rickshaw and its impact on the economy and society.

Sailing Against the Wind by Trygve Bolstad and Eirik Jansen illustrates with over 100 colour photographs of traditional sailing boats which are sadly being replaced by motorised vessels.

Tanti by John Warren looks at handloom weaving and traditional weavers in a series of superb colour and B&W photos.

There are a number of field guides to birdwatching in the Bangladesh region.

Pictorial Guide to the Birds of the Indian Subcontinent, though unwieldy, is the best field guide specific to the area. The 1994 edition is now available in the UK and US.

Where to Watch Birds in Asia by Nigel Wheatly is a good, hands-on guide to particular areas on the continent.

FILMS

Dhaka, or Dhallywood as the local movie fanzines call it, has a thriving film industry. Around 150 to 200 films are produced annually, usually with crowd-pleasing titles

Taslima Nasrin and the Politics of Shame

Dubbed the 'Salman Rushdie of Bangladesh', Taslima Nasrin became Bangladesh's most internationally famous writer with the publication of her book *Lajja* (*Shame* in its English title) in 1993.

Shame is the fictional story of the Dutta family; Bangladeshi Hindus victimised by Islamic extremists. It is based on real events. In 1992 the destruction of the Babri mosque in India by Hindu extremists unleashed religious violence in India and in Bangladesh. In Bangladesh Hindus were attacked by mobs, their temples smashed and their property destroyed. *Shame* details at length atrocities committed against an innocent minority, and the Dutta's indignation at being classed as second-class citizens in their own country. Some critics say the book is not her best work – Nasrin herself said she was so incensed by the violence against Hindus that she 'wrote the book almost in a trance ... it was ready for the press in just a few days'. But it is an important book, a raw emotional plea backed with hard facts, written by a member of the majority for the rights of a minority.

Born in 1963, Nasrin had worked as a gynaecologist in public hospitals. Besides writing 15 other Bangla-language books, she began writing for Bangladeshi newspapers and magazines in 1989. Nasrin had first drawn the ire of Islamic extremists in a series of newspaper features in 1990 in which she criticised some Islamic statutes, describing herself as an atheist and at one point calling the Quran 'obsolete'. Nasrin has since said 'I don't believe in the Quran ... I've called for the abolition of Quranic law on the grounds that it is a discriminatory law which oppresses women in Bangladesh.' Her three marriages also count against her in fundamentalist eyes.

The *Shame* controversy heated up when the Bharatiya Janata Party (BJP), the right-wing Hindu Indian political party behind the destruction of the Babri mosque, translated and printed many copies of *Shame* in India. The BJP used it to show Hindus were being persecuted in Bangladesh, written by none other than a Muslim writer. As a result, Islamic radicals accused Nasrin of being an Indian agent. Street protests by Islamic militants began calling for her death, *hartals* were held for her arrest, and some Islamic clerics declared a *fatwa* or death sentence for blasphemy against her. The controversy reached the international media. Begum Khaleda Zia's government had confiscated her passport, but she managed to escape to Europe with the help of the international writers' group PEN in 1994. That year the European Union gave her the Sakharov prize for freedom of thought.

Some Bangladeshi intellectuals and feminists have mixed feelings about Nasrin. Though they agree with the crux of her arguments against the oppression of women and Hindus, they feel she went too far and stirred too much of a reaction. People who argue for increased freedom for women are accused of being her supporters. On the other hand Bangladeshi Hindus support her strongly.

Nasrin returned to Bangladesh in September 1998 to be with her cancer-stricken mother. The protest calling for her death started anew, and the government issued an arrest warrant on the grounds that she had 'hurt people's religious feelings'. In January 1999 Nasrin had to flee Bangladesh a second time. Her mother had died, and Islamic extremists had reissued an offer of Tk 200,000 (US$2000) to anyone who murdered her. She now lives in exile in Sweden.

such as *The Poor Also Fight!* Every commercial movie follows the immortal formula of romance, comedy, violence and song-and-dance, often spliced together in ways gloriously free of western notions of plot continuity. They may not be high art but they are certainly entertaining to watch, not least for the audience participation, and you don't need to know a word of Bangla to follow the plot.

NEWSPAPERS & MAGAZINES

The press in Bangladesh is relatively free. Newspaper ownership and content, for example, are not subject to government restriction, and there are hundreds of daily and weekly publications, mostly in Bangla. However, the government does seek to influence newspapers through the placement of advertising, one admitted criterion being the objectivity of the reporting.

There are eight English-language daily newspapers. The ones with the most international news and, reputedly, the most unbiased reporting are the *Independent* and the *Daily Star*. The *Bangladesh Observer* is also fairly good. Others include the *New Nation*, the *Financial Express*, the *Daily Star* and the *Bangladesh Times*. Most are about 16 pages long and cost Tk 5.

The best weekly is the *Dhaka Courier*; it's independently minded and critical of both leading political parties. The TV column is wonderfully cruel about the shortcomings of ATN Bangla, the national broadcaster. *Holiday* often has some interesting articles as well. Both cost Tk 10.

French-language weekly newspapers can be found at the Sonargaon and Sheraton hotels, but for copies of the most recent weeklies and monthlies visit the library at Alliance Française (for more information see Libraries under Information in the Dhaka chapter). *Le Fleuve* (The River) is a monthly newspaper on Bangladeshi culture published jointly by Alliance Française and the French embassy.

RADIO & TV

Satellite TV has revolutionised local viewing habits, with up to 30 channels, mostly entertainment channels from India such as Star, Zee TV and Sony, but also CNN, Discovery, BBC and other European channels.

The national broadcaster is ATN Bangla; it has nightly news in English, as does Radio Bangladesh. Bangladesh's first private television channel, Ekushey TV (ETV), commenced broadcasting in June 2000. Check local newspapers for broadcast times.

PHOTOGRAPHY

Rural Bangladesh is extremely photogenic. The landscape looks best at sunrise or sunset. People look better too – traditionally women are first introduced to potential husbands at sunset. A polarising filter will help reduce glare and intensify colours, especially for river photographs. Avoid taking landscape photos in the middle of the day – the tropical sun has a tendency to wash out colours.

Film & Equipment

Colour print film is available everywhere and processing is quite good. Slide film, mainly Fujichrome, is available at a few places in Dhaka – see the Film & Photography section in the Dhaka chapter. When buying film check the expiry date carefully, and be aware that the storage conditions the film has been in can be less than ideal.

Photographing People

One aspect of photography unique to Bangladesh is the people. Rather than being turned down by individuals who don't want you to take their picture, you'll have to be quick if you don't want the whole village in your photograph of a sunset over the river.

Candid photos will have to be fast for the same reason, so you'll find an autofocus lens invaluable. If there are two of you, each can take turns being the 'decoy' who attracts most of the attention while the other gets the shots. Children flock to cameras like moths to a flame and it often works to point your camera in the opposite direction of the scene you want to photograph. They'll all congregate in front of your lens, allowing you to turn quickly and take your picture. You'll undoubtedly end your trip with some great crowd shots.

TIME

Bangladesh has one time zone: one hour behind Thailand, 15 minutes in front of Nepal, half an hour ahead of India, six hours ahead of GMT, 10 hours ahead of New York (11 hours during daylight-saving time), four hours behind EST in Australia and five hours ahead of France.

ELECTRICITY

Assuming there is any, the electricity is 220V, 50 cycle AC. The two-prong connection is round rather than flat; various adaptors are available at most hardware shops but they may not fit all plugs.

WEIGHTS & MEASURES

Officially Bangladesh is metric, but some local measures are still in use. The *tola*, used by goldsmiths and silversmiths, equals

11.66g, and 16 *ana* equals one *tola*. For weights in general, a *seer* equals 850g and a *maund* is 37kg. Land may be measured using *katha,* 80 sq yd, and *bigha,* 1600 sq yd. Large amounts of taka are invariably quoted in *lakh* (100,000) and *crore* (10 million). Yards are used interchangeably with metres, and miles are often confused with kilometres.

LAUNDRY

There are no do-it-yourself laundrettes in Bangladesh. There are dry cleaners in Dhaka, Chittagong and some other major cities. It's usually possible to arrange for washing to be done at your hotel, however; around Tk 50 for a large load of clothes at a budget hotel is a fair price. The hotel boys will pass the job on to the sweeping lady, so try to make sure she gets the bulk of the money and not them. It is probably easier to do it yourself. Most cheap hotel rooms have small washbasins in attached bathrooms (but no plugs).

TOILETS

In mid-range and top-end hotels and restaurants you'll find sitdown toilets that flush, but most toilets are mildly malodorous squat types. There are also some weird hybrids with foot-rests on a sitdown toilet. The ritual in squat toilets is to use your left hand and water rather than toilet paper. A strategically placed tap and jug is usually at hand. If you can't master the local method, toilet paper is widely available. Sometimes a basket is provided where paper and tampons can be discarded.

Some women report that when trying to use toilets in cheap restaurants, they've been told the facilities are unsuitable. There are very few facilities at bus stations, and what facilities there are tend to be pretty awful. It pays to do your thing back at the hotel. Finding a toilet is not always possible in the rural areas, nor is privacy. For women in a desperate situation, a long skirt will make this awkward position a little less so.

HEALTH

Travel health depends on your predeparture preparations, your daily health care while travelling, and how you handle any medical problem that does develop. While the potential dangers can seem quite frightening, in reality few travellers experience anything more than an upset stomach.

Predeparture Planning

Immunisations Plan ahead for getting your vaccinations – some of them require more than one injection, while some vaccinations should not be given together. Note that some vaccinations should not be given during pregnancy or to people with allergies – discuss this with your doctor.

It is recommended that you seek medical advice at least six weeks before travel. Be aware that there is often a greater risk of disease with children and during pregnancy.

Discuss your requirements with your doctor, but vaccinations you should consider for this trip include the following (for more details about the diseases themselves, see the individual disease entries later in this section). Carry proof of your vaccinations, especially yellow fever, as this will be needed to enter Bangladesh (see Yellow Fever later in this section).

Vaccinations that travellers to Bangladesh should consider include:

Hepatitis A Hepatitis A vaccine (eg, Avaxim, Havrix 1440 or VAQTA) provides long-term immunity (possibly more than 10 years) after an initial injection and a booster at six to 12 months. Alternatively, an injection of gamma globulin can provide short-term protection against hepatitis A – two to six months, depending on the dose given. It is not a vaccine, but a ready-made antibody collected from blood donations. It is reasonably effective and, unlike the vaccine, it is protective immediately, but because it is a blood product there are current concerns about its long-term safety. A hepatitis A vaccine is also available in a combined form, Twinrix, with hepatitis B vaccine. Three injections over a six-month period are required, the first two providing substantial protection against hepatitis A.

Hepatitis B You should consider vaccination against hepatitis B if you are planning on staying in Bangladesh for a long time. The course involves three injections, with a booster at 12 months. More rapid courses are available.

Diphtheria & Tetanus Vaccinations for these two diseases are usually combined and are recommended for everyone. After an initial course of three injections (usually given in childhood), boosters are necessary every 10 years.

Japanese B Encephalitis Consider vaccination against this disease if you're spending a month or longer in a high risk area (parts of Asia), making repeated trips to a risk area or visiting during an epidemic. It involves three injections over 30 days.

Malaria Antimalarial drugs do not prevent you from being infected, but they kill the malaria parasites during a stage in their development and significantly reduce the risk of becoming very ill or dying. Expert advice on medication should be sought, as there are many factors to consider, including the area to be visited, the risk of exposure to malaria-carrying mosquitoes, the side effects of medication, your medical history, and whether you are a child, an adult or pregnant. Travellers to isolated areas may like to carry a treatment dose of medication for use if symptoms occur.

Polio Everyone should keep up to date with this vaccination, which is normally given in childhood. A booster every 10 years maintains immunity.

Rabies Vaccination should be considered by those who will spend a month or longer in Bangladesh, where rabies is common, especially if they are cycling, handling animals, caving or travelling to remote areas, and for children (who may not report a bite). Pre-travel rabies vaccination involves having three injections over 21 to 28 days. If someone who has been vaccinated is bitten or scratched by an animal, they will require two booster injections of vaccine; those not vaccinated will require more.

Tuberculosis The risk of TB to travellers is usually very low, unless you will be living with or closely associated with local people. Vaccination against TB (BCG) is recommended for children and young adults living in Bangladesh for three months or more.

Typhoid Vaccination against typhoid may be required if you are travelling for more than a couple of weeks in most parts of Asia, Africa, Central and South America, and Central and Eastern Europe. It is now available either as an injection or as capsules that allow the vaccination to be taken orally. A combined hepatitis/typhoid vaccine has recently been developed, although its availability is limited – check with your doctor to find out its status in your country.

Yellow Fever Bangladesh itself is not a region prone to yellow fever. However, anyone, including infants, who arrives by air or sea without a yellow fever vaccination certificate will be detained for a period of up to six days if they arrive within six days of leaving an infected area, or if they have been in transit through an infected area. The Bangladeshi government defines an infected area as any country that reports a case of yellow fever. At the time of writing this list was composed mainly of countries from Africa and Central and South America.

Health Insurance Make sure that you have adequate health insurance. See Travel Insurance under Visas & Documents earlier in this chapter for details.

Travel Health Guides Lonely Planet's *Healthy Travel Asia & India* is a handy pocket size and packed with useful information including pre-trip planning, emergency first aid, immunisation and disease information and what to do if you get sick on the road. *Travel with Children* from Lonely Planet also includes advice on travel health for younger children.

There are many excellent travel health sites on the Internet. From the Lonely Planet home page there are links at www.lonely planet.com/weblinks/wlheal.htm to the World Health Organization and the US Centers for Disease Control & Prevention.

Other Preparations Make sure you're healthy before you start travelling. If you are going on a long trip make sure your teeth are OK. If you wear glasses take a spare pair and your prescription.

If you require a particular medication take an adequate supply, as it may not be available locally. Take part of the packaging showing the generic name rather than the brand, which will make getting replacements easier. It's a good idea to have a legible prescription or letter from your doctor to show that you legally use the medication – this can help you avoid any serious problems.

Losing your glasses can be a real problem, although at DIT II Circle in Gulshan, Dhaka you can get new spectacles competently made up in approximately four days for about Tk 1000, possibly faster if you pay extra.

Dhaka has some excellent dentists, and if you have a lot of work to do (eg, root canals) you can probably pay for your trip by using them instead of a more expensive dentist in the west.

Basic Rules

Food There is an old colonial adage that says: 'If you can cook it, boil it or peel it you can eat it ... otherwise forget it.' Vegetables and fruit should be washed with purified water or peeled where possible. Shellfish such as mussels, oysters and clams should be avoided as well as undercooked meat, particularly in the form of mince. Steaming does not make shellfish safe for eating.

If a place looks clean and well-run and the vendor also looks clean and healthy, then the food is probably safe. In general, places that are packed with travellers or locals will be fine, while empty restaurants are questionable. The food in busy restaurants is cooked and eaten quite quickly and is probably not left to stand or reheated.

Ice cream is usually OK if it is a reputable brand such as Igloo or Polar, but beware of ice cream from street vendors and of ice cream that has melted and been refrozen; if there's any doubt (eg, a power cut in the last day or two), steer well clear.

Street food that is fried on the spot is usually quite safe. However, rice dishes and curries sold on the street, typically for rickshaw-wallahs, are questionable because the dishes are cooked at home and reheated on the streets. Restaurants which depend largely on repeat business are generally OK.

Water The number one rule is *be careful of the water,* especially ice. If you don't know for certain that the water is safe, assume the worst. Reputable brands of bottled water or soft drinks are generally fine, although in some places bottles may be refilled with tap water. Only use water from containers with a serrated seal – not tops or corks. Take care with fruit juice, particularly if water may have been added. Milk should be treated with suspicion as it is often unpasteurised, though boiled milk is fine if it is kept hygienically. Tea or coffee should also be OK, since the water should have been boiled.

Medical Kit Check List

Following is a list of items you should consider including in a medical kit – consult your pharmacist for brands available in your country.

- ☐ **Aspirin or paracetamol (acetaminophen in the USA)** – for pain or fever
- ☐ **Antihistamine** – for allergies, eg, hay fever; to ease the itch from insect bites or stings; and to prevent motion sickness
- ☐ **Cold and flu tablets, throat lozenges and nasal decongestant**
- ☐ **Multivitamins** – consider for long trips, when dietary vitamin intake may be inadequate
- ☐ **Antibiotics** – consider including these if you're travelling well off the beaten track; see your doctor, as they must be prescribed, and carry the prescription with you
- ☐ **Loperamide or diphenoxylate** – 'blockers' for diarrhoea
- ☐ **Prochlorperazine or metaclopramide** – for nausea and vomiting
- ☐ **Rehydration mixture** – to prevent dehydration, which may occur, for example, during bouts of diarrhoea; particularly important when travelling with children
- ☐ **Insect repellent, sunscreen, lip balm and eye drops**
- ☐ **Calamine lotion, sting relief spray or aloe vera** – to ease irritation from sunburn and insect bites or stings
- ☐ **Antifungal cream or powder** – for fungal skin infections and thrush
- ☐ **Antiseptic (such as povidone-iodine)** – for cuts and grazes
- ☐ **Bandages, Band-Aids (plasters) and other wound dressings**
- ☐ **Water purification tablets or iodine**
- ☐ **Scissors, tweezers and a thermometer** – note that mercury thermometers are prohibited by airlines

Water Purification The simplest way of purifying water is to boil it thoroughly.

Consider purchasing a water filter for a long trip. There are two main kinds of filter. Total filters take out all parasites, bacteria and viruses and make water safe to drink. They are often expensive, but they can be more cost effective than buying bottled water. Simple filters (which can even be a nylon mesh bag) take out dirt and larger foreign bodies from the water so that chemical solutions work much more effectively; if water is dirty, chemical solutions may not work at all. It's very important when buying a filter to read the specifications, so that you know exactly what it actually removes from the water. Simple filtering will not remove all dangerous organisms, so if you cannot boil water it should be treated chemically. Chlorine tablets will kill many pathogens, but not some parasites like giardia and amoebic cysts. Iodine is more effective for and is available in tablet form. Follow the directions carefully and remember that too much can be harmful.

Medical Problems & Treatment

Self-diagnosis and treatment is risky. You should always seek medical help. Embassies, consulates or five-star hotels can usually recommend a local doctor or clinic. Although we give drug dosages in this section, they are for emergency use only. Correct diagnosis is vital. In this section we have used the generic names for medications – check with a pharmacist for brands available locally.

Note that antibiotics should ideally be administered only under medical supervision. Take only the recommended dose at the prescribed intervals and use the whole course, even if the illness seems to be cured earlier. Stop immediately if there are any serious reactions, and don't use the antibiotic at all if you are unsure that you have the correct one. Some people are allergic to commonly prescribed antibiotics such as penicillin; carry this information (eg, on a bracelet) when travelling.

Environmental Hazards

Jet Lag Jet lag is experienced when a person travels by air across more than three time zones (each time zone usually represents a one-hour time difference). It occurs because many of the functions of the human body (such as temperature, pulse rate and emptying of the bladder and bowels) are regulated by internal 24-hour cycles. When we travel

Nutrition

If your diet is poor or limited in variety, if you're travelling hard and fast and therefore missing meals, or if you simply lose your appetite, you can soon start to lose weight and place your health at risk.

Make sure your diet is well balanced. Cooked eggs, tofu, beans, as well as lentils (dhal in India) and nuts are all safe ways to get protein. Fruit you can peel (bananas, oranges or mandarins, for example) is usually safe and a good source of vitamins. Melons can harbour bacteria in their flesh and are best avoided. Try to eat plenty of grains (including rice) and bread. Remember that although food is generally safer if it is cooked well, overcooked food loses much of its nutritional value. If your diet isn't well balanced or if your food intake is insufficient, it's a good idea to take vitamin and iron pills.

In hot climates make sure that you drink enough – don't rely on feeling thirsty to indicate when you should drink. Not needing to urinate or voiding small amounts of very dark yellow urine is a danger sign. Always carry a water bottle with you on long trips. Excessive sweating can lead to loss of salt and therefore muscle cramping. Salt tablets are not a good idea as a preventative, but in places where salt is not used much, adding salt to food can help.

long distances rapidly, our bodies take time to adjust to the 'new time' of our destination, and we may experience sensations of fatigue, disorientation, insomnia, anxiety, impaired concentration and loss of appetite. These effects will usually be gone within three days of arrival, but to minimise them:

- Rest for a couple of days prior to departure.
- Try to select flight schedules that minimise sleep deprivation; arriving late in the day means you can go to sleep soon after you arrive. For very long flights, try to organise a stopover.
- Avoid excessive eating (which bloats the stomach) and alcohol (which causes dehydration) during the flight. Instead, drink plenty of noncarbonated, nonalcoholic drinks such as fruit juice or water.

- Avoid smoking.
- Make yourself more comfortable by wearing loose-fitting clothes and perhaps bringing an eye mask and ear plugs to help you sleep.
- Try to sleep at the appropriate time for the time zone you are travelling to.

Motion Sickness Eating lightly before and during a trip will reduce the chances of motion sickness. If you are prone to motion sickness try to find a place that minimises movement – near the wing on aircraft, close to midships on boats, near the centre on buses. Fresh air usually helps. Commercial motion-sickness preparations, which can cause drowsiness, have to be taken before the trip commences. Ginger (available in capsule form) as well as peppermint (including mint-flavoured sweets) are natural preventatives.

Heat Exhaustion Dehydration and salt deficiency can cause heat exhaustion. Take time to acclimatise to high temperatures, drink sufficient liquids, and do not do anything too physically demanding. Salt deficiency is characterised by fatigue, lethargy, headaches, giddiness and muscle cramps; salt tablets may help, but adding extra salt to your food is better.

Anhidrotic heat exhaustion is a rare form of heat exhaustion that is caused by an inability to sweat. It tends to affect people who have been in a hot climate for some time, rather than newcomers. It can progress to heatstroke. Treatment involves removal to a cooler climate.

Heat Stroke This serious, occasionally fatal condition can occur if the body's heat-regulating mechanism breaks down and the body temperature rises to dangerous levels. Long, continuous periods of exposure to high temperatures and insufficient fluids can leave you vulnerable to heatstroke.

The symptoms are feeling unwell, not sweating very much (or at all) and a high body temperature (39° to 41°C or 102° to 106°F). Where sweating has fully ceased, the skin becomes flushed and red. Severe, throbbing headaches and lack of coordination will also occur, and the sufferer may be confused or aggressive. Eventually the vic-

Everyday Health

Normal body temperature is up to 37°C (98.6°F); more than 2°C (4°F) higher than this indicates a high fever. The normal adult pulse rate is 60 to 100 per minute (children 80 to 100, babies 100 to 140). As a general rule the pulse increases about 20 beats per minute for each 1°C (2°F) rise in fever.

Respiration (breathing) rate is also an indicator of illness. Count the number of breaths per minute. Between 12 and 20 is normal for adults and older children (up to 30 for younger children, 40 for babies). People with a high fever or serious respiratory illness breathe more quickly than normal. More than 40 shallow breaths a minute may indicate pneumonia.

tim will become delirious or convulse. Hospitalisation is essential, but in the interim get victims out of the sun, remove their clothing, cover them with a wet sheet or towel and then fan continually. Give fluids if they are conscious.

Prickly Heat Prickly heat is an itchy rash caused by excessive perspiration trapped under the skin. It usually strikes people who have just arrived in a hot climate. Keeping cool, bathing often, drying the skin and using a mild talcum or prickly-heat powder or resorting to air-conditioning may help.

Sunburn In the tropics you can get sunburnt surprisingly quickly, even through cloud. Use a sunscreen, a hat, and a barrier cream for your nose and lips. Calamine lotion or a commercial after-sun preparation are good for mild sunburn. Protect your eyes with good quality sunglasses, particularly if you will be near water or sand.

Smog Pollution is something you'll become very aware of in Asia if you are travelling in urban environments, especially in India, Bangladesh, China or the Philippines. Dhaka is one of the most polluted cities in the world. Air pollution can be a health hazard, particularly if you suffer from a lung disease such as asthma. It can also aggravate coughs, colds and sinus problems and cause eye irritation. Consider avoiding badly polluted areas such as central Dhaka, especially if you have asthma, or you could invest in a surgical mask.

Infectious Diseases

Diarrhoea Simple things like a change of water, food or climate can all cause a mild bout of diarrhoea, but a few rushed toilet trips with no other symptoms is not indicative of a major problem.

Dehydration is the main danger with any diarrhoea, particularly in children or the elderly as dehydration can occur quite quickly. Under all circumstances *fluid replacement* (at least equal to the volume being lost) is the most important thing to remember. Weak black tea with a little sugar, soda water, or soft drinks allowed to go flat and diluted 50% with clean water are all good. With severe diarrhoea a rehydrating solution is preferable to replace minerals and salts lost. Commercially available oral rehydration salts (ORS) are very useful; add them to boiled or bottled water. In an emergency you can make up a solution of six teaspoons of sugar and a half teaspoon of salt to a litre of boiled or bottled water. You need to drink at least the same volume of fluid that you are losing in bowel movements and vomiting. Urine is the best guide to the adequacy of replacement – if you have small amounts of concentrated urine, you need to drink more. Keep drinking small amounts often. Stick to a bland diet as you recover.

Gut-paralysing drugs such as loperamide or diphenoxylate can be used to bring relief from the symptoms, although they do not actually cure the problem. Only use these drugs if you do not have access to toilets, eg, if you *must* travel. These drugs are not recommended for children under 12.

In some situations antibiotics may be required: diarrhoea with blood or mucus (dysentery), any diarrhoea with fever, profuse watery diarrhoea, persistent diarrhoea not improving after 48 hours, and severe diarrhoea. These suggest a more serious cause and in such cases gut-paralysing drugs should be avoided.

In these situations, a stool test may be necessary to diagnose what bug is causing your diarrhoea, so you should seek medical help urgently. Where this is not possible the recommended drugs for bacterial diarrhoea (the most likely cause of severe diarrhoea in travellers) are norfloxacin (400mg twice daily for three days) or ciprofloxacin (500mg twice daily for five days). These are not recommended for children or pregnant women. The drug of choice for children would be cotrimoxazole with dosage dependent on weight. A five-day course is given. Ampicillin or amoxycillin may be given in pregnancy, but medical care is necessary.

Fungal Infections Fungal infections occur more commonly in hot weather and are usually found on the scalp, between the toes (athlete's foot) or fingers, in the groin, and on the body (ringworm). You get ringworm (which is actually a fungal infection, not a worm) from infected animals or other people. The presence of moisture encourages these infections.

To prevent fungal infections wear loose, comfortable clothes, avoid artificial fibres, wash frequently and dry yourself carefully. If you do get an infection, wash the infected area at least daily with a disinfectant or medicated soap and water, and rinse and dry well. Apply an antifungal cream or powder like tolnaftate. Try to expose the infected area to air or sunlight as much as possible. Wash all of your towels and underwear in hot water, change them often and allow them to dry in the sun.

Hepatitis Hepatitis is a general term for inflammation of the liver. It is a common disease worldwide. There are several different viruses that cause hepatitis, and they differ in the way that they are transmitted. The symptoms are similar in all forms of the illness, and include fever, chills, headache, fatigue, feelings of weakness and aches and pains, followed by loss of appetite, nausea, vomiting, abdominal pain, dark urine, light-coloured faeces, jaundiced (yellow) skin and yellowing of the whites of the eyes. People who have had hepatitis should avoid alcohol for some time after the illness, as the liver will need time in order to recover.

HIV & AIDS Infection with the human immunodeficiency virus (HIV) may lead to acquired immune deficiency syndrome (AIDS), which is a fatal disease. Any exposure to blood, blood products or body fluids may put the individual at risk. The disease is often transmitted through sexual contact or use of dirty needles – vaccinations, acupuncture, tattooing and body piercing can be potentially as dangerous as intravenous drug use. HIV/AIDS can also be spread through infected blood transfusions; some developing countries cannot afford to screen blood used for transfusions.

If you do need an injection, ask to see the syringe unwrapped in front of you, or take a needle and syringe pack with you.

Nobody really knows how common HIV is in Bangladesh. Because of the country's close proximity to India (which has a very high incidence), high STD (sexually transmitted disease) rates, high rates of migration and large number of prostitutes, the country is a prime candidate for an epidemic.

Intestinal Worms These parasites are most common in rural, tropical areas. The different worms have different ways of infecting people. Some (eg, tapeworms) may be ingested via food such as undercooked meat and some (eg, hookworms) enter through your skin. Infestations may not show up for some time, and although they are generally not serious, if left untreated some can cause severe health problems later. Consider having a stool test when you return home to check for these and determine the appropriate treatment.

Sexually Transmitted Diseases HIV/AIDS and hepatitis B can be transmitted through sexual contact – see the relevant sections earlier for more details. Other STDs include gonorrhoea, herpes and syphilis; sores, blisters or rashes around the genitals and discharges or pain when urinating are common symptoms. In some STDs, such as wart virus or chlamydia, symptoms may be less marked or not observed at all, especially in women. Chlamydia infection can cause infertility in men and women before any symptoms have been noticed. Syphilis symptoms eventually disappear completely, but the disease continues and can cause severe problems in later years. While abstinence from sexual contact is the only 100% effective prevention, using condoms is also effective. The treatment of gonorrhoea and syphilis is with antibiotics. The different sexually transmitted diseases each require a specific antibiotic treatment.

Typhoid Typhoid fever is a dangerous gut infection caused by contaminated water and food. Medical help must be sought.

In its early stages sufferers may feel they have a bad cold or flu on the way, as early symptoms are a headache, body aches and a fever that rises a little each day until it is around 40°C (104°F) or more. The victim's pulse is often slow – unlike a normal fever where the pulse increases. There may also be vomiting, abdominal pain, diarrhoea or constipation.

In the second week the fever and slow pulse continue and a few pink spots may appear; trembling, weakness and dehydration may occur as well as complications such as pneumonia, perforated bowel or meningitis.

Insect-Borne Diseases

Malaria This potentially fatal disease is spread by mosquito bites. It is not a problem in Dhaka but in other areas of the country, especially the Chittagong Hill Tracts, it is becoming increasingly endemic. If you are travelling in endemic areas it is extremely important to avoid mosquito bites and to take tablets to prevent this disease. Symptoms can range from fever, chills and sweating, headache, diarrhoea and abdominal pains to a vague feeling of ill-health. Seek medical help immediately if malaria is suspected. Without treatment malaria can rapidly become more serious and can be fatal.

If medical care is not available, malaria tablets can be used for treatment. You need to use a malaria tablet that is different from the one you were taking when you contracted malaria. The standard treatment dose of mefloquine is two 250mg tablets and a further two six hours later. For Fansidar, it's a single dose of three tablets. If you were previously taking mefloquine and cannot obtain Fansidar, then other alternatives are Malarone (atovaquone-proguanil; four tablets once daily for three days), halofantrine (three doses of two 250mg tablets every six hours) or quinine sulphate (600mg every six hours). There is a greater risk of side effects with these dosages than in normal use if used with mefloquine, so medical advice is preferable. Be aware also that halofantrine is no longer recommended by the WHO as an emergency standby treatment because of its side effects, and should only be used if no other drugs are available.

Travellers are advised to prevent mosquito bites at all times. The main messages are:

- Wear light-coloured clothing.
- Wear long trousers and long-sleeved shirts.
- Use mosquito repellents containing the compound DEET on exposed areas (prolonged overuse of DEET may be harmful, especially to children, but its use is considered preferable to being bitten by disease-transmitting mosquitoes).
- Avoid perfumes or aftershave.
- Use a mosquito net impregnated with mosquito repellent (permethrin) – it may be worth taking your own. Impregnating clothes with permethrin effectively deters mosquitoes and other insects.

Dengue Fever This viral disease is transmitted by mosquitoes and is fast becoming one of the top public health problems in the tropical world. Unlike the malaria mosquito, the *Aedes aegypti* mosquito, which transmits the dengue virus, is most active during the day, and is found mainly in urban areas, in and around human dwellings.

Signs and symptoms of dengue fever include a sudden onset of high fever, headache, joint and muscle pains (hence its old name, 'breakbone fever') and nausea and vomiting. A rash of small red spots sometimes appears three to four days after the onset of fever. In the early phase of illness, dengue may be mistaken for other infectious diseases, including malaria and influenza. Minor bleeding such as nose bleeds may occur in the course of the illness, but this does not necessarily mean that you have progressed to the potentially fatal dengue haemorrhagic fever (DHF). This is a severe illness, characterised by heavy bleeding, which is thought to be a result of a second infection due to a different strain (there are four major strains) and usually affects residents of the country rather than travellers. Recovery even from simple dengue fever may be prolonged, with tiredness lasting for several weeks.

You should seek medical attention as soon as possible if you think you may be infected. A blood test can exclude malaria and indicate the possibility of dengue fever. There is no specific treatment for dengue. Aspirin should be avoided, as it increases the risk of haemorrhaging. There is no vaccine against dengue fever. The best prevention is to avoid mosquito bites at all times by covering up, using insect repellents containing the compound DEET and mosquito nets – see the Malaria section earlier for more advice on avoiding mosquito bites.

Fortunately, unlike in Sri Lanka, cases of dengue fever in Bangladesh are extremely rare and travellers have little to worry about.

Japanese B Encephalitis This viral infection of the brain is transmitted by mosquitoes. Most cases tend to occur in rural areas, since the virus exists in pigs and wading birds. Symptoms include fever, headache and alteration in consciousness. Hospitalisation is necessary for correct diagnosis and treatment. There is a high mortality rate among those who have symptoms; of those who survive many are intellectually disabled. The prevalence of this rare but serious disease in Bangladesh is not precisely known, but given that one of the carrier species includes waterbirds, it's not impossible that it exists here as well.

Cuts, Bites & Stings

See Less Common Diseases later in this section for details of rabies, which is passed through animal bites.

Bedbugs & Lice Bedbugs live in various places, but particularly in dirty mattresses and bedding, evidenced by spots of blood on bedclothes or on the wall. Bedbugs leave itchy bites in neat rows. Calamine lotion or a sting relief spray may help.

All lice cause itching and discomfort. They make themselves at home in your hair (head lice), your clothing (body lice) or in your pubic hair (crabs). You catch lice through direct contact with infected people or by sharing combs, clothing and the like. Powder or shampoo treatment will kill the lice, and infected clothing should be washed in hot, soapy water and dried in the sun.

Bites & Stings Bee and wasp stings are usually painful rather than dangerous. However, if people are allergic to them severe breathing difficulties may occur and require urgent medical care. Calamine lotion or a sting relief spray will give relief and ice packs will reduce the pain and swelling. There are some spiders with dangerous bites but antivenins are usually available. Scorpion stings are notoriously painful and in some parts of Asia, the Middle East and Central America they can actually be fatal. Scorpions often shelter in shoes or clothing.

Cuts & Scratches Wash well and treat any cut with an antiseptic such as povidone-iodine. Where possible avoid bandages and Band-Aids, which can keep wounds wet.

Jellyfish Avoid contact with these sea creatures, which have stinging tentacles – seek local advice. Stings from most jellyfish are simply painful, rather than life-threatening. Dousing in vinegar will deactivate any stingers that have not 'fired'. Calamine lotion, antihistamines and analgesics may reduce the reaction and relieve the pain.

Leeches & Ticks Leeches may be present in damp rainforest conditions; they attach themselves to your skin to suck your blood. Salt or a lighted cigarette end will make them fall off. Do not pull them off, as the bite is then more likely to become infected. Clean and apply pressure if the point of attachment is bleeding. An insect repellent may keep them away.

You should always check all over your body if you have been walking through a potentially tick-infested area as ticks can cause skin infections and other more serious diseases. If a tick is found attached, press down around the tick's head with tweezers, grab the head and gently pull upwards. Avoid pulling the rear of the body as this may squeeze the tick's gut contents through the attached mouth parts into the skin, increasing the risk of infection and disease. Smearing chemicals on the tick will not make it let go and is not recommended.

Snakes To minimise your chances of being bitten always wear boots, socks and long trousers when walking through undergrowth where snakes may be present. Don't put your hands into holes and crevices, and be careful when collecting firewood.

Snake bites do not cause instantaneous death and antivenins are usually available. Immediately wrap the bitten limb tightly, as you would for a sprained ankle, and then attach a splint to immobilise it. Keep the victim still and seek medical help, if possible with the dead snake for identification. Don't attempt to catch the snake if there is a possibility of being bitten again. Tourniquets and sucking out the poison are now comprehensively discredited.

Less Common Diseases

The following diseases pose a small risk to travellers, and so are only mentioned in passing. Seek medical advice if you think that you may have contracted any of these diseases.

Cholera This is the worst of the watery diarrhoeas and medical help should be sought. Outbreaks of cholera are generally widely reported, so you can avoid such problem areas. *Fluid replacement is the most vital treatment* – the risk of dehydration is severe as you may lose up to 20L a day. If there is a delay in getting to hospital, then begin taking tetracycline. The adult dose is 250mg four times daily. It is not recommended for children under nine years nor for pregnant women. Tetracycline may help shorten the illness, but adequate fluids are required to save lives.

Filariasis This is a mosquito-transmitted parasitic infection found in many parts of Africa, Asia, Central and South America and the Pacific. Possible symptoms include fever, pain and a swelling of the lymph glands; inflammation of lymph drainage areas; swelling of a limb or the scrotum; skin rashes; and blindness. Treatment is available to eliminate the parasites from the body, but some of the damage already caused may not be reversible. Medical advice should be obtained promptly if the infection is suspected.

Rabies This fatal viral infection is found in many countries. Many animals can be infected (such as dogs, cats, bats and monkeys) and it is their saliva that is infectious. Any bite, scratch or even lick from an animal should be cleaned immediately and thoroughly. Scrub vigorously using soap and running water, and then apply alcohol or iodine solution. Medical help should be sought promptly to receive a course of injections to prevent the onset of symptoms and death.

Tetanus This disease is caused by a germ that lives in soil and in the faeces of horses and other animals. It enters the body via breaks in the skin. The first symptom may be discomfort in swallowing, or stiffening of the jaw and neck; this is followed by painful convulsions of the jaw and whole body. The disease can be fatal. It can be prevented by vaccination.

Tuberculosis (TB) TB is a bacterial infection usually transmitted from person to person by coughing, but which may be transmitted through consumption of unpasteurised milk. Milk that has been boiled is safe to drink, and the souring of milk to make yoghurt or cheese also kills the bacilli. Travellers are usually not at great risk as close household contact with the infected person is usually required before the disease is passed on. You may need to have a TB test before you travel – this can help diagnose the disease later if you become ill.

Women's Health

Gynaecological Problems Antibiotic use, synthetic underwear, sweating and contraceptive pills can lead to fungal vaginal infections, especially when travelling in hot climates. Thrush or vaginal candidiasis is characterised by a rash, itch and discharge. Nystatin, miconazole or clotrimazole pessaries are the usual treatment, but some people use a more traditional remedy involving vinegar or lemon-juice douches, or yoghurt. Maintaining good personal hygiene and wearing loose-fitting clothes and cotton underwear may help prevent these infections.

Sexually transmitted diseases are a major cause of most vaginal problems. Symptoms include a smelly discharge, painful intercourse and sometimes a burning sensation when urinating. Medical attention should be sought and male sexual partners must also be treated. For more details see the section on Sexually Transmitted Diseases earlier. Besides abstinence, the best thing is to practise safer sex using condoms.

Pregnancy It is not advisable to travel to some places while pregnant as some vaccinations normally used to prevent serious diseases are not advisable during pregnancy (eg, yellow fever). In addition, some diseases are much more serious for the mother during pregnancy, and may actually increase the risk of a stillborn child (eg, malaria).

Most miscarriages occur during the first three months of pregnancy. Miscarriage is not uncommon and can occasionally lead to severe bleeding. The last three months should also be spent within reasonable distance of good medical care. A baby born as early as 24 weeks stands a chance of survival, but only in a good modern hospital. Pregnant women should avoid all unnecessary medication, although vaccinations and malarial prophylactics should still be taken where needed. Additional care should be taken to prevent illness and particular attention should be paid to diet and nutrition. Alcohol and nicotine, for example, should be avoided.

WOMEN TRAVELLERS
Attitudes Towards Women
Bangladesh is generally very safe for women travellers, but it's wise to be a little careful. It is easier here than in some other Muslim countries, and gender discrimination is an issue among educated people. This is partly due to Bangladesh's relatively relaxed attitudes and partly because of the large part women played in taking up arms during the Liberation War. You might find that women consider themselves to be Bangladeshis and Muslims first; feminism is a means of improving their society, not creating a new one.

Keep in mind that women are not touched by men in this society. Even a casual tap on the shoulder is not appropriate, but because you're a foreigner, it might happen. The best thing to do is to show clearly, yet tactfully, that you object to being touched. That should end the matter. Most people are genuinely friendly and interested in what you're doing; it's a matter of not letting things get out of hand.

In a Bangladeshi middle-class home you would most likely be expected to eat first with the men while the women of the household tuck themselves away in another part of the house, or dutifully serve the meal. In rural areas, you might not eat with either, but be served first, and separately, as a gesture of respect. Accept either graciously. Protest would cause great embarrassment on the part of your host.

Most mosques don't allow women inside, although a few do have a special women's gallery. If in doubt, ask.

Women, with or without men, are sometimes unwelcome in budget hotels, usually because the manager thinks the hotel is not suitable. This knee-jerk reaction can sometimes be overcome if you hang around long enough. On the other hand, staying in one of these cheaper establishments, especially

A Woman's Experience

I'm surprised how easy it is to be a female traveller in Bangladesh. You always get a seat on the buses (in the front), and people will always move away and let you through when it's crowded. I could walk into any crowded, cheap restaurant for a coke or snacks and the locals would squeeze together and clear a table for me. I would be served immediately even though quite a few others were waiting. I lined up in a terrible, long queue at the post office but was immediately directed to the front of the line. You've got to get used to people staring at you though. After all they don't see many tourists.

Hanne Finholt, Norway

if you are going solo, can be more trouble than it is worth. It's hard to change attitudes that are so deeply ingrained in the culture. Mid-range hotels that are accustomed to foreigners are the best bet. Unmarried couples are better off simply saying they're married, although this leads to questions about children and the number of years married and so on.

On BIWTC (Bangladesh Inland Waterway Transport Corporation) boats there's sometimes a special section for women, although it's usually very crowded. There are often women's waiting rooms at railway stations. On buses, unaccompanied women are expected to sit at the front, and if you want to find a seat, glaring at a man in a seat near the front will usually procure one.

Safety Precautions
Practically anything out of the ordinary attracts a crowd in Bangladesh, and foreigners, both men and women, are the biggest drawing cards. Conforming to the local notion of a respectable woman is your best protection, although just being a solo traveller raises doubts. The other side of the harassment coin, and almost as much of a nuisance, is that people are constantly making elaborate arrangements to protect you from harassment.

How you carry yourself also subtly determines how you are treated. Women who are tentative, appear unsure or seem to be helpless are potential targets for harassment. A woman who is assertive can ask for space and usually gets it.

Avoid travelling alone at night; Bangladeshi women avoid going out alone at night as much as possible. On local transport, don't sit next to the driver in a baby taxi.

What to Wear
Modest clothing is a must, although opinions differ as to whether it's bare arms or ankles which are most likely to mark you as disreputable. While Bangladeshi men often wear western clothes, almost no women do, so investing in a *salwar kameez* (a long dress-like tunic worn over baggy trousers) is a good idea. A *dupatta* (long scarf) to cover your head increases the appearance of modesty and is a handy accessory. Some foreign women make the mistake of wearing a sari undershirt, which is rather like a T-shirt. Unfortunately this is comparable to walking around in the street in your underwear, and is likely to cause a reaction.

That said, foreign women tend to be exempt from many social customs. You can get away with wearing baggy trousers and a long loose-fitting shirt in most parts of the country. Long, loose skirts are also acceptable and provide the added advantage of a modicum of privacy in the absence of a public toilet.

Organisations
A good place to find out about the situation concerning women in Bangladesh is the feminist bookshop run by UBINIG in Dhaka (see Bookshops in the Dhaka chapter).

GAY & LESBIAN TRAVELLERS
In a country with such strong taboos against any mingling between sexes, it's little wonder that there is a high degree of sexual repression in Bangladesh, and not surprising that authorities deny the existence of homosexuality. You may hear people say that gays in Bangladesh are a product of western cultural pollution. Unofficially, many believe homosexuality is quite prevalent. Bangladeshi society can be privately tolerant towards homosexuality among young men, but only if it is a 'phase' and doesn't interfere with marriage prospects. Lesbians have to stay even deeper in the closet.

The criminal code (left over from the Raj) punishes male homosexual acts with deportation, fines and/or prison, but these laws are hardly ever used. Lesbianism is studiously denied by the legal system. Gay travellers would be wise to be discreet in Bangladesh.

DISABLED TRAVELLERS
While Bangladesh struggles with its own impoverished people, little has been done to accommodate disabled travellers. In fact, with the terminally cracked (or absent) footpaths, Asian-style squat toilets, overcrowded buses, and absence of elevators in all but the finest buildings in Dhaka, it would seem that the country has contrived to keep out all but the most fit and able. While this is not the case, the fact of the matter is that disabled travellers to Bangladesh will face many obstacles. On the other hand, hiring help to check out accessible hotels and restaurants, toilets and other facilities, and to help with getting around, is going to be quite cheap. Disabled travellers tour around India with a car and an assistant, so there's no reason it can't be done here.

Several western organisations offer general advice on travel for disabled people, plus listings of wheelchair-friendly destinations, airports, hotels etc, though none have specific information on Bangladesh. They include:

Holiday Care Service (☎ 01293-77 4535, fax 78 4647) Imperial Buildings, Victoria Road, Horley, Surrey RH6 7PZ

Mobility International USA (✉ info@miusa.org), PO Box 10767, Eugene, OR, 97440, USA, publishes *A World of Options: A Guide to International Exchange, Community Service and Travel for Persons with Disabilities*.

RADAR, the Royal Association for Disability & Rehabilitation (☎ 020-7250 3222, fax 7250 0212), at 12 City Forum, 250 City Road, London EC1 8AF, UK, focuses on European travel.

Travelcare (☎ 0181-295 1797, fax 467 2467), 35A High St, Chislehurst, Kent BR7 5QAE, specialises in travel insurance for the disabled.

There's also a Web site for and by disabled travellers (www.travelhealth.com/disab.htm).

SENIOR TRAVELLERS

Stifling heat for much of the year, basic facilities (if that), simple accommodation, uninspired cuisine, and rough public transport would all seem to deter senior travellers to Bangladesh. There are, however, a fair number of older people working as volunteers, many on a short term basis, while others have come to visit family members. Many have enjoyed their experiences and discovered in the process that Bangladesh is not the 'basket case' the world press would have everyone believe.

Older people are given an enormous amount of respect in Bangladeshi culture and you are sure to find that the local people are hugely helpful. A number of clean, comfortable hotels and guesthouses in the more popularly visited regions serve to provide a pleasant haven for travellers who don't want to 'rough it', and private vehicles with drivers are available almost anywhere for getting around. In more remote areas older travellers find it easier to stay at circuit houses and other government resthouses than the typical youthful backpacker does.

TRAVEL WITH CHILDREN

In a society with an abundant child population, travelling with children in Bangladesh can be quite pleasant. Children are an integral part of Bangladeshi life, and foreign children are especially fascinating and draw a lot of attention. You may find yourself fending off would-be nannies who want to take your child on a tour of the village, or perhaps you'll happily take advantage of the impromptu childcare service! Older children will find instant playmates wherever they go.

From a health standpoint, dishes of boiled rice and unspiced dhal, scrambled or boiled eggs, oatmeal and a variety of fruits and vegetables should be enough to keep the little ones satisfied.

If long journeys on cramped public transport is asking too much of little travellers, private transport is a reasonable option that allows for periodic rest stops and space for catnaps. Most hotels and guesthouses happily accommodate travellers with children, and you'll find that throughout Bangladesh special effort is made for those with children in tow. Lonely Planet's *Travel with Children*, by Maureen Wheeler, is a collection of experiences from travelling families, and includes practical advice on how to avoid the hassles and have a rewarding experience when travelling with your kids.

DANGERS & ANNOYANCES

Bangladesh is a very friendly country, and to travellers arriving from India this is immediately obvious and a great relief. There are few serious dangers – the worst annoyance is an accumulation of minor irritations. After a while the crowds and the constant staring get on your nerves, the baksheesh demands become infuriating, and you don't even want to discuss the possibility of sponsoring an immigrant to your country.

Bangladeshis are quite a volatile people – loud arguments in public places are a constant background noise – so be careful about venting your frustrations too openly.

Despite the poverty the crime rate is surprisingly low. Even pickpocketing on the crowded buses is not as endemic as in some other Asian countries. *Dacoity* (armed robbery) on buses is on the increase and night buses are more prone to attack. Don't be tempted to use your size advantage in the unlikely event that you're confronted with bandits – messy weapons like knives, acid bulbs and home-made shotguns are popular. You're in much more danger from more mundane robbery like bag-snatching, although even this isn't particularly common.

Crowds are one thing any foreigner will have to get accustomed to. They appear wherever you may go, but are especially inquisitive in the rural areas, where they are less likely to have seen foreigners before.

One of the standard questions you'll be asked is 'What is your religion?' If your answer is 'atheist', be prepared for some startled reactions – things might even get a little heavy. Saying you are 'humanist' might be better.

Drugs

As with neighbouring countries, cheap grass is quite common in Bangladesh. But unlike India you are unlikely to be hassled to buy any, except in those parts of Dhaka where foreigners congregate. And unlike India we haven't had any reports of people being set up for drug busts.

Bangladesh has the death penalty for trafficking in drugs. Commuted sentences are not an option. Don't trust the dealers either – turning you in for some baksheesh isn't likely to bother gentlemen whose stock of merchandise includes their sisters. One of the major substances of abuse in Bangladesh is Phensidyl, an alcohol-based medicine smuggled in from India.

If a man furtively asks 'Smoking?', it's usually an invitation to give him a cigarette, not a prelude to offering you drugs.

Getting Things Done

Government paperwork is about average for a developing country. However, Islamic good manners mean that in almost any official dealing your status is that of an honoured guest with privileges, rather than a customer with rights. Being rude or losing your temper definitely doesn't work here – Bangladeshis are proud people and their clerks aren't a ground-down *babu* class. Just accept that things will take time and be prepared to drink a lot of tea.

Coping with Beggars

A few of the more disturbing aspects of travelling in Bangladesh are encounters with extreme poverty and the preponderance of beggars. Many travellers find themselves taken aback by the impoverishment that confronts them at seemingly every turn. After a little time travelling around the country, one becomes better able to distinguish true poverty from the simple, hard-working lifestyle and things begin to look a little more optimistic.

Despite this, there are very needy people everywhere and begging is a way of life for many of them. Begging is an accepted practice and giving alms is an important requirement of Islam.

There are different sorts of beggars. The 'professionals' are the most insistent and will not necessarily be content with a few taka from a wealthy foreigner. Many of these beggars, mostly found in the larger cities, are controlled by the mafia. Sadly, much of what they receive is turned over to the *mustans* (bosses). Women with babies, and small children are the major recruits, probably because of their vulnerability. Independent beggars will gratefully accept what is offered and move on to the next potential source. The word most commonly used by beggars is 'baksheesh', which in this case means alms or donation. In other contexts, it can be used to refer to a tip or a bribe.

Begging tends to stir up conflicting emotions and many travellers agonise over this issue. Dealing with it is a personal decision. Some opt to give nothing, realising that there will always be someone else who needs help and a single taka will not cure what ails this country. Others, recognising their privileged position, choose to have small change readily available. Some resolve to give money to reputable development organisations, either in Bangladesh or back home, which have a philosophy of self-sufficiency as opposed to hand-outs. But there is no easy answer.

The advantage in giving is that the beggar will move on as soon as he/she has received something, but otherwise often lingers in case you change your mind.

The disadvantage is that although it generally will only take a taka or two to satisfy beggars, you'll be making the situation more difficult for future travellers, especially in Dhaka, Chittagong and Cox's Bazar, where their presence is most acutely felt.

Hartals

Hartals (strikes) can not only ruin your itinerary but even be dangerous. 'Hartal' is a

Gujarati word, popularised by the Indian political leader Mahatma Gandhi during the struggle against British rule. Hartals have been a constant feature of Bangladesh's roughhouse politics. The opposition parties frequently call hartals to try and bring down the government.

Party workers and hired goons ensure that shops and markets are closed, vehicles stay off the road and industries stay shut for periods of 12 hours, 24 hours, or sometimes several days. Trains and ferries (run by the government) usually still operate. National hartals are normally announced a few days in advance, but regional or local strikes can come into effect with little warning.

There's little you can do during a hartal except stay in your hotel with a book, or perhaps take a walk. However, it can be dangerous even to walk around, depending on how nasty the local gangs of hartal enforcers are. Get advice from the hotel manager, and heed local warnings on places to avoid. Main roads and areas near opposition party offices are usually the worst places to venture. It may be possible to get past a roadblock gang of a dozen or so men, but if you try to pass a larger one there is a serious risk you could be attacked.

Dhaka sees the worst disturbances during hartals, including violent demonstrations and street battles with police or gangs hired by the governing party. See the Dhaka chapter for more information specific to how hartals affect the capital.

LEGAL MATTERS

Drug offences are very stiff in Bangladesh and can result in the death penalty if the quantities seized are considerable. Any person, including foreigners, caught smuggling virtually any amount of drugs or gold often ends up with a prison sentence for life. As a matter of practice, the courts permit those charged with crimes to have access to a lawyer.

Sad to say, if you are in a serious or fatal traffic accident (or, God forbid, you're responsible), the local custom is to flee if you can. Newspaper reports of bus crashes typically end with the words 'the driver ab-

sconded on foot'. The reason is that they fear a lynch mob appearing, since no-one has much faith in the police or justice system.

BUSINESS HOURS

Banking hours on Monday to Thursday are 9 am to 3 pm, and on Saturday from 9 am until noon. The official day off is Friday. Government offices are open Saturday to Thursday from 9 am to 2 pm. Private businesses generally operate between 9 am to 6 pm except Fridays, while consumer shopping, including bazars, tends to vary from 9 or 10 am to 8 or 10 pm. There are many individual shops that close on Fridays, but each bazar tends to have its very own particular closing day.

PUBLIC HOLIDAYS

The following holidays are observed nationally, and government offices, banks and most businesses are closed.

Amar Ekushe 21 February – Also known as Shaheed Day or the National Day of Mourning, this holiday is a tribute to the students who successfully opposed the government's attempts to deny Bangla the status of state language. On 21 February 1952 several students from the Language Movement were killed, and subsequently awarded martyr status. This is a potentially chaotic day as it celebrates a crucial event on the path to independence but it also legitimises student protest, and all the rival factions attempt to claim the mantle of saviours of the country.
Birthday of the Father of the Nation 17 March – Sheikh Mujibur Rahman's birthday
Independence Day 26 March
Pohela Boisakh 14 April – Bengali New Year
May Day 1 May
Bank Holiday 30 June
National Mourning Day 15 August – anniversary of the death of Sheikh Mujibur Rahman
National Revolution Day 7 November
Biganj Dibash 6 December – Victory Day
Christmas Day 25 December – known as *Bara Din* (big day); churches are adorned with lights and some churches hold cultural evenings with dances and prayers
Bank Holiday 31 December

SPECIAL EVENTS

A festival in Bangladesh is usually called a *mela*. Melas are generally times when all

Islamic Festival Dates

Event	2001	2002	2003	2004	2005
Shab-e-Barat	3 Nov	23 Oct	13 Oct	2 Oct	18 Sep
Jamat-ul-Wida	17 Nov	6 Nov	27 Oct	16 Oct	5 Oct
Eid-ul-Fitr	16 Dec	6 Dec	25 Nov	10 Nov	30 Oct
Eid-ul-Azha	5 March	22 Feb	11 Feb	1 Feb	21 Jan
Ashura	5 April	25 March	14 March	3 March	20 Feb
Eid-e-Miladunnabi	4 June	25 May	14 May	26 June	21 Apr

religions – Muslims, Hindus, Buddhists and Christians – join in the celebrations. Melas could be likened to a spectator sport, but one where everybody joins in despite their allegiances. Festivals may be related to harvests and other religious rites and ceremonies of the Hindus and Buddhists. Minor melas are mainly related to weddings, exhibition fairs or even election victories.

Islamic Festivals

Muslim holidays, known as *Eids*, follow a lunar calendar. The dates depend on the physical sighting of the moon, and fall about 11 days earlier each successive year. Along with public holidays, these special events are observed nationally, and government offices, banks and most businesses are closed. Projected dates for major Muslim events in the next few years are in the table following.

September-November

Shab-e-Barat – This holiday marks the sighting of the full moon 14 days before the start of Ramadan. The night of *barat* (record), according to Mohammed, is the time that God registers all the actions men are to perform in the ensuing year. It is a sacred night when alms and sweets are distributed to the poor.

Jamat-ul-Wida – Start of the month of Ramadan and the fasting period.

Ramadan – Referred to as *Ramzan* in Bangladesh, this month-long period of fasting is not technically a festival (nor is it a month-long period of public holidays), but warrants mention here as an important Muslim ritual. Fasting, the third pillar of Islam, incurs merit whenever observed, but is an absolute duty during Ramzan. For the entire month, between sunrise and sunset, abstinence from food, liquids, including swallowing one's own saliva, smoking, impure

thoughts, and physical pleasures is obligatory. The fast begins at dawn as soon as a white thread is distinguishable from a dark one, though in most villages and cities the broadcast morning call to prayer is signal enough. When the evening call to prayer is heard, the fast is broken with the *iftar* (meal). *Iftari* (food eaten at iftar) is wonderful. Traditional offerings include samosa, shingara, piaju, beguin, alu chop, various kabobs, and moori and cheera preparations. The meal taken about 30 minutes before dawn is called *Sehri*. For many reasons, extreme poverty being the best one, many Bangladeshis do not fast during Ramzan. Snack shops in the larger cities will stay open during the day, but put up curtains across the door so that diners have a little anonymity. In smaller villages it may be more difficult to come up with a meal during the day. Plan accordingly.

November-December

Eid-ul-Fitr – One of the two major Muslim holidays, it celebrates the end of Ramzan with the sighting of the new moon. It's a holiday as important to Muslims as Christmas is to many westerners. Shops close for a couple of days, government offices fill up for a week, and transportation becomes a nightmare because many Bangladeshis travel to their home villages. The festival is characterised by alms-giving and prayer, along with feasting, merriment, new clothes and gifts. Eid Mubarrak or Happy Eid are the common greetings.

January-March

Eid-ul-Azha – Known as the Eid of Sacrifice or informally as Bloody Eid, this two-day festival, the other major Muslim holiday, is 69 days after Eid-ul-Fitr. It remembers Abraham's sacrifice of his son Ishmael, celebrated with the slaughter of a cow, sheep or goat. After the morning prayers, the head of the family takes the animal out to the entrance of the house, faces it toward Mecca and kills it with a quick slash of the throat. The meat is divided equally among the poor, friends and family. During the week preceding the festival, open-air fairs do a brisk trade in cattle and goats. The animals are brightly adorned with ribbons, garlands and tassels. This festival also marks the beginning of the hajj (pilgrimage) to Mecca.

Ashura – The Ashura festival (also just called Muharram) takes place in the Muslim month of Muharram. It commemorates the martyrdom of Hussain, grandson of the prophet Mohammed, on the battlefield of Kerbala in modern-day Iraq in the Christian year 680. The leadership of the Islamic world had come into the hands of the Umayyad dynasty. A huge army pursued Hussain's household and small band of loyal soldiers to press him to accept the supremacy of the Umayyad Caliph Yazid. Hussain refused to do so, and the entire group was massacred.

April-June
Eid-e-Miladunnabi – Birth of the Prophet Mohammed.

Hindu Festivals
Hindu holidays also follow a different calendar but they generally fall at much the same date each year. They usually mark the changing of the seasons.

January
Saraswati Puja – Towards the end of January, clay statues of Brahma's consort Saraswati are made in preparation for this ceremony held around the beginning of February. The goddess of knowledge is always depicted playing a *veena* (an Indian stringed instrument) and accompanied by a swan, but outside these limitations there's a lot of variety.

February-March
Holi – The Festival of Colours is celebrated in late February/early March in Bangladesh. Commonly known as the spring festival, it is celebrated, less so here than in other countries, with the throwing of coloured water and powders and the consumption of foodstuffs containing bhang (powdered marijuana).

June-July
Rath Jatra – This festival celebrates Jagannath, the lord of the world and a form of Krishna, along with his brother and sister. These three images are set upon a Jagannath (chariot) and pulled through the streets by devotees. The seven-metre chariot in Dhamrai, 32km northwest of Dhaka, is typical. It's used in the big mela held there every year during the full moon

in late June/early July. Smaller festivals take place in other towns.

October
Durga Puja – The most important Hindu festival celebrated in Bangladesh. Statues of the goddess Durga astride a lion, with her 10 hands holding 10 different weapons, are placed in every Hindu temple. Celebrations last for four days, culminating on the day of the full moon when the statue is moved to the banks of a river or pond amidst much dancing and drum-beating. Sometime after sunset the goddess is carried into the water to dissolve. A huge festival takes place along the Buriganga in Dhaka. Country boats can be hired to watch the celebrations from the middle of the river.

LANGUAGE COURSES
The best place for learning Bangla is at HEED (Health Education Economic Development) Language Centre (☎ 810 2423, fax 810 3482, ✉ elgin@dhaka.agni.com) at House 38, Road 11, Block G, Banani, Dhaka. The basic course lasts three months and costs Tk 5500 per month, with a one-off Tk 500 registration fee. If you don't have three months to spare, you could pay for just one month and then drop out.

WORK
Work in Bangladesh is fairly limited. People with special teaching skills are sometimes able to land jobs at the American or the French School. There are also donor agencies that occasionally need people with certain skills on a temporary basis. Rather than wait until you get to Bangladesh before you start looking of work, the best thing to do is to contact a charity in advance in order to find out whether or not you are needed.

For information on specific charities in Bangladesh, contact them in your own country. If you are interested in a long-term post, the following organisations may be able to help:

Australian Volunteers International (03-9279 1788, fax 03 9419 4280, ✉ ozvol@ozvol .org.au) PO Box 350, Fitzroy VIC 3065
Coordinating Committee for International Voluntary Service (☎ 01-45 68 27 31) c/o Unesco, 1 rue Miollis, F-75015 Paris, France

International Voluntary Service (IVS) (0131-226 6722) St John's Church Centre, Edinburgh EH2 4BJ, UK

Peace Corps of the USA (☎ 202-606 3970, fax 606 3110) 1990 K St NW, Washington, DC 20526, USA

Voluntary Service Overseas (VSO) (☎ 020-8780 7200, fax 8780 7300) 317 Putney Bridge Rd, London SW15 2PN, UK

ACCOMMODATION

There are international-standard hotels in Dhaka but most accommodation in Bangladesh is well down the price scale.

Unmarried couples won't find things as difficult as in some Muslim countries, but there will be the odd cheap hotel unwilling to condone such behaviour. Lodgings in remote villages tend to be less forward-thinking.

Hotels

The word 'hotel' can mean a hotel or restaurant; the correct term for a hotel is 'residential hotel'. Lower-end establishments often make this distinction on their signs, and you'll avoid confusion by using this term when looking for a cheap hotel.

Many hotels don't have English signs and there are lots of buildings that look like they might be hotels but aren't, so it's useful to learn to recognise the word 'hotel' in Bangla script. An example of this is given in the Language chapter at the end of this book.

Although you can find very cheap accommodation, you get what you pay for. Very tiny rooms with fans and shared bathrooms, maybe mosquito nets as well, typically cost around Tk 40/60 for singles/doubles. Apart from their deficiencies in space and hygiene, bottom-end places sometimes refuse to accept foreigners; you'll get a queer look and be told that there's no room. This is particularly true of the central area in Dhaka. Outside of Dhaka, this happens only rarely. If it's late and you're really desperate, you might try hanging around the foyer for a while. An English speaker might strike up a conversation with you and be able to help you get a room.

The biggest hassles are the over-friendly room boys, some of whom simply won't leave you alone. Banging on your door at midnight to ask if you need anything is not uncommon. If you stay at the very cheapest hotel in town you may find that your door is made with two or three slabs of wood; cracks between them offer scope for Peeping Toms.

Mid-range hotels are better value, and there are lots of them. Expect to pay around Tk 80/120 for singles/doubles with attached bathroom, more in Dhaka. For this you'll usually get a small room with a slightly softer bed (beds in Bangladesh are usually larger and more comfortable than those in India) and a bathroom with a cold shower and an Asian-style squat toilet, usually quite clean. Almost all rooms have fans and mosquito netting – in this guide, unless stated otherwise, you can assume that mid-range hotels have them.

Parjatan motels are expensive by Bangladeshi standards (eg, Tk 500 to Tk 800 for a room), but they're usually modern and decent.

Government Rest Houses & Circuit Houses

There are government rest houses and circuit houses (guesthouses) in every district but they aren't officially accessible to travellers. However, if there are rooms available and you say something about being embassy-connected with suitable poise and dignity, the district commissioner will often let you stay if there are no mid-range or top-end hotels in town. Older travellers seem to have more luck here than younger ones. Having your own car or campervan is often a sign that you are important enough to stay at circuit houses. These circuit houses are often the nicest places in town. Rooms are generally spacious and you can usually eat there as well.

The Archaeology Department has rest houses at Paharpur, Mainimati and Mahasthan. They accept travellers if there's room, and are quite pleasant and comfortable. If you just show up, there's still a fair chance of getting a room. The rooms are basic but cheap, typically Tk 150 for a double room, and there will usually be a caretaker there to prepare food.

The Forestry Office has guesthouses in four forest areas: Sundarbans, Cox's Bazar, Madhupur Forest Reserve near Mymensingh, and Bhawal National Park north of Dhaka. Foreigners are allowed to stay at them but you must, without exception, book a room in advance with the Forestry Officer of the region where the park is located. These guesthouses vary widely in price, from nothing to Tk 800 for a room. Reservations by phone are sometimes possible.

Many companies, such as the Water and Power Development Authority (WAPDA) or the Rural Electrification Board (REB) have guesthouses all over the country; occasionally it's possible to stay at them, sometimes without prior booking in Dhaka. They're usually very cheap at around Tk 60 a person.

If you're cycling or camping around Bangladesh, finding a place to sleep in small villages is not nearly as difficult as you might think. Many villages too small to support a hotel have guesthouses with one or two rooms so they can offer government officials a place to stay, should they come to town. Foreigners are always welcomed to stay provided there's space. The price is typically Tk 30 a room and they're usually quite decent and spacious.

FOOD

Bangladeshi food is influenced, like the rest of the Indian subcontinent, by the regional variations of its history. Bangladesh, once an outpost of the Mughal Empire, now retains part of this heritage through its cuisine. Spicy *kebabs*, *koftes* (meatballs) and *biryanis* (meat mixed with rice) of all kinds are available. This has combined to form a mix with the more southern, vegetarian cuisine.

Budget restaurants are all very similar; a plain room where men shovel down rice, dhal and maybe a meat curry as quickly as possible. Notions of hygiene are pretty basic; extra rice might be served by hand, for instance. In low-end restaurants, it's rare to see women eating, but they are welcomed. Some restaurants have family rooms, often just a curtained booth, where women and families are supposed to eat. These offer a welcome opportunity to go 'off stage' for both men and women.

In Dhaka you can also find excellent Indian, Thai, Chinese and Korean restaurants, but outside Dhaka the only cuisine that you'll find besides Bangladeshi food is Chinese, or rather a Bangladeshi interpretation of Chinese (Chinadeshi?). There are Chinese restaurants everywhere, even in small towns such as Savar and Benapole. Prices typically range from Tk 60 a dish, and double that in Dhaka.

Snacks

Breads and biscuits are available everywhere, and in some small towns they might be all that you feel like eating. 'Salt' biscuits are usually not salty, just not the usual extremely sweet variety.

Local 'fast foods' are plentiful and rarely cost more than Tk 3 or Tk 4, but try to find them freshly cooked and hot. Some of the more common snacks include:

aloe – a fried vegetable cutlet
chapati – round and thin bread made from grilled unfermented dough
chokputi – hot chickpeas with potato, egg, spices and tamarind sauce
luchi – a tasty and crusty fried preparation, usually with dhal
moghlai paratha – a paratha stuffed with vegetables and spices, delicious for breakfast
paratha – thin flat bread (like a chapati) lightly fried in oil or butter
puri – deep-fried bread stuffed with dhal
samosa – an Indian-style, wheat-flour pastry triangle stuffed with vegetable or minced meat with spices
shingara – very similar to a samosa but round with a slightly heavier filling, typically of potatoes or liver, and spices

Fruit

Stalls everywhere sell fruit. The golden rule is *don't eat it unless you can peel it*. Oranges and bananas are safe for this reason, and they are the most common fruits on sale in winter. Major fruit-growing areas include the hilly fringes of Sylhet division, the Chittagong Hill Tracts and Rajshahi division. Fruit-growing is a major occupation for tribal groups such as the Khashias and Chakmas.

Mangoes have a cult following. The orchards along the banks of the Padma in Rajshahi division are said to grow the best mangoes. The mango season coincides with the hottest months of the year, and the sweet pulpy fruit is very refreshing.

There are many different varieties of banana on sale. Generally the smaller varieties are the sweetest. Have a close look at the quality of the fruit before you buy – storage and handling is very basic. If you see bunches of bananas being stacked 5km high on trucks you understand why they can arrive a bit mushy. The Bengali words for some basic fruits can be found in the Language chapter.

Main Dishes

Overall, Bangladeshi food is not nearly as varied as Indian food, and many dishes begin to look and taste the same after a while. A typical meal would include a curry (or masala) made with beef, mutton, chicken or fish, or egg and vegetables cooked in a hot spicy sauce with mustard oil; yellow watery lentils (dhal or jhal) and plain rice. Rice is considered a higher status food than bread, therefore at people's homes you will generally not be served bread.

Bhuna (or bhoona), which you'll find on lots of menus, is a cheaper cut of meat in a rich, spicy gravy. Another common dish is *dopiaza*, which is served with the same kinds of meat or fish. Finding purely vegetarian dishes can be quite difficult because in Bangladesh meat is highly prized. Ask for *bhaji*, which can be any kind of fried vegetable, such as squash or green beans. A mixed vegetable dish would probably be *shabji bhaji*. At fancy dinners, an all-vegetarian meal would not be well received.

The three main forms of rice dishes that you're likely to encounter are *biryani*, rice with chicken, beef or mutton; *pulao* (or pilao), fried and spiced like the biryani but without the meat; and *baht*, which is just plain rice. Rice and dhal mixed together and cooked is called *khichuri*. In restaurants,

chicken tikka is also common and usually served with Indian-style *naan*, a slightly puffed whole-wheat bread cooked in a tandoori oven.

Fish is part of the staple diet, but as river fish become scarce, more sea fish is appearing on menus. During the summer, when storms keep fishers from the Bay of Bengal, sea fish served in restaurants is likely to be frozen and a little suspect. Make sure river fish is properly cooked, and beware of heads and entrails as they can contain some nasty parasites.

The fish you are most likely to eat – broiled, smoked or fried – is *hilsa* or *bekti*. Smoked hilsa is very good, but is mainly available at five-star prices in big hotels. Bekti is a variety of sea bass with lots of flesh and few bones. It's one of the best fish you'll eat and is served in middle-range restaurants along with prawn and crab dishes.

Beef is widely available, although the quality is low. Cows are rumoured to be smuggled across from India, leaving their 'sacred' status at the border.

Kebabs come in a wide variety including *sheesh kebab*, which is prepared with less spice and usually with mutton or beef, and *shami kebab*, made with fried minced meat. *Koftes* are minced meatballs cooked in gravy.

A Bengali breakfast is usually dhal or yellow peas on roti bread. It's not always vegetarian though – sometimes there's a lump of bone served on top.

Desserts

The Bangladeshis have a sweet tooth and many sugar-loaded desserts are made. Even their yoghurt, known as *misti doi*, is sweetened. It's virtually impossible to get normal fresh yoghurt without difficulty in the bigger cities. Other sweet things include:

firni – rice pudding cooked with milk, sugar, flavouring and nuts, popular at Eid celebrations
halva – a common light-brown dessert made with carrot or pumpkin, butter, milk and sugar
jarda – yellow sweet rice with saffron, almonds and cinnamon
keora – a milk and sugar combination flavoured with a floral extract, usually rose
kheer – rice pudding with thick milk

molidhana – another milk-based dessert similar to halva

pais – similar to firni

pitha – a blanket term for all kinds of cakes or pastries including specific varieties such as *chitol, dhupi, takti, andosha, puli, barfi* and *pua*

ras malai – round sweets floating in a thick milk

rasgula & kalojam – two popular Indian-style desserts, milk-based and made with sugar, flour and ghee

sooji – wheat cream, almond and pistachio nuts

sundesh – a milk-based dessert, one of the best available

shemai – vermicelli cooked in milk and sugar

shirni – rice flour with molasses or sugar

zorda – sweetened rice with nuts

DRINKS

There are very few sources of drinking water in the country that are guaranteed to be safe. Some expatriates say they brush their teeth in Dhaka tap water without problems, others abhor the very idea. People in Dhaka are advised to boil and filter tap water. In a restaurant, even if the water comes from a tube well, it can easily be contaminated by the glass.

It's possible to buy bottled water nearly everywhere. Because it's locally bottled, the price is not high (Tk 15 to Tk 20, Tk 25 in restaurants), but local newspapers have revealed that quite a few brands are made by companies that don't actually filter the water all the time. If the filter breaks, for example, they might choose not to jeopardise their business by stopping production. When buying bottled water from outdoor stalls, make sure that the plastic cap has not been tampered with in any way. Recycling takes many forms, including 'rebottling' water.

Nonalcoholic Drinks

The milky sweet tea known as *chai* usually costs Tk 2 a cup and is available everywhere. It's slightly better than the Indian version as each cup is made individually, rather than stewing all day. This also means that it's no problem getting tea without sugar (say *chini na* or *chini sera*), but as sweetened condensed milk will be used it doesn't make much difference.

The magic words to get a pot of tea, usually with just one weak tea bag, are 'milk separate'. Miming a tea bag produces hilarity but not much else. Coffee is difficult to find and those who can't do without should consider buying a jar of the instant stuff in Dhaka.

International soft drinks, such as Pepsi, Coke and Sprite, are quite readily available throughout the country and cost between Tk 10 and Tk 15. Getting them cold or 'cool-ish' is fairly easy. Fresh lime sodas are generally available at the better restaurants in Dhaka and at some of the top-end hotels outside Dhaka.

Coconut milk is a fine, safe and refreshing drink. A whole young coconut costs about Tk 5. On the other hand, *lassi*, the refreshing yoghurt drink found throughout India, is not so common in Bangladesh.

Alcoholic Drinks

Every major town has at least one government-owned shop selling alcohol, but they're invariably hidden in very discreet locations (to avoid upsetting Islamic sensibilities). The selection is usually hard liquor such as whiskey. In Dhaka, Chittagong, Cox's Bazar and Teknaf you can sometimes find Asian whisky and cans of Heineken or Tiger beer sold on the sly; the price is at least Tk 150 per can.

Hindu and tribal people are generally not averse to drinking alcohol, typically their own brews made of rice. On the tea estates, which are worked predominantly by Hindus, the drinking of local brew, especially during festival time, is quite common. The liquor made in the Chittagong Hill Tracts kicks like a mad mule.

In the countryside you may encounter a drink called *tari*, made from coconut palms. When it's fresh it is cool and sweet, but when fermented it becomes the local beer. Many palm trees have a decidedly notched appearance due to repeated tapping. It is known as 'coconut toddy', but only found in tribal areas like the Chittagong Hill Tracts. *Kesare rose* is the rural liqueur, made from date molasses. It is mixed with hot water and tastes like brandy or cognac. A bottle costs about Tk 10.

ENTERTAINMENT

There are plenty of cinemas in Bangladesh but only one (in Dhaka) that shows western films; the rest are Bangladeshi or Indian. If you have access to a video there are plenty of video shops in larger towns.

The large American and British communities have social clubs in the Gulshan area of Dhaka (the American Recreation Association and the Bagha Club), as do the Australians, Germans, Canadians, Dutch and Scandinavians. On certain days, members from other clubs are welcomed and club members are likely to invite you in as their 'guest' even though they've just met you at the gate.

Another way to meet foreigners is to join the Hash House Harriers on their twice-weekly runs in Dhaka. Call the Marines at the US embassy, the British high commission or the Bagha Club for the location, which is different for each run.

SPECTATOR SPORTS

A knowledge of events in the world of cricket is a good conversational standby. Cricket has become enormously popular in recent years, possibly because of the spread of Indian satellite TV which broadcasts cricket practically non-stop. The national team, led by Aminul Bulbul, has played in one-day match tournaments for a few years. The team qualified for the 1999 World Cup for the first time in 20 years, and became national heroes by beating Pakistan. This rare victory was the cause of national rejoicing, and the Prime Minister described it as the greatest day in the country's history. In June 2000 Bangladesh was granted test-playing status by the International Cricket Council, allowing it to take its place alongside other subcontinental teams such as India, Pakistan and Sri Lanka.

The popularity of football (soccer) waxes and wanes, but a new national league with corporate sponsorship could see it rise again. Football crowds can get as unruly as those in the west when minor skirmishes escalate into major brawls.

Women don't play much sport, except for badminton, which is one of the country's most popular sports. Floodlit village courts are everywhere, and if you can play you'll have no problem in meeting people – if you're male.

SHOPPING

You don't get hassled to buy things here, mainly because there isn't very much produced with a tourist market in mind. Even quality postcards are hard to come by.

Things *not* to buy are products made from wild animals and reptiles, all of which are under pressure to survive in this crowded country. Even if a leopard skin for sale really is 20 years old, how do you think the stock will be replenished if you buy it? There is also trade in the country's artistic treasures, which are often plundered from Hindu temples.

Souvenirs include jewellery, garments, brasswork, leatherwork, ceramics, jute products, artwork, woodcarvings and clay or metal sculptural work. Unique items include pink pearls, fine muslin, *jamdani* or silk saris, jute doormats, wall pieces, glass bangles, seashells, conch shell bangles, and reed mats. Quality is generally quite high and the prices are very low.

Jute carpets, if you have the room, are a real deal. The better ones look exactly like and feel similar to oriental wool carpets. There is a good selection of colours, designs and sizes. They don't last as long as the real thing, but a two metre by three metre (six feet by nine feet) jute carpet costing US$50 will last five or more years. The Sonargaon Hotel in Dhaka has a jute carpet shop where the affordable prices are fixed by the government.

You may decide to replace everything in your backpack, or improve your stock of T-shirts. The garment industry is one of the biggest producers of western clothing, and you can buy seconds and overruns at the enormous Banga Bazar, sometimes referred to as Gulistan market. Clothing ranges from Calvin Klein jeans to baby rompers. The Westecs stores in Dhaka have fixed prices, changing rooms and sell only production line overruns, not imperfect or poor quality goods. See Shopping in the Dhaka chapter for more details.

One distinctly Bangladeshi souvenir is a piece of authentic rickshaw art. It's lightweight and easy to pack in the flat of your bag or backpack. Rickshaw art is not a tourist industry, so you'll have to shop where the rickshaw-wallahs shop. The few centrally located shops are on Bicycle Street, a local name for the area where most bicycle parts, and a few whole bicycles, are sold. (See Bangsal Rd in the Old Dhaka section of the Dhaka chapter for details.) You'll see painted rectangular tin and vinyl pieces and how they are attached to the rickshaw. The tin pieces are cheaper and last longer than the vinyl pieces, which tend to crack when folded. Quality varies among shops, but expect to pay Tk 50/100 for a tin/vinyl piece. If you don't see what you like, ask to see some others, which are usually stored in bundles tucked behind the counter.

The chain of Aarong shops has a good range of high-quality goods, although the fixed prices are higher than what could be bargained for on street stalls. Aarong has shops in Dhaka, Chittagong, Khulna and Sylhet; see the city sections in the relevant chapters for locations.

Getting There & Away

AIR

With the exception of Biman Airlines flights between Kolkata (Calcutta) and Chittagong, Dhaka's Zia International Airport is the only international gateway into Bangladesh.

International airlines that fly to Bangladesh include Air France, British Airways, Emirates Air, Malaysia Airlines and Singapore Airlines. See the Getting There & Away section in the Dhaka chapter for more information about airlines.

Some travel agencies may insist that you need a return ticket to Bangladesh and threaten you that the airline won't allow you on board without one. This isn't true; either the travel agencies have been given false advice or they are just angling to sell you a return ticket.

While fares from Europe and Bangkok are often bargains, fares out of Bangladesh are expensive. And compared to fares for flights originating in India, those from Dhaka seem even more expensive. In general, fares out of India are half those originating in Dhaka. Flying from Dhaka to Kolkata, for example, costs US$66, while flying from Kolkata to Dhaka is US$43. So if you're headed from Dhaka to, say, Karachi, you'll save big money going to Kolkata and purchasing your ticket there.

There are many good travel agents in Dhaka. If the agency doesn't have a computer facility, find one that does. The best agencies are listed in the Dhaka chapter, and all of them accept payment by credit card or by travellers cheques. Biman also accepts travellers cheques, but if you cancel you won't get a refund until the cheques have been cleared. If you pay in cash, make sure that they endorse your encashment certificate.

Departure Tax

The airport departure tax for international flights is Tk 300, which is included in the price of nearly all tickets.

The USA

Discount travel agents in the USA are commonly known as consolidators (although you won't see a sign on the door saying Consolidator). San Francisco is the consolidator capital of America, although some good deals can be found in Los Angeles, New York and other big cities. Consolidators can be found through the *Yellow Pages* or the major daily newspapers. The *New York Times*, the *Los Angeles Times*, the *Chicago Tribune* and the *San Francisco Examiner* all produce weekly travel sections in which you will find travel agency ads.

Council Travel, America's largest student travel organisation, has 60 offices in the USA; its head office (☎ 800-226 8624) is at 205 E 42 St, New York, NY 10017, and its Web site is at www.ciee.org. STA (☎ 800-777 0112) has offices in Boston, Chicago, San Francisco and other major cities. Call the toll-free 800 number for office locations or visit its Web site at www.statravel.com.

Air Travel Glossary

Cancellation Penalties If you have to cancel or change a discounted ticket, there are often heavy penalties involved; insurance can sometimes be taken out against these penalties. Some airlines impose penalties on regular tickets as well, particularly against 'no-show' passengers.

Courier Fares Businesses often need to send urgent documents or freight securely and quickly. Courier companies hire people to accompany the package through customs and, in return, offer a discount ticket which is sometimes a phenomenal bargain. However, you may have to surrender all your baggage allowance and take only carry-on luggage.

Full Fares Airlines traditionally offer 1st class (coded F), business class (coded J) and economy class (coded Y) tickets. These days there are so many promotional and discounted fares available that few passengers pay full economy fare.

Lost Tickets If you lose your airline ticket an airline will usually treat it like a travellers cheque and, after inquiries, issue you with another one. Legally, however, an airline is entitled to treat it like cash and if you lose it then it's gone forever. Take good care of your tickets.

Onward Tickets An entry requirement for many countries is that you have a ticket out of the country. If you're unsure of your next move, the easiest solution is to buy the cheapest onward ticket to a neighbouring country or a ticket from a reliable airline which can later be refunded if you do not use it.

Open-Jaw Tickets These are return tickets where you fly out to one place but return from another. If available, this can save you backtracking to your arrival point.

Overbooking Since every flight has some passengers who fail to show up, airlines often book more passengers than they have seats. Usually excess passengers make up for the no-shows, but occasionally somebody gets 'bumped' onto the next available flight. Guess who it is most likely to be? The passengers who check in late.

Promotional Fares These are officially discounted fares, available from travel agencies or direct from the airline.

Reconfirmation If you don't reconfirm your flight at least 72 hours prior to departure, the airline may delete your name from the passenger list. Ring to find out if your airline requires reconfirmation.

Restrictions Discounted tickets often have various restrictions on them – such as needing to be paid for in advance and incurring a penalty to be altered. Others are restrictions on the minimum and maximum period you must be away.

Round-the-World Tickets RTW tickets give you a limited period (usually a year) in which to circumnavigate the globe. You can go anywhere the carrying airlines go, as long as you don't backtrack. The number of stopovers or total number of separate flights is decided before you set off and they usually cost a bit more than a basic return flight.

Transferred Tickets Airline tickets cannot be transferred from one person to another. Travellers sometimes try to sell the return half of their ticket, but officials can ask you to prove that you are the person named on the ticket. On an international flight tickets are compared with passports.

Travel Periods Ticket prices vary with the time of year. There is a low (off-peak) season and a high (peak) season, and often a low-shoulder season and a high-shoulder season as well. Usually the fare depends on your outward flight – if you depart in the high season and return in the low season, you pay the high-season fare.

There are basically two ways to Bangladesh from the US. From the west coast, virtually everyone flies to Dhaka via Bangkok or Singapore. You can also fly direct to India and connect from there, but it costs more. Return fares from the west coast to Dhaka via Bangkok start at around US$1125.

From the east coast of the US, most people fly via Europe. Biman has the only direct flights from North America to Dhaka, and Gulf Air offer the best deals. Biman's DC 10s depart from New York and stop en route at Brussels or Amsterdam and Delhi without needing to change planes. The fare is around US$1300. If you purchase this through a consolidator, the price will be less.

Gulf Air offers lower fares from New York and its service is reputedly better. You must switch planes en route but connections are good. The return fare from New York is US$1050 (including tax).

If you live near a city serviced by British Airways or KLM, you can often get special return excursion fares flying all the way with those airlines for around US$1400. You could fly, for instance, on KLM to Amsterdam and connect with its twice-weekly flights to Dhaka, or on British Airways to London and connect with one of its four weekly flights from London to Dhaka.

Australia

From Australia, the easiest way to get to Bangladesh is to fly to Bangkok, Singapore or Kuala Lumpur and fly from there to Dhaka, or to fly to Kolkata in India and fly or travel by land into Bangladesh. See the following Asia section for more details of transport from Bangkok or Kolkata. Advance purchase air fares from the Australian east coast to Bangkok are from A$800 one way or A$1340 return on Malaysia Airlines. You should be able to find similar fares without the advance purchase restrictions through travel agents.

Quite a few travel offices specialise in discount air tickets. Some travel agents, particularly smaller ones, advertise cheap fares in the travel sections of weekend newspapers such as the *Age* in Melbourne and the *Sydney Morning Herald*.

The UK

Airline ticket discounters are known as 'bucket shops' in the UK. Despite the somewhat disreputable name, there is nothing under-the-counter about them. Discount air travel is big business in London. Advertisements for many travel agents appear in the travel pages of the weekend broadsheets, such as the *Independent* on Saturday and the *Sunday Times*. Look out for the free magazines, such as *TNT*, that are widely available in London – start by looking outside the main railway and underground stations.

For students or travellers under 26, popular travel agencies in the UK include STA Travel (☎ 020-7361 6161), which has an office at 86 Old Brompton Rd, London SW7 3LQ, and other offices in London and Manchester. Visit its Web site at www .statravel.co.uk. Usit Campus (☎ 020-7730 3402), at 52 Grosvenor Gardens, London SW1 WOAG, has branches throughout the UK. Their Web site can be found at www .usitcampus.com. Both of these agencies sell tickets to all travellers but cater especially to young people and students.

Other recommended travel agencies include Trailfinders (☎ 020-7938 3939), 194 Kensington High St, London W8 7RG; Bridge the World (☎ 020-7734 7447), 4 Regent Place, London W1R 5FB; and Flightbookers (☎ 020-7757 2000), 177-178 Tottenham Court Rd, London W1P 9LF.

The best deals are with Middle Eastern airlines, including Kuwait Airlines (£350; change planes in Kuwait) and Emirates (£365; change planes in Dubai). British Airways flies direct for £420.

Continental Europe

Though London is the travel discount capital of Europe, there are several other cities where you can find a range of good deals. Generally, there is not much variation in air fare prices for departures from the main European cities. All the major airlines are usually offering some sort of deal, and travel agents generally have a number of deals on offer, so shop around.

Across Europe many travel agencies have ties with STA Travel. Outlets in major cities include Voyages Wasteels (☎ 08 03 88 70 04 – this number can only be dialled from within France, fax 01 43 25 4625 – this number can be dialled internationally), 11 rue Dupuytren, 756006 Paris; STA Travel (☎ 030-311 0950, fax 313 0948), Goethestrasse 73, 10625 Berlin; and Passagi (☎ 06-474 0923, fax 482 7436), Stazione Termini FS, Gelleria Di Tesla, Rome.

France has a network of student travel agencies that can supply discount tickets to travellers of all ages. OTU Voyages (☎ 01 44 41 38 50) has a central Paris office at 39 ave Georges Bernanos (5e) and another 42 offices around the country. Their Web site is at www.out.fr. Acceuil des Jeunes en France (☎ 01 42 77 87 80), at 119 rue Saint Martin (4e), is another discount travel agency.

In the Netherlands, NBBS Reizen is the official student travel agency. You can find them in Amsterdam (☎ 020-624 0989) at Rokin 66, and there are several other agencies around the city. Another recommended travel agent in Amsterdam is Malibu Travel (☎ 020-626 3230), at Prinsengracht 230.

In Switzerland, SSR Voyages (☎ 01-297 1111) specialises in youth, student and discount fares. There is a branch in Zurich at Leonardstrasse 10, and there are others in most major Swiss cities. The Web address is www.ssr.ch.

The best airlines serving Dhaka from Europe are British Airways and KLM. Quite a few Middle Eastern airlines have connections between Europe and Bangladesh, with a stop in their home country. At the time of writing, Kuwait Airlines was offering the cheapest flights: from Zurich for Sfr780, from Paris for 3150FF and from Frankfurt for DM1000.

Asia

There are flights between all neighbouring Asian countries – Thailand, India, Nepal, Bhutan, Myanmar (Burma) – and Bangladesh. All connections are direct to Dhaka's Zia International Airport except for Biman flights between Chittagong and Kolkata.

India Biman and Indian Airlines have frequent flights between Dhaka and Kolkata.

Both airlines charge the same for the 35-minute flight. However, the fare is US$43 if you purchase the ticket in Kolkata and US$66 if you purchase it in Dhaka.

Biman also has twice-weekly flights between Chittagong and Kolkata for US$85.

Nepal There are flights five days a week between Dhaka and Kathmandu; Biman and Royal Nepal Airlines Corporation are the airlines serving this route. The flight takes 65 minutes and the one-way fare is US$107 on either airline.

Thailand Thai Airlines, Biman and Druk Air fly Bangkok to Dhaka. Thai Airlines has flights every day and Biman has almost as many; the Biman fare is US$220 while Thai charges US$264. However, if you purchase your ticket from one of the many discount agencies in Bangkok, you'll get a much better deal.

Myanmar The only flight between Yangon (Rangoon) and Dhaka is Biman's weekly flight every Sunday. The one-way fare for the 90 minute flight is US$184. Flying via Bangkok, which you can do almost daily, costs 65% more, ie, US$304 one way.

Bhutan Druk Air offers the only service between Dhaka and Paro, and the fare is high (US$175 one way). There are only two flights a week. If the schedule isn't convenient you could also fly to Paro via Kolkata, using Druk Air and Biman; connections are good and the cost is only marginally more.

LAND

India is still the only official land border crossing for foreigners to/from Bangladesh. While the idea of crossing into Myanmar may appeal, it is unlikely to become possible in the immediate future.

India

Road Permit If, having entered by air, you leave via a land border crossing, a road permit is officially required. This can be obtained in Dhaka at the Immigration & Passport Office (☎ 955 6020), at 127 New

Eskaton Rd, Mogh Bazar. It's open from 10 am to noon Saturday to Thursday. Two passport photos are required but there is no fee (officially). The process usually takes 24 hours, sometimes 48 hours, and you don't have to leave your passport. We have received reports that people at this office try to extract bribes from people who need the permit before their visas expire. We've also had reports that this permit will not always be asked for at the border, especially at some of the more obscure crossing points. The following is the opinion of an expatriate who has lived in Bangladesh for 20 years:

Nobody knows for sure what the regulations are regarding road permits, least of all the immigration and border people. Cash works wonders. Supposedly one needs permission to change the port/mode of entry/exit (airport vs overland). This is available at the Immigration office in Dhaka, and the place is infested with 'agents' and 'entrepreneurs' more than willing to help out for a small fee. The border officials would settle for less. I used to drive to Nepal once or twice a year, and never had any problems. At least nothing that between Tk 2 and Tk 500 couldn't solve.

If you drive from Bangladesh in your own vehicle, a permit is required from the Indian high commission (☎ 506346), at House 120, Road 2, Dhanmondi, Dhaka, as well as one from the Bangladesh Ministry of Foreign Affairs (☎ 956 2950/1/2), on Park Ave, facing the Supreme Court in Segun Bagicha (in the city centre).

Border Crossings The main crossings in India on the western side are found at Benapole/Haridaspur (near Jessore, on the Kolkata route), Chilahati/Haldibari (in the far north, on the Shiliguri-Darjeeling route), and on the eastern side at Tamabil/Dawki, in the north-east corner on the Shillong route, and east of Akhaura to Agartala in Tripura. If officials tell you that you cannot cross elsewhere, be sceptical because we have letters to the contrary from travellers. In recent years travellers have crossed at Bhurungamari/Chengrabandha (in the north, well east of Chilahati, an alternate route to Shiliguri and Darjeeling), Hili/

Balurghat (north-west of Bogra) and Godagari/Lalgola (west of Rajshahi on the Padma River, an alternate route to Kolkata). It is also possible to pass at Satkhira (south-west of Khulna).

The problem is that these lesser crossings witness so few foreigners passing through (maybe only once or twice a year) that everyone assumes it's impossible. Getting the correct story from Indian and Bangladeshi officials is virtually impossible. The truth is probably that crossing at these lesser routes is simply more variable and never certain. If you do use one of the minor crossings, be sure you don't leave the border without a stamp in your passport, otherwise you're sure to run into problems when leaving the country.

Via Benapole This is the main overland route into Bangladesh, made generally by train from Kolkata. It's a half-hour rickshaw ride to the immigration checkpost, then walking distance to the actual border. Inside Bangladesh it is a Tk 6 rickshaw ride to the bus station in Benapole, where you can catch buses to Jessore (one to 1½ hours). Because this is such a crowded crossing point, you can easily spend two hours going through immigration on both sides. See the Benapole section in the Khulna Division chapter for more details.

Via Chilahati This is the main overland route into Bangladesh from the north and is generally made by bus or train from Darjeeling or Shiliguri to Haldibari. It's a 30-minute rickshaw ride from Haldibari to Hemkumari at the Indian border; slow buses also cover this stretch. From Hemkumari to Chilahati (5km), the Bangladeshi border town, is about a 4km hike. From there you can take the twice-daily local train or a bus south to Saidpur; either way the trip takes several hours. See the Chilahati section in the Rajshahi Division chapter for more details.

Via Tamabil The bus from Sylhet to Tamabil takes about 2½ hours. The border at Tamabil/Dawki opened up to foreigners in 1995, providing direct passage to/from Shillong. If border officials mention anything about a permit, remain steadfast. No permit is required unless you're taking a vehicle.

Via Godagari One traveller reports that this infrequently used crossing is 'open for Bangladeshis' but 'variable for foreigners'. Another notes that leaving through Godagari poses no problem but if you're coming from Lalgola on the Indian side, it would be difficult to find this crossing as there is a lot of walking through fields involved. You need both rupees and taka for ferry crossings on the way and there are no exchange facilities either at the border or in Lalgola.

Via Hili Regarding this equally minor crossing, one recent traveller reports:

At Balurghat/Hili, crossing for foreigners is a very painful experience. After a long rickshaw ride (1½ hours along a deteriorating brick road) to Hili, the customs formalities took forever; everything in my rucksack was examined in minute detail and my camera opened. The strange demand that I take off my boots (on three separate occasions) later became clear as it was explained that the last foreigner to go through (four months before) had been a German caught smuggling gold hidden in his boots. So maybe I was just lucky. It is possible to cross this way, however, and on the Indian side there is a regular bus from the border to Balurghat from where there is a direct overnight luxury bus service to Kolkata.

Via Bhurungamari The border crossing in the north at Bhurungamari, north-east of Rangpur, is rarely used by travellers. If you're entering Bangladesh here, you'll find getting to the Indian border town of Chengrabandha from Shiliguri is easy. There are buses every 45 minutes between 6 am and 1 pm (the last bus); the fare is Rs 20 and the 70km trip takes 2½ hours. The Indian immigration office opens at 9 am. Outside, you can change your rupees into taka. Exporting rupees from India is illegal and they will be confiscated if found on you. Officials are usually very friendly, however, and don't perform searches.

Upon entering Bangladesh, you'll be questioned by officials and then told that you can proceed to Bhurungamari, 1km away. It's a tiny village, and if you're caught here for the night your only option may be to sleep on the floor of one of the bus offices. There are also a few very basic food stalls. You can take buses direct to Rangpur (5½ hours, Tk 50) and Bogra (eight hours, Tk 80).

Myanmar (Burma)

Overland routes between the subcontinent and Myanmar have been closed since the early 1950s. Even if the border were to be opened to foreigners in the future (it is periodically opened for Bangladeshis), roads across the frontier are in bad condition.

Given the understandable fascination that Myanmar's off-limits border areas have for many travellers, some people have been tempted to make a discreet trek across the Bangladeshi border into Rakhine (Arakan) state. However, while this may have been fun in the past, and the eventual punishment meted out by the government was formerly not too severe, things are different now – the Myanmarese army has planted minefields along the border. Crossing here is not recommended.

Getting Around

Internal transport in Bangladesh is so cheap that everyone uses it all the time, whether it be air, land or water transport. The rule is: if you want a seat get there early and learn to shove, kick and gouge like the rest of your travelling companions.

The distinguishing feature of internal travel in Bangladesh is the presence of a well-developed and well-used system of water transport. You will find that in a country where rivers and streams outstretch roads in total distance, water transport is very interesting, especially on the smaller rivers where you can see life along the banks.

Nevertheless, travelling by boat is slow compared to travelling by bus and it's usually avoidable, so many travellers never go out of their way to take a long trip, settling instead for a short ferry ride across a river or two. This is a big mistake – going to Bangladesh and not taking a trip down a river is like going to the Alps and not skiing or hiking. Travelling on river boats is a high point of a visit to Bangladesh for many travellers.

AIR

Bangladesh currently has three domestic airlines; Biman Airlines, GMG Airlines, and Air Parabat.

Biman's planes have done an awful lot of air miles and the interiors are a bit tattered, but the pilots are enormously experienced. Some expatriates recommend Biman if you have to fly during the stormy monsoon season. Biman is more prone to delays than the other airlines, as it flies more routes with its domestic fleet.

The privately owned GMG is the classiest of the three, operating Canadian-built Dash 8 turboprop aircraft fitted out with comfy leather seats. GMG also wins for punctuality and service.

Air Parabat, the fledgling airline has had two accidents since it started and is experiencing difficulty winning back confidence.

Domestic Air Services

All flights are one way from Dhaka, and include the Tk 75 domestic departure tax.

destination	Biman (Tk)	GMG (Tk)	Air Parabat (Tk)
Barisal	–	1470	970
Chittagong	1865	1870	1670
Cox's Bazar	2365	2395	2070
Jessore	1075	1470	970
Rajshahi	1125	1470	–
Saidpur	1325	–	–
Sylhet	1765	1770	1150

Flights on Biman between Saidpur and Rajshahi cost Tk 775.
Flights on Biman between Chittagong and Cox's Bazar cost Tk 550.

At the time of writing it was offering substantial discounts compared to the other two carriers, but it remains to be seen if it can stay in business.

All the airlines fly between Dhaka and regional cities; there are no direct flights between regional cities.

Domestic Departure Tax
There is a Tk 75 departure tax on internal flights, included in the ticket price.

BUS
Bus drivers in Bangladesh are among the world's most reckless, as shown by the incredible number of bus accidents occurring every day. Each time (as the newspapers invariably report) the driver – knowing full well that if he stays around, the angry survivors will beat him to death – absconds from the scene and is nowhere to be found.

The number of buses on the highways is hard to believe. Travelling between Dhaka and Comilla (a two-hour trip) you'll pass about 500 buses – an average of four buses every minute!

The country has an extensive system of passable roads. The main problem with them is that they aren't really wide enough for two buses to pass without pulling onto the verge, which is inevitably crowded with rickshaws and pedestrians. All this involves a lot of swerving, yelling and horn blowing, and can be extremely hard on the nerves.

When your bus encounters a river crossing it generally comes on the ferry with you, and the smoky queues of buses waiting to be loaded is one of the more frustrating aspects of travel here. If you don't mind paying another fare you can always leave your bus and get on one at the head of the queue.

For the lengthy ferry crossings of the mighty Padma, you may have to leave your bus and pick up another one from the same company waiting on the other side. These major inland *ghats* (landings) are a mass of boats, people and vehicles, so expect to be confused – pick out someone on your bus and follow them off the ferry. In any case, the bus assistant continues with the passengers, so you're unlikely to get left behind if you take a while finding your bus after the crossing.

It's illegal to ride on top of a bus like the locals do, but the police won't stop you. If you do ride on top, though, remember that low trees kill quite a few people each year.

Most bus stations are located on the outskirts of towns, often with different stations for different destinations. This helps reduce traffic jams in town (if you've come from India you'll appreciate the difference) but it often means quite a trek to find your bus. Chair-coach companies, however, usually have their own individual offices, often in the centre of town, and it's at these offices, not at the major terminals, that you must reserve your seat.

Chair Coach Buses

Chair coaches are distinguished by their adjustable seats and extra leg room. Where possible, take one of these large modern buses on journeys of more than three or four hours. They are not faster on the road – nothing could possibly go faster than the usually out-of-control ordinary buses!

However, departure hours are fixed and seats must be reserved in advance, so unlike regular buses there's no time wasted filling up the seats and aisles. In addition they are less crowded, often with no people in the aisles. And, most importantly for taller people (ie, more than about five foot ten inches tall), there's plenty of leg room.

Bus Adventures

Travelling from Sylhet to Dhaka, we expected just another teeth-cracking hair-pulling bus ride typical of Bangladesh bus travel. What we got was so much more. The first hour and a half was smooth enough. Then trouble struck. A dump truck full of stones simply would not let us pass. Our driver's hands were calloused from honking the horn and the male passengers on our bus were visibly (and audibly) impatient. Finally, on a slow section of road, a man jumped from our moving bus and ran up to the truck driver's window. A few sharp words (and blows!) were exchanged and our man returned. We were then allowed to pass.

But the adventure wasn't over; the incident demanded further road justice. Our driver forced the truck to stop on the shoulder and 10 or 12 passengers on our bus ran to the truck, pulled the driver and passengers from the truck, and beat them for a few minutes. Our passengers returned, vindicated, and we were off again. As our bus blared into the next small town, we hit a traffic jam and it all flared up again. This time about 20 were involved with the melee. Luckily, the local law arrived to cart the whole kicking-yelling-pushing bunch down to the police station. After two hours, the groups (apparently reconciled) returned and we were back on the road for the remaining ride into Dhaka.

Todd Kirschner & Rick Hamburger, US

Most chair-coach services travelling between Dhaka and cities on the western side of the country operate at night, typically departing sometime between 5 and 9 pm and arriving in Dhaka at or before dawn. Chair coaches plying the Dhaka-Chittagong route, however, travel mostly during the day.

There are two classes of chair coach – those with air-con and those without. Aircon chair coaches cost about twice those without air-con. All chair coaches are express buses, but not vice versa.

In Rajshahi division some of the best chair-coach companies are RE and Keya Paribahan: in Khulna and Barisal divisions there's Shohagh Paribahan; in Sylhet there's SylCom; and to Chittagong there are half-a-dozen major companies including Soudia, Shohagh Paribahan, Neptune and Borak. Not only do their waiting rooms have air-con, but snacks and drinks are served on board and the buses screen videos. Service is punctual, nonstop and slightly faster than the train.

Ordinary Buses

Among the ordinary buses, there are express buses and local ones that stop en route. The latter charge about 25% less but are slow. In more remote areas, local buses may be your only option. Most buses are large, but there are a few minivans (coasters).

The government's Bangladesh Road Transport Corporation (BRTC), whose buses generally leave from a separate BRTC station, is being driven out of business by the private companies. It may be just as well, as BRTC buses tend to be in much worse condition. On the other hand, they are sometimes slightly cheaper and tend to be slower, which in Bangladesh can not only be a blessing but also a life saver.

Ordinary buses are seemingly made for midgets; the leg room does not allow anyone to sit with their knees forward. On long trips, this can be exceedingly uncomfortable, so try and get an aisle seat.

Women travelling alone sit together up the front, separate from the men. Women travelling with their husbands normally sit in the men's section. Bus attendants often treat women with a bit of disdain, but with foreigners, both women and men, they are usually very helpful and try to give them the best seats.

On long-distance bus trips, chai stops can be agonisingly infrequent and a real hassle for women travellers – toilet facilities are rare indeed and sometimes hard to find when they do exist.

TRAIN

Trains are a lot easier on the nerves, knees and backside than buses, and those plying the major routes aren't too bad, at least in 1st class. However, travelling between Dhaka and western Bangladesh is complicated by unbridged rivers requiring ferry crossings, circuitous routing to the north via Mymensingh and different gauges.

The longest river crossing is on the Jamuna between Dhaka and Rajshahi divisions, where there's a three-hour ferry crossing and a change of trains to contend with. Travelling from, say, Bogra to Dhaka takes twice as long by train than by bus, while between Dhaka and Chittagong the travel time by either is virtually the same.

In the eastern zone of the country, the railway system may be improving slightly with the recent purchase of 20 trains from Germany. In contrast, the railway system in the western zone (Rajshahi and Khulna divisions), which has had only one station renovated since independence and relies on engines purchased from Hungary 40 years ago, continues to deteriorate.

Classes

Inter City (IC) trains are frequent, relatively fast, clean and reasonably punctual, especially in the eastern zone. Fares in 1st class are fairly high, about a third more than an air-con chair coach, but in *sulob* (2nd class with reserved seating and better carriages than ordinary 2nd class) the fare is comparable to that in a chair coach without air-con and the trip is a lot more pleasant.

There really isn't much difference between 1st class and sulob except space – 1st class has three seats across, facing each other and separated by a table, while sulob has four seats across without tables. Air-con 1st class is popular but limited; you'll have to reserve at least several days in advance to get a seat.

There are generally no buffet cars, but sandwiches (eg, hamburgers), Indian snacks and drinks are available from attendants. Second-class cars with unreserved seating are always an over-crowded mess and on mail trains your trip will be even slower. However, you may come out of the experience with a few good stories.

The only sleepers are on the night train between Dhaka and Sylhet, Chittagong and Sylhet, and Chittagong and Dhaka. The fare is about 40% more than 1st class. However, on many other trains the 1st-class compartments are sleeping compartments, and who's to stop you climbing into an upper bunk for a nap? If the carriage is full of other people with the same idea there's a fair chance that few of them have 1st-class tickets – the conductor will evict them if you ask. While locals often use baksheesh to upgrade their tickets, it's unlikely that you'll get away with it.

There is no longer a 3rd class, but the distinction is semantic, as 2nd class on the poorly maintained local trains is very crowded and uncomfortable, though it is remarkably cheap – less than a third the price of 1st class. Unreserved 2nd class has at least two levels above it (1st class and sulob, and sometimes 1st air-con and 1st sleeping), so it's really 3rd class and feels like it. On some trains, such as between Dhaka and Mymensingh, there are only 2nd-class compartments.

Reservations

For IC and mail trains, ticket clerks will naturally assume that you, as a seemingly rich foreigner, want the most expensive seats unless you make it clear otherwise. Buying tickets on local trains is a drag because they don't go on sale until the train is about to arrive, which means that while you're battling the ticket queue all the seats are being filled by hordes of locals. It's almost always better to take a bus than a local train.

Printed timetables are not available, so understanding the convoluted rules of train

travel is not easy, even for railway staff. It usually isn't too difficult to find a station master who speaks English.

Dhaka's modern Kamalpur station is the exception; schedules are clearly marked on large signs in Bangla and English, but you'll have to double check to make sure they are correct. Some schedules, particularly on the Dhaka-Sylhet route, change by half an hour or so between the summer and winter seasons, and the signs may not have been updated. You can phone the station, but inquiries in person are more likely to yield a reliable result. When making inquiries, it's best to keep things as simple as possible – specify when and where you want to go, and which type of train you want to catch.

If your queries are too much for counter staff, try the District Information Officer (DIO) at Kamalpur station (in the administration annexe just south of the main station building) – where you'll at least get a cup of chai.

If the crowds who silently follow you around the platform get you down (and they will), ask for the waiting room to be unlocked, or establish yourself in the office of an official who speaks English. Rural railway stations are prone to power failures – hang onto your luggage if the lights go out.

BOAT
Ferry

The river is the traditional means of transport in a country that has 8000km of navigable rivers, though schedules, even for the ferries crossing the innumerable rivers, are prone to disruption. During the monsoon, rivers become very turbulent and flooding might mean relocation of ghats; during the dry season riverbeds choked with silt can make routes impassable. Winter fogs can cause long delays, and mechanical problems on the often poorly maintained boats are not unknown.

The main routes are covered by the Bangladesh Inland Waterway Transport Corporation (BIWTC), but there are many private companies operating on shorter routes and some competing with the BIWTC on the main ones. Private boats tend to be slower and less comfortable but

In a country with so many rivers, ferries are a popular mode of transport.

cheaper than BIWTC boats. It always seems to be private boats that are involved in the occasional disaster. Bangladesh averages about five major ferry sinkings a year, frequently at night and with an average of 100 people drowning each time.

Classes

There are four classes of ticket on Bangladeshi boats: 1st, 2nd, inter and deck class. 1st and 2nd class are fairly straightforward, but travellers may be less familiar with the other two. Deck class simply means a space on deck. You'll need to bring your own bedding, mattress, food and water. Inter stands for intermediate, and gives you a berth in a cabin with 10 to 16 wooden-slat bunks. It's quite unusual for a foreigner to use either the intermediate or deck classes.

On all craft with 1st-class tickets you must book in advance to be assured of a cabin. On popular routes, especially the Rocket (paddle wheel) route between Dhaka and Khulna, you may have to book a couple of weeks ahead during the dry season. If you're catching a boat at one of the smaller stops, your reservation for a 1st-class cabin will have to be telegraphed to another office and may take some time. Inter-class and

deck-class tickets can be bought on board, so there's always a scramble for room. In deck class you may find your ability to sleep in cramped, noisy spaces stretched to the limit. Bedding is provided only in 1st class.

If you haven't managed to book a 1st-class cabin, it's worth boarding anyway and buying a deck-class ticket, as you may be offered a crew member's cabin. Renting a crew cabin is a common and accepted practice, but it's technically against the rules, so there's scope for rip-offs. Don't necessarily believe the crew member when they tell you that the fee you pay them is all that you will have to pay – you need to buy at least a deck-class ticket to get out of the ghat at the other end of the trip, and other hastily-thought-of hidden charges may crop up. Some travellers have even had these sorts of problems when renting the captain's cabin.

It's a hassle finding the ship assistant, but if you want to avoid the possibility of minor rip-offs, involve him in negotiations for a crew cabin. He is responsible for matters relating to passengers and accommodation.

If you travel deck or inter class (and having a crew berth counts as deck class), you can't use the pleasant 1st-class deck, from where the best views are to be had. You

Ferry Routes

from	to	frequency (each way)
Barisal	Chandpur & Dhaka	daily
Bahadurabad	Chilmari	daily
Barisal	Chittagong	2 weekly
Barisal	Hularhat (Sea truck)	6 weekly
Chittagong	Hatiya Island	2 weekly
Chittagong	Kutubdia Island	daily
Dhaka	Barisal/Mongla/ Khulna (Rocket)	4 weekly
Kumira	Guptachara (Sondwip Is)	daily
Manpura	Mirzakalu	1 weekly
Steamerghat	Hatiya Island	daily

might of course be able to sneak in, but don't complain too loudly if you're thrown out. You aren't *really* special, just rich. Anyway, you can insinuate yourself onto the walkway near the wheelhouse, where the views are better – but it's rare to find yourself more than five metres above water level in Bangladesh.

Travellers on a really tight budget who can't even afford the crew berth might try going up to the 1st-class dining room to sleep there. Once again, it's a bit arrogant to complain if you're thrown out.

Tips

In winter, thick fog can turn a 12-hour trip into a 24-hour one, although the captain sometimes doesn't decide that it's unsafe to proceed until he has a very close encounter with a riverbank. If you're travelling deck class, make sure that you're sleeping somewhere that you won't roll off the boat if it comes to a sudden stop!

Porters waiting to leap on docking ferries jostle and fidget like swimmers on the starting blocks – if you don't fancy a swim, don't stand in front of them. The BIWTC routes are shown in the 'Ferry Routes' table. Also, see the relevant sections in the Division chapters for schedules and fares.

The country's major ferry crossing is at Aricha, which is at the confluence of the country's two largest rivers, the Jamuna and the Padma. Ferries operate between Aricha (east bank), Nagarbari (west bank) and Daulatdia (Goalundo Ghat). So if you're heading from Dhaka north-west to, say, Bogra, you'll take the Aricha-Nagarbari ferry (usually about three hours, including bus changes), and if you're heading west to Khulna Division, including Jessore, you'll take the Aricha-Daulatdia ferry (about two hours).

Ferries from Aricha to Daulatdia or Nagarbari depart approximately hourly between 6 am and 10 pm and take about 40 vehicles; the last ferries from Daulatdia and Nagarbari depart at midnight and 1.30 am respectively.

If you're heading for the Khulna Division you can also take the Mawa-Kaorakandi Ghat ferry. This ferry crossing is slightly shorter than at Aricha, but the wait may well be longer because there are less frequent crossings.

It's amazingly relaxing just watching the countryside drift by. If you're lucky you may spot a sluggish Gangetic river dolphin. Sometimes you find yourself gliding over thick growths of water hyacinth close to the jungle-covered bank; at other times you're churning along a river so wide that neither of the banks are visible.

The Rocket

This is the generic name that is given to special BIWTC boats that run daily between Dhaka and Khulna, stopping at Chandpur, Barisal, Mongla and five other lesser ports en route. If you're heading to the Sundarbans, Kolkata or the Muslim ruins at Bagerhat, travelling by the Rocket is a great way to go for a major part of the journey. The journey all the way to Khulna takes about 30 hours, departing from Dhaka at 6 pm and arriving at Khulna at 3 am the following night.

There are four Rockets, the best two being the *Ghazi* and the *MV Masood*, which are the most recently refurbished. These two Rockets are not particularly glamorous by Mississippi paddle-wheel standards, but they do have paddle wheels, two levels and in 1st class a protected deck with comfortable cane seats. On rare occasions the BIWTC has to substitute a non-paddle wheeler for the real thing. The Rocket operating on your trip is pretty much hit or miss. Regardless of which boat you take, 2nd class (Tk 220) and deck class (Tk 135) are crowded, but possible if you are on a budget.

The front half of the upper deck of the old paddle-wheel steamer is reserved for 1st-class passengers, most of them, typically, Bengalis – this is not a tourist boat. There are eight cabins in this section – four doubles and four singles. The cost is Tk 915 if you go the entire distance. Inside, floors are carpeted and each cabin has a washbasin and a narrow bunk bed or two with reasonably comfortable mattresses, freshly painted white walls, wood panelling and good lighting. Bathrooms with clean toilets and showers are shared.

The central room has overhead fans to cool things off, a long sofa and four tables for dining. Guests have a choice between Bengali and western meals and they're both quite adequate, although the choice doesn't vary much. Outside, you can sit on the deck in cushioned wicker chairs and have the stewards serve tea and biscuits as you cruise the Ganges delta.

In Dhaka, tickets are available from the well-marked BIWTC office in the modern commercial district, Motijheel, a block down from the landmark Purbani Hotel. Book in advance. The boat leaves from Badam Tole, a pier 1km north of Sadarghat terminal on the Buriganga River. Leaving from Khulna, you should be allowed to sleep the night before in your cabin; departure is at 3 am. They move the boat to a different anchorage for the night so get aboard early. Sometime after midnight the boat steams back to the loading dock.

The paddle-wheel steamers known as Rockets are a great way to see the waterways of Bangladesh.

The Rocket Experience

On the riverbanks the panorama changed continuously – from lush, tropical jungle with mangroves, to vast expanses of paddy fields dotted with brightly coloured figures at work. Sometimes we saw people leading their cattle or goats across narrow bridges made of no more than a couple of palm-tree trunks; at other times there were fisherpeople's huts on stilts with nets hanging out to dry. But most memorable was a potters' village of humpbacked, thatched roofs opposite the ferry terminal at Kawkhali, where newly fired terracotta pots were stacked in herring-bone patterns along the bank. What a contrast to the enormous brick factories with tall industrial chimneys that lined the approach to Dhaka the following morning.

Hallam & Carole Murray

Traditional River Boats

There are about 60 types of boats plying the rivers of Bangladesh. Steamers are only one type; the remaining 59-odd are traditional wooden boats of all shapes and sizes, some with sails but most without. It's a big mistake to think that steamers are the only way to travel in Bangladesh. Some travellers prefer the smaller rivers plying the smaller rivers; this is the only way to see the life along the riverbanks. Out on the wide Padma, you'll see lots of big launches, traditional boats and maybe some river dolphins, but you won't see people fishing with their nets, children waving from the shore, farmers working in the paddy fields, or women walking along the banks in their colourful saris.

The problem with taking boats on the minor rivers – and the reason why travellers almost never do this – is finding out where to take them and where they're heading. There is no 'system'; you simply have to ask around. If you see two towns on a map with a river connecting them, you can be sure that boats travel between them, and if there's no obvious road connecting them there will be lots of passenger boats plying the route.

A great river for taking a cruise is right in the Dhaka area – the Tongi (TONG-gee) River. See the Around Dhaka section in the Dhaka chapter for details.

CAR

Travelling by car has two possibilities: either you'll be driving your own vehicle or you'll be the passenger in a rental car, which comes complete with its own driver.

Owner-Drivers

The import of a vehicle requires a *carnet de passage en douane* from the country in which the vehicle is registered (see Driving Licence under Visas & Other Documents in the Facts for the Visitor chapter). Later, the vehicle must be exported. Driving in Bangladesh, especially within 100km of Dhaka and on the Dhaka-Chittagong highway it takes a bit of guts. On the major highways you'll be pushed onto the curb every few minutes by large buses hurling down the road. Dhaka presents its own unique driving perils because of the vast number of rickshaws and baby taxis (three-wheeled auto-rickshaws).

The incredibly dexterous rickshaw-wallahs and mad baby-taxi drivers dart in and out of lanes, causing near misses every few seconds. And just because you're in a one-way lane doesn't mean you can't expect to face a vehicle or two coming straight at you, seemingly oblivious to the road laws (if there are any). Traffic is heavy and when jams occur you'll be surrounded by so many rickshaws you may think you'll never get out.

Rental

Self-drive rental cars are not available in Bangladesh, and that's probably a good thing – even the biggest and the shiniest cars here are covered in scratches and dents, and the road laws are vague at best. Fortunately, renting cars with drivers has become very easy and the price is lower than in Europe and North America. Considering the ease and low cost of renting cars in Bangladesh, it's surprising how rarely travellers do it.

[Continued on page 98]

Bangladesh by Bike

Upon our arrival in Bangladesh, we decided to see a bit of the country that would be our home. A bicycle trip would give us a good preview and Kolkata (Calcutta), less than 50km from the Bangladesh border, was a suitable destination. A return to Dhaka by air would let us cover maximum distance in minimum time.

Kolkata is about 240km from Dhaka as the crow flies, so we followed the crows and avoided the heavily used highway.

The route was wonderfully conceived. Except for the first 30km out of Dhaka and the last 30km into Kolkata, there was virtually no traffic. (Not to mention that somewhere in the middle 65km section there was virtually no road!) Using the best available map (a scrap of paper with certain village checkpoints highlighted), we pedalled along the backroads of Bangladesh.

The village checkpoint system was our key to success. Each preselected village was within a day's walk of the next, ensuring that almost any local we asked would know of its location.

At the main traffic circle south of Dhaka, we took the Khulna road, crossed the Chinese Friendship bridge and headed for Mawa (checkpoint No 1) on the Padma River. There we waited for the big ferry, drank a few cold Cokes and provided the main entertainment for a crowd of about 40.

Once across the river, we headed down the near-deserted road toward Bhanga (checkpoint No 2). Rice paddies and rural settlements flashed by in a series of instant replays. Bhanga is a hub of activity. Buses, rickshaws, food stalls and people competing for space at dusty intersections. We bolted down a dinner of samosas and chapatis while straddling our bikes and fending off the ever-swelling crowd.

At the main intersection of Boritola (checkpoint No 3), an astonished traffic policeman pointed out the right-hand turn to Mukshudpur (checkpoint No 4). The air was thick with mosquitoes at sunset and the bumpy brick road gradually deteriorated into an even bumpier, potholed track.

We left Dhaka too late in the morning to make it to Mukshudpur before nightfall. We were still pedalling when darkness settled around us with black finality.

That day we'd mastered the art of small-boat ferrying. These country rowboats, sitting inches out of the water, routinely transport cycles and other cumbersome objects. The first crossing or two (there would be many before we saw Kolkata) were a little precarious until we got used to the shifty balance. Our last such crossing for the day would have been at Mukshudpur but the boatman had gone home for the night. Our only option was a narrow, bamboo-pole bridge about 15cm wide, spanning 10m of wet, murky darkness.

As we pondered the physics of guiding two fully loaded bikes across the rickety structure, out of nowhere came a local who silently shouldered the first bike and deftly crossed the bridge. A second trip had us both across without a hitch. Our next problem was solved by another 'guardian angel' who led us to a nearby guesthouse.

The Mukshudpur guesthouse would have been difficult to recognise without help. What looked like a deserted, semi-deteriorated building in the dark, opened to reveal a room with a double bed complete with fresh sheets, mosquito netting and a clean basic toilet. The wizened man who, as the appointed caretaker, went about his caretaking duties with a practised formality, added to a sense of unreality.

After a blissful sleep, we glided silently out of Mukshudpur in the wet, predawn mist toward the village of Kashiani (checkpoint No 5). The entire scene could not have been more rural. The track narrowed to a footpath as we vied for space with men carrying farm tools and women balancing water urns on their hips. Naked children greeted us and field labourers paused as we rolled past. Pungent bursts of onion and coriander punctuated the air, and only occasional bursts from a nearby generator interrupted the serenity.

Bangladesh by Bike

Footpaths and bumpy tracks slowed our progress, but it was great to be out and we felt no urge to hurry. Past Kashiani we hardly noticed the several short ferry crossings, and all too quickly we were in Kalna (checkpoint No 6) and then Lohagara (checkpoint No 7). By the time we got to Narail (checkpoint No 8), the road improved considerably. In another 15km we were in Jessore. It seemed we were going to make it after all.

It was early afternoon when we navigated Jessore's traffic-laden streets, an abrupt change from the peaceful countryside. Overcoming the temptation to stop, we pushed on the last 30km to the border town of Benapole.

Our experience of Bangladesh was slight, but in no time we knew that Benapole was not one of its highlights. The town is one long, gravelly, dusty street, haphazardly lined with trucks and food stalls. Guesthouse is not a term used here.

After a number of enquiries, we were finally led down a narrow alley to a shed-like structure. The concrete room was a jumble of unmade beds and mosquito netting. Smiles masked our misgivings, and we decided to look at the other options. Within an hour, we were out of options, humbly returning to bargain for the room.

The border formalities the next morning were straightforward despite the lines of people and the officer's request for our nonexistent road permit. As the main attraction, we proceeded to the front of the line for processing, and an hour later were pedalling down the tree-lined Indian highway toward Kolkata.

The first difference we noticed was that even the smallest of settlements had refrigeration. The first cold lime soda went down so sweetly that it was hard to resist stopping at every village.

By mid-afternoon the third day we reached the outskirts of Kolkata. No signs suggested its proximity, but the increase in overloaded buses and smoke-spewing trucks was enough. We rode as far as the airport on the eastern edge of the city and called it quits.

We found a guesthouse, the Tutimeer, a few kilometres west of the airport, with hot water and air-con for a very reasonable price. Alternating between streams of hot water and blasts of cool air, we soaked in the comfort, enjoyed a sense of accomplishment and relished the thought that we would not have to straddle a bike for at least another week.

Alex Newton

RICKSHAW ART

RICHARD I'ANSON

You hardly need to walk in Bangladesh. Once you reach a street or road, a rickshaw (or several rickshaws) will appear, with the little bell tinkling to get your attention. It takes a little practice to climb into the seat gracefully, but once you're ensconced and your destination is settled, the driver steps up from the seat, brings all his weight to bear on the pedals, and the journey begins.

The roads are full of obstacles, and in the villages the paths are often bumpy, brick-paved and narrow. More than likely you'll be caught in traffic. Rickshaw traffic. The divine law of Bangladeshi roads is that every driver must pull in front of the next and cut them off. This tends to create problems in the orderly flow of vehicles. The most pleasant journeys can be at night, when the traffic is lighter and the rickshaws have little kerosene lamps flickering beneath the undercarriage. On cool nights and mornings the driver's blanket flows out behind him as you tinker along.

Foreigners will probably find you're being overcharged a little, but since it's only a few cents it barely matters and at least your money is literally helping the man on the street. And for people with wider hips than the average Bangladeshi, fitting two people on a rickshaw is a lesson in discomfort.

Art moving by on wheels needs to be bold and eye-catching, able to be taken in quickly. Rickshaw artists aim to decorate the vehicles with as much drama and colour as possible, and paint images that are both simple and memorable. This is street art for the ordinary man, and it is unashamedly commercial. Rickshaw builders compete to win contracts from the rickshaw fleet owners, who in turn compete among themselves to own the fanciest vehicles.

Rickshaw drivers are usually rural migrants. With no other opportunities they turn to a rickshaw fleet owner, called a *malik*. The malik rents out a vehicle from his fleet (which could be anything from less than 10 rickshaws to several hundred) and usually also provides meals and basic dormitory-style accommodation for a fee.

The maliks commission rickshaw makers called *mistris* to build and decorate the machines to their specification. The artists working in the mistri's workshop learn on the job, maybe starting out as young as 10, when they work decorating the upholstery and smaller sections of the vehicle.

The main 'canvas' is recycled tin, from a drum of cooking oil for example. This forms the backboard of the rickshaw. Enamel paints are used. The artist may also decorate the seat, handlebars, the curved back of the seat, the chassis, the hood, and just about every other surface. The handlebar

There are many different stages that a rickshaw goes through before it is completed. From the initial assembly to the final decoration stages, the process requires dexterity and an artistic sensibility.

ALL PHOTOGRAPHS BY RICHARD I'ANSON

Rickshaws on the streets of Dhaka are often decorated with images from movies, pictures of animals and a multitude of tassels and bells.

RICHARD I'ANSON

decorations in particular can be wildly elaborate, with intricate coloured plastic tassels 20cm long.

All the dreams of the working man appear on rickshaws. Common backboard painting themes include idealised rural scenes, wealthy cities crammed with cars, aeroplanes and high-rise buildings, unsullied natural environments, and dream homes with sports cars parked outside. Images from Bangladeshi and Indian fantasy movies are the most popular (as well as a few Hollywood stars altered to local taste, like Leonardo Di Caprio with distinctly Bangladeshi features). The portraits often make the actors plumper than in real life – a slim figure isn't a fantasy when so many go hungry. The images of women with heart-stopping stares are a great contrast to the real women on the street, who by custom avoid eye contact with unfamiliar men.

Another theme is animals behaving as humans. Many are just playful: birds playing music, or lions, tigers and deer dancing and singing in a wedding procession. Others have coded messages, such as a fat lion sitting in the back of the rickshaw roaring at a skinny pedal-pushing deer, or a tiger (Bangladesh?) feasting on a cow (India?).

In the more pious Muslim towns such as Sylhet and Maijdi, rickshaw paintings have fewer human and animal figures, due to the Islamic injunction against depicting living creatures. In their place appear landscapes and religious imagery such as crescent moons and stars, Arabic calligraphy, Mecca and the Taj Mahal. Islamic green is the main colour used on these rickshaws.

Mass-produced images of film stars applied to the backboard are increasingly challenging hand-painted backboard art, especially in Dhaka. The rise of motorised traffic in the big cities is another threat to the non-polluting rickshaw industry. Some people say that nowadays the smaller towns of Mymensingh and Tangail have the freshest and most original rickshaws tinkling by on the streets.

Top: In a rickshaw traffic-jam, everybody comes to a standstill.

[Continued from page 93]

In Dhaka there are innumerable companies in the rental business; the best ones are listed under Car in the Getting Around section of the Dhaka chapter. Expect to pay about Tk 1500 a day for a car without aircon and about Tk 2000 for a vehicle with air-con, plus petrol (which costs only Tk 14 a litre). There are no other extras except one: when you stay out of town overnight, you must pay for the driver's lodging (about Tk 60 a night) and food (Tk 50 a meal is reasonable). They don't try to hide this, but make sure you determine beforehand what those rates will be so as to avoid any misunderstandings. Insurance isn't required because you aren't the driver.

Outside of Dhaka, the cost of renting vehicles is typically about a third less if you don't go through Parjatan – around Tk 1000 a day plus petrol for a van without air-con. In cases where no information is available your best bet is to go to the top hotel in town and ask the manager who to contact. You negotiate with the driver but if you go through Parjatan they rake off 50% from the driver's price. If this approach fails, try a development organisation in the area, such as Care or Danida; the chances are that they or their drivers will know of someone in the business. Outside of Dhaka, any taxi is also a rental car, but there are so few taxis available that finding one can be difficult – try the airport when a plane arrives. You will not find taxis outside of Dhaka, Sylhet, Khulna, Saidpur and Rajshahi.

BICYCLE

Bangladesh is great for cycling and this is an interesting way to see the country. With the exception of the tea-estate regions in the Sylhet Division, the Chittagong Hill Tracts and the road between Chittagong and Teknaf, it is perfectly flat; you can pedal around very easily with a single-gear bike.

Just because you may be travelling around the Indian subcontinent without a bike doesn't preclude cycling in Bangladesh. You can buy a new Chinese bike for around Tk 3000 to Tk 4000. In Dhaka, Bicycle Street in the old section is the best of several places to look. When you leave the country, there's a good chance that you will be able to sell it for half the price. You might even set up a purchase-back scheme with the bike seller. Tools for repair are hardly needed because everywhere you go you'll find people who can repair bikes. Remember – rickshaws are everywhere.

The cities, particularly Chittagong and especially Dhaka, are not easy places to cycle. The traffic is a maelstrom, the fumes and dust are unpleasant, and heading out of Dhaka in any direction is a major hassle. However, if you're on your way by 5.30 am, you'll zip out of there (or any city) without much problem. Alternatively, hop on a train with your bike, get off when you arrive at a major town and start your trip from there. When you're arriving at Dhaka or Chittagong and you don't want to deal with the traffic you can simply hail any bus or baby taxi and ride in from there, with your bike on top.

The trick to cycling in Bangladesh is to avoid the major highways as much as possible; two buses trying to pass another bus at the same time is a frequent sight. All you can do is try to get out of their way.

While keeping off the major highways is not always possible, look for back roads that will get you to the same destination. Unfortunately, maps of Bangladesh lack sufficient detail or are too notoriously bad to be of help here.

Nevertheless, it's possible to travel to areas where maps show no trails and if you're travelling between two major towns, trails virtually always exist between them. So long as you're not in complete marshland there is bound to be a path. Most paths are bricked and in good condition, and even if it's just a dirt path, bikes will be able to pass during the dry season. A river won't hinder your travel, since there's invariably a boat of some sort to take you across. See the Around Dhaka section of the Dhaka chapter and the Sylhet Division chapter for some suggested cycling routes.

The ideal time to go cycling is in the dry season from mid-October to late March;

during the monsoon many tracks become impassable.

HITCHING

Hitching is never entirely safe in any country in the world, and we don't recommend it. Travellers who decide to hitch should understand that they are taking a small but potentially serious risk. People who do choose to hitch will be safer if they travel in pairs and let someone know where they are planning to go.

LOCAL TRANSPORT

Bangladesh has an amazing range of vehicles; on any highway you can see buses, cars, trucks, rickshaws, baby taxis, tempos, tractors with trays laden with people, motor-bikes, scooters, bicycles carrying four people, bullock and water-buffalo carts and bizarre home-made vehicles all competing for space. One local favourite in Rajshahi division is a sort of mini-tractor powered by incredibly noisy irrigation pump motors.

In Dhaka and Chittagong, motorised transportation has increased tremendously over the last 10 years; traffic jams in central Dhaka are a nightmare. The problem continues to be due more to rickshaws than cars, but motorised vehicles are now causing traffic jams.

What is most disturbing to people is the total chaos that seems to pervade the streets, with drivers doing anything they please – certainly the police can't control them. The foolish traveller, unable to control anything in this mad environment, will fret to no end. Others will sit back in their baby taxi or rickshaw and enjoy the crazy scene. Accidents do happen and sometimes people are killed, but the odds of your being involved are still fairly slim.

Taxi

Outside of Dhaka there are precious few taxis in Bangladesh. In Dhaka, Capital Cab has a modern fleet. The only place you'll find them are at the airport and at the Sonargaon and Sheraton hotels – you cannot hail a taxi in the street. In Chittagong, the same applies – you'll find a few taxis at the airport and at the city's leading hotel, the Agrabad. In Sylhet, Khulna, Saidpur and possibly Rajshahi, you'll see no taxis except for a few at the airport. They are not marked, so you'll have to ask someone to point them out to you. At Zia International Airport in Dhaka, taxi drivers now demand Tk 400 to virtually anywhere in the city.

Rickshaw

In Bangladesh, all rickshaws are bicycle driven. Unlike in Kolkata, there are none of the human-puller variety. Rickshaw-wallahs (drivers) usually do not speak English and often don't know much of the layout of their town beyond their own area, so if you'll be going a good distance and you're not sure where you're going, don't expect them to be able to help much in locating your destination; you probably won't be able to explain yourself anyway.

Fares vary a lot and you must bargain if you care about paying twice as much as locals, but it still isn't very expensive. In any case it is simply unrealistic to expect to pay exactly what Bangladeshis do. If you can get away with paying a 25% premium you'll be doing exceptionally well. Around Tk 30 per hour or Tk 3 per km with a minimum fare of Tk 5 is normal, and up to double that in Dhaka. To hail a rickshaw, stick your arm straight out and wave your hand downwards – the usual way of waving your arm upwards used in the west appears to a Bangladeshi as 'Go away! To hell with you!'

It's important to get a firm agreement on the fare to avoid hassles at the other end – a nod of the head doesn't count. When bargaining, make your first offer only a taka or two below the fair price, as rickshaw-wallahs seem satisfied if they've beaten you up by any amount. If you have no idea of the correct fare it's hard to get the wallah to make an offer, even to the extent of losing the fare to another rickshaw – try offering Tk 4 or Tk 5.

If the wallah yells the agreed fare at the other wallahs and they start laughing, that's your cue to get out and take another rickshaw for half the price. If the driver doesn't understand you, pull out the amount you want to pay and show him; he'll understand that.

Driving a Rickshaw

Most travellers, even those who frequently travel in these colourful vehicles, never bother to get on a rickshaw and pedal it for a few metres. Try it – and give your rickshaw-wallah a big laugh. It takes more effort than you would imagine and once you've tried it you'll definitely empathise with the driver. (You might not even feel so bad when you think you've overpaid him.) After steering one of these tipsy machines, you'll really appreciate the drivers' dexterity in avoiding all manner of potential accidents at the last second. Try turning a corner as you would on a bicycle and you'll end up in a ditch.

We met two travellers who gave the rickshaw driving experience a try for a kilometre or so. The wallahs of course had never seen a foreigner driving a rickshaw. For them it was a real hoot, not only watching their awkward attempts, but being pulled as well. One warning: choose a wide, empty road to practise. Rickshaws are brutes to steer and slow to stop. And, it's amazing how much damage they can cause if you run into something!

Baby Taxi

In Bangladesh, three-wheeled auto-rickshaws are called baby taxis. Like rickshaws, baby taxis are covered with paintings and trimmings, making them unquestionably the most colourful three-wheelers on earth. Also like the rickshaws, the drivers almost never own their vehicles; they're owned by powerful fleet owners called *mohajons* who rent them out on an eight-hour basis. Like rickshaws, they're designed to take two or three people, but entire families can and do fit. Unlike rickshaws, they pollute the air, but if you patronise the baby taxis you'll be helping to keep rickshaw art alive and well.

In Dhaka and Chittagong, baby taxis are everywhere – most people use these instead of regular taxis. Rickshaws are also used all over these two cities but generally for shorter distances. Faster and more comfortable than rickshaws on most trips, baby taxis cost about twice as much. You'll also find them at Dhaka and Chittagong airports, and they charge less than half the taxi fare. Outside of these two metropolises, baby taxis are much rarer. In towns such as Rangpur, Dinajpur and Barisal, they virtually do not exist.

You can go from one side of Dhaka to the other for Tk 50; from the airport you'll pay double because of their waiting time. The minimum fare is about Tk 20 compared to about Tk 5 for rickshaws, so for short distances rickshaws are much more economical. For long distances, the price difference can be minuscule.

In addition to colourful baby taxis, every so often you'll see a similar vehicle that is slightly narrower and, if you look closely, is driven by a motorised chain like a bicycle. It will be devoid of rickshaw art decoration. This is a *mishuk* (mee-SHUK).

Tempo

This is a larger version of a baby taxi, with a cabin in the back. Tempos run set routes, like buses, and while they cost far less than baby taxis, they're more uncomfortable because of the small space into which the dozen or so passengers are squeezed. On the other hand, they're a lot faster than rickshaws and as cheap or cheaper. Outside Dhaka and Chittagong they're a lot more plentiful than baby taxis; you will find them even in relatively small towns.

ORGANISED TOURS

There are a handful of private companies offering tours; the small tourist industry can't support many. For example Parjatan, the national tourism body, seems to have largely given up on running tours other than day trips around Dhaka. The most popular tours cover the Sundarbans, the Chittagong Hill Tracts and river cruises.

Bangladesh Ecotours (☎ 018-318345, in USA fax 987-285 6214, ✆ bangladeshecotours@yahoo .com) This Chittagong agency specialises in hiking and tours in the Chittagong Hill Tracts. See under Organised Tours in the Chittagong Hill Tracts section of the Chittagong chapter for more information.
Web site: www.geocities.com/bangladeshecotours

Contic (☎/fax 02-819 5935, 018-211 601, 018-211 603, ✉ contic@bangla.net). Run by the husband and wife team of Runa and Yves Marre, Contic offers river cruises. Their Fleche D'Or boat tours along the Turag and Buriganga rivers near Dhaka, while the B613 does longer cruises on the Jamuna and Padma Rivers. The 30m-long wooden B613 is a converted livestock freighter (former capacity: 200 cattle) with six well-appointed double cabins and plenty of deck space. One-day B613 cruises cost US$60 per person, two-day cruises US$150, three-day cruises US$350, including transport to and from Dhaka and all meals. Tours around Dhaka cost US$25 for a half-day, US$35 for a full day, including lunch and transport. Contic cruises get excellent reviews.

The Guide Tours (☎ 02-988 6983, fax 988 6984, ✉ theguide@bangla.net) Rob Super Market, DIT II Circle, Gulshan. A long-established agency that offers a similar range of tours to tours of the Sundarbans, the Chittagong Hill Tracts, Cox's Bazar and Teknaf, and Rajshahi division.

Unique Tours and Travels (☎ 988 5116, fax 818 3392, ✉ unique@bangla.net) 51/B Kemal Ataturk Ave, Banani. Unique offer similar tours to The Guide, including the Sundarbans, Chittagong Hill Tracts, Buddhist sites and tea estates.

Dhaka

☎ 02 • pop 6,487,000

Bangladesh's capital is growing uncontrollably into one of the world's biggest cities. It is the place of last resort for the dispossessed and desperate from the countryside, who pour into the city whenever a natural disaster strikes, straining the city's resources even more. From a population of around one million in 1971, Dhaka has exploded to something like 12 million and rising. But Dhaka is also the centre of the emerging middle class, the success stories of the slow but steady economic expansion. New cars choke the roads, and together with other motor vehicles they seem to be pushing rickshaws off the major roads. The air pollution is among the worst in the world. The only way to escape the pandemonium of the crowded streets is to head out of town.

Dhaka does, however, have a mad charm of its own, not unlike the Bangkok of 20 years ago. Dhaka is the rickshaw capital of the world. There are more here (over 600,000) than anywhere in the world, and they are by far the most colourfully painted as well. Riding one is always a highlight of any trip here.

Budget travellers usually stay in the central city area, while long-term visitors congregate in the wealthy suburbs of Gulshan, Banani and Baridhara.

HISTORY

Dhaka, once merely a small town dating from the 4th century, first received principal status during the reign of the Mughal Emperor Jahangir. In 1608 Emperor Jahangir appointed Islam Khan Chisti as the subedhar (provincial governor) of Bengal. Khan then proceeded to transfer the capital from Rajmahal to Dhaka, which, upon his arrival in 1610, he renamed Jahangirnagar. It lost its provincial capital status in 1704, but for over half a century afterwards it remained the commercial centre of the region until the British centralised everything in Calcutta,

Highlights

- **River Trip** – a boat ride on one of the rivers around the city shows a fascinating variety of boats and activities
- **Museums** – the National Museum features the remarkable artworks of Zainul Abedin, while the Liberation War Museum covers the country's tumultuous birth
- **Bazars** – Dhaka's vibrant commercial life offers everything from rickshaw art to cheap clothes to second-hand books

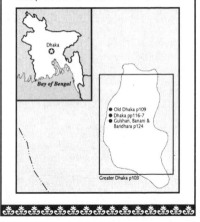

reducing Dhaka to a district headquarters. By the end of the 18th century Dhaka had lost almost three-quarters of its population and the muslin cloth trade almost completely vanished.

During the Mughal period, Dhaka became the chief commercial emporium, so much so that forts were built along the riverbanks to protect the city from Portuguese and Mogh pirates. In 1626 the Mogh pirates and their Portuguese allies briefly took Dhaka, and from 1639 to 1659 the capital was moved to Rajmahal, leaving Dhaka as the administrative centre. This had the effect of encouraging a much greater

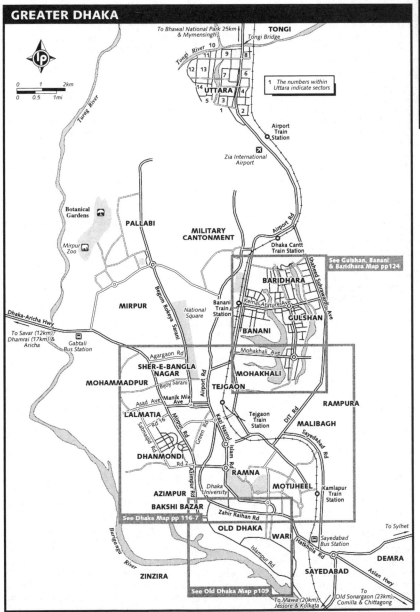

GREATER DHAKA

To Bhawal National Park 25km
& Mymensingh

TONGI

Tongi Bridge

Tongi River

10
11   9   8
12 13   7   6
14   5 3 1 4 2

UTTARA

1 | The numbers within
Uttara indicate sectors

Turag River

0   1   2km
0   0.5   1mi

Airport
Train
Station

Zia International
Airport

Botanical
Gardens

PALLABI

MILITARY
CANTONMENT

Airport Rd

Dhaka Cantt
Train Station

Mirpur
Zoo

See Gulshan, Banani
& Baridhara Map pp124

BARIDHARA

MIRPUR

Begum Rokeya Sarani

National
Square

Banani
Train
Station

Kemal Ataturk Ave

GULSHAN

Shaheed Suhrawardi Ave

BANANI

Dhaka-Aricha Hwy

To Savar (12km),
Dhamrai (17km) &
Aricha

Gabtali
Bus Station

Agargaon Rd

Mohakhali Ave

SHER-E-BANGLA
NAGAR

Bijoy Sarani

MOHAKHALI

MOHAMMADPUR

Airport Rd

TEJGAON

RAMPURA

Asad Ave   Manik Mia
Ave

DIT Rd

MALIBAGH

LALMATIA

Rd 16

Mirpur Rd

Kazi Nazrul Islam Rd

Green Rd

Tejgaon
Train
Station

Sayedabad Rd

Salimulgi Rd

DHANMONDI

Rd 2

Azimpur Rd

RAMNA

Dhaka
University

MOTIJHEEL

Kamlapur
Train
Station

AZIMPUR

BAKSHI BAZAR

See Dhaka Map pp 116-7

Zahir Raihan Rd

To Sylhet

OLD DHAKA

WARI

Sayedabad
Bus Station

Hatkhola Rd

DEMRA

Burigonga River

Islampur Rd

Asian Hwy

ZINZIRA

See Old Dhaka Map p109

To Mawa (20km),
Jessore & Kolkata

SAYEDABAD

To
Old Sonargaon (23km),
Comilla & Chittagong

concentration of commerce; and maritime trade brought with it industry, Islamic education and increasing sophistication in the arts. As many as 100 vessels arrived annually to unload their cargo at Narayanganj and to load up with rice, sugar, fats, oilseeds and wax. Exotic goods were imported from Central Asia, Persia, Afghanistan and Turkey, and the influx of foreign money resulted in cowrie shells being replaced by silver as the local currency.

Dhaka remained the capital under the Mughals until 1704, when they moved it to Murshidabad. Under the Mughals, Dhaka's prosperity was considerably enhanced – they built mosques, palaces, *caravanserais*, bazars and gardens. This development began to attract European traders from southern India.

Five Augustinians, led by Father Bernard de Jesus, arrived in Dhaka in 1599 and established the first Christian mission in the area. In 1616 it became their official missionary centre for the region. They were followed by Portuguese traders who were given the area of Ichamata, about 18km from the city centre, now called Ferringi Bazar. Some of these traders entered the service of the Mughals.

They were soon followed by the Dutch, who established trading posts in Dholai Khal, a more favoured place in the centre of the commercial area. In 1682 the French arrived and, like the Dutch, sided with the Mughals against the Portuguese and Mogh pirates. The area north of Dholai Khal was assigned to the Europeans by the Mughals, and it was in this part of the city that they had their headquarters, residences and churches.

The Church of Our Lady of the Holy Rosary was built there by the Portuguese in 1677. It's the oldest church in Bangladesh. The Portuguese, the Dutch and the French all vied for influence with the Mughals. Armenian and Greek merchant families also arrived on the scene.

Like the Greeks, the Armenians concentrated on inland trade and it was they who pioneered the jute trade in the second half of the 19th century until they were overtaken by the British monopolies. In 1666

Counting Rickshaws

The Dhaka police estimate there are something like 600,000 rickshaws in the city. However, the Revenue Department of Dhaka City Corporation, the body responsible for collecting licence fees from rickshaw-wallahs, has a different figure. When a newspaper reporter asked a top official from the department about the number of rickshaws in Dhaka, the official replied, 'There are 88,700 and something rickshaws in the city'. When the reporter pointed out that other estimates were somewhat higher, the official replied, 'As far as we are concerned there are only 88,700 and something rickshaws in the city. If you disbelieve me, why don't you start counting?'

the British East India Company established a trading post in Dhaka, but fell afoul of Shaista Khan, the Mughal viceroy. Dhaka's decline as a maritime trade centre had already begun, however, as Narayanganj began to lose ground to the new port of Satgaon, later to become Calcutta.

The British East India Company extended its power to such an extent that by 1757 it controlled all of Bengal except Dhaka, which it took eight years later. The Mughal nawab of Bangala, Naim Nizamat, was allowed to govern under the British. It was under British auspices during the late 18th and early 19th centuries that the dominant forms of current economic development were established: vast plantations of indigo, sugar, tobacco, tea and, of course, jute. At the same time the other European powers were eased out – the Dutch surrendered their property to the British in 1781. In 1824, after almost six decades of indirect rule, the British finally took over direct control and administration of the city.

In 1887 Dhaka became a district capital of Bangladesh, and in 1905 Bengal was divided into east and west, the eastern section incorporating Assam (with Dhaka as its winter capital). From this point on Dhaka again began to assume some measure of importance as an administrative centre. Government buildings, churches, residential enclaves and educational institutions transformed it into a city of prosperity. During the existence of East Pakistan Dhaka was classed as a subsidiary capital, and it was not until independence in 1971 that Dhaka once again achieved its former capital-city status.

ORIENTATION

Dhaka is not too difficult to figure out. When you're in the streets surrounded by hundreds of rickshaws, however, you'll probably have a different opinion. Three facts stand out about the city's plan. Firstly, it's basically oriented along a line from south to north, with the bustling Buriganga River forming the southern boundary and the satellite town of Uttara being the northern limit.

Secondly, the city can be conveniently divided into three areas. Old Dhaka is a compact maze of crowded bazars and equally crowded narrow streets lying between the northern bank of the Buriganga and Fulbaria Rd. About 2km to the north is where the much larger 'modern' city begins, stretching about 7km northward to the military cantonment. Beyond are the suburbs, including the cantonment (a restricted area) and the upmarket quarters of Banani, Gulshan and Baridhara. Virtually all of the city's top restaurants are located in these three quarters, as are the best guesthouses, almost all of the embassies and their clubs, and many of the best shops. There are also bookshops, travel agencies, banks and even an Internet cafe to be found in this part of the city.

Thirdly, most major arteries run north-south. Starting in the east these include: DIT Rd/Shaheed Suhrawardi Ave, which starts in Malibagh and extends north to the east of Baridhara; Airport Rd, which starts as Mogh Bazar Rd in the city centre and heads northward past Banani, eventually connecting with Shaheed Suhrawardi Ave and passing Zia International Airport; Kazi Nazrul Islam Rd, which starts in the heart near Dhaka University and passes the National Museum and the Sheraton and Sonar-

gaon hotels en route to the busy Farm Gate intersection where it becomes Airport Rd and later Sadar Rd; the shorter Begum Rokeya Sarani starts in the area around the National Assembly building and heads north towards Mirpur; and Mirpur Rd, which starts out as Azimpur Rd near the Lalbagh Fort in Old Dhaka, runs past New Market and continues through Dhanmondi towards the Gabtali (GAB-toh-lee) bus station.

The heart of the modern city is Motijheel (moh-tee-JEEL), which is also the commercial district. Major landmarks that can be found here include the National Stadium, the Shapla (Lotus Flower Fountain) Circle on Inner Circular Rd and the Raj-era Supreme Court located just north of Dhaka University.

An important road connecting Old Dhaka and the central area is North-South Rd, heading south from Kakrail Rd past the GPO and the Gulistan (Fulbaria) bus station into Old Dhaka, leading indirectly all the way towards the Buriganga River. The intersection of North-South and Fulbaria Rds is known as Gulistan Crossing. In the old section, streets become much narrower, and wandering around becomes rather confusing. Some of the major landmarks include, from east to west, the busy Sadarghat boat terminal, where most boats dock on the Buriganga; Islampur Rd; the Chowk Bazar Shahid Mosque in Chowk Bazar; and Lalbagh Fort.

Even in the modern section, travelling around is complicated by the fact that the main roads are known by the names of the areas through which they pass, and rarely by their official name. Adding to the confusion is the fact that side streets and lanes often take the same name as the nearby main road. If the driver of your rickshaw, bus or baby taxi doesn't speak English, you'll be better off giving sections of the city or landmarks, and addresses only after you get there.

Between 5 and 8 pm the streets are especially full of people going home. The traffic jams are phenomenal. Friday morning is the best time for wandering around and, although few commercial businesses are open, a number of public markets and tourist sites can be visited. Some shops reopen in the afternoon, when traffic on the streets picks up.

INFORMATION
Tourist Offices

The main office of Parjatan (☎ 811 7855/6, fax 811 7235), the national tourism organisation, is on Airport Rd, just north of the intersection with Bijoy Sarani. It's not really set up to give general tourist advice; the only things it can offer you by way of information and advice are its tourist brochures, car rentals and various tour options. Parjatan also has offices at Zia International Airport (☎ 819 4416) and the Sheraton Hotel (☎ 509479). The car rental division (☎ 811 9193) is adjacent to the main office.

Money

There is a small but growing number of ATMs located around the city, belonging either to ANZ Grindlays or HSBC. There are two to be found in Gulshan on Gulshan Ave, as well as the ANZ Grindlays branches in Dhanmondi and at the Sheraton office complex, right next to the Sheraton Hotel. There is an HSBC ATM located in Motijheel on DIT Avenue, next to the Dhaka Inn. Banks that have branches based in Dhaka include:

American Express (☎ 956 1751/2) Inner Circular Rd, just south of Shapla Circle, Motijheel; (☎ 912 0908/9) Sonargaon Hotel; (☎ 818 3635) Gulshan Ave (north of DIT II Circle), Gulshan
ANZ Grindlays Bank (☎ 955 0181) 2 Dilkusha Rd, Motijheel; (☎ 816 4240) corner of Mirpur Rd & Road 5, Dhanmondi; (☎ 988 4783) 116 Gulshan Ave, Gulshan; (☎ 811 2019) Kazi Nazrul Islam Ave, between Farm Gate and the Sonargaon Hotel
Citibank (☎ 956 2355/9) 122-4 Motijheel, north of Dilkusha II Circle
Eastern Bank (☎ 236360/1) Dilkusha II Circle, Motijheel
HSBC (☎ 988 5141) Corner of Gulshan Ave and Road 5, Gulshan; (☎ 966 7076) 1/C DIT Ave, Motijheel

Janata Bank (☎ 924 0000) Dilkusha I Circle, Motijheel
Pubali Bank (☎ 923 0622, 923 6505) 18 Dilkusha Rd, Motijheel
Sonali Bank (☎ 955 0426/7) Shapla Circle, Motijheel; (☎ 819 4437) Zia International Airport
Sonargaon Hotel (☎ 811 2011, 811 1005) Kazi Nazrul Islam Ave, Kawran Bazar (will change cash and travellers cheques at fair rates)
Standard Chartered Bank (☎ 956 1465/6) Inner Circular Rd just south of Shapla Circle, Motijheel; (☎ 881718/9) 14 Kemal Ataturk Ave, Banani

Post & Communications

The GPO is near the Baitul Mukarram Mosque on Abdul Gani Rd on the corner of North-South Rd, open 9.30 am to 8 pm (closed Friday). You may need to sew parcels in cloth and seal them, especially if the package is large. If sewing is required, check another branch to see if it's more flexible. There are parcel-wallahs who sew packages up hanging out in a shelter near the GPO.

Receiving parcels takes persistence and determination, as there's only one clerk in the entire building who is prepared to admit that he knows what's involved in the procedure. Make sure that you don't lose the scrap of paper from poste restante that notified you that a parcel had arrived, or things will take even longer to resolve.

If you prefer to use a courier for sending parcels, try DHL (☎ 956 0108), located at

---

Smog Alert

There is no need to say Dhaka is said to have some of the worst pollution in the world – it's a fact that it does. And while the government has made some comforting noises about cutting out two-stroke-engined vehicles, nothing is happening about it. In the same way that there are seven times more unlicensed rickshaws in Dhaka than licensed ones, the government does not seem to have the will or the ability to get rid of two-stroke engines.

Auto-rickshaw drivers are quite a powerful lobby, and even if they get banned they can always bribe someone for a fake license.

94 Motijheel, and also at House 1, Road 95, Gulshan (☎ 600191). Also recommended are Federal Express (☎ 956 5114) at 95 Motijheel, and also at Bilquis Tower, Road 46, Gulshan (☎ 818 7771).

There are small business centres all around the city offering fax, telephone or photocopying. Some also have one or two computers with Internet access, usually for Tk 5 per minute. However, their Internet connections are usually slow, highly subject to breakdowns, and you're likely to have people breathing down your neck as you type.

The best Internet cafe in town is the very cool Cyber Cafe at Dolce Vita-La Galerie, 2nd floor, 54 Kemal Ataturk Ave, Banani. Open every day (including hartals) from 10 am to 10 pm. Internet use costs Tk 3 per minute and connections are pretty reliable. It also functions as a bookshop, art gallery, coffee shop and ice-cream parlour.

Film & Photography
There are lots of photo studios around the city. A roll of colour film (36 prints) costs between Tk 120 (Fujicolor) and Tk 200 (Kodachrome), and around Tk 300 to develop. Most photo studios give same-day service, and some have one-hour service. The quality of the processing is quite good. Some do B&W passport photos; the cost is around Tk 100 for four and Tk 250 for 10.

Travel Agencies
In the central area, one of the best travel agencies for making airline reservations is Bengal Airlift (☎ 241337/8, fax 816 3945), at 54 Motijheel Ave, not far from Shapla Circle. Also in Motijheel, you could try Beacon Travel (☎ 955 2942) on the ground floor of the Adamjee Court Building on Dilkusha II Circle. Another agency in Motijheel is Hac Enterprise (☎ 955 2208), at 5 Inner Circular Rd, 150m south of Shapla Circle.

Pacific Overseas Travel (☎ 955 2069), 21 Topkhana Rd is another reputable travel agency in the centre of the city.

Vantage Travel (☎ 811 3021) is a big agency with offices at the Sonargaon Hotel.

There are many travel agencies in the Gulshan area, including Travel House

(☎ 818 1726), ABC Tower, 8 Kemal Ataturk Ave, Banani; Regency Travels (☎ 818 8373), 18 Kemal Ataturk Ave, Banani; and Travel Channel (☎ 988 1082), 33/6 Gulshan Ave, Gulshan (south of DIT I Circle). Bengal Airlift (☎ 988 6634) also has an office at DIT II Circle, in the Landmark Building.

Bookshops
In the central area, the best place for books about Bangladesh is University Press. It's on the 2nd floor of the Red Crescent building at 114 Motijheel, just west of the Biman Airlines office, and is very poorly marked. It's open Saturday to Thursday from 9 am to 5 pm, and has an excellent catalogue. The University Press Booskhop is in Motijheel, on Dilkusha I circle.

The New Market complex on Azimpur Rd has several good bookshops, including the Zeenat Book Supply (shop 190) and Mohiuddin & Sons (shop 143).

The Sheraton and Sonargaon hotels both have bookshops that carry international newspapers and magazines, maps of Dhaka and Bangladesh, a few interesting books on Bangladesh, plus some recent blockbusters. For second-hand books, try New Market on Azimpur Rd. Entering the market from the south, turn left and head towards the end, which is where all the book and map stalls are located.

In the Gulshan area the biggest bookshop is Boi Bichitra, on Kemal Ataturk Ave in Gulshan, across the road from Wimpy, with a wide range of novels, blockbusters and arty tomes. There's an excellent newsagent on the same road closer to DIT II circle, selling all the major news magazines.

UBINIG, at 5/3 Barabo Mahanpur Ring Rd in Shamoli, runs a feminist bookshop.

Finally, there's The Bookworm, on Airport Rd between the Prime Minister's office and the military cantonment. It's just beneath the jet fighter. It has a range of blockbusters from Grisham to King, and also carries books on Bangladesh.

Libraries & Cultural Centres
Travellers desperate for books and conversation in English should try the British

Council & Library (☎ 861 8905) at 5 Fuller Rd in the Dhaka University area. The Alliance Française (☎ 816 1557) at 26 Mirpur Rd, just north of Road 3 in Dhanmondi, is a very active cultural centre that holds art exhibitions and poetry evenings and has published several books. There's also a French library here. The Goethe Institut (☎ 912 6526) is nearby at House 23, Road 2, Dhanmondi, and also holds art exhibitions.

Libraries in Dhaka include Dhaka University Library (☎ 950 5161/2); and the Dhaka Public Library (☎ 950 3242) on Kazi Nazrul Islam Ave near the National Museum.

Medical Services

For emergency medical care, contact the British High Commission Medical Centre, Elizabeth House (☎ 603590) at 23 Park Rd (at the corner of Road 6), Baridhara.

Another option is Dr Wahab (☎ 882 1454, 882 7553). His office is at House 3 on Road 12 in Baridhara. Closer to the central city you could try the Monowara Hospital (☎ 813 9529) in Mogh Bazar, 1km east of the Sheraton Hotel.

There is a Traveller's Clinic (☎ 600171/8) at the highly respected International Centre for Diarrhoeal Disease Research Bangladesh (ICDDRB) Hospital in Mohakhali, east of Airport Rd.

Another recommended medical centre is the Japan-Bangladesh Friendship Hospital (☎ 818 7575), House 27, Road 114, Gulshan.

There are pharmacies all over the city and they keep long hours, usually until 10 pm. There is a 24-hour pharmacy at Banani Mall on Kemal Ataturk Ave in Banani.

Two recommended dentists in Dhaka are Dr David Johnston (☎ 818 6789), House 52, Road 11, Banani, and Dr Ronald Halder (☎ 818 5107), House 28, Road 17A, Banani.

Emergency

Dhaka doesn't have any central emergency numbers, but police, fire and ambulance can be contacted on the following numbers:

Ambulance
 ICDDRB Hospital ☎ 881 1751/2/3
 Holy Family Hospital ☎ 831 1721/2/3

Fire Station
 ☎ 955 5555
Police
 Dhaka Metropolitan Police ☎ 832 2501/2/3
 Gulshan Police Station ☎ 988 0234

Dangers & Annoyances

The biggest annoyance is the air pollution, which is just about the worst in the world. Most days the city's air is a chewable cloud of filthy brown smog, a dense soup of lead, partially unburned hydrocarbons and construction dust. People react differently, but after a few hours in the central city or Old Dhaka you're likely to have itching eyes, a sore throat and a headache. Various plans to ban old vehicles and two-stroke engines come and go, as the transport industry is a powerful lobby. The health risks to residents are enormous, especially to children. On top of all this, the city's traffic jams are horrendous, and likely to get worse as the number of vehicles inexorably rises. If you're staying in the centre of the city and need to get to the airport during daylight hours, allow yourself 90 minutes or so of travel time to be on the safe side.

Bag-snatchings and even muggings are not unknown, so be a little cautious. Pay particular care if you are withdrawing money from an ATM. The train and bus stations are quite dodgy after dark, so try to avoid leaving or arriving at night.

In the current political climate hartals and accompanying violent demonstrations are quite common.

During the strikes known as *hartals* it is safe enough to drive around the Gulshan area, and it is usually possible to move around the central city area by rickshaw. Rickshaw-wallâhs know which areas to avoid, such as opposition party offices. If you have to get to the airport during a hartal, you can either go by rickshaw or find a auto-rickshaw driver who knows a safe route. If you happen to arrive at the airport during a hartal, a cunning method of transport awaits you. Believe it or not, ambulances will be there to take you wherever you want to go (shame about the people who might actually need to go to hospital).

OLD DHAKA
Sadarghat & Badam Tole

If you have time to do only one thing in Dhaka, then take a small boat out on the Buriganga River from Sadarghat boat terminal. The panorama of river life is fascinating. In the middle of the river, which is roughly 500m wide, you'll see an unbelievable array of boats – uncovered and covered boats, cargo boats, speed boats, tugs and motor launches – going in every direction. You'll see crew painting boats, bathing, cooking or just resting and observing, while hordes of people cross the river in small

canoes, and both large and small ships ply up and down the river.

If you look hard along the river's edge, you may also spot some of the ancient house boats called *baras*. These worn-out boats, some half a century old, are popular floating restaurants catering to the poorest of the poor, where meals are served from 8 am until midnight.

It costs Tk 2 to enter Sadarghat boat terminal. You'll find large ferries stationed there during the day, many heading south for Barisal in the evening. Among all the large ships are the tiny wooden ones that you can

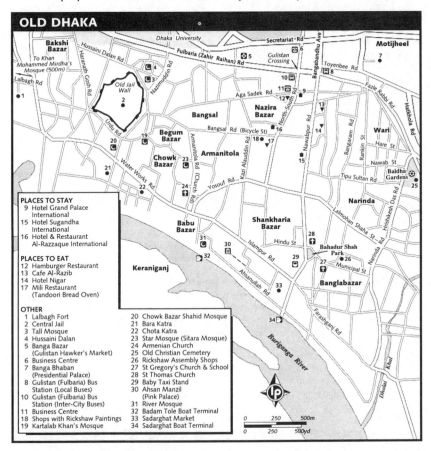

OLD DHAKA

PLACES TO STAY
9 Hotel Grand Palace International
15 Hotel Sugandha International
16 Hotel & Restaurant Al-Razzaque International

PLACES TO EAT
12 Hamburger Restaurant
13 Cafe Al-Razib
14 Hotel Nigar
17 Mili Restaurant (Tandoori Bread Oven)

OTHER
1 Lalbagh Fort
2 Central Jail
3 Tall Mosque
4 Hussaini Dalan
5 Banga Bazar (Gulistan Hawker's Market)
6 Business Centre
7 Banga Bhaban (Presidential Palace)
8 Gulistan (Fulbaria) Bus Station (Local Buses)
10 Gulistan (Fulbaria) Bus Station (Inter-City Buses)
11 Business Centre
18 Shops with Rickshaw Paintings
19 Kartalab Khan's Mosque
20 Chowk Bazar Shahid Mosque
21 Bara Katra
22 Chota Katra
23 Star Mosque (Sitara Mosque)
24 Armenian Church
25 Old Christian Cemetery
26 Rickshaw Assembly Shops
27 St Gregory's Church & School
28 St Thomas Church
29 Baby Taxi Stand
30 Ahsan Manzil (Pink Palace)
31 River Mosque
32 Badam Tole Boat Terminal
33 Sadarghat Market
34 Sadarghat Boat Terminal

hire for the trip or by the hour. Bargaining is difficult because the boat owner is unlikely to understand your itinerary. A reasonable price would be Tk 50 per hour, but to get that rate you may have to bargain awhile. Foreigners are rarely seen doing this, so not all boat operators will demand an outrageous fee. Still, expectations may be rising.

Badam Tole, where the Bangladesh Inland Waterway Transport Corporation (BIWTC) Rocket ferries dock, is 1km north-west along the river-side lane, Buckland Bund, which runs the length of the waterfront and is always packed with people, rickshaws and colourful trucks.

Walking from Sadarghat to Lalbagh Fort is a good way to get to know Old Dhaka, or at least to discover how easy it is for someone to get lost in its winding lanes. Islampur Rd (which becomes Water Works Rd at the western end) is the major road connecting the two. It runs parallel to the river, passing through Chowk Bazar and south of the large Central Jail.

Ahsan Manzil

Around 600m west of Sadarghat is Ahsan Manzil (the Pink Palace), one of the most interesting buildings in Dhaka. The best feature is the interior – it's one of the few buildings furnished in the style of the era in which it was built. Dating from 1872, it was built on the site of an old French factory by Nawab Abdul Ghani, the city's wealthiest *zamindar* (landowner). Some 16 years after the palace's construction, it was damaged by a tornado and in the reparation was substantially altered in appearance, becoming even grander than before. Lord Curzon stayed here whenever he came to visit. After the death of the Nawab and his son, the family fortune was dispersed and the palace eventually fell into disrepair. It was saved from oblivion by a massive restoration job in the late 1980s.

It's a magnificent pink-coloured building with an imposing staircase leading to the 2nd floor, and it is topped by a lofty dome. In each of the 23 grand rooms there is a photograph of the room dating from around 1902. Having these photos allowed the accurate restoration of the furnishings and draperies, so when you take a tour you'll be taking a walk back in time to the high point in the palace's history.

The museum gives a good insight into the life of the ruling classes of Bengal during the Raj, with historical background to the

Nawab Abdul Ghani

Nawab Ghani, born in 1830 of Kashmiri descent, was the most influential person in East Bengal in the last half of the 19th century. Unlike most zamindars, the nawab was Muslim. Ghani, his son, Nawab Ahsanullah, and his grandson, Salimullah Bahadur, contributed greatly to Dhaka's development. Along with elephants, horses, boats and other materials donated to the British government, they also contributed large sums to local colleges.

As Ghani's land holdings grew to include most of Dhaka, he ruled like a king over the residents. He ordered them to settle their disputes in the arbitration court of his zamindars before going to the government courts. In effect, every conflict among his 'subjects' was settled at Ahsan Manzil.

Politically astute, he participated in both Hindu and Muslim festivals and both groups admired him. He also introduced professional horse racing to Dhaka. When he returned from a voyage to Calcutta by steamer, flags were flown along the river, a band played lively tunes and guns were fired.

The demise of the family occurred when Ahsanullah, for whom Ahsan Manzil (the Pink Palace) was named, died suddenly in 1901 without a will. Under Islamic law the monolithic estate was broken into nine parts and his son, Salimullah, received only one. Salimullah, although residing at the Pink Palace, was reduced to a relatively poor man. Nevertheless he contributed more to Muslim schools than anyone in the city's history, and founded Dhaka Medical School. Because of this he is revered today perhaps even more than his illustrious grandfather.

building and period, and displays of items found on the site. There are also paintings of various Bengali notables and an excellent view over the river from the 1st floor verandah. Admission is Tk 2. It's open Saturday to Wednesday from 10.30 am to 5.30 pm and Friday from 4 to 7 pm.

Shankharia Bazar

Often called Hindu Street by foreigners, this is the most fascinating street in Dhaka and a must see. It's near Sadarghat and the Pink Palace, so a stroll down this narrow lane is easy to include in a visit to the area. It's the most densely populated area in Dhaka, and it contains an interesting row of ancient houses sheltering countless *shankharis* (Hindu artisans), most notably the conch shell bangle makers.

Shankharis first came here over 300 years ago, but these days their art is slowly dying out. If you pass a shop and hear some faint grinding sounds out the back, ask to see the tiny quarters where they make the jewellery; some owners will be delighted to show you around. There are machines which cut the shells into rough rings and bangles, and with these the crafts people initiate their carving. Other artisans on the street include drum makers, gravestone carvers, wedding-hat vendors and kite sellers. Any day is good for visiting, including Friday, which is a work day for shankharis.

To find Shankharia Bazar head north along Nawabpur Rd from Sadarghat. After two long blocks you'll pass a small square on your right called Bahadur Shah Park, which has a cenotaph to commemorate the Indian Uprising of 1857. From the northwest corner, cross the street and head west, parallel to the river. After 100m you'll come to some small shops selling tombstones – that's the beginning. It continues for about 400m until it merges with Islampur Rd.

If you'd also like to see some rickshaws being made, head east of Bahadur Shah Park along Municipal St for about 150m and take a left (north) along a tiny lane, opposite St Gregory's Church. About 100m down that narrow, winding lane you'll find five or six shops.

Conch Shell Jewellery

To the Hindus, conch shells are a symbol of good fortune and purity. Hindu scriptures instruct married women to wear conch shell bangles on both wrists and to break them when the husband dies. Nowadays, Muslim and Christian women wear these bangles as well.

Three centuries ago, conch-shell artisans migrated from India to the Dhaka area, and Shankharia Bazar has been the centre of their trade since then. The conditions here are appalling. The tiny rooms are claustrophobic and the low ceilings allow little ventilation or sunlight. You have to stoop to enter the work areas. The artisans work hard and only earn about Tk 80 a day. Many have moved on to other pursuits, such as making gold ornaments, stone spice-grinders or harmoniums and other musical instruments.

The craft faces an uncertain future. The shells come from the seas of India and Sri Lanka, and are not always available. Also, more and more Hindu women are unable to afford these bangles, opting to buy the much cheaper plastic lookalikes.

Armenian Church

About 1km north-west of Sadarghat and north of Badam Tole is an area called Armanitola, so named after the Armenian colony that settled here late in the 17th century. Even during the height of their influence in the mid-19th century, they numbered no more than about 40 families. However, because of their close business ties with the British East India Company, many Armenians became rich zamindars with palatial houses.

The Armenian Church of the Holy Resurrection, which can be found on Armanitola Rd and dates from 1781, is fascinating and well worth considering a visit. Mr Martin (☎ 017-561 497) took over as caretaker in the mid-1980s and he has done much to restore it, including throwing out the squatters. Unfortunately, during the course of the Liberation War, the silver setting and organ were stolen and many of the graves were desecrated.

Now in reasonably good shape, the church is an oasis of tranquillity in the heart of the crowded city, and about twice a year the Armenian Archbishop from Australia comes here to hold ceremonies, which is by far the best time to visit. It is open every day except when the caretaker leaves the premises. Mr Martin speaks English and delights in giving personal tours. There's no fee for this but donations, which finance the restoration work, are most welcome.

The church is a small chapel with a balcony and the original wooden pews seat about 100 people. The grounds cover nearly a hectare and are paved with old gravestones, some quite ornately carved, with some fruit trees down the back. Judging by the ages of those buried here, the local climate didn't do the Armenians much harm.

From the intersection of Hindu St and Islampur Rd, head west along Islampur for about 700m until you come to Armanitola Rd (or Church Rd); head north one block (150m) along that road and the church is on your left. Alternatively, from Badam Tole, head north for two blocks to Islampur Rd, then go left for one block and right for one block.

Sitara Mosque

About four blocks (350m) north of the Armenian church, on the same street, you'll come to Sitara Mosque, popularly named Star Mosque. This picturesque mosque is one of the city's most popular tourist attractions because of its striking mosaic decoration of coloured glass set in white tiles. It is also distinctive for its low-slung style and the absence of a minaret. While the mosque is quite old, dating from the early 18th century, it has been radically altered. It was originally built in the typical Mughal style, with four corner towers. Around 50 years ago, when mosaic decoration became popular in Bengali buildings, a local businessman financed its redecoration with Japanese and English china tiles and the major addition of a new eastern verandah substantially altering the overall structure. If you look hard, you can see tiles illustrated with pictures of Mt Fuji.

Bara Katra & Choto Katra

These are two of the oldest buildings in Dhaka, which is why they're in most tourist brochures. However, these Mughal-era structures are very dilapidated, especially Choto Katra, which is in total ruins. Bara Katra (BORE-ah KAT-rah), which was once a palace with monumental dimensions, was built in 1644 and now has a street running through its once-magnificent arched entrance. It was originally quadrangular, with 22 rooms around a central courtyard, and gates to the north and south. While only a small portion of the original structure is still standing, the building is still occupied and has a small prayer room on top. If you walk up to the roof, three storeys up, you can get some excellent views of Old Dhaka.

Choto Katra, which dates from 1663, was a caravanserai for visiting merchants. It was similar in design to Bara Katra, but there's not much left. However, if you go down the passage immediately before the south-east corner you'll come to a soap factory, with lakes of boiling soap in metal vats. Deeper in the bowels of the ancient foundations is a maze of smoky rooms where the soap is moulded. By night it's like something out of Dante's *Inferno*.

Few locals know about Bara Katra, so don't expect help from them to find it. Head west along Water Works Rd (the continuation of Islampur Rd) for the landmark Chowk Bazar Shahid Mosque, which has a very tall red-brick tower – you can't miss it. Bara Katra is located 100m south from the mosque, towards the river. Finding Choto Katra is a little more difficult. From Bara Katra head south and take the first left. Follow this road for a few hundred metres and the Choto Katra is along a street to your left.

Lalbagh Fort

This unfinished fort is touted as Dhaka's premier tourist attraction, but if you're expecting something like Delhi's Red Fort you'll be disappointed. Regardless, it's definitely worth a visit and along with Sadarghat it's one of the two best places to begin a tour of the Old City. You'll find it near the intersection of Dhakeswari and Azimpur Rds.

Construction of the fort began in 1677 under the auspices of Prince Mohammed Azam, third son of Aurangzeb, who then handed it over to Shaista Khan for completion. The death of Khan's daughter, Pari Bibi (fair lady), was considered such a bad omen that the fort was never completed. However, three architectural monuments within the complex, all in the Bangla-Mughal style of architecture, were finished in 1684 and remain in good condition – the Diwan (Hall of Audience), the Mausoleum of Pari Bibi and the Quilla Mosque. The expansive complex and its serene formal gardens are enclosed by a massive wall.

On the eastern side of the fort, to your far left as you enter, is the residence of the governor containing the Hall of Audience. It's an elegant two storey structure with a symmetrical facade and a central hall. Inside, there's a small museum of Mughal miniature paintings and beautiful examples of calligraphy, along with the usual swords and firearms. Beyond, on the western side, a massive arched doorway leads to the central square *hammam* (a place for having baths and body massages, keeping hot and cold water, and going to the toilet). In the winter it was heated from below. It's a low masonry structure with a glazed tile floor and topped by a dome. Adjacent to this chamber are the baths and toilets (not so very different from today's models).

The mosque on the western side of the complex is quite attractive but the middle building, the Mausoleum of Pari Bibi, is a unique and important structure. It's the only building in Bangladesh where black basalt and white marble (from Bangladesh) and encaustic tiles of various colours have been used to decorate an interior. At each corner are four graceful turrets capped by ribbed cupolas. The roof is covered with a false copper dome and crowned by a tall finial (ornament). Inside where Pari Bibi is buried, the central chamber is entirely veneered in white marble.

Admission to the fort is free. Entry to the museum and the hammam is Tk 1. Winter opening hours are Sunday to Wednesday from 10 am to 5 pm; Friday from 2.30 to 5.30 pm (closed Thursday and holidays). From April to October, opening and closing times are half an hour later.

Khan Mohammed Mirdha's Mosque

Some 400m west of Lalbagh Fort, on Lalbagh Rd, is Khan Mohammed Mirdha's Mosque, one of the most beautiful mosques in Dhaka. Erected in 1706, several decades after the fort, this Mughal structure is of similar inspiration to Lalbagh Fort. It is built on a large raised platform, up a flight of 25 steps. Three squat domes, with pointed minarets at each corner, dominate the rectangular roof, and the wall surface is profusely relieved with plaster panels. To get a good view of this walled mosque, you must enter the main gate, which is off the main road. Unfortunately, unless you're here during prayer times (eg, around 1 pm), you'll probably find the gate locked.

Dhakeswari Temple

About 1km north-east of Lalbagh Fort, up a short alley off Dhakeswari Rd, is the city's main Hindu temple, dating from the 12th century. There are two sets of buildings. The one often seen in tourist photos consists of four adjoining *rekha* temples (buildings with a square sanctum on a raised platform with mouldings on the walls) covered by tall pyramidal roofs of the typical curvilinear bangla style. It's been modernised and is nothing special, but it is colourful and you are likely to find some long-haired *sadhus* (itinerant holy men) hanging around smoking ganja.

Hussaini Dalan

A block north of the Central Jail, on Hussaini Dalan Rd in Bakshi Bazar, is a historic building that looks more like a Hindu *rajbari* (zamindari palace) than a mosque. It was built in the 18th century near the end of the Mughal period as the house of the Imam of the Shia community; the Ashura festival on the 10th day of the Islamic month of Muharram is celebrated here. See Islamic

Durga Puja

This colourful festival occurs around the second week of October and is a good time to visit Dhakeswari Temple. The festival commemorates the victory of this mighty warrior goddess. The green-skinned buffalo demon Mahishasura had led an army of demons and conquered the throne of heaven. The gods were driven out, and appealed to Brahma, Shiva and Vishnu for help. The three great gods combined their powers to create Durga, who led a vast new army onto the earth. One by one the division of demon armies were drawn back to earth and defeated, until Mahishasura was forced to face the goddess himself.

After an epic battle in which the demon changed from buffalo to man to elephant and finally back to a buffalo, Mahishasura was cornered at last. The gruesome monster said to the goddess, 'Durga, I have dreamed of you and in the dream I worshipped you. I will be glad to die in your hands. I only ask that you ensure that along with you I am worshipped by all.' Durga agreed, and after holding him down under her left foot and spearing him, he remained frozen in this form for eternity. The surviving demons fled to the far corners of the earth.

On the last day of the five-day festival, devotees gather with their colourful goddesses made of bamboo and clay to pray to the goddess Durga. Around 5 pm they parade their effigies through the streets toward Sadarghat, arriving there at nightfall. Durga, seated on a lion and holding a long spear that is piercing Mahishasura, is then placed on a boat and sent to the middle of the Buriganga for immersion. This ends the simple but colourful ceremony. Foreigners, even those who just show up, are often treated as honoured guests and have an easier time amid the throngs of people around the boat terminal.

Around Durga Puja, usually the last Saturday in September, there's a colourful boat race on the Buriganga near Postagola. It's quite a spectacle and is inaugurated each year by the President of Bangladesh. Each long boat is crammed with roughly 60 oarsmen and the competition ensues amidst continuous clapping by the spectators. Advance publicity is poor so foreigners never hear about it. Call Parjatan for details.

Festivals under Special Events in the Facts for the Visitor chapter for more details.

The architecture of this Shia mosque, with its four large Doric columns supporting a grand porch, seems baroque in inspiration. The original building, however, was purely Mughal as it lacked the porch and had an elevated roof and minarets at all four corners. This changed with the 1897 earthquake, when the roof collapsed – you can see a silver filigree model of the original building in the National Museum (see National Museum, later in this chapter).

Baldha Gardens & Christian Cemetery

One of the hidden gems of Dhaka is the Baldha Gardens in Wari, at the eastern end of Tipu Sultan Rd and a block south of Hatkhola Rd. The two walled enclosures, Cybele and Psyche, were once the private gardens of Narendra Narayan Roy, a wealthy zamindar whose grandson gave them to the government in 1962 as a tribute to the family.

Started in 1904, these gardens house about 1500 plants and 672 species. Many of these are rare plants procured from about 50 different countries, including an Egyptian papyrus plant such as was used to make paper centuries ago, and a century plant that apparently blooms once every 16 years. Inside the buildings are an orchid house, a cactus house and a green house. The gardens are also a bit whimsical – you can't help wondering how all that Royal Doulton got smashed to make the free-form mosaic. Pysche has a lovely lily pond, while inside Cybele are the tombs of Roy and his son. Admission is Tk 2 and the gardens are open Saturday to Thursday from 9 am to 5 pm, with a two-hour break at lunch. Keep your eye out for the resident mongoose.

Across the street to the east is the old Christian Cemetery, which dates from the mid-18th century. Dominating the whole cemetery is the interesting Mughal-inspired tomb of Columbo-Saheb. It's a high octagonal tower-like structure with eight arched windows surmounted by a dome. No-one has a clue as to who Columbo-Saheb was.

Bangsal Rd (Bicycle St)

For a souvenir of Bangladesh, you can't beat **rickshaw art**. The art is painted on strips of tin and vinyl that fit within most suitcases and cost only around Tk 40 each, sometimes more if it's special. Bargaining is required, of course. The place to find this art is on Bangsal Rd, popularly known as Bicycle Street. This is also the best place to buy cheap Chinese bikes (about Tk 3500), which you'll see everywhere in this country; there are lots of spare parts as well.

The street begins 700m south of the ever-crowded Gulistan Crossing near Banga Bazar. The rickshaw art and bicycle section lasts only one block, starting just west of North-South Rd, one block south of the well marked Hotel Al-Razzaque International.

CENTRAL DHAKA

North of Old Dhaka is the old European zone, now the modern part of town.

Banga Bhaban & Baitul Mukarram Mosque

Banga Bhaban, the official residence of the president, the country's titular head, is just south of the modern commercial district of Motijheel. Photography, even of the gate, is forbidden.

Just west of Motijheel is the modern Baitul Mukarram Mosque. Designed in the style of the holy Ka'aba of Mecca, this 'national mosque' does not permit non-Muslims to enter. While it is the city's largest mosque, it's not very interesting except at night when it's lit up.

Dharmarajikha Buddhist Monastery

Other noteworthy structures in Dhaka include the modern Kamlapur train station and, beyond it, the Dharmarajikha Buddhist Monastery. It's the largest Buddhist cultural centre in the country containing one huge bronze and one beautiful marble statue of Buddha. There's a peaceful pond here too; bring a book and get some reading done. The monastery is open during daylight hours (vague, but true). Take off your shoes before entering the temple, don't take photos of shrines without permission, and behave respectfully if prayers are being held.

Old High Court

This imposing white building, once the governor's residence, is a good kilometre west of Motijheel, just north of Dhaka University. It's the finest example in Dhaka of the European Renaissance style, with few or no Mughal features. Similar in size to the Pink Palace and also surmounted by a graceful dome, it features a prominent central porch with two wide verandahs on either side. Nearby is the newer **Mausoleum for Three Martyrs** and to the right is the better-maintained **Supreme Court**.

Suhrawardi Park

Beginning near the Old High Court and stretching all the way up to the National Museum, the Suhrawardi Park covers an enormous area with quiet, well-maintained parkland. This was once the Race Course, where both the Bangladeshi Declaration of Independence and the surrender of Pakistani occupation forces took place in 1971. The park is open daily between 6 am and 10 pm.

East of Suhrawardi Park is **Ramna Park**, which is well tended and has a boating lake.

Dhaka University & Curzon Hall

Dating from 1921, Dhaka University (DU) has some fine old buildings spread over a large area to the north-west of Suhrawardi Park. In the same area is the **British Council Library** and immediately north of the university is the **Institute of Arts & Crafts**, which has an art gallery.

On the main campus, south of the Old High Court, is **Curzon Hall**, which houses the science faculty and is the university's architectural masterpiece. It's a fine example

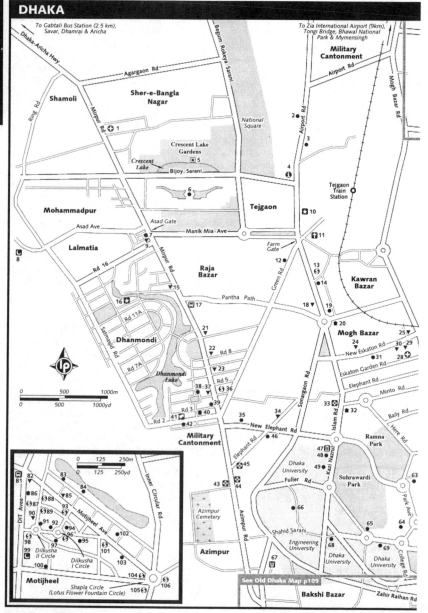

DHAKA

To Gabtali Bus Station (2.5 km), Savar, Dhamrai & Aricha

Dhaka-Aricha Hwy

Ring Rd

Agargaon Rd

Shamoli

Mirpur Rd

Sher-e-Bangla Nagar

Begum Rokeya Sarani

National Square

To Zia International Airport (9km), Tongi Bridge, Bhawal National Park & Mymensingh

Military Cantonment

Airport Rd

Mogh Bazar Rd

Airport Rd

2

3

4

Crescent Lake Gardens

Crescent Lake

5

Bijoy Sarani

6

Tejgaon

Tejgaon Train Station

10

Mohammadpur

Asad Gate

Asad Ave

Manik Mia Ave

Lalmatia

11

Farm Gate

8

9

Rd 16

Mirpur Rd

Raja Bazar

Green Rd

12

13

14

Kawran Bazar

Salimullah Rd

15

16

Rd 11A

Pantha Path

18

19

17

Dhanmondi

20

21

Mogh Bazar

25

Rd 7A

22

Rd 8

24

New Eskaton Rd

30 29

28

31

Dhanmondi Lake

23

Rd 5

Eskaton Garden Rd

36

Elephant Rd

Minto Rd

38 37

39

33

32

Baily Rd

Rd 3

40

35

34

Sonargaon Rd

Islam Rd

Here Rd

41

42

New Elephant Rd

Military Cantonment

Elephant Rd

46

47

48

Kazi Nazrul

Ramna Park

45

Dhaka University

49

Suhrawardi Park

63

Inner Circular Rd

43

44

Azimpur Rd

Fuller Rd

Azimpur Cemetery

66

65

64

Azimpur

Shahid Sarani

Engineering University

68

69

Dhaka University

Dhaka University

67

Park Ave

College Rd

See Old Dhaka Map p109

Bakshi Bazar

Zahir Raihan Rd

Motijheel inset

DIT Ave

82

81

83

84

Motijheel Ave

86

85

88

93

87

90

89

91

92

94

96

97

98

95

102

99

Dilkusha II Circle

100

101

103

Dilkusha I Circle

104

Motijheel

Shapla Circle (Lotus Flower Fountain Circle)

105

106

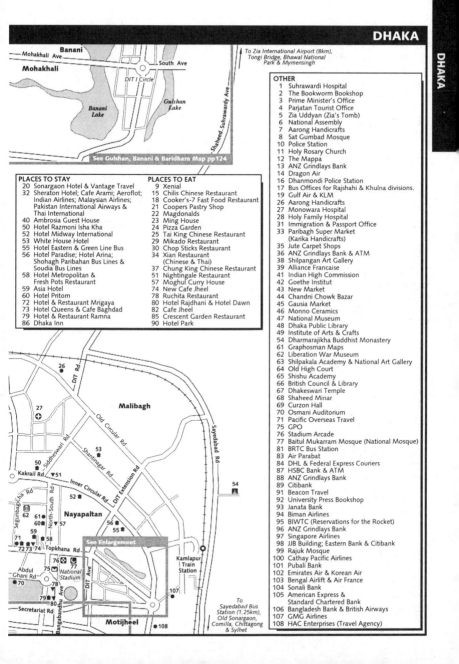

Banani
Mohakhali Ave
Mohakhali
South Ave
DIT I Circle
Banani Lake
Gulshan Lake
Shaheed Suhrawardy Ave

To Zia International Airport (8km),
Tongi Bridge, Bhawal National
Park & Mymensingh

See Gulshan, Banani & Baridhara Map pp124

PLACES TO STAY
20 Sonargaon Hotel & Vantage Travel
32 Sheraton Hotel; Cafe Arami; Aeroflot;
Indian Airlines; Malaysian Airlines;
Pakistan International Airways &
Thai International
40 Ambrosia Guest House
50 Hotel Razmoni Isha Kha
52 Hotel Midway International
53 White House Hotel
55 Hotel Eastern & Green Line Bus
56 Hotel Paradise; Hotel Arina;
Shohagh Paribahan Bus Lines &
Soudia Bus Lines
58 Hotel Metropolitan &
Fresh Pots Restaurant
59 Asia Hotel
60 Hotel Pritom
72 Hotel & Restaurant Mrigaya
73 Hotel Queens & Cafe Baghdad
79 Hotel & Restaurant Ramna
86 Dhaka Inn

PLACES TO EAT
9 Xenial
15 Chilis Chinese Restaurant
18 Cooker's-7 Fast Food Restaurant
21 Coopers Pastry Shop
22 Magdonalds
23 Ming House
24 Pizza Garden
25 Tai King Chinese Restaurant
29 Mikado Restaurant
30 Chop Sticks Restaurant
34 Xian Restaurant
(Chinese & Thai)
37 Chung King Chinese Restaurant
51 Nightingale Restaurant
57 Moghul Curry House
74 New Cafe Jheel
78 Ruchita Restaurant
80 Hotel Rajdhani & Hotel Dawn
82 Cafe Jheel
85 Crescent Garden Restaurant
90 Hotel Park

OTHER
1 Suhrawardi Hospital
2 The Bookworm Bookshop
3 Prime Minister's Office
4 Parjatan Tourist Office
5 Zia Uddyan (Zia's Tomb)
6 National Assembly
7 Aarong Handicrafts
8 Sat Gumbad Mosque
10 Police Station
11 Holy Rosary Church
12 The Mappa
13 ANZ Grindlays Bank
14 Dragon Air
16 Dhanmondi Police Station
17 Bus Offices for Rajshahi & Khulna divisions.
19 Gulf Air & KLM
26 Aarong Handicrafts
27 Monowara Hospital
28 Holy Family Hospital
31 Immigration & Passport Office
33 Paribagh Super Market
(Karika Handicrafts)
35 Jute Carpet Shops
36 ANZ Grindlays Bank & ATM
38 Shilpangan Art Gallery
39 Alliance Francaise
41 Indian High Commission
42 Goethe Institut
43 New Market
44 Chandni Chowk Bazar
45 Gausia Market
46 Monno Ceramics
47 National Museum
48 Dhaka Public Library
49 Institute of Arts & Crafts
54 Dharmarajikha Buddhist Monastery
61 Graphosman Maps
62 Liberation War Museum
63 Shilpakala Academy & National Art Gallery
64 Old High Court
65 Shishu Academy
66 British Council & Library
67 Dhakeswari Temple
68 Shaheed Minar
69 Curzon Hall
70 Osmani Auditorium
71 Pacific Overseas Travel
75 GPO
76 Stadium Arcade
77 Baitul Mukarram Mosque (National Mosque)
81 BRTC Bus Station
83 Air Parabat
84 DHL & Federal Express Couriers
87 HSBC Bank & ATM
88 ANZ Grindlays Bank
89 Citibank
91 Beacon Travel
92 University Press Bookshop
93 Janata Bank
94 Biman Airlines
95 BIWTC (Reservations for the Rocket)
96 ANZ Grindlays Bank
97 Singapore Airlines
98 JJB Building; Eastern Bank & Citibank
99 Rajuk Mosque
100 Cathay Pacific Airlines
101 Pubali Bank
102 Emirates Air & Korean Air
103 Bengal Airlift & Air France
104 Sonali Bank
105 American Express &
Standard Chartered Bank
106 Bangladesh Bank & British Airways
107 GMG Airlines
108 HAC Enterprises (Travel Agency)

DIT Rd
Malibagh
Old Circular Rd
Siddheswari Rd
Shantinagar Rd
Inner Circular Rd
DIT Extension Rd
Sayedabad Rd
Kakrail Rd
Segunbagicha Rd
North-South Rd
Nayapaltan
Kamlapur Train Station
Topkhana Rd
See Enlargement
Abdul Ghani Rd
National Stadium
DIT Ave
Secretariat Rd
Bangabandhu Ave
Motijheel

To
Sayedabad Bus
Station (1.25km),
Old Sonargaon,
Comilla, Chittagong
& Sylhet

of the European-Mughal style of building erected after the first partition of Bengal in 1905. A red-brick building with many eye-catching details, it has an elegant facade with a central projecting bay and wide arched horseshoe-shaped portals.

Two blocks west, on Secretariat Rd and just north of the College of Medicine, is a modern monument, the **Central Shaheed Minar**, built to commemorate the historic Language Movement of 1952.

If you're looking for a place to meet DU students, try Madhu's Canteen. It's a rustic yellow-coloured building where the political minds of the campus meet.

National Museum

A visit to the National Museum is a must. If you're short of time skip the top floor, which displays reproductions of western paintings (no nudes, of course) and portraits of historical figures. The displays are poorly executed and not all items are of museum quality, but you can learn a good deal about the country from a trip here.

There are displays from Bangladesh's Hindu, Buddhist and Mughal past, but the real value of the museum is in the extensive collection of fine folk art and handicrafts. Check out the models of the many varieties of 'country' boats, most of which you'll still see on the rivers. One of the highlights is the collection of paintings and charcoal drawings by Zainul Abedin depicting the 1943 Great Bengal Famine. The stark images of stick-thin figures in a scorched landscape, stalked by carrion birds, are very powerful. There's also a simple but extremely moving display on the Liberation War. Exhibits include the first Bangladeshi flag (made by hand) and a Pakistani torture box, evil in its bland hi-tech design.

Admission is Tk 2; free on Friday. It's open daily from 10 am to 4.30 pm, Friday from 3 to 7 pm and is closed Thursday.

Liberation War Museum

This new museum has a very moving display on the 1971 War of Independence, with lots of English and Bangla newspaper reports, photographs (some quite graphic) and memorabilia. The lines on the floor take you on a chronological tour of the conflict. It's one of the best museums in the country. There are English-speaking guides. From Topkhana Rd head north up Segunbagicha Rd about 400m, and it's on the second street on the right. Admission is Tk 3. It's open daily from 10.30 am to 6.30 pm.

National Assembly

Sher-e-Bangla Nagar, north of Dhanmondi, is where the striking National Assembly building, Sangshad Bhaban, is located. In 1963 the Pakistanis commissioned Louis Kahn, a world-renowned American architect, to design a regional capital for East Pakistan. Due to the liberation movement and ensuing war the building wasn't completed until 1982. The building often features in books on modern architecture, and is regarded as among Kahn's finest works.

A typical Kahn structure, it's a huge assembly of concrete cylinders and rectangular boxes sliced open with bold, multistorey circular and triangular apertures instead of windows. The marble strips between the concrete layers have been likened to pinstripes on a finely tailored suit. The interior, which includes the octagonal Assembly hall, features bizarre Piranesi-inspired spaces. You can't take photos inside. Around the structure is a large lake, with red-brick apartments to one side where parliamentarians from outside Dhaka stay when the Assembly is in session.

Tours are only by special appointment but a few travellers have managed to arrange tours on the spot. Ask for a seat in the visitor's gallery; if Parliament is in session and you're lucky, you might be given one for a session several days later.

Sat Gumbad Mosque

Dating from 1680, Sat Gumbad (Seven Domed) Mosque is the finest example of the pure Mughal style mosque in Dhaka. The mosque's most notable feature is its seven bulbous domes crowning the roof and covering the main prayer hall.

Not many years ago, the mosque's location was ideal, overlooking the Turag River, but the views are now completely blocked by ugly buildings. Try to come at prayer time (1 and 5 pm) when the gate is open.

Unfortunately, few travellers see Sat Gumbad because of its somewhat remote location in Jafarabad. Getting here is quite simple. As the crow flies, it's 4km west of the National Assembly. Head north from Dhanmondi on Mirpur Rd to Asad Gate, take a left through it and go to the end of the road (1.5km), then begin asking; it's nearby, towards the river. Suitably clothed women are admitted, but there is no entry to any non-Muslim during prayer times.

SUBURBAN DHAKA
Mirpur Zoo
On the north-western outskirts of Dhaka, 16km from the city centre, is Mirpur Zoo. As with many zoos in the developing world, this one is rather depressing. But if you want to see a Royal Bengal tiger, come here – you're unlikely to see one elsewhere in the country, including the Sundarbans. The zoo contains over 100 species of animals. Quite a lot of animal teasing by the thousands of visitors goes on as well. It's open daily from 8 am to 6 pm, and admission is Tk 5.

The birds are some of the best wildlife here. There is a large lake within the northern perimeter of the zoo. During the winter this area is a rich habitat for a great number of ducks, cranes and other waterfowl, both wintering and migrant species. Migratory birds such as bar-headed geese, widgeon and whistling duck are among the species you're likely to see at the lake. During the high season in January, the noise is deafening.

To get here, take a bus from Farm Gate or Gulistan bus station to Mirpur via Begum Rokeya Sarani. The route does not, unfortunately, run directly to the zoo, but stops short by a couple of kilometres. Remind the conductor of your destination and take a rickshaw from the drop-off point (Tk 5).

Botanical Gardens
Next to the zoo, these shady tranquil gardens stretch over 40 hectares and contain over 1000 species of local and foreign plants. If you're looking for respite from the city's

mass of humanity, come and enjoy the serenity here. In the distance you'll see the Turag River. It's open every day from dawn to dusk. The entrance is next to the zoo's entrance.

These gardens are probably the best place in the city for bird-watching. The quiet early mornings are especially good. For birdwatchers keeping count, you can spot as many as 40 species in a single three-hour visit. The gardens are open 9 am to 5 pm from Saturday to Thursday. Admission is free.

ART GALLERIES
Dhaka is the centre of a vibrant modern art scene, and it's well worth checking out a few exhibitions. The Cyber Cafe in Banani has information on current exhibitions (see Post & Communications, earlier in this chapter), as does the Alliance Française in Banani (see Libraries and Cultural Centres, earlier in this chapter). For displays of work by students, check the Zainul Gallery at Dhaka University's Institute of Fine Arts & Crafts. Leading Bangladeshi abstract artists include Shahabuddin, who is best known for his bold drawings; Khalid Mahmood Mithu, a well-known Dhaka photographer and artist; and Kanak Chanpa, a Chakma from the Chittagong Hill Tracts. Other leading artists are Mahbubur Rahman (sculpture) and Ranjit Das and Mahmudul Huq (both working in abstract oils). There are many commercial art galleries at the two storey DIT II Shopping Centre on Gulshan Ave. In Dhanmondi a good contemporary gallery is Shilpangan (☎ 816 4246), at House 25, Road 5.

SWIMMING
Nonguests can use the pools at the Sonargaon and Sheraton hotels for Tk 550.

LANGUAGE COURSES
The Heed Language Centre in Dhaka is the best place to go if you want to take lessons in Bangla. See the Language Courses section in the Facts for the Visitor chapter for more information.

ORGANISED TOURS
Parjatan's tour division (☎ 811 7855/6, fax 811 7235), on Airport Rd, north of the

DHAKA

intersection with Bijoy Sarani in Tejgaon, offers a four to five-hour city tour by minibus. It includes Curzon Hall, Dhakeswari Temple, the National Assembly, the Liberation War Museum and various national monuments. The tour doesn't venture into Old Dhaka because of the traffic. It costs Tk 150, and leaves from the Sheraton Hotel every Friday at 9 am. There must be a minimum of 10 people before the tour will begin.

There are several other companies offering city tours that don't require so many people. The company with the best reputation is The Guide (☎ 988 6983, fax 988 6984, ✆ theguide@bangla.net), at Rob Super Market, DIT II Circle, Gulshan. Half-day tours cover Sadarghat, Lalbagh Fort, the Liberation War Museum and other sights, and they cost US$15 per person; full-day tours include Savar or Sonargaon and cost US$25. The minimum group size is four people. The Guide also runs day trips to a pottery village near Savar (US$30 per person, minimum two people) and overnight stays in a village (US$60 per person). You could also try Unique Tours and Travels (☎ 988 5116, fax 818 3392, ✆ unique @bangla.net), at 51/B Kemal Ataturk Ave, Banani.

Alternatively, hire a rickshaw and navigate your way around. The going rate is about Tk 40 per hour. Rickshaw-wallahs who speak English can generally be found outside five-star hotels. These guys charge around Tk 75-100 per hour and expect a tip. Convincing them that sex and drugs aren't on the itinerary can be difficult.

River Trips

There are several companies offering trips on the rivers encircling Dhaka.

A river cruise specialist, Contic (☎ 819 5935, 018-211601/3, ✆ contic@bangla.net) has an elegant boat, the *Fleche D'Or*, which cruises along the Turag River, west of the city, down to the Buriganga River. Tours cost US$25 for a half day, US$35 for a full day, including lunch and transport. Contic cruises get excellent reviews. See the Organised Tours section of the Getting Around chapter for information on longer river cruises.

The Guide also runs boat cruises. On Monday, Friday and Saturday, it offers a 4½-hour cruise on the Sitalakhya River on its yacht, the *SB Ruposhi*, departing from Demra, a river town about 15km east of Dhaka. You'll get to stop at a village of *jamdani* (muslin cloth) weavers en route, and swimming is also possible. The US$25 per person cost (US$15 for children) includes dinner on board. On Wednesday this boat trip is combined with a half-day sightseeing tour of the city for US$30 per person. The minimum size group is six people. On Sunday, Tuesday and Thursday the trip starts at 4 pm, returning to Demra at 9.30 pm. Dinner is served on board for US$25 per person.

The tour division of Parjatan (☎ 811 7855/6) offers a five-hour cruise on the *ML Shalook* on the Sitalakhya on Friday and Saturday, but only for groups of at least 10 people. The boat departs from Paglaghat (near Narayanganj) at 10 am and returns at 3 pm. Buses leave from the Sonargaon and Sheraton hotels at 9.10 and 9.15 am respectively. The tour costs Tk 700 a person and includes snacks, lunch and a cultural performance. When booking, which is necessary, you might ask how many people are signed up. When it fills up, this small double-decker boat, which seats 72 people, is far too crowded for comfort.

PLACES TO STAY

Accommodation is more expensive in Dhaka than elsewhere in Bangladesh, but it's still cheap by international standards. The highest concentration of budget and mid-range hotels is in the area extending from Inner Circular Rd down to Old Dhaka. It's within walking distance of Motijheel, Old Dhaka and a number of attractions. Unfortunately, most of the budget hotels in this area don't accept foreigners, so finding a place for less than Tk 120 per person can be quite frustrating.

The two big luxury hotels are further north, between New Elephant Rd and Farm Gate. You'll get much better value, however, staying in the Gulshan area, where all the top restaurants are located. There are roughly 50 guesthouses there and most frequent travellers to Dhaka prefer them.

If you arrive late at night by plane, one option is to stay at the airport. Leave the arrival area (but not the building) and go upstairs to the departure area, where you'll find a waiting room. Although there are only moulded plastic chairs, it gets you out of the crowds for the night. There is likely to be a small fee.

PLACES TO STAY – BUDGET

If you arrive late at night at Gabtali bus station (which isn't advisable), you could stay at the well-marked six-storey *Hotel Turag* across the street. It charges Tk 150/180 for singles/doubles, and is reasonably decent.

Old Dhaka

Most places in Old Dhaka refuse foreigners, including virtually all of the 10 or so hotels along Nawabpur Rd. One that bucks the trend is *Hotel Sugandha International*, at 243 Nawabpur Rd, 1km south of the stadium. The small, clean rooms cost Tk 100/150 for singles/doubles with fans, soft mattresses and attached bathrooms.

The well-marked *Hotel Al-Razzaque International* (☎ 956 6408), at 29/1 North-South Rd, 600m south of Gulistan Crossing, is also friendly to foreigners. Small singles/doubles with attached bathrooms cost Tk 120/250. It's neat and has reasonably soft mattresses, plus it has one of the area's best restaurants. See Places to Eat later in this chapter for more details.

Dhaka

You'll find lots of cheap hotels along Topkhana Rd near the GPO, some of which don't accept foreigners; the following do.

The *Asia Hotel* (☎ 956 0709), up a side alley at 34/1 Topkhana Rd, is in a quiet location, is well maintained and has relatively large rooms. Singles with common bath cost Tk 130, rooms with attached bath are Tk 200/300.

Hotel Mrigaya (☎ 955 4049), nearby on Topkhana Rd, has small rooms, but the bathrooms are tiled and it has clean sheets. Singles/doubles cost Tk 160/300. There's also a restaurant here. Another option a few doors away is the *Hotel Queens*, where rooms cost Tk 160/250.

PLACES TO STAY – MID-RANGE
Dhaka

The well-marked *Hotel Grand Palace International* (☎ 956 1623) is actually in Old Dhaka, on North-South Rd, a block south of Gulistan Crossing. It's a clean place with small singles/doubles for Tk 200/300. Very basic economy doubles cost Tk 250, while air-con rooms cost Tk 400/500. There's a choice between a quiet room with no window, or a noisy room with a window. The entrance is on a side street.

Three blocks north, on North-South Rd (the official address is 45 Bangabandhu Ave), you'll find the massive *Hotel Ramna* (☎ 956 2279). It charges Tk 230/350. The hotel is big enough to escape some of the street noise, and the balconies surrounding each floor have wide views over the city. Reception is on the 2nd floor and can be difficult to find in the maze of tailor shops.

Hotel Metropolitan (☎ 955 8460), just north of Topkhana Rd, is drab but functional. Rooms cost from Tk 250/350.

On Inner Circular Rd, east of DIT II Extension Rd, you'll find several hotels that are slightly better value for money. One is the seven-storey *Hotel Eastern* (☎ 410090/1, fax 956 9828) at 12 Inner Circular Rd (or Fakirapool Rd). The Green Line bus (to Chittagong) has its office here. It's not outstanding but the beds are comfortable and the bathrooms are well-maintained. Singles/doubles cost Tk 170/270.

Nearby, the popular *Hotel Paradise* (☎ 831 8337) has decent rooms for Tk 175/300, all with attached bath. The mattresses are pretty tough but the elderly staff are friendly, and the signs by the elevator to 'be courteous' and 'maintain your dignity' set the tone. The *Hotel Arina* (☎ 409503), next door, has rooms for Tk 120/200; they are basic and small, with battered furniture.

For a few more taka, you can get quite decent accommodation. The *Hotel Midway International* (☎ 831 5360, fax 831 6935), 1km north-west at 30 Inner Circular Rd (Nayapaltan), features parking and a doorman. It charges Tk 400/600 for standard rooms and Tk 1000 for deluxe doubles. The rooms are not spacious but they are fairly

DHAKA

clean and have armchairs and desks, and there's a restaurant (see Places to Eat later in this chapter).

PLACES TO STAY – TOP END
Dhaka

Top honour goes to the 325-room *Sonargaon Hotel* (☎ 811 2011, fax 811 3324, ✉ bizcenter@panpac.com), Mogh Bazar. It charges US$150 plus 32.5% tax for deluxe rooms with cable TV. Amenities include a pool, tennis court, squash court, health club, car rental, disco and shopping arcade. Further south on the same road the older 256-room *Sheraton Hotel* (☎ 816 3391, fax 813 2915) has the same amenities except for the disco. Its standard rooms cost US$182, including tax.

The *Hotel Razmoni Isha Kha* (☎ 832 2426/9, fax 831 5369, ✉ razmoni@bdcom .com), on Kakrail Rd, 1.5km north-west of Motijheel, charges Tk 2400 plus 5% tax for a carpeted room, including satellite TV, minibar, phone and modern bathrooms with tubs and showers. 'Superior' deluxe doubles cost Tk 3300. The decor seems to have come from the Roger Moore era of James Bond movies.

For cheaper accommodation, try the *White House Hotel* (☎ 813 4601, fax 813 7720) at 155 Shantinagar Rd, 1km north of Motijheel. It has rooms with satellite TVs, a business centre and a restaurant; singles/doubles with air-con cost Tk 1200 to Tk 1500/Tk 1700 to Tk 1800. It also has some cheaper units at the back.

In Motijheel, the new *Dhaka Inn* (☎ 983 4592, fax 982 1472), on DIT Ave, has clean doubles for Tk 500, and air-con doubles for Tk 900. All rooms have spotless bathrooms with hot water and satellite TV.

In Dhanmondi there's the pleasant *Ambrosia Guest House* (☎ 501505, fax 966 8502), on the corner of Road 2 and Road 3. It has rooms for Tk 1550/1800 including breakfast and laundry service, and there's a small garden.

Gulshan Area

The greater Gulshan area, including Banani and Baridhara, has 50 or so guesthouses

that offer a cosy ambience and much cheaper rates than the Sonargaon or Sheraton. Nearly all accept major credit cards. All offer discounts for stays of more than a fortnight or so. There's a concentration of them in Banani north of Kemal Ataturk Ave, so if you're staying for a while it pays to look around until you find one that suits. There are also a handful of new upmarket hotels.

One of the best guesthouses is the *Tropical Inn Guest House* (☎ 881 3313, 882 6028, fax 882 3941, ✉ tropical@citechco.net, House 19, Road 96, Gulshan). Air-con singles/doubles cost US$60/70, including laundry service. Rooms include phones, satellite TVs and VCRs, and there is free Internet use. It has a restaurant (curries, Chinese and western dishes) overlooking a garden area with a fountain and outdoor seating.

Eastern House (☎ 988 7470, fax 882 6298, House 4, Road 24, Gulshan) is an attractive apartment building between DIT I and DIT II. Rooms cost from US$45/50, and it's US$75 for a suite, including local calls, breakfast, satellite TV and airport transportation.

In Baridhara, arguably Dhaka's most attractive neighbourhood, try the homely *Golden Inn Guesthouse* (☎ 881 0239, fax 882 3849, House 30, Road 10). For comfortable air-con rooms with satellite TVs and minibars, it charges US$40/US$45 (US$52 for super deluxe).

The *Excelsior Guest House* (☎ 882 5139, fax 882 3007, House 38J, Road 18, Banani) is similar to many of the smaller guesthouses in this area. It's a well-to-do family home that has been partly converted into a guesthouse. It costs US$20 for standard single room and has deluxe rooms for US$45/50 and super deluxe rooms for US$50/60.

The popular *Green Goose Guest House* (☎ 988 0050, fax 882 6432, House 30, Road 38, Gulshan) has comfortable modern rooms, which will cost you US$40 for a single, US$45 for a double, and US$50 for a suite.

Golden Goose Guest House (☎ 988 0372, fax 882 3827, House 46, Road 41) is an older establishment with a garden and a view of Banani Lake. Single rooms cost from Tk 1800, doubles from Tk 3000.

Rosewood Residence (☎ *988 0458, fax 882 6784, House 54, Road 16, Banani)*, has rooms for Tk 1500/2000. The rooms are quite clean and have hot showers (Tk 2000 with full baths), air-con, satellite TVs, mini-bars and phones. The restaurant offers a wide selection of Chinese and western dishes.

One of the best hotels is the *Hotel De Crystal Garden* (☎ *882 3147, fax 882 7076,* @ *crytlhtl@citechco.net, House 28, Road 63, Gulshan)*. It's a large business-oriented hotel with all mod cons and large rooms. Standard singles cost US$65, deluxe rooms are US$75 and suites US$85, including airport transportation and breakfast. It also has a business centre, an attractive restaurant and 24-hour room service.

Hotel De Castle (☎ *881 2888, fax 881 0182,* @ *hdel@bdcom.com, House B-72, Road 21, Banani)* also has a good reputation. Standard rooms cost US$60, super deluxe rooms US$80 and suites US$95. Facilities include a business centre, health club and an excellent restaurant. One guest has been staying there since the day it opened.

In Baridhara the *Asia Pacific Hotel* (☎ *881 4125, fax 881 4125,* @ *asiaphtl @vasdigital.com, House 2, Road 2, Baridhara)* is a tall building with fine views. As with the Hotel de Castle and Crystal Garden most of the staff used to work at the Sonargaon and Sheraton hotels. The rooms are light and airy, and cost US$65 for a standard single, US$90 for a deluxe with king-sized bed and US$130 for a suite.

PLACES TO EAT
Local Cuisine
In Old Dhaka, it's hard to beat the popular *Hotel Al-Razzaque International* at 29/1 North-South Rd (see Places to Stay earlier in this chapter). There's no menu but some waiters speak English. You can get rice chicken (or mutton or fish) for around Tk 40. Women eat in separate cabins with curtains. You'll find cheap eateries along Nawabpur Rd to the east, in particular *Cafe Al-Razib*, which gets lots of customers.

In the mod[...] *Rajdhani* on the [...] and Rajuk Aves. It's a[...] very popular. Some trav[...] the restaurant on the 7th fl[...] *Ramna* on North-South Rd as a g[...] to get away from the street noise and[...] the city.

One block further north from Hotel Ramna and to your right is the *Ruchita Restaurant*, which has Bangladeshi, Chinese and English dishes, mostly in the Tk 30 to Tk 60 range, such as chicken dopiaza and vegetable chow mein.

For good food and clean surroundings, it's hard to beat the popular *New Cafe Jheel,* further north on Topkhana Rd, 200m west of North-South Rd. It has fresh hot Indian naan bread, chicken tikka and beef kebabs.

There are numerous other late-night restaurants here worth checking out, including *Cafe Baghdad* at 20 Topkhana Rd, near Hotel Queens, which serves delicious hot kebabs right off the grill with sauce for Tk 8 each. On North-South Rd opposite the Hotel Pritom, the *Moghul Curry House* is somewhat dark but it's relaxing and it does a fine prawn masala for Tk 50.

Over in Motijheel, there's another *Cafe Jheel* (not to be confused with the New Cafe Jheel) on the corner of DIT Extension Rd and Motijheel Ave. Two blocks along Motijheel is the *Crescent Garden Restaurant*. It's also very popular and a bit more upmarket, with chicken biryani (Tk 60), mutton curry (Tk 70) and chicken curry (Tk 52), among other dishes. *Hotel Park,* just north of Dilkusha II Circle, is another popular place. It displays a menu outside, including chicken biryani (Tk 30), vegetable biryani (Tk 35) and chicken masala (Tk 35).

The only places in the Gulshan area specialising in Bangladeshi food are the *Kushum Restaurant,* at 37 Kemal Ataturk Ave in Banani, and the excellent *Kalapata Restaurant* (Bangla sign only), on the corner of Gulshan Ave and Road 132, just north of DIT Circle I.

The *Plaza*, an ordinary Bengali restaurant, and *Zafrani Biriani* both face onto

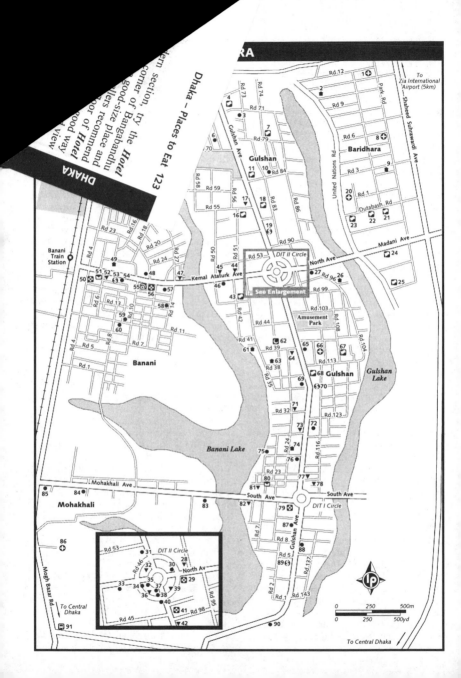

GULSHAN, BANANI & BARIDHARA

PLACES TO STAY
2 Golden Inn Guesthouse
5 Hotel De Crystal Garden
9 Asia Pacific Hotel
14 Rosewood Residence
15 Excelsior Guest House
26 Tropical Inn Guest House
49 Hotel De Castle
61 Golden Goose Guest House
63 Green Goose Guest House
74 Eastern House

PLACES TO EAT
17 New Arirang
28 Spaghetti Jazz
32 Ninfa's Restaurant &
   Landmark Shopping Centre
36 Don Giovanni's Sizzler
   Restaurant
39 Plaza Restaurant &
   Zafrani Biriani Restaurant
42 Hong Kong Restaurant
44 Saffron Restaurant
45 Wimpy
47 Kushum Restaurant
52 Sky Room Restaurant;
   Travel House;
   GMG Airlines
64 King's Kitchen Restaurant
71 Wakana Japanese Restaurant
73 La Boheme Chinese
   Restaurant
77 Kalapata Restaurant
78 Cathay Restaurant
81 Sajna Restaurant
82 Aangan Restaurant

EMBASSIES
4 Pakistani High Commission
7 Italian Embassy
11 Australian High Commission
13 Thai Embassy

16 Swedish Embassy, Danish
   Embassy & Danida
18 German Embassy
21 Chinese Embassy
22 Japanese Embassy
23 British High Commission &
   Club, ODA
24 American Embassy
25 Nepalese Embassy
43 Canadian High Commission
   & CIDA
67 French Embassy
68 Myanmar Embassy

OTHER
1 Dr Wahab's Clinic
3 Bagha Club (British)
6 American Club
8 British High Commission
   Medical Centre (Elizabeth
   House)
10 European Economic
   Community (EEC)
12 Japanese International
   Cooperation Agency (JICA)
19 American Express
20 US Embassy Medical Unit
   (Suvastu House)
27 DHL Couriers
29 DIT II Market
30 The Guide Tours
31 Singapore Airlines
33 Newsagent
34 Lucky Enterprise Fax Centre
35 Monno Ceramics & Federal
   Express Couriers
37 Fuji Color & Brightway
   Business Centre
38 Kodak Photo Shop & Good
   Tailors
40 Sausly's (German Meat Shop)
41 DIT II Shopping Centre

46 Boi Bichitra Bookshop
48 Unique Tours & Travels
50 UAE Shopping Centre/Banani
   Mall; 24-Hour Pharmacy;
   Shetuli Handicrafts
51 GPO & Petrol Station
53 Standard Chartered Bank
54 Regency Travels
55 Cyber Café at Dolce
   Vita-La Gelarie
56 Banani Market
57 Saptagram Nari Swanirvar
   Handicrafts
58 Dentist
59 Dentist
60 HEED Language Centre
62 Gulshan Central Mosque
65 British Airways
66 Japan-Bangladesh Friendship
   Hospital
69 Kumudini Handicrafts
70 ANZ Grindlays Bank & ATM,
   British Airways & Rose
   Garden Guesthouse
72 Pollywog (Yoghurt, Brown
   Bread, Cookies, Peanut Butter)
75 German Technical
   Cooperative Agency (GTZ)
76 Canadian Club
79 DIT I Market
80 GPO
83 BRAC Headquarters
84 Shetuli Handicrafts
85 Dhaka District Forestry Office
86 ICDDRB Hospital &
   Traveller's Clinic
87 Travel Channel
88 Westecs (Clothing)
89 HSBC Bank & ATM
90 Aarong Handicraft
91 Mohakhali Bus Station
   (Mymensingh & Tangail Buses)

DIT II Circle in the Gulshan area. There are also small places at DIT Mall and at Banani Mall on Kemal Ataturk Ave serving snack food, such as samosas for Tk 8.

The fancy restaurants at the Sonargaon and Sheraton hotels are very expensive. Both have large buffet lunches for around Tk 700. You could eat enough to last until dinner. At the Sheraton, *Cafe Arami* is open around the clock – good for midnight snacks. Both hotels also have bars and excellent but expensive pastry shops.

The air-con *Kasturi* on North-South Rd opposite the Pritom Hotel is also noted for its Bengali food; a meal there will cost around Tk 100 to Tk 150. The menu includes curries made with a variety of local fish, including rui, koi, pavda, and king-size freshwater lobsters.

Fast Food
If you crave western junk food there's the *Wimpy* hamburger-and-fries place on Kemal Ataturk Ave in Gulshan.

In the Sonargaon Hotel area, try *Cooker's-7 Fast Food Restaurant*, 200m north of the hotel. It has lots of dishes in the Tk 25 to Tk 50 range, including hamburgers, chicken sandwiches and fried rice. *Pizza Garden,* one block south of the Sonargaon, has standard ready-made pizzas. Farm Gate and Mogh Bazar are also good areas for finding local restaurants and samosa stalls.

In Dhanmondi there are snack shops along Mirpur Rd, including *Coopers Pastry Shop* opposite Dhanmondi Lake. It has the usual breads, cakes and beef pies, and the standard pizza and hot dogs.

Chinese

It doesn't take very long to become totally numbed by the array of Chinese restaurants serving almost exactly the same food at similar prices. They tend to cater to Bangladeshi tastes, so the food is a bit oily and salty – less so at the more expensive establishments. Many of these are in the Gulshan area.

In the city centre there are a number of Chinese restaurants along Inner Circular Rd. One of the best for the price is *Nightingale Restaurant* at 35/1 Inner Circular Rd, near North-South Rd. Most dishes are in the Tk 70 to Tk 100 range, including hot and sour chicken (Tk 80), fish with vinegar (Tk 95) and beef with vegetables (Tk 100).

Fresh Pots Restaurant, on North-South Rd, near the Hotel Metropolitan, features primarily Chinese cuisine. Most dishes are in the Tk 50 to Tk 70 range, but many dishes on the menu aren't available and the service is slow.

Another street known for Chinese restaurants is New Eskaton Rd, a block south of the Sonargaon Hotel. These include the long-standing *Chop Sticks Restaurant* at No 133, the *Mikado Restaurant* and the *Tai King Chinese Restaurant* (☎ 400194). Tai King is attractive inside and seems the best. The long menu includes chop suey (Tk 65), sweet and sour prawns (Tk 80) and shredded beef (Tk 100). Prices at the others are similar.

The best Chinese restaurant in this area is *Xian Restaurant* at 126 Elephant Rd. It features both Chinese and Thai cuisine, and dishes are generally in the Tk 100 to Tk 175 range. The place is a bit dark but the service is excellent and there's classical music in the background.

Another area for Chinese restaurants is Dhanmondi, particularly along Mirpur Rd. The best two are *Chilis Chinese Restaurant*, on Mirpur Rd just north of Dhanmondi Lake, and *Xenial*, at House 365 on Road 16. Prices of dishes at both places are mostly in the Tk 120 to Tk 175 range. Both places are quite attractive, especially Xenial, and Chilis also offers a few Thai selections.

If price is your main concern, there is cheap Chinese to be had on Mirpur Road. *Chung King Chinese Restaurant* faces ANZ Grindlays Bank; *Magdonalds* has numerous TVs playing while diners eat; and *Ming House* at least doesn't have noisy TVs. Two kilometres north in Mohammadpur you'll find the *VIP Chinese Restaurant*. Most dishes at the VIP are in the Tk 80 to Tk 100 range and the food is ordinary.

In the Gulshan area there are many Chinese restaurants. The better places include the *Cathay*, at House 6, Road 133, Gulshan; the colourful *King's Kitchen* at 79 Gulshan Ave; *La Boheme* at 65 Gulshan Ave; and the *Hong Kong*, on the corner of Gulshan Ave and Road 98.

Other Cuisines

For mid-range meals, the city's best restaurants are in Gulshan and Banani, with new ones cropping up almost every month. The top three Indian restaurants are *Sajna*, at 10 South Avenue (200m west of DIT I Circle); *Aangan*, across the street; and *Saffron*, on the corner of Road 51 and Kemal Ataturk Ave in Gulshan, which has wide windows overlooking a pleasant garden. A typical meal costs anywhere from Tk 250 to Tk 500 a person. You can also get good Indian food at *Ninfa's*, which overlooks DIT II Circle in Gulshan.

For Indonesian food, there's the swish *Sky Room*, 8 Kemal Ataturk, Banani, on the 12th floor of the ABC building.

The best Korean and Japanese food is served at *New Arirang*, at 12 Gulshan Ave.

It's so popular with the Korean community that it serves as their informal club. Expect to pay Tk 500 per person. The **Wakana Japanese Restaurant**, at House 5A, Road 32, Gulshan is a simpler, more basic Japanese restaurant that serves alcohol.

For grilled steaks and freshly made pasta, you can't beat the popular **Don Giovanni's Sizzler Restaurant**, which has a fairly rustic laid-back setting. It's on the small street south-east of DIT Circle II. Another recommended Italian restaurant is **Spaghetti Jazz**, which also has wonderful pasta and costs around Tk 500 per person for dinner. It's on Road 91, almost on the corner of North Avenue, a short walk from DIT Circle II.

ENTERTAINMENT
Traditional Music & Dance
The best place for cultural performances is **Shilpakala Academy** (☎ 956 2801), which is in the city centre in Segunbagicha, just east of the Supreme Court down a side street, next to the National Art Gallery. This is the national academy of fine art and the performing arts. The major cultural event of the year is the month-long Asian Art Biennial, which occurs in November. The exhibition, which spills over into Osmani Auditorium and the National Museum, attracts top modern artists and the quality is very high.

For other events, consult the *Daily Star*; it sometimes announces events in advance. Generally, however, you cannot find out about upcoming events through the newspapers, so you'll have to contact Shilpakala Acdemy for details.

Cultural events are also held at **Shishu Academy**, which is south-west of the Supreme Court; the **National Museum**, 1km north-west of the Supreme Court; **Osmani Auditorium** on Abdul Gani Rd, 1km south-east of the Supreme Court; and Dhaka University. Finding out about events proves to be a bit of a challenge – they seem to be only advertised among the cultural elite. Your best option is to try asking at the Shilpakala Academy itself or to inquire at the Alliance Française. Sometimes cultural events will be listed in the English-language press.

Bars
Various embassy social clubs including the American Club, Bagha Club, British Club, Swedish Club and the Australian Club in Gulshan have happy hours on Thursday nights and special events. These clubs are usually open only to ticket holders, but it is possible to get temporary membership or to enter under the auspices of a member. Expats are usually happy to help you get into a club.

SPECTATOR SPORT
There are often cricket, soccer or hockey matches at the National Stadium; the spectators are all males. Women don't go to sporting events – it's considered unseemly. Check English-language newspapers for details.

SHOPPING
Handicrafts
The city has numerous handicraft shops, and they all offer a slightly different assortment of textiles (especially local clothing, robes, silk pillow covers and bedspreads), jute products and pottery. The biggest name in quality handicrafts is the Aarong chain, whose outlets are almost like department stores.

The leading handicraft shops are:

Aarong
  Gulshan-Tejgaon Link Rd
  Corner Mirpur Rd & Manik Mia Ave
  4 New Circular Rd, Mogh Bazar
Karika Handicrafts
  Paribag Super Market, Kazi Nazrul Islam Rd
  Sheraton Hotel Shopping Arcade
Kumudini
  97 Gulshan Ave, Gulshan
  Sonargaon Hotel
Saptagram Nari Swanirvar
  60E Kemal Ataturk Ave, Banani
Shetuli
  UAE Shopping Centre/Banani Mall
  91 Mohakhali

One of the cheaper shops is Karika Handicrafts, which has Bangladeshi fabrics and jute products as well as bronze work, leatherwork, purses, handbags and jewellery.

Many shops accept credit cards. Most open daily between 9 and 10 am and close between 7 and 9 pm, and are closed Friday.

Halima Handicrafts, 12/24 Sir Syed Rd in Mohammadpur, is a project to help abandoned and widowed women to support themselves and their children by producing goods such as wall hangings, bedspreads, cushions and tablecloths.

The Sonargaon and Sheraton hotels have handicraft shops in their shopping malls and are probably the best places for purchasing jute carpets. You can pay less elsewhere, including at the row of shops on New Elephant Rd, but the selection won't be as good. Kumudini specialises in jute products and Saptagram specialises in clothes.

For modern ceramics, head for Monno Ceramics, which has an outlet at 334 New Elephant Rd in the city centre and at DIT II Circle in Gulshan.

For jewellery, consider items made of white conch shells, particularly bangles. They're made by Hindu artisans in Shankharia Bazar (see Shankharia Bazar earlier in this chapter) and are sold at most handicraft shops.

Bangladesh is also noted for its pink pearls. You can find them sold individually and set in jewellery all over the city. Reliable shops include Mona Jewellers, 28 Baitul Mukarram market in the city centre (closed Thursday afternoon and all day Friday); Pearl Paradise, 20 Baitul Mukarram (and the Sonargaon); and New Pearls Heaven, upstairs at 62/7 Kemal Ataturk Ave in Banani.

Clothing

Dhaka is a fantastic place for purchasing cheap ready-made garments, all of which are produced locally for export. If you're ready to haggle then head for Banga Bazar; it's a block west of Gulistan bus station. Although some of the clothes are seconds, with small flaws, most are over-runs. The items include cotton shorts (Tk 40), dress shirts (Tk 80 to Tk 100), cotton pants (Tk 100), saris, colourful nylon jogging suits (Tk 260), winter jackets (Tk 300) and blue jeans (up to Tk 200).

Bargaining is required; you can usually get things for a third of the asking price. Speaking a few words of Bangla will help.

The kids who hang around the market are experts at seeking out particular garments. They expect a tip of course. Banga Bazar is usually closed on Friday, but ask around because opening hours are frequently disrupted by strikes (see Hartals under Dangers and Annoyances in the Facts for the Visitor chapter). Also, normal opening hours may be disregarded before holidays.

Westecs, a clothing store on Gulshan Ave three blocks south of DIT I Circle, is an easier place to shop for cheap clothes. It has changing rooms, for instance. Shirts that sell for US$50 or more in the west with a designer label stuck on them sell here for between Tk 100 and Tk 200, while jeans cost around Tk 300.

New Market & Chandni Chowk Bazar

The city's largest market is New Market at the southern end of Mirpur Rd. You can find a bit of everything, including maps of Dhaka and Bangladesh, material, saris and household items. Chandni Chowk, to the east across the street, is best for local fabrics, which vary extensively from the glittery to the more conservative. Both markets are closed on Monday afternoon and all day Tuesday.

Other Markets

Stadium Arcade, which is just west of the National Stadium and the National Mosque, has a similar array of items including electrical goods and cassettes of local music. It's closed Thursday afternoon and all day Friday.

DIT II Market has about 10 antique shops, and DIT I Market has a few more. Some items, particularly Hindu brass statues, are small and portable and make good buys. Many items, such as clocks, wooden items made in Myanmar (Burma) and old Dutch 'country' china, come from ships demolished at Chittagong. Prices tend to be ridiculously high, so shop around in order to compare prices and variety before purchasing.

[Continued on page 129]

NAKSHI KANTHA

Once found among a woman's private posses-
sions, the embroidered quilts called *nakshi
kanthas* can be seen in Bangladesh hanging on
the walls of upmarket hotels, offices and in
museums. The humble but indigenous nakshi
kantha has become an artistic symbol not just of
Bangladeshi women but the nation as well.

Traditionally, nakshi kantha-making was mostly
done in the central and western divisions of
Bangladesh. Rajshahi nakshi kanthas tended to be thicker, due to the
colder winters. Jessore nakshi kanthas incorporated more Hindu motifs
than quilts from Dhaka division. They were made from worn-out clothing material, especially saris. Six or so layers of material were stitched
together with a special stitch, which gave a rippled surface. Thread from
a sari border is used to stitch the patterns. They could be made as
wedding gifts to a daughter leaving home, or given to a grown son as
a reminder of his mother. Practical uses included wrapping for precious
clothes, pillow covers, prayer mats and light blankets for the cool nights
of winter and the monsoon season. Besides the usefulness of recycling
old material, there is also a folk belief that a nakshi kantha made from
old material brings good luck. The jealous gods won't harm someone
dressed in rags – infants were often dressed in nakshi kantha nappies
for this reason.

Nakshi kanthas share many motifs with another female art, the
ground drawings made with powder called *alpanas*. Alpanas have an

Right: The special
stitching used
gives the quilt a
rippled surface.

GLENN BEANLAND

old connection to religious rites held to bring rain, protect families, celebrate the harvest and secure a successful new rice sowing. The lotus symbol, often the central symbol, evokes both sun and water. The plant opens as the sun rises and, seemingly dead in the dry season, revives as soon as the water rises. The tree-of-life motif is an ancient fertility symbol. In one old ritual a newlywed couple plant a banana sapling to mark their new life together. Patterns made of twined leaves relate back to the tree-of-life. Images of fish and rolling waves reflect the dominance of the rivers on the Bangladeshi landscape. Weavers add images of the articles in their daily life – agricultural tools and cooking utensils, as well as symbols of the good life such as combs, mirrors, cosmetics and betel-nut cutters. Wedding symbols are also depicted, such as the palanquin brides are carried in and even the nakshi kanthas given as wedding presents. Religious symbols like the Islamic crescent moon and star and Hindu temples and goddesses are another theme. *Nakshi Kantha Maath* (The Field of the Embroidered Quilt) is a famous poem by Jasimuddin, which tells of a woman who stitches her life story onto her kantha.

The nakshi kanthas that are available for sale these days are mostly produced by Nongovernment Organisation handicraft projects. To find a commercial market they use a wider range of colours than the traditional black, red and blue, and instead of worn-out clothes, cotton or silk is used as the surface, with synthetic fibres to stitch the patterns. Some are really tapestries rather than multi-layered quilts. Regional differences have faded. But what was once a dying tradition seen only in the domestic world is now a living, recognised artform.

Top: Images of daily life are often depicted in nakshi kantha. This quilt shows people gathered around a boat at the side of a river, a typical Bangladeshi scene.

[Continued from page 128]

GETTING THERE & AWAY
Air

Zia International Airport (☎ 819 4350), located north of the city centre on the road to Uttara, 12km from the city centre, handles both international and domestic flights. The airport compares favourably with several regional airports (eg, Delhi) and it has a bank that is open for most flight arrivals, a restaurant and the 'welcome offices' for the Sonargaon and Sheraton hotels. There's no left-luggage facility available at the airport but there is one available at Kamlapur train station. Offices and agencies for the major airlines include:

Aeroflot (☎ 816 9556) Sheraton Hotel
Air France (☎ 955 3050/9) 54 Motijheel Rd, Motijheel
Air Parabat 1st floor, 95 Motijheel (north of Motijheel Rd); (☎ 980 3777) Zia airport
Biman Airlines (☎ 956 0151/2) Dilkusha Circle I, Motijheel (open 9 am to 7.30 pm every day); (☎ 989 4771) Zia International Airport
British Airways (☎ 956 4870/1) Sena Kalyan Bhaban Bldg, Shapla Circle, 195 Motijheel Ave, Motijheel; (☎ 881154) 116 Gulshan Ave, Gulshan
Dragon Air (☎ 812882, 311630) between Farm Gate and Sonargaon Hotel, Kazi Nazrul Islam Rd
Druk Air (Bhutan Airlines) (☎ 811 3021) Vantage Travel, Sonargaon Hotel
Emirates Air (☎ 956 3813) 64 Motijheel Ave, Motijheel
GMG Airlines (☎ 602703) ABC House, 8 Kemal Ataturk Ave, Banani; (☎ 328172, 011 865761) Sonargaon Hotel; (☎ 956 7561) Sena Kalyan Bhaban Bldg, Shapla Circle, 195 Motijheel Ave, Motijheel
Gulf Air (☎ 956 3930) Travel Trade, 10 Kawran Bazar, opposite Sonargaon Hotel; (☎ 955 3050/9) Bengal Airlift, 54 Motijheel Ave, Motijheel
Indian Airlines (☎ 816 3611, 256533) Sheraton Hotel
KLM (☎ 811 5354) 4th floor, 10 Kawran Bazar, opposite Sonargaon Hotel
Korean Air (☎ 956 3828) 64 Motijheel
Malaysia Airlines (☎ 912 9141) Sheraton Hotel
Pakistan International Airways (☎ 816 3391) Sheraton Hotel
Singapore Airlines (☎ 817 1250) 7th floor, Gulshan Tower, DIT II Circle, Gulshan
Thai International (☎ 813 4711/2) Sheraton Hotel

Bus

There are four main bus stations. The largest is Gabtali bus station on the north-western side of town on Aricha Rd (extension of Mirpur Rd), about 8km from the heart of the city (Tk 5 by bus from Gulistan bus station). It serves destinations in the north-west and south-west, eg, Savar, Bogra, Pabna, Rangpur, Dinajpur, Rajshahi, Kushtia and Jessore. It's a madhouse and you definitely must be on the guard for pickpockets, but in general people are very friendly and helpful. It's much riskier after dark.

An express bus will cost you Tk 5 to Savar and Tk 120 to Kushtia. Express/chair coach bus fares are Tk 100/120 to Bogra, Tk 120/150 to Rangpur, Tk 125/170 to Saidpur, Tk 135/200 to Dinajpur, Tk 120/150 to Rajshahi, Tk 110/160 to Jessore, Tk 130/180 to Khulna and Tk 110/140 to Barisal.

Leaving Gabtali for Dhaka

When taking a local bus from Gabtali bus station into Dhaka, don't just jump onto the first bus you see. Rather, go down the line until you find one that is nearly full. Buses depart only when full and choosing a near-empty one means you'll spend time waiting while the bus drives around the station looking for passengers – especially frustrating if you've just ended an all-night bus trip.

Long-distance chair coaches increasingly leave during the day to avoid bandits who attack at night. One of the best bus companies serving Jessore, Khulna, Kushtia and Barisal is Metro Paribahan, which is located at Gabtali, and has expresses and chair coaches, including air-con chair coaches, to Jessore (Tk 280) and Khulna (Tk 300). New Green Line, which serves Khulna, is another good line but it doesn't have air-con buses. Hasna Enterprise at Counter 41 serves Rajshahi (Tk 260).

Many air-con coach companies serving Rajshahi and Khulna divisions also have offices on Mirpur Rd, in the vicinity of the junction with Pantha Path, across from Dhanmondi Lake.

For destinations in the south and west, Sayedabad bus station is located on the south-eastern side of town on Hatkhola Rd, 1km before Jatrabari Circle. Express/chair coach fares are Tk 35/60 to Comilla, Tk 70/110 to Maijdi, Tk 90/125 to Chittagong and Tk 120/160 to Sylhet. For Sylhet, check SylCom at Sayedabad bus station. Fares to Barisal, Jessore, Khulna and Kushtia are the same as those from Gabtali. They depart for Chittagong between 7 am and midnight.

For Chittagong, the best chair coach companies are along a one-block stretch on Inner Circular Rd in Fakirapool, near the Hotel Paradise and Hotel Arina. They all charge Tk 125 for chair coaches (Tk 230 with air-con). The trip should take six hours if the traffic isn't too awful. There are also buses from here to Cox's Bazar (Tk 220/350, 10 hrs). The return trip departs from Cox's Bazar at 4 pm. Three comparable bus companies are Shohagh Paribahan, Neptune and Soudia Bus. Bilash, which serves Maijdi, is also on Inner Circular Rd and has three or four chair coaches a day (Tk 110).

Buses heading north for Gazipur, Mymensingh, Tangail and Jamalpur depart from Mohakhali bus station on Mogh Bazar Rd, 2km south of Banani. There are no chair coaches on these routes. Expresses charge Tk 30 to Tangail and Tk 50 to Mymensingh, and depart throughout the day.

Finally, there's Gulistan (Fulbaria) bus station, in the heart of town on North-South Rd at Gulistan Crossing. Most buses depart from a block east at the chaotic intersection of Bangabandhu Ave and Toyenbee Rd. It's extremely crowded and traffic jams in the area are constant. Most buses are local and people are stuffed into them like sardines. Destinations include greater Dhaka as well as many towns within 30km or so of Dhaka, such as Mograpara (Old Sonargaon). The government BRTC also has a station (in Motijheel) but it's best forgotten as the service is far inferior to that of the private lines.

Train

Dhaka's main train station is the modern Kamlapur station in Motijheel. Buying tickets is easy and there's a large timetable in English. Double check it for accuracy because the schedules change slightly in the summer and the board may not reflect this. The inquiry counter, which is open until 11 pm, and the Chief Inspector are both helpful. See the Express Trains from Dhaka table for some examples.

Express Trains from Dhaka		
destination	departure	duration (hr)
Chittagong	8.10 am	6
Chittagong	5 pm	7
Chittagong	11 pm	7
Maijdi	1 pm	6
Noakhali	7.30 am	6
Noakhali	10.30 pm	8
Sylhet	7 am	7
Sylhet	3.30 pm	8
Sylhet	10 pm	8

Boat

Book 1st and 2nd-class Rocket tickets at the well-marked BIWTC office (☎ 955 9779) in Motijheel, a block east of Dilkusha Circle I. It's open Sunday to Wednesday until around 5 pm, Thursday until 2 pm, and is closed Friday and Saturday. There's precious little printed information in English.

The Rocket ferries usually depart from Badam Tole Ghat, 1km north of Sadarghat.

However, on occasion they leave from Sadarghat. The departure point will be written on your ticket, but it sometimes changes, so get there in plenty of time. The trip to Khulna takes about 33 to 36 hours.

Those travelling deck class may want to ensure a good seat by hiring a boat to get out to the Rocket in order to stake a place before the hordes arrive. Others have been known to pay a local to occupy a place for them, sitting all day for a fee of around Tk 30.

Boats depart daily at 6 pm sharp. Fares to Khulna are: 1st class, Tk 915; 2nd class, Tk 555; inter class, Tk 139; and deck class, Tk 94. For an explanation of classes, see Classes under Boat in the Getting Around chapter.

Private launches operate up and down the major rivers but most head south. A cartel of about 30 launch owners runs these services. The Sadarghat boat terminal is only about 200m long, but there are often so many launches docked there that you need to allow yourself some time to determine which one you want to use. Short-distance launches travel during the day. The large long-distance launches travel at night, arriving at Sadarghat in the morning and remaining there all day until departure at around 6 or 7 pm. Tickets are usually sold on board on the day of departure. There are no launches to Chittagong.

Short-distance destinations reached by services from Dhaka include:

Bandura (30km west of Dhaka) Many boats depart on the six-hour trip between 5.30 am and 2.10 pm daily. First/deck class costs about Tk 30/20.
Munshiganj (25km south-east of Dhaka) There are frequent departures for this two-hour trip. Deck class costs Tk 8.
Srinagar (20km south-west of Dhaka) At least one boat daily, at 11.30 am; it's a five-hour trip and costs Tk 25/15.

Long-distance destinations reached by services from Dhaka include:

Barisal (110km south of Dhaka) Four or five launches leave daily between 6 and 7 pm; the trip takes 12 to 15 hours. Deck class costs Tk 60 but prices of 1st-class cabins, which usually have fans and common bathrooms, vary according to the boat, from Tk 250 to Tk 300 for a single and up to Tk 600 for a double. Two boats that make this run are the *MV Sadia* and the *Jalkaporte*. Their 1st-class cabins are inferior to those of the Rocket, which also goes to Barisal four times a week.
Bhola (30km east of Barisal) Two launches *(Coco-1* and *Coco-2)* depart daily at 7 and 7.30 pm, and cost Tk 200 per person for 1st class and Tk 50 for deck class.
Chandpur (60km south-east of Dhaka) Boats depart hourly between 7 am and 1.30 pm and take five hours. Deck class costs Tk 25 or Tk 30. The best launch on this route is the yacht-like *Mayour*, operated by the Flying Birds Corp. It departs from Sadarghat daily at 1.30 pm, and charges Tk 142 for an air-con 1st-class cabin, Tk 50 for 2nd class and Tk 25 for deck class. Another launch on this route is the *MV Matlab*, which departs daily at 12.30 pm and charges Tk 120 for a 1st-class cabin and Tk 60 for deck class.
Madaripur (60km south-west of Dhaka) Three launches daily at 8, 8.30 and 9 pm. First/deck class costs about Tk 200/40.
Patuakhali (40km south of Barisal) Two launches depart daily at 6 and 6.30 pm. First/deck class costs Tk 250/60.

GETTING AROUND
To/From Zia Airport

The cheapest way to get to the city centre is by bus. Buses are extremely crowded, however, so this may not be a viable option if you have much luggage. You'll find buses out on the main highway, a five-minute walk from the airport. The fare is only about Tk 5 to most destinations, including Farm Gate. After 8 pm you may have difficulty finding one.

To get to the airport, buses and coasters leave Gulistan bus station throughout the day and cost Tk 5.

Baby taxis (auto-rickshaws) have no fixed rates, so you must bargain. It should cost about Tk 50 or Tk 60, though some of the drivers will open the bidding at as high as Tk 250. If they won't budge, walk out to Airport Rd and try there. Rickshaws aren't allowed at the airport or on the major highway (Airport Rd) passing the airport.

DHAKA

The Mustans

If you get a baby taxi from one of the larger taxi stands, you may see the driver give a young man a Tk 2 note before departing. This money ultimately goes to one of the *mustans* who wield Mafia-like power over their territories. Baby taxi drivers have to pay for the privilege of using a public space to park. A man carting cargo through a mustan's area may be stopped by one of his lieutenants and forced to pay a small fee for the right to pass on a public street. Roadside food vendors also have to pay regular tolls to mustans. These thugs levy similar tolls on slum-dwellers occupying public lands. Refusal often draws a beating.

Mustans operate all over the country. In Dhaka alone, the number of mustans is estimated to be anywhere between 300 and 1000. Their lieutenants collect money from a large number of sources and operate throughout the city, including Dhaka University. Popular belief is that the most powerful mustans are connected with the major political parties and, if true, this might account for much of the violence on campus.

The airport has taxis outside. Coming out of the airport you'll be surrounded by scores of young men offering you rides. This is not a dangerous situation, just a confusing one. Most are not the drivers; they simply help the drivers make the arrangements. There's a fixed-rate taxi booth just outside the airport but Bangladeshis never use it, preferring to bargain down the price with the drivers. Fares to most places in the city, however, are around Tk 400 for foreigners.

Expect to pay Tk 200 to Tk 300 for a taxi from the central city area to the airport, and factor in plenty of time for traffic jams. Capital Cabs can be called on ☎ 935 2847/8/9.

Bus

Cheaper than cheap, buses have no signs in English and their numbering is in Bangla. Furthermore, they are always overcrowded so boarding between major bus stops is virtually impossible. Bus fares vary from Tk 0.50 to Tk 5. There are lots of double-decker buses – if you leap on one near the Gulistan bus station you might get an upper-storey window seat and a cheap tour of Dhaka.

The BRTC is now vastly outnumbered by private bus lines. It does, however, operate a number of female-only services. These are distinguished by the word *mohilla* written in Bangla (examples are shown below), which translates as 'ladies'; you can't just go by the number. For an example of this

script, see the Language chapter at the end of this book.

Buses to the towns of Narayanganj, Mograpara (Old Sonargaon), Murapara and other outlying towns and villages can be found at Gulistan bus station. If you're heading north-west for Savar and Dhamrai, you must go to Gabtali bus station.

Rickshaw

You will find rickshaws everywhere and in crowded streets they're no slower than baby taxis. Aim for a basic fare of about Tk 5 for the first kilometre, and Tk 4 per kilometre after that.

Baby Taxis

Although twice the price of rickshaws over short distances, baby taxis and *mishuks* (the slightly narrower ones without rickshaw art) cost little more for distances of 5km or more and they're a lot faster. The baby taxi fare to Gulshan, including some searching for the address, should be around Tk 40 from the main GPO and Tk 50 to Tk 60 from Sadarghat boat terminal. Some feel that as baby taxis produce more than their share of air pollution, they should be avoided on principle.

Tempo

Fast and cheap, tempos are a convenient way to travel if you aren't carrying very much luggage and don't mind feeling like a sardine. The close quarters might make women feel uncomfortable. A trip from Gabtali bus station to Farm Gate costs around Tk 5.

Car

A good way to do an all-day tour of the city would be to rent a car; you can do this for as little as Tk 1500 (US$30). Renting them outside Dhaka costs only slightly more. All rental cars come with drivers, which is obligatory. Prices include everything except petrol; there are no hidden extras. Your driver can act as a guide as well but don't expect him to know much more than how to get where you want to go. If you go outside Dhaka, you'll have to pay him directly for his meals (Tk 50 per meal) and lodging (Tk 50 to Tk 100). All of them will offer a better deal if you rent for several days or by the month.

There are dozens of businesses around town where you can rent cars; two which seem to be reliable are:

Bangladesh Tours (☎ 313094) DIT Rd in Kawran Bazar, next door to the Sonargaon Hotel; Tk 1500/1000 (with/without air-con) to hire a car (Tk 2000/1500 outside Dhaka) and a minibus for Tk 1600/2500
Dhaka Tours (☎ 500979) 3 Link Rd, 1½ blocks south-west of the Sonargaon; Tk 1500/1000 for a car (Tk 2000/1500 outside Dhaka) and Tk 2200/1600 for a minibus. It also has an office on Minto Rd, opposite the Sheraton Hotel.

Around Dhaka

Many locations in Dhaka division make interesting day trips from Dhaka. Here are just a few.

TONGI-KALIGANJ ROAD

The crowded town of Tongi, which is 1km north of Mohakhali bus station, is a good starting point for a cycling trip. It is also a good route out of Dhaka. When you cross the Tongi River bridge on the main road north to Mymensingh, go about 1km further north into town and turn right. Head east from there. For the first kilometre or

so you'll ride past shops and at the 3km point you'll cross over the railway tracks, where you'll leave the town behind. The road is good and follows the railway line, so you can cycle all the way to Kaliganj (20km) on the Sitalakhya River. From there, the easiest way back is to retrace your path.

TERMOUK ROAD

This is a somewhat more adventurous back-road cycling route that connects with the same route (Tongi-Kaliganj Rd) via Termouk (tair-MOUK). Heading north towards Tongi, about one kilometre south of the Tongi River bridge you'll pass the last red-light intersection before the bridge. Take a right (east) for Termouk (7km), which is a major crossing point (not a village) on the Tongi River. The brick-road route is not direct, so you'll have to ask directions along the way. At Termouk you can get a canoe to take you across the river; get off on the eastern bank. From there, have someone point you towards Ulukala (ou-LOUK-ah-lah), which is on the same bank and several kilometres to the north. From Ulukala you can continue northward, heading for the Tongi-Kaliganj Rd, which runs east-west. That portion will take about half an hour and you must ask directions (for the Tongi Rd). If you'd prefer to end up at Kaliganj, simply ask directions for that more north-eastwardly route (about 45 minutes). During the rainy season, either way could be slippery.

TONGI RIVER BOAT RIDE

The Tongi is a great river for taking a boat ride and its proximity to the city makes logistics relatively simple. The Tongi splits off from the Turag River west of Tongi and heads eastward past Tongi to Termouk (6km from Tongi), then south to Demra on the southern edge of the city, just off the Chittagong highway. There, it spills into the Sitalakhya River which, in turn, continues south past Narayanganj.

· Even though the Tongi is close to the city, you'll never sense it because of the rural scenery. The only signs are an occasional glimpse of tall buildings in the far distance. The flood season is June to October; during these months the river overflows its boundaries and becomes very wide. During the remainder of the year the river is quite narrow, which greatly facilitates the view of life along the river. During the dry season, you'll be able to see irrigated paddy fields everywhere.

The best starting point is the bridge at Tongi. The motorised passenger boats plying the river are called *tolars* (toh-LARS) and can take up to about 50 passengers. The launching point for the tolars is on the northern bank, about 300m west of Tongi Bridge. Most tolars are headed to Ulukala, which costs Tk 5, takes 1½ hours, and is 25 minutes past Termouk, where the river forks. The left fork (a tributary) heads north for Ulukala; the right fork (the main river) heads south for Hardibazar and Demra. From Ulukala, you can either return to Tongi by boat or take a rickshaw to Kaliganj on the Sitalakhya. This takes about 70 minutes over rough dirt roads with great scenery, and costs about Tk 50. At Kaliganj, your options include taking a bus back to Dhaka, the 2nd-class train back to Dhaka via Tongi (ride on top like some local men do), or another tolar to Demra (Tk 15) on the wide Sitalakhya, which takes about 4½ hours. You could shorten the journey by getting off in Murapara (three hours, Tk 10) and catching a local bus back to Dhaka (one hour, Tk 10). Most tolars leave Kaliganj in the morning (just south of town on the western bank) before 9 am but there's also one available in the afternoon, leaving at 2.30 pm.

Another possibility is trying to go from Tongi to Demra all the way via the Tongi River. This is quite difficult as there are no tolars direct to Demra and you may have to turn around for lack of connections. There are occasionally tolars from Tongi to Hardibazar; get to Tongi by 8 am as the best time to find one is in the early morning. They cost about Tk 7 and take about two hours from Tongi. It's very difficult to find onward connections from Hardibazar, but if you can get to the next few villages by any type of boat, you should eventually find one with onward connections to Demra.

Dhaka Division

Dhaka division, the most densely populated area of the country, is surrounded to the west, south, and east by the other five divisions, with the Indian state of Meghalaya to the north. Except for the Faridpur region, which is south of the Padma, all of Dhaka division lies east of the mighty Jamuna (Brahmaputra) and Padma (Ganges) Rivers and north of the wide Meghna. Most of the division is closely settled farmland; only in the far north can you find some of the gradually shrinking woodland.

The northern part of Dhaka division reaches the Indian border at the base of the low, wooded Garo Hills chain. It is the largest district of Bangladesh, located in the heart of the deltaic region of the Jamuna (Brahmaputra) and the Meghna Rivers. Neglected by its Mughal overlords, the region boomed under the British when jute was an important crop. The whole region became one vast jute plantation; jute grew better here and was of a higher quality than anywhere else.

HISTORY

There are traces of ancient Buddhist settlements in the southern region around Savar and Vikrampur. When Muslim rule was established in northern Bengal in 1204, the Hindu Senas fled southward and settled in Vikrampur. Rivalry with their fellow-Hindu Devas in Sonargaon weakened their resistance against increasing Muslim attacks, and in 1278 Vikrampur fell. Sonargaon lasted another decade and continued as a subsidiary capital, with Gaud as the principal capital city.

In 1338 the sultanate of Bangala was established, and as maritime trade with South-East Asia flourished, Sonargaon became the capital. According to some chroniclers, the city stretched for 60km by 30km at the confluence of the Meghna and the Sitalakhya Rivers.

Early in the 17th century the sultanate of Bangala collapsed under pressure from the

Highlights

- **Sonargaon** – site of the old capital of Bengal, with a fine folk art museum and a good area for cycling
- **Madhupur Forest** – home to monkeys, langurs and many species of bird, with tribal Mandi villages nearby
- **Savar** – site of Bangladesh's national monument, with some interesting villages in the vicinity

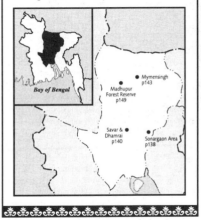

Mughals. Sonargaon was taken in 1611 but it was too exposed to attacks and Dhaka was chosen as the site of the new capital.

In 1757 the whole of Bangala fell into the hands of the British. With the exception of Dhaka, the Mughal rulers had never really regarded this region as possessing any particular significance. Neither did the British during their period of rule indicate that they had any particular interest in developing it. That is, until the farming and harvesting of jute became a commercially valuable enterprise and the northern district of Mymensingh was transformed into the centre for growing this in-demand 'golden fibre'.

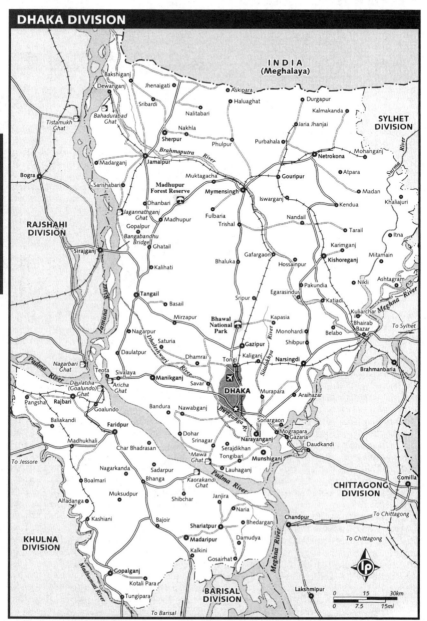

SONARGAON

One of the best day trips from Dhaka is an excursion to Sonargaon (sometimes known as Old Sonargaon), the country's first capital. An hour away from Dhaka, it's just off the Dhaka-Chittagong Highway, some 23km south-east of Dhaka. Today it is nestled between the Meghna and the modest Sitalakhya River, but when it was capital the Sitalakhya was the main channel of what is the now the Jamuna River. These days the Sitalakhya is a relatively minor river, and the mighty Jamuna has changed course, flowing into the Padma, which is some 90km away.

Many visitors to Sonargaon mistakenly believe that its buildings are remnants of the ancient capital city. Except for several mosques, a bridge, a few tombs and stupas, and some indistinguishable mounds scattered around the area, nothing remains of the original city. The area also has two newer but much smaller villages: Mograpara and Painam Nagar.

Unfortunately, the government's archaeological department has done precious little to preserve the buildings of Sonargaon. Reportedly, some of the poorer occupants sell the bricks from these ramshackle buildings to be broken into gravel for construction work. Since independence, only Goaldi Mosque, a pre-Mughal bridge and a single *rajbari* (zamindari palace) called Sardarbari have been restored.

Mograpara

A thriving village located on the Dhaka-Chittagong Highway, Mograpara claims most of the remains of the old capital, including the tomb of Sultan Ghiyasuddin Azam Shah (the oldest surviving Muslim monument in Bangladesh), the Panch Pir Dargah tombs and Fetah Shah's mosque. Most of these are 1km or 2km west of Mograpara. These monuments aren't very impressive and most visitors, believing only Painam Nagar to be Old Sonargaon, don't even know they exist.

Folk Art Museum

Sadarbari, built in 1901, is a beautiful rajbari and an appropriate building for a folk art museum. About 50m in length and accommodating more than 50 rooms, this two-storey building has two facades. Facing the street, ornamental verandahs lined with

DHAKA DIVISION

Sonargaon

The ancient capital of Sonargaon ('Golden Town' in Hindi) flourished as the region's major inland port and centre of commerce during the pre-Muslim period. By the 13th century it was the Hindu seat of power. With the Muslim invasion and the arrival of the sultan of Elhi in 1280, its importance magnified as the region's de facto Islamic capital. Some 42 years later, the first independent sultan of East Bengal, Fakhruddin Mubarak Shah, officially established his capital here.

For the next 270 years, Sonargaon, known as the 'Seat of the Mighty Majesty', prospered as the capital of East Bengal and the Muslim rulers minted their money here. Mu Huany, an envoy from the Chinese emperor, visited Sultan Ghiyasuddin Azam Shah's splendid court here in 1406. He observed that Sonargaon was a walled city with broad streets, great mausoleums and bazars where business of all kinds was transacted. In 1558, famous traveller Ralph Fitch noted that it was an important centre for the manufacture and export of *kantha* (traditional muslin) cloth, the finest in all of India. Ancient Egyptian mummies were reportedly wrapped in this indigo-dyed muslin exported from Bengal.

When the invading Mughals ousted the sultans, they regarded Sonargaon's location along the region's major river as too exposed to Portuguese and Mogh pirates. So in 1608, they moved the capital to Dhaka, thus initiating Sonargaon's long decline into oblivion. Yet its legendary fame for incredibly fine muslin fabric continued undiminished until foreign competition from the British and their import quotas ruined the trade.

columns and accented by a roof-top band of plaster floral relief overlook a bathing pond. This view, with steps leading down to the water and life-size English horsemen in stucco on either side, is one of the most picturesque in Bangladesh. The other facade, at the museum's entrance, is profusely embellished with a mosaic of broken china and stucco floral scrolls.

Most of the interior is exceedingly plain, consisting of small unadorned rooms with various objects and handicrafts on display, including swords, waistbands, necklaces, anklets, beautiful beadwork, fishing baskets, Hindu statues and crude sickles. One room has a whole array of nutcrackers. There is also a new building with more exhibits. Admission costs Tk 2.

The museum is 2km north-east of Mograpara, down a narrow road, and has a small handicrafts shop. There is a larger display of local crafts at the Handicrafts Centre, 300m further down the same road, on your right.

Goaldi Mosque

Across from the Handicrafts Centre you'll find a winding dirt road heading west towards Goaldi Mosque, 1km away. Built in 1519, it's the most impressive of the few extant monuments of the old capital city. A good example of pre-Mughal architecture, it's a graceful single-domed mosque measuring about 10m square, with some original decorations surviving on the front wall, especially in the three *mihrabs* (niches facing Mecca). The central mihrab, constructed of black basalt, is beautifully embellished with carved floral and arabesque relief, while the side ones are decorated in red brick and fine terracotta work.

Some 50m beyond Goaldi is a second, and historically less important, single-domed mosque, built in 1704 during the Mughal period. Yet another single-domed mosque in the Mograpara area is Fateh Shah's Mosque, which predates Goaldi Mosque by 35 years. It has been renovated rather than restored and, consequently, is not so interesting.

Painam Nagar

Continue past the Folk Art Museum and Handicrafts Centre and you'll come to Painam Nagar. This town is unusual in that its layout suggests that it was planned to foster social cohesion. Constructed almost entirely between 1895 and 1905 on a small segment of the ancient capital city, this tiny settlement consists essentially of a single narrow street, less than 500m long, lined with around 50 dilapidated mansions, which were built by wealthy Hindu merchants. At the time of Partition in 1947, many of the owners fled to India, leaving their elegant homes in the care of poor tenants who did nothing to maintain them. The remaining owners pulled out during the anti-Hindu riots of 1964, which led up to the 1965 Indo-Pakistan war.

Today, Painam Nagar has a delightful ghost-town quality, with its buildings choked with vines and their facades slowly crumbling away. One mansion, Awal Manzil, is a textile factory, while another near the far end,

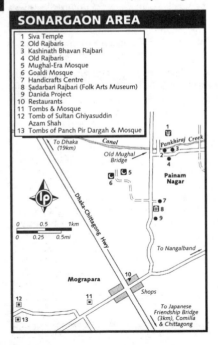

SONARGAON AREA

1 Siva Temple
2 Old Rajbaris
3 Kashinath Bhavan Rajbari
4 Old Rajbaris
5 Mughal-Era Mosque
6 Goaldi Mosque
7 Handicrafts Centre
8 Sadarbari Rajbari (Folk Arts Museum)
9 Danida Project
10 Restaurants
11 Tombs & Mosque
12 Tomb of Sultan Ghiyasuddin Azam Shah
13 Tombs of Panch Pir Dargah & Mosque

To Dhaka (19km)
Canal
Old Mughal Bridge
Pankhiraj Creek
Painam Nagar
Dhaka-Chittagong Hwy
To Nangalband
0   0.5   1km
0   0.25   0.5mi
Mograpara
Shops
To Japanese Friendship Bridge (3km), Comilla & Chittagong

Cycling Around Old Sonargaon & Murapara

For a delightful bicycle day trip that combines peaceful rural scenery with some interesting historical sights and good river views, try the areas around Sonargaon and Murapara. Take your bike by baby taxi to Sayedabad bus station in Dhaka and catch a Comilla bus (departing every five minutes). Tell the driver you want to get off at Mograpara – he will not know what you mean by Sonargaon.

As you pedal around the greater Sonargaon area, don't limit yourself to Painam Nagar.

Afterwards, head north along the Dhaka-Chittagong Highway to the long bridge over the Sitalakhya River (11km). Just before crossing it, turn right (north) onto the Sylhet road and peddle to Murapara junction (11km). Cycle west to Murapara (5km) and south along the scenic eastern bank of the river, passing Murapara Palace, and back to the junction with the Chittagong road (10km more). If you can't hail a Dhaka-bound bus there, go over the bridge and catch one at the crowded intersection just beyond.

The Chittagong and Sylhet roads can be hair raising with buses flying by, but otherwise there is not much traffic.

marked 'Sonargaon Art Gallery', is rented from the government by artist Aminul Islam, whose paintings are on display.

Getting There & Away
Bus Buses for Mograpara depart from Gulistan bus station. Look out for conductors yelling 'Meghna' (the river just beyond Mograpara); they can drop you off in Mograpara, which is 3km before the Japanese Friendship Bridge. The fare is only Tk 10. If you're short of time, get a Comilla bus (about Tk 35) at the Sayedabad bus station (further south at the western end of Sayedabad Rd) and ask to be let off at Mograpara. This will cost you about Tk 30, but you'll find one departing almost instantly.

Car Mograpara is 20km south-west of Jatrabari Circle, the Dhaka junction for Comilla and Chittagong. About halfway to Mograpara you'll cross the Sitalakhya River; it's another 11km to Mograpara, which is the first crowded settlement along the highway after the bridge. If you're lucky, you might see the small 'Folk Art Museum' sign.

MURAPARA
For a full-day outing you can combine a trip to Sonargaon with a visit to the rajbari at Murapara, which is 20km up the Sitalakhya River from Narayanganj, on the eastern

bank. Built in 1889, this rajbari now houses a small tertiary college. It is reasonably impressive, with a 65m frontage overlooking a spacious lawn with the river just beyond.

In the front of the main building, you'll see two small Hindu shrines, both still in reasonably good condition. Built largely in carved red stone, the attractive stucco decorations and ornate roofs make good backdrops for photographs.

Getting There & Away
Bus Murapara is located 26km from Jatrabari Circle in Dhaka. Buses from Gulistan bus station cost Tk 10. Buses from Murapara leave from a stand just south of the college.

Car About 9.5km south-east from Jatrabari Circle, just over the Sitalakhya River, you'll come to a junction where you should take a left (the road to Sylhet) and continue 11km to Murapara junction, the first major settlement on this highway. If you pass a petrol station, you've gone too far. Take a left (west) to the river, then another left (south) along the river through Murapara to the college just beyond.

SAVAR
☎ 06626
A popular day excursion for Dhaka locals is a trip to Savar (SHAH-var). The town, called Savar Bazar, is on the Dhaka-Aricha

Highway, 15km north of Gabtali bus station in Dhaka. The main attraction is the historic Savar memorial, which is 8km further along this highway, just off the road. Tuesday is market day in Savar Bazar, which becomes very animated, especially along the banks of the Bangsi River just west of town.

National Martyrs' Memorial
Savar is home to the Jatiya Sriti Saudha, the tapering 50m-high memorial to the millions who died in the struggle for independence. The beautifully kept grounds contain a number of grassy platforms that cover the mass graves of some of those slaughtered in the Liberation War. This is an important place for Bangladeshis and on weekends it gets very crowded. Just across the road there's a reasonable restaurant run by Parjatan, as well as some souvenir stalls, and down the road towards Dhaka is the bus stand.

Snake Charmers' Village
The Badhi river gypsies are famous for their skill as snake charmers. Their village, Bodapara (or Purabari), is on the outskirts of Savar, along the river and to the north. A few speak English, so asking for a snake-charming demonstration should be no problem. The rather unimpressive performance comes complete with a crowd of interested onlookers, but the variety of snakes is interesting. For this Bangladeshis probably wouldn't pay more than Tk 10, but foreigners will be expected to pay much more. Try to keep the amount to a reasonable Tk 50. For a more elaborate performance with dancing, you'll have to pay more but it might be more memorable.

Places to Eat
There is a well-marked *Chinese Restaurant* on the main drag in the centre of Savar Bazar.

Getting There & Away
Buses for Savar leave from Gabtali bus station. The fare is Tk 5 by bus and Tk 50 by baby taxi to Savar Bazar (15km), and Tk 10 by bus to the memorial (23km), or about Tk 80 for a baby taxi. You could also take an Aricha-bound bus from Gabtali or Farm

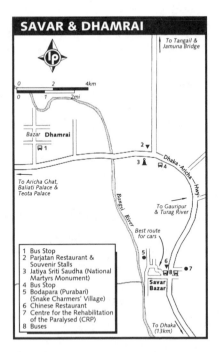

SAVAR & DHAMRAI

To Tangail & Jamuna Bridge

0   2   4km
0   1   2mi

Bazar **Dhamrai**

To Aricha Ghat, Baliati Palace & Teota Palace

Dhaka-Aricha Hwy

To Gauripur & Turag River

Bangsi River

Best route for cars

Savar Bazar

To Dhaka (13km)

1 Bus Stop
2 Parjatan Restaurant & Souvenir Stalls
3 Jatiya Sriti Saudha (National Martyrs Monument)
4 Bus Stop
5 Bodapara (Purabari) (Snake Charmers' Village)
6 Chinese Restaurant
7 Centre for the Rehabilitation of the Paralysed (CRP)
8 Buses

Gate and get off at Savar, but you'll pay slightly more. If you want the actual town, ask for 'Savar Bazar', otherwise the driver will probably think you want to go to the memorial further on.

To get to the snake charmers' village, go to the centre of Savar Bazar along the Dhaka-Aricha Highway, take the crowded road west through the heart of town towards the Bangsi River as far as you can (1.5km), and then take a right (north) along a dirt track for another 1.5km to Bodapara. If you're driving, the only route available is more complicated but it's paved and quite passable; see the Savar & Dhamrai map for more details.

DHAMRAI
If you're in the Savar area, make a side trip to Dhamrai, which is only 5km west of the monument and 1km north off the Dhaka-Aricha road. Known for its artisans who work with brass and *jamdani* (embroidered muslin

Centre for the Rehabilitation of the Paralysed (CRP)

CRP (☎ 06226 464/5) is an inspired organisation that has been operating since 1975, helping paralysed people develop skills that will enable them to become economically self-sufficient and cope with life in general. The founder, Valerie Taylor, continues to keep the organisation going with money raised from donations. Today, the number of patients is about 80. There is a sizeable Bangladeshi staff whose work is supplemented by volunteers from around the world.

Three of the centre's money-making projects are making crafts for Dhaka handicraft shops, fabricating wheelchairs for the local market and export, and selling milk and eggs. The centre, which is the only one of its kind in the country, is on the north-eastern outskirts of Savar Bazar on the Dhaka-Aricha Highway. Visitors are most welcome at this sprawling complex; various training sessions and workshops are held daily from 8 am to 1 pm and from 3 to 6 pm. The centre is closed Thursday afternoon and Friday. Purchasing a few handicrafts is usually possible.

or silk) cloth weavers, it's a predominantly Hindu town with a friendly atmosphere. Old Hindu homes dress up the place a bit. Unlike Sonargaon, with its Raj-era buildings in ruins, most of them are in good shape and are inhabited by some of the town's wealthiest citizens.

On market days, including Saturday, the main drag is lined with vegetable stands. Behind these are the artisans' shops. Further on sits the town's multi-storey wheeled *Jagannath* (chariot) that has images from Hindu mythology painted on the sides and is paraded down the street during Rath Jatra, the *mela* (festival) held here during the full moon in late June/early July. See Hindu Festivals under the Special Events section in the Facts for the Visitor chapter for more information.

Getting There & Away
Buses to/from Dhaka cost Tk 15 and depart in Dhaka from Gabtali bus station. The trip takes about an hour. Buses between Savar and Dhamrai cost about Tk 5.

MANIKGANJ
☎ 0651

If you have the means to explore further, you could check two rarely visited rajbaris further west in the Manikganj district, roughly 30km beyond the Savar memorial. The first, **Baliati Palace**, is one of the finest rajbaris in Bangladesh. It's also the largest, with a frontage of approximately 125m, an area of about eight hectares and over 200 rooms. Originally owned by descendants of Govinda Ram Saha, the impressive Renaissance frontage, with its attractive array of tall fluted Corinthian columns lining a wide corridor, is reminiscent of a neo-classical English country house.

Further west, on the banks of the Jamuna River, is **Teota Palace**, which dates from the mid-19th century and was built by the zamindars of the Joy Sankar estate. The highlights are the large Hindu temple and the smaller family shrine. The well-preserved temple, built in 1858, resembles the impressive Shiva Temple in Puthia (see the Puthia section in the Rajshahi Division chapter). The nearby family shrine has five semi-circular arched doorways as its entrance.

Getting There & Away
Baliati Palace is about halfway between Savar memorial and Aricha Ghat. Turn left (south) at Kalampur, which is about 8km before (east of) Manikganj on the Dhaka-Aricha Highway. Teota Palace is 30km or so further west at Sivalaya, which is several kilometres south of Aricha Ghat by tarred road and along the Jamuna River.

BHAWAL NATIONAL PARK
Located at Rajendrapur, and only one hour north of Dhaka, Bhawal National Park is far less interesting than Madhupur Forest Reserve (see Around Mymensingh later in this chapter). Its accessibility ensures it is more

frequented, especially as a picnic spot on weekends.

There's angling and boating on the long meandering lake, ponies to ride and pleasant walking through stands of young *sal* trees, but it's no wilderness. Although the area was virgin forest until a few decades ago, the trees you'll see are regrowth, and they're still not very tall or interesting. In a country with so few forests, however, it's a welcome sight. Admission to the park is Tk 15 per person.

Getting There & Away

The park is on the Dhaka-Mymensingh Highway, 38km north of Dhaka and 15km beyond Shandana (shan-dah-NAH), the four-way intersection for Gazipur. Express buses headed for Mymensingh from Mohakhali bus station in Dhaka (see Bus under Getting There & Away in the Dhaka chapter) run right past the well-marked park entrance, which is on your right. The trip takes an hour by car or express bus.

TANGAIL
☎ 0921

Tangail has one of the country's real gems – Atia Mosque. Other than the mosque, however, there is nothing to see. The city itself is singularly unattractive, with incredible traffic jams for its modest size.

If you're plannign on heading north to Madhupur Forest Reserve (45km) and want to camp or stay at the guesthouse there (see Around Mymensingh later in this chapter), Tangail is a necessary stopover. You can only get the required permission (routinely granted) from the director of the District Forestry Office (☎ 3524, 4129; fax 4254) in Tangail; you cannot obtain permission in Madhupur, Mymensingh or even Dhaka. The office is on the 3rd floor of the well-marked Water Development Board building, a block north of the post office, which is on Victoria Rd. Rooms at the Madhupur Forest Guesthouse cost Tk 500.

Atia Mosque

Built in 1609, this fascinating transitional-phase mosque, depicted on the 10 taka note, shows a happy blend of pre-Mughal elements with imperial Mughal architectural features. Beautifully restored to its former glory, it's a four domed mosque with a large hemispherical dome over the square prayer hall and three small domes in front, just behind the entrance. Turrets at all four corners are relieved with plaster panels and give the building a fortress-like appearance.

The exterior walls, which are relieved with plaster panels fused harmoniously with terracotta floral scrolls, are unique. It's as though the entire building was draped with a textured Indian material. Entering through one of the three arched openings in front, you'll see more terracotta work in the closed rectangular verandah area, which leads into the large prayer hall.

This well-known mosque is located 5km south of Tangail on the tarred road to Nagarpur. Coming from Dhaka, you'll have to go completely through town, along Victoria Rd and the crowded Six Annas Market Rd, before coming to the intersection of Delduar and Nagarpur Rds on the southern edge of town. Veer to your right into Nagarpur Rd and continue for around 4km. The turn-off on your left is marked by a sign in Bangla; the mosque is several hundred metres down that dirt road by a pond.

Places to Stay & Eat

Tangail supports only a few hotels. The best is the *Polashbari Hotel (☎ 3154)*, which is a four-storey establishment on Masjid Rd, near the heart of town and east of the market, with a sign in Bangla. It's decent enough, with singles for Tk 70 and doubles from 100 to Tk 120. The rooms are small but they're clean and have fans, reasonably comfortable single mattresses and attached bathrooms.

If it's full, try the two-storey *Residential Hotel* (Bangla sign only) just across the street. It's quite clean and has similarly priced rooms.

For a meal, you could try the friendly *Rasa Hotel* (Bangla sign only), a small clean restaurant across the street from the Polashbari. Meals of rice with chicken, fish or mutton cost Tk 22. You'll find three or

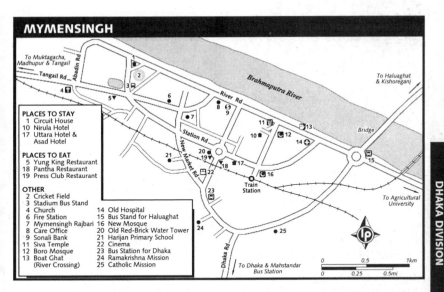

MYMENSINGH

To Muktagacha,
Madhupur & Tangail

Tangail Rd

Abadin Rd

To Haluaghat
& Kishoreganj

Brahmaputra River

River Rd

Station Rd

New Market Rd

Bridge

PLACES TO STAY
1 Circuit House
10 Nirula Hotel
17 Uttara Hotel &
   Asad Hotel

PLACES TO EAT
5 Yung King Restaurant
18 Pantha Restaurant
19 Press Club Restaurant

OTHER
2 Cricket Field
3 Stadium Bus Stand
4 Church
6 Fire Station
7 Mymensingh Rajbari
8 Care Office
9 Sonali Bank
11 Siva Temple
12 Boro Mosque
13 Boat Ghat
   (River Crossing)

14 Old Hospital
15 Bus Stand for Haluaghat
16 New Mosque
20 Old Red-Brick Water Tower
21 Harijan Primary School
22 Cinema
23 Bus Station for Dhaka
24 Ramakrishna Mission
25 Catholic Mission

Train
Station

To Agricultural
University

Dhaka Rd

To Dhaka & Mahstandar
Bus Station

0   0.5   1km
0   0.25   0.5mi

DHAKA DIVISION

four more restaurants serving similar food at the intersection of Dhaka and Mymensingh Rds.

Getting There & Away
Ordinary buses from Tangail to Dhaka, Mymensingh and Jamalpur all cost Tk 30. Chair coaches (which cost Tk 40) exist, but they are harder to find. They all leave from the main bus station on Mymensingh Rd, 2km north of the intersection with Dhaka Rd.

Buses for Tangail depart from Mohakhali bus station in Dhaka.

MYMENSINGH
☎ 091
The outskirts of Mymensingh are slightly deceptive, with many modern buildings housing various colleges and the Kumudini Hospital greeting the newly arrived visitor. The further one goes into the town, the more this original impression diminishes. The scene reverts to the usual chaos of Bangladeshi urban life. Despite this, the town has a comfortable, unhurried atmosphere, with a huge fleet of rickshaws. The local rickshaw owners are in fierce competition to see who has the most colourfully decorated fleet.

Information
The central section of the city, the *sadar*, is hidden by trees and walls from the main road. Some pleasant Raj buildings also adorn the city centre. A minaret, enlarged and modernised, towers over it all. The train station is here, just near a small church. Numerous post-independence structures mixed with the old contribute to the hotchpotch nature of the sadar.

An old channel of the Brahmaputra River separates the city from the jute plantations and mills of the village of Samoganj, 2.5km away. Near the river is a picturesque old Shiva temple, looking much more at home than the nearby huge Boro Mosque.

Mymensingh Rajbari
This well-kept palace, built between 1905 and 1911, is an outstanding building in the middle of the city overlooking the Brahmaputra River. It is now the Women's Teachers' College, but much of the original structure has been left, complete with crystal door handles, marble floors, etched glass door panes and ornate chandeliers.

[Continued on page 146]

ARCHITECTURE

TONY WHEELER

There are more temples and palaces in Bangladesh than most people realise, and hunting for these old structures can be half the fun. In a country with little stone and an extreme tropical climate, buildings don't last long when they aren't maintained or are damaged by iconoclasts of opposing religions. Nevertheless, the government has done a reasonably good job at preserving the major Muslim and Buddhist historical monuments and many of them are quite beautiful.

Pre-Mauryan & Mauryan (4th to 2nd Century BC)

The term bangla is associated with the indigenous architecture of this period. The bamboo-thatched hut with a distinctively curved roof, still seen in villages today, known as a bangla, is the most ancient architectural form known in the country. This word is most likely a derivation of bangala, which means 'the people who live on mounds'. Bang was the name of the tribe and ail means divider. Even then the annual rains and floods of the delta made it essential to live on elevated mounds.

Gupta Buddhist (4th to 8th Century AD)

The traditional design of a stupa for this period consisted of a square plinth surmounted by a circular one and topped by a solid dome which tapered off sharply near the top. The design of the cell which the monks lived in, a three metre square cube, was established during this period. The only variation was the addition of an ornamental pedestal placed in a few cells, like those found in Paharpur.

The great brick temples and monasteries at Mahasthangarh and Comilla were already in existence during this time, however, it is not known if the great Paharpur temple dates from this period.

Architecture seems to have fallen from favour during the Pala period (8th to 12th century) because no important structures, either Buddhist or Hindu, have been discovered from this era.

Sena Dynasty (12th to 13th Century)

During this period Hindu temples were constructed which had a pronounced Indian influence. Perfect specimens are to be found in Puthia, near Rajshahi. Much later, the Indian design of Hindu temples was replaced by purely local architecture. The temple in Kantanagar near Dinajpur is a good example.

The Muslim Period (12th to 17th Century)

From the 12th to 16th century a variety of Muslim styles penetrated the region's architecture.

The Turkistan Khiljis period from the 13th to 15th centuries is noted mainly for its mosques, such as the numerous ones around Bagerhat (near Khulna), including the famous Shait Gumbad Mosque, the Goaldi

Bottom: The Kantanagar Temple is Bangladesh's major *nava-ratha* (nine-towered) shrine.

MIKE WOODCOCK

The Rose Garden rajbari in Dhaka emulates European styling.

Ahsan Manzil rajbari, Dhaka

Dhaka's Baldha Gardens

Muslims praying before the mihrab of the Sitara Mosque in Dhaka

The Armenian Church, Dhaka

A Mughal-era bridge in Sonargaon, Bangladesh's former capital

Dhaka's famous National Assembly Building

Ornate markings on a rajbari door in Sonargaon

Terracotta tiles inside the Atia Mosque, Tangail

The structure of Tangail's Atia Mosque blends pre-Mughal elements with imperial Mughal architecture.

Mosque at Sonargaon, and the Kusumbha Mosque north of Rajshahi. From 1576 to 1757 the Mughals ruled Bengal and made some improvements on the simple design of preceding Muslim architecture although they did not follow the traditional designs employed in India. The best examples are the Lalbagh Forte and the Sat Gumbad Mosque, both in Dhaka.

British Raj Period

The most notable buildings constructed during the British Raj were the Hindu rajbaris, mostly built a century ago, and some public buildings, constructed during the first two decades of the 20th century.

Rajbaris With Hindus dominating economic life under the Raj, it was natural that the most substantial houses were built by them. Rajbaris is the generic name for the palaces built by the big zamindar landowners who often adopted the title of raja (ruler or landlord). European Renaissance styles had become popular in Europe and was emulated by rich Hindu zamindars in Bangladesh.

Although they are essentially very large Georgian or Victorian country houses, the cosmopolitan ideas of their owners were usually expressed in a barrage of neo-Renaissance features, such as Corinthian, Ionic and Doric columns. The architects also adopted domes, which were often decorated with a series of windows and columns. The decoration is often a mixture of various styles. Today, most rajbaris are in ruins, having been vacated at partition, and the more intact examples are now usually neglected government buildings or schools. A few in the rural areas are deserted and you can roam through them at will. Two rajbaris are in excellent condition: Ahsan Manzil in Dhaka, which is now a museum, and Dighapatia Palace in Natore, which is now a government building.

Public Buildings Most of the public structures built during the British era combine Renaissance and Mughal styles. Examples of this combination include Curzon Hall and Salimullah Muslim Hall at Dhaka University and Carmichael College in Rangpur. Their layout is typically Renaissance but the ornamentation is mostly Mughal: horseshoe arches, octagonal minarets, towering pinnacles and ornamented parapets.

Many of the old government Circuit Houses resemble the British bungalow style, with high-pitched corrugated iron roofs and low verandahs. The most notable example is the one in Chittagong (now a museum).

Bottom: The Kusumbha Mosque dates from the Turkistan Khiljis period.

Modern Buildings

The most notable modern building in Bangladesh is the National Assembly building, designed by the American architect Louis Kahn. Typical of Kahn's style, it incorporates bold geometrical patterns. The Baitul Mukarram Mosque's orthodox Islamic architecture is interpreted with very sharp and spare lines. At night its moodily lit wall looming out of the darkness at ithe top of Nawabpur Rd looks a little like a drive-in movie screen.

MIKE WOODCOCK

[Continued from page 143]

An ornamental marble fountain with a classical statue of a semi-nude nymph lies just beyond the arched gateway entrance. Behind the main building is the Jal-Tungi, a small two- storey bathhouse once used as the women's bathing pavilion. Visitors are allowed to roam the grounds, but permission to enter the building must be obtained from the registrar's office in the west wing of the main building.

Harijan Poly
This is a community of members of the Hindu untouchable caste, known today as *Harijans* (meaning 'God's children') or *Dalits* (meaning 'the oppressed'). It's an interesting area to walk through, if only to experience being among Hindus in a predominantly Muslim culture. By following the main track leading into the community to the end and taking a left, you'll come to a small Hindu shrine and see a red metal gate opposite. Behind the gate lies the Harijan Primary School, founded and run by an unflagging Clara Biswas. The school provides basic education and skills to about 400 children between the ages of four and 13 years.

Agricultural University
Situated 2km south of the city centre, the well-known Agricultural University lies on sprawling, landscaped grounds. It is a peaceful environment for roaming around; even a quiet picnic is possible here. There is a bricked trail that starts at a public park near the university and goes for about 800m along the banks of the Brahmaputra River.

Places to Stay
The *Nirula Hotel* is a good budget option. It's a five-storey building in Chowk Bazar, near the Boro Masjid. Clean, though windowless, singles/doubles with attached bathrooms cost Tk 60/80. The problem of smelly bathrooms has been solved by putting them on the balcony.

On Station Rd not far west of the railway station, the *Uttara Hotel* is not very clean and has rooms with attached bathroom for Tk 60/120. The *Asad Hotel,* just around the corner, is similar, with claustrophobic singles for Tk 50 and roomier doubles for Tk 80. Neither of these have signs in English, and both can be quite noisy from the street traffic below.

The government-run *Circuit House*, down a small lane off River Rd, sits on the edge of a spacious green park area where locals practise football and cricket. The government rate is Tk 150 for foreigners. Permission to stay is granted by the district commissioner, whose office is nearby.

Places to Eat
There's a small restaurant at the railway station, supposedly only for 1st-class ticket holders, but no-one checks. Behind the old red-brick water tower off Station Rd, the *Press Club Restaurant* on the 2nd floor serves a set meal of chicken biryani and a variety of snacks. It is open for lunch and dinner from noon to 9 pm.

The *Yung King* Chinese restaurant on Shehora Rd is a little expensive but the food is good and the place is reasonably clean. The *Pantha Restaurant*, two blocks south of Station Rd, offers good local food and is open for lunch and dinner.

Getting There & Away
There are three main roads out of Mymensingh that eventually end up in or near Dhaka. The buses take the shortest route, which goes directly south, passing west of Gazipur and more or less parallel to the railway line. The old Dhaka Highway through Tangail is more circuitous, but offers interesting side trips along the way, including Madhupur Forest. Now that the Bangabandhu Bridge is completed, connections with Rajshahi division are much improved, but the Tangail road is much busier.

Train connections to Rajshahi division involve a three-hour ferry crossing, at least until the rail link over the Banghabandhu Bridge is completed.

Bus As the bus stations are widely scattered, it's simpler to go to one of the private bus depots about 1km south of the city centre. There are frequent departures. From the main bus station at Mahstandar, south-west of the city centre on the Dhaka road, buses leave for Dhaka every 40 minutes from 6 am to 6 pm, and cost Tk 30/55 for local buses/expresses. There are no chair coaches on this route. For buses south-west to Madhupur and Tangail (Tk 30), head for the Stadium bus stand.

The route to Sylhet or Comilla is circuitous and runs south via the ferry crossing at Bhairab Bazar, where buses leave from the old bus station. It's simpler to take a train to Comilla or Akhaura (there's a rail bridge at Bhairab Bazar) or to go via Dhaka.

Train Mymensingh is on the Dhaka-Rangpur route and there are four intercity (IC) trains which operate six days a week (with different days off for each train) in either direction. Departures for Dhaka are at 4.15 and 6.15 am, and 3 and 5.10 pm, and cost Tk 220/60 in 1st class/economy class for the two-hour trip.

AROUND MYMENSINGH

To the north, the hill country of the Indian state of Meghalaya beckons enticingly, but there is no border crossing here. The area may be divided politically, but culturally it shares a common heritage among the tribal hill people – Mandi (known as Garos across the border in India), Hanjongis and Kochis – who are ethnically distinct from the others around them.

Haluaghat

This is the end of the line, so to speak; the metalled road ends here, but a number of potholed dirt roads take off in various directions for smaller villages along the Indian border. Haluaghat, one of the Mandi tribal centres for the area, is a typical bustling town less than two hours north of Mymensingh. It's one big market, with vendors selling a variety of rice, dried peppers, melons in season and so on. Blacksmiths work in small shops next to silversmiths and cloth dealers.

Oxford Mission The Oxford Christian Mission, founded in 1910, welcomes visitors. The mission operates a boys and girls high school, with a combined enrolment of about 1000. If you're interested in getting out further into some of the smaller Mandi villages, such as Askipara, Padre Babu may be able to help with directions or provide one of the children as a guide.

The spacious compound is tucked away off the main street. Many locals don't seem to know where it is; asking directions may prove futile. Basically, follow the main road north through town past some modern-looking buildings (grain storage warehouses) on your left (west). About 50m further is a large mosque; take the narrow road leading west and follow it for about 300m. The red metal gate on your left past the grain warehouses is the entrance to the mission.

Getting There & Away Buses from Mymensingh leave for Haluaghat frequently from the bus stand near the Brahmaputra Bridge. The fare is about Tk 15.

Askipara

This Mandi village is in a beautiful area north of Haluaghat, near the Indian border, and is about as remote as you can get in Bangladesh. The predominantly tribal area is officially 'restricted', requiring permission from the district office in Haluaghat, but you may be able to get around that. A local guide could be your 'host', or you could get lucky and not be checked going into the area. There are no official checkpoints, only an occasional roaming police troupe. At worst, without permission, you would only be turned back.

In Askipara, you might be able to stay with the 'richman' – a well-to-do Mandi who welcomes visitors. There are wonderful walks in the area, and some distance away right on the border is Pani Hata, an Anglican mission surrounded by beautiful teak trees. On the hilltop above the mission is a wonderful view looking out over the plains to the hills of Meghalaya.

There is no public transport to Askipara, but a rickshaw can be hired from Haluaghat for the two-hour trip (Tk 100).

DHAKA DIVISION

Muktagacha

Situated 12km west of Mymensingh on the old Tangail-Dhaka road is the little village of Muktagacha. It is said that sometime during the early 18th century, a local smith named Muktaram presented the eldest son of the region's ruler with a brass *gacha* (lamp) as a sign of loyalty. In recognition of the gift, the son named the town Muktagacha.

The rajbari here draws the occasional visitor, but the town is best known throughout Bangladesh for its famous sweet shop, **Gopal Pali Prosida Monda**, which makes the best *monda* in the country. Two hundred years ago, the Pal family cooked these delicious sweetmeats for the zamindar, who liked them so much that he employed the family. When the landowner's family left during Partition, the Pal family opened up shop and have been in business ever since.

The western palate may not appreciate the subtleties of this famous monda, which, to the uninitiated, tastes a bit like a grainy, sweetened yogurt cake. Still, if you're in town, stop by and try one. The shop, with a lion motif over the door, looks more like a sitting area than a sweet shop, as there is no display area or cash counter.

If arriving from Mymensingh on the Tangail road, take the second road leading north-east (right) into Muktagacha. Go down about three blocks and the shop will be on your right.

Twenty feet past the shop, to the left, are old concrete pillars marking one of the entrances to the **Muktagacha Rajbari**. The rajbari is definitely worth seeing if you're heading to Madhupur Forest. This palace, dating back to the early-to-middle 19th century, is now mostly in ruins. It includes several different blocks and spreads over ten acres. It is a very special estate, even in disrepair, bedecked with Corinthian columns, high parapets and floral scrolls in plaster. The Rajeswari Temple and the stone temple, believed to be dedicated to Shiva, are two of the finer temples within the complex.

Madhupur Forest Reserve

Some 50km south-west of Mymensingh on the road to Tangail, Madhupur (MODE-uh-

The Rubber Tree Fiasco

Some years ago, the forestry department received a grant to help farmers in the Madhupur forest area supplement their incomes by planting rubber trees. The intention was for farmers to plant trees wherever the land was already cleared, thus filling in open patches and easing the pressure to cut down existing forests.

But the farmers began clearing new patches in the forest, claiming them as old clearings and requesting assistance. Initially, forestry officials turned a blind eye to this. When the facts were uncovered, the assistance was terminated. As you go through forested areas you may see rows of rubber trees planted during that time.

poor) town is nothing special, but the surrounding area is definitely unique. The biggest attraction is Madhupur Forest Reserve, a tract of land roughly 50 sq km just north-east of town. About 8km from Madhupur town, on the highway to Mymensingh, you'll arrive at the forest's south-western edge. It continues for around 8km along both sides of the highway, but the principal section lies to the north. There are some secluded spots that are perfect for camping.

This is the last remnant in Bangladesh of the moist deciduous old-growth forest which at one time extended for hundreds of kilometres across Dhaka division. Unfortunately, government conservation efforts have been ineffective and there has been considerable felling in the area.

Exploring the forest will likely turn up some rhesus monkeys and golden-coloured capped langurs, which look like bushy-tailed monkeys. There are also three species of civets here. This area was also once famous for tigers.

Madhupur is also very good for birdwatching. There are numerous species, but serious bird-watchers will be most interested in spotting the dusky owl, the brown fish owl, the spotted eagle owl and the famous brown wood owl, which is a speciality of the forest. This time of year is also more favourable for hiking when the lower swampy areas dry up after the monsoon.

Places to Stay In addition to camping, you can stay at the Forestry Guesthouse in the forest. The setting is lovely. Visitors use *Chuniya Cottage*. It has three bedrooms, common areas and a caretaker. The other guesthouse appears to be exclusively used by forestry personnel. Camping, which is only allowed in the area of the forest reserve, may be less than peaceful on weekends. Potable water is available.

Permission to camp or stay at Chuniya Cottage is obtained from the District Forestry Office in Tangail (see the earlier Tangail section for more information). The cost is Tk 500 for a room, and although it's possible that the caretaker might provide food with advance warning, you should bring your own to be on the safe side.

Getting There & Away Madhupur is about halfway between Mymensingh and Tangail. There are frequent buses (Tk 80) between the two. By bus or car, it takes about 45 minutes from Mymensingh, and a bit longer from Tangail. From town, the entrance is about 15km to the north-east along the Mymensingh Highway. Take a tempo or hop on any bus heading for Mymensingh.

The main entrance to the forest is on the northern side of the Mymensingh-Madhupur road at the eastern end of the forest, just before it abruptly ends and paddy fields begin. At the entrance you'll find the main forestry headquarters; those driving must register their vehicles here. Chuniya Cottage and the camping area are about 6km up the road on your right.

Dhanbari Nawab Palace

Some 15km north of the town of Madhupur, is the old Dhanbari Nawab Palace, which is well worth visiting. It was originally owned by Dhanwar Khan, a Hindu, but it fell into the hands of Muslims, which is why it has, most unusually, a mosque. Within the complex there is also a main palace and a large *kutchery* building (clerks' office), in poor-to-fair condition, but still intact.

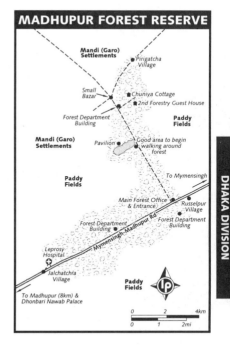

MADHUPUR FOREST RESERVE

The main building has an impressive 65m-long facade with an arched entrance and 10 pairs of Corinthian columns. What's most impressive about the long kutchery nearby is the very fanciful *do-chala*, or hut-shaped pavilion, on top.

The interior of the elegant three-domed mosque, which was renovated in 1901, is marvellous – the inner walls are covered from floor to ceiling with mural decorations made from broken china pieces.

To get here from the town of Madhupur, take the tarred road north towards Jamalpur and after about 15km you'll see the palace on your right, just off the highway.

Gouripur Rajbari

About 18km east of Mymensingh, across the Brahmaputra River and a few kilometres off the road to Kishoreganj, is the town of Gouripur. Here the Gouripur Palace, built in the 19th century, serves as the headquarters of the *upazila* (local-level government) of the

Mandi Settlements

Far into the Madhupur Forest, where there are fewer trees, are some small Mandi settlements. The atmosphere of these enclaves is quite distinct from that of Muslim villages. A matrilineal group, the Mandi, or Garo as they are commonly called by outsiders, may have originally migrated from Myanmar (Burma). They are peaceful and accustomed to living in a spacious forest. Primarily Christians or animists, they seem to be more at ease with foreigners than your average Bangladeshi.

Unfortunately for the Mandi, neighbouring Bengalis are slowly encroaching on their lands and cutting down their forests. Accustomed to having their own space, the Mandi, although the original inhabitants of this region, are selling off their lands and heading to more remote areas further north. The rate of deforestation is high and poorly paid forestry officials are turning a blind eye to the destruction. If something doesn't change, this reserve is doomed.

Mymensingh district. This palace was the seat of the famous Gouripur zamindars. The scattered remains of palaces are still visible amidst the overgrown jungle thickets.

Egarasindur

Further south along the Mymensingh-Kishoreganj route, some 15km beyond (south of) Kishoreganj on the Narayanganj fork, lies the small town of Pakundia. Here a side road toward the river leads to the village of Egarasindur, about 3km away. The village has two lovely old mosques that are well worth checking out.

The **Sadi Mosque** of 1652 is a grand building with a large dome towering over two smaller ones. The **Shah Mohammed Mosque** of 1680 has a single dome and one wall sparsely relieved with terracotta panels of geometric and floral patterns. It is fronted by a brick structure which is considered to be the real attraction. It resembles a common reed hut and served as a *dachala*, or gatehouse.

FARIDPUR
☎ 0631

Though part of Dhaka division, Faridpur is geographically more a part of the Khulna division, south of the Padma River. There are a couple of Hindu temples in Faridpur district, but the only reason you're likely to pass through this backwater town is if you're attempting to travel between Barisal and the western part of Khulna division.

Still, it's a pretty place, with leafy suburbs and picturesque old ponds (or 'tanks') scattered about.

There's a Ramakrishna Mission on the north-west outskirts, which may have information on Hindu sights and festivals.

Places to Stay & Eat

Hotel Luxury, near the bus stand, is a so-so place with singles/doubles with attached bathrooms for Tk 50/90.

The best place to eat is the *Peking Restaurant*, which is some way from the town centre (a pleasant Tk 5 rickshaw ride), though the food is ordinary.

Getting There & Away

If you're headed east to Dhaka, take a bus to Rajbari (Tk 10) and Goalundo Ghat (Daulatdia Ghat) for the river crossing to Aricha. Buses south to Barisal cost around Tk 45.

AROUND FARIDPUR

Located in the village of Khalia, the **Raja Ram Temple** is an early-18th-century *mandir* (Hindu temple) built in the form of the Jagannath Temple in Puthia (see the Puthia section in the Rajshahi Division chapter).

In Ujani Gopalpur, the 17th-century **Math Shrine** is a fine example of *chauchala* hut design, which is characterised by a corniced brick hut-shaped roof. The design, which imitates bamboo rafters and a thatched roof, is purely decorative.

Khulna Division

Situated in the south-west of the country, half of Khulna division is marshland or dense jungle and a haven for wildlife.

Khulna borders the state of Bangla (West Bengal) in India. In the north, the Padma (Ganges) River separates it from Rajshahi division, while Barisal division forms the eastern boundary.

The dense jungles and numerous rivers formed natural barriers to any invasion from the west or east. Even after its late settlement Khulna division remained relatively neglected by the Mughals, and it was not until the arrival of the British that it started to be developed. The people of Khulna division are said to speak the purest form on Bangla in the country.

Nowadays the region remains the centre of the declining jute industry, once the backbone of the economy, while the fish and shrimp processing industry is thriving. The city of Khulna is the country's third biggest urban centre, and products from the nearby Khulna Export Processing Zone are shipped out from the country's second international port at Mongla.

In the south of Khulna division are the Sundarbans ('beautiful forest'), a huge, almost untouched tract of waterlogged jungle. Many travellers count a boat trip through the waterways of the Sundarbans as a highlight of their visit to Bangladesh. Between Khulna city and Barisal, the monuments and mosques scattered around Bagerhat make another worthwhile excursion.

JESSORE
☎ 0421

If you've crossed from India at the Benapole border, you'll arrive almost immediately at Jessore (JOSH-or) on your way to Dhaka, Khulna or points north. The Bhairab River, which runs through the heart of town, and the city's impressive court building, which dates from the British Raj, add charm to this otherwise fairly ordinary city. Once you're beyond the congested central area, the town,

- **The Sundarbans** – vast watery jungle, home to the royal Bengal tiger; only accessible by boat
- **Bagerhat** – historic Islamic monuments and shrines in a lush rural setting
- **Tagore Lodge** – old home of Nobel laureate Rabrindranath Tagore, on the bank of the Padma River near Kushtia

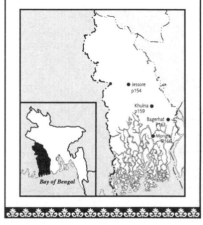

which has many shady streets, takes on a more tranquil air. Khulna division's only airport with commercial flights lies west of the city in the military cantonment.

Of the country's modern cities, including Khulna, Dhaka and Sylhet, Jessore is the oldest. As a district headquarters outreach from Kolkata (Calcutta), it was far more prominent than Khulna during the Raj era, and the huge court here handled cases from far and wide. There is still a train line to Kolkata but it is not used. Jessore Zilla School is the country's oldest high school, built around 1860.

Jessore was the scene of the decisive conflict of the 1971 Liberation War. The Jessore cantonment had been one of the Pakistani army's most important strongholds, and

KHULNA DIVISION

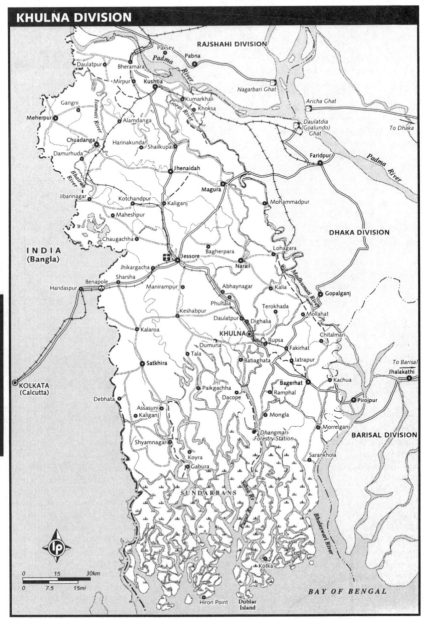

KHULNA DIVISION

RAJSHAHI DIVISION

Padma River

Paksey
Pabna
Daulatpur
Bheramara
Mirpur
Kushtia
Nagarbari Ghat
Aricha Ghat
Gangni
Kumarkhali
Khoksa
Meherpur
Alamdanga
Daulatdia
(Goalundo)
Ghat
To Dhaka
Chuadanga
Harinakunda
Shailkupa
Damurhuda
Faridpur
Padma River
Jhenaidah
Jibannagar
Magura
Kotchandpur
Kaliganj
Mohammadpur
Maheshpur
DHAKA DIVISION
Chaugachha
INDIA
(Bangla)
Bagherpara
Lohagara
Jessore
Jhikargacha
Narail
Sharsha
Benapole
Manirampur
Abhaynagar
Kalia
Haridaspur
Gopalganj
Phultala
Terokhada
Keshabpur
Daulatpur
Dighalia
Mollahat
Kalaroa
KHULNA
Rupsa
Chitalman
Dumuria
Fakirhat
Tala
Batiaghata
Jatrapur
To Barisal
Jhalakathi
Satkhira
Bagerhat
Kachua
KOLKATA
(Calcutta)
Debhata
Paikgachha
Ramphal
Pirojpur
Assasuni
Dacope
Kaliganj
Mongla
Morrelganj
Shyamnagar
Dhangmari
Forestry Station
BARISAL DIVISION
Koyra
Gabura
Sarankhola
SUNDARBANS
Kotka
BAY OF BENGAL
Hiron Point
Dublar
Island

Ismail River
Gorai River
Bhairab River
Madhumati River
Bhadrabati River

0   15   30km
0   7.5   15mi

after India declared war on 3 December a huge battle was expected here. In fact the Pakistani army at Jessore gave up on 7 December with little resistance, and the war was over less than 10 days later.

The town doesn't have much to offer visitors; if nothing else it's a very typical Bangladeshi country town.

Orientation

To the north, the Bhairab River meanders through town, and the city's principal bazar begins just east of the intersection. A further 1.5km along Municipal Rd is the Moniher Cinema intersection, where the bus stations are located. Between these intersections is where you'll find most hotels, restaurants and banks. The GMG Airlines office is on Rail Rd where it intersects with Municipal Rd.

Biman and most of the development organisations, on the other hand, are at the leafier western end of town. One NGO in this part of town is Banchte Shekha, which has a guesthouse.

There is no tourist information office in Jessore. The staff of Banchte Shekha and the managers of the Mid-Town and Magpie hotels may be able to give information.

Places to Stay – Budget

Most hotels are in the centre of town, east of High Court Morh, and further east around Moniher Cinema intersection. One of the best for the money is *Hotel Al-Hera* (no sign in English), a two-storey establishment on K'Purti Rd. It has reasonably clean and spacious singles/doubles with fans, mosquito nets and common bathrooms for Tk 40/60 (Tk 60/100 with attached bathrooms). It's under pious (but friendly) Muslim management who may not accept unmarried women.

Another possibility is *Hotel Nayan* (☎ 6535), which is two blocks away on the same street and well marked in English. It's overpriced at Tk 100/170 for small rooms with attached bathrooms, fans and mosquito nets (Tk 70 for tiny singles with common bathrooms), but it's clean enough.

You might also check out *Hotel Rena,* nearby on Bazar Rd, close to the Morh. It's

priced midway between the Al-Hera and the Nayan, but is a better deal than the Nayan.

Hotel Taj Mahal (☎ 65320), on RN Rd, 100m or so west of the busy intersection with Dhaka-Kushtia Rd, is dirt cheap. Rooms with common bathrooms cost Tk 50/80. From the outside this place appears to be a complete dump, but the rooms, which are reasonably clean and have windows, are marginally better than you'd expect.

About 400m east along RN Road is the large blue *Hotel Coco (☎ 73551).* Rooms with common bathroom cost Tk 60/100, or Tk 80/150 with attached bathroom. The rooms are basic but decent enough, with overhead fan and mosquito net. The manager speaks English and is friendly.

The six-storey *Hotel Mid-Town (☎ 6501),* just off Chowrasta Morh, has friendly staff – the manager seems rather dour at first but is actually quite helpful. Rooms are a little more expensive than most of the cheapies in town but they are also relatively bright and roomy with lots of windows. Singles cost Tk 85, doubles Tk 120 and triples Tk 145 (all with bathrooms).

Places to Stay – Mid-Range & Top End

The *Hotel Magpie (☎ 72162),* on High Court Morh, is a particularly unsightly multistorey jumble of concrete but it is also the town's only top-end hotel, and it has private parking. Thankfully the rooms are nicer than the exterior. Ordinary rooms cost Tk 200/400, while air-con rooms with carpet and satellite TV cost Tk 400/800. There's also an air-con restaurant here.

Banchte Shekha (BACH-tah SHAY-kah) *(☎ 6436),* on Airport Rd (just east of the bypass road to Benapole), is a good place to stay, especially for women. Coming from the airport you'll pass the centre's sign on your left, 150m after crossing Kushtia Rd. One of the country's largest PVOs (private voluntary organisations), it offers destitute women a wide range of training programs aimed at helping to empower them socially and economically. The staff here are exceedingly friendly, which makes staying here all the nicer.

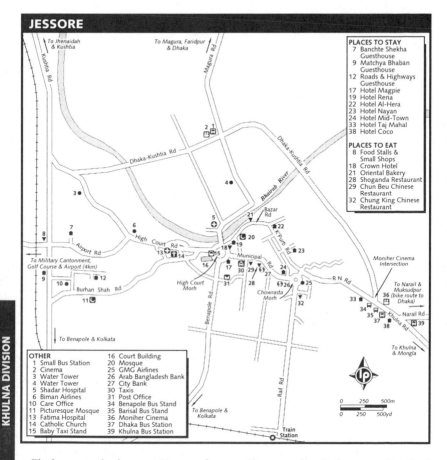

JESSORE

To Jhenaidah & Kushtia
To Magura, Faridpur & Dhaka

Kushtia Rd
Magura Rd

Dhaka-Kushtia Rd

Dhaka-Kushtia Rd

Bhairab River

Airport Rd

To Military Cantonment, Golf Course & Airport (4km)

High Court Rd

Bazar Rd

Municipal Rd

High Court Morh

Burhan Shah Rd

Benapole Rd

To Benapole & Kolkata

Chowrasta Morh

R N Rd

Moniher Cinema Intersection

To Narail & Muksudpur (bike route to Dhaka)

Narail Rd

Khulna Rd

To Khulna & Mongla

Rail Rd

To Benapole & Kolkata

Train Station

PLACES TO STAY
7 Banchte Shekha Guesthouse
9 Matchya Bhaban Guesthouse
12 Roads & Highways Guesthouse
17 Hotel Magpie
19 Hotel Rena
22 Hotel Al-Hera
23 Hotel Nayan
24 Hotel Mid-Town
33 Hotel Taj Mahal
38 Hotel Coco

PLACES TO EAT
8 Food Stalls & Small Shops
18 Crown Hotel
21 Oriental Bakery
28 Shoganda Restaurant
29 Chun Beu Chinese Restaurant
32 Chung King Chinese Restaurant

OTHER
1 Small Bus Station
2 Cinema
3 Water Tower
4 Water Tower
5 Shadar Hospital
6 Biman Airlines
10 Care Office
11 Picturesque Mosque
13 Fatima Hospital
14 Catholic Church
15 Baby Taxi Stand
16 Court Building
20 Mosque
25 GMG Airlines
26 Arab Bangladesh Bank
27 City Bank
30 Taxis
31 Post Office
34 Benapole Bus Stand
35 Barisal Bus Stand
36 Moniher Cinema
37 Dhaka Bus Station
39 Khulna Bus Station

0   250   500m
0   250   500yd

KHULNA DIVISION

The huge complex has over 70 rooms for housing trainees and visitors. To stay in a four-bed dormitory room costs Tk 60, or there are double rooms for Tk 250 (Tk 500 with air-con). The double rooms are spotless and well lit, with fans and carpets, and the bathrooms have hot-water showers. Reservations are advisable but if you just show up, chances are that you'll get a room, provided there's space. If you let them know in advance, you can join in their family-style meals – typically fried fish, rice and dhal (watery lentils) for Tk 50 per day. There's also food at the busy intersection nearby.

The tranquil, single-storey ***Roads & Highways Guesthouse*** (☎ 6632) is about 1km away from Banchte Shekha, 300m from the Care office on an unmarked, paved back road. There are three spacious guest rooms, two with twin beds and a third with a single large bed and air-con for Tk 150. Getting a room is not difficult provided you call ahead, and you can eat here if you order well in advance.

The ***Matchya Bhaban Guesthouse*** (☎ 5752), on the busy bypass road to Benapole, belongs to the Fisheries Department, and has one single and three double rooms in a pleasant modern building away from the main administrative offices (Tk 200/400). The compound has private parking. Since accommodation is limited, it's a good idea to call in advance.

Places to Eat

Two inexpensive places in the centre serving typical Bangladeshi food are the clean *Crown Hotel*, on Bazar Rd just east of High Court Morh, and the *Shoganda Restaurant* (no English sign) on Municipal Rd, 1½ blocks east of the same circle. At the Crown you can get a Coke, two portions of dhal, and one portion each of spinach, rice and salad for around Tk 25. Make sure your order is clear – the staff have a habit of bringing dishes not ordered. For a good range of biscuits and cakes, try the *Oriental Bakery* on Bazar Rd, a block beyond the Crown Hotel.

The two best restaurants are both Chinese and near the centre of town – the *Chun Beu Chinese Restaurant* (☎ 6141), on Municipal Rd, and *Chung King Chinese Restaurant* (☎ 4057), several blocks further east on Rail Rd. The attractive air-con Chun Beu, which is poorly signed, is on the 2nd floor of a building at an intersection. Open every day from 11 am to 4 pm and 6 to 11 pm, this friendly establishment offers a wide range of dishes for around Tk 80 to Tk 100, including Chinese chop suey, Mandarin fish and chicken fried rice. The colourfully painted two-storey Chung King is hard to miss and similar in most respects.

Getting There & Away

Air Biman, GMG and Air Parabat each have several daily flights to and from Dhaka. The fare is Tk 1075 on Biman and Tk 1470 on GMG. Biman (☎ 5023) has an office in town on the road leading to the airport and at the airport (☎ 5026). GMG (☎ 73280) has an office on the corner of Rail Rd and Chowrasta Morh. Air Parabat only seems to have an office at the airport (☎ 4044, 5827).

Bus There are buses to Dhaka all day, from around 6 am to 10.30 pm. Several companies including Druti Paribahan have offices

around the Dhaka bus station; they all cost around Tk 170 for ordinary coaches, or Tk 280 for air-con buses. The trip often takes about seven hours (around 2½ hours to the ferry crossing), but sometimes up to 10 hours if there's a long wait for the ferry across the Padma River. In Dhaka, buses for Jessore leave from Gabtali bus station.

Buses for Khulna (Tk 20 for chair coach and Tk 15 for ordinary) leave from the same general area about every 10 minutes and take 90 minutes.

Minibuses for Benapole (Tk 15) also leave periodically from 6 am. The trip takes one to 1½ hours. There are also cheaper local buses to Benapole (Tk 7), leaving from the western outskirts of Jessore, but by the time your rickshaw has found the right place you'll have paid almost as much as you would have if you had taken a faster and more comfortable minibus. If you're headed to Kolkata, count on about six hours for the entire trip.

Buses for Barisal cost Tk 110 (Tk 160 for a chair coach) and depart from Moniher Cinema intersection between 6 am and 12.15 pm. Because of the numerous ferry crossings involved, the trip takes at least eight hours. There are also several buses a day to Rajshahi (Tk 85) and Bogra (Tk 105). These buses usually depart in the morning and in the early afternoon.

Train The train station (☎ 5019) is 2km south of the central area at the end of Rail Rd. The express to Rajshahi departs at 8.15 am and costs Tk 215/56 in 1st class/sulob (upper 2nd class with reserved seating). It's usually quicker, however, to take the next train to Ishurdi (five daily) and change trains there. Most trains for Ishurdi (Tk 170/60 in 1st class/sulob) continue on to Saidpur (Tk 370/110); the express train, which departs from Jessore at 9.40 am and 10.15 pm, is the best.

It's simpler to travel by bus on the short journey to Khulna, although this would probably be a good opportunity for the experience of taking a train in Bangladesh, as there are six departures daily. The trip takes just 1½ hours and costs Tk 85/35 in 1st class/sulob.

There are two local trains daily to Bena-pole, at 8.35 am and 3.45 pm, for Tk 15.

AROUND JESSORE
Baro Bazar Mosque
This old pre-Mughal mosque, dating from the 15th or early 16th century, is a good example of a single-domed mosque following the tra-ditional Khan Jahan style, with thick walls, arched doorways, a square shape, sparse ex-terior embellishment and a low semicircular dome. Not well-known by the locals, it's about 18km north-east of Jessore on the Jes-sore-Magura highway at Baro Bazar.

Sonabaria Temple
The Sonabaria Shyam Sundar Temple, built in 1767, 15 years after the magnificent Kan-tanagar Temple of Dinajpur, is of the same *nava-ratna* (nine-towered) style. Like Kan-tanagar, it's a square structure, rising in three diminishing storeys, and it is exten-sively decorated with terracotta art. It's only about half the size of Kantanagar, however, and not as beautiful or well preserved.

As the crow flies, it's about 30km south-west of Jessore, near the Indian border. To get there from Jessore, take the road west towards Benapole for 25km to the tiny vil-lage of Navaron (about two-thirds the dis-tance to Benapole), where you'll find a country road heading south. It's about 15km along that road.

BENAPOLE
Benapole (also spelt Benapol) is the border town situated on the overland route from Kolkata. The border officials see quite a few travellers crossing here and things are relatively efficient. Travellers have reported being surprised by the friendliness of Bangladeshi border officials after dealing with their Indian counterparts, but watch out for minor rip-offs when changing money. The town itself is as ugly as they come – a single road, 2km long, lined from end to end with huge trucks waiting to cross the border. If you arrived in Bangladesh by air, you should obtain a 'road transit permit' in Dhaka to allow you to cross the border. Although travellers have succeeded in get-ting across without one, it's really not worth the risk.

Crossing the Border
The border is officially open between 7 am and 8 pm but the form can take hours to fill in, so get there early.

Changing Money There are 'authorised' moneychangers on the Indian side. If you have taka, don't flash wads because the rule about not bringing in more than Tk 100 is given at least lip service. Currency dec-laration forms are no longer used in Bangladesh.

If you're departing from Bangladesh, sell your excess taka to the moneychangers be-fore crossing. Rates are not the best, so don't try to change large amounts. As for changing other currencies into Indian ru-pees, you'll do better waiting to change your money on the Indian side where you'll get better rates.

Entering & Exiting Be sure to arrive at the border in plenty of time. With so many people passing through here, the formalities can easily take up to two hours. Travelling from the railway station at Bangaon in India to the border costs Rs 30 by baby taxi. Due to the amount of traffic it may be easier to take a rickshaw (Rs 15 per person) – the trip takes about 30 minutes.

After the immigration checkpoint, don't take the first bus on the right for Jessore (Tk 6) unless you want to be crammed in with all the luggage. Instead, go to the bus stand, which is 1km away (Tk 6 by rickshaw), and get a minibus (Tk 12); these are faster and cleaner, and well worth the extra hike and cost. Even if you have reserved a seat, grab it immediately as it is very difficult to evict local passengers once they have settled in your seat. There are minibuses departing for Jessore every 20 minutes, which is the major transit point for Dhaka, Khulna and points north.

Leaving Bangladesh for the Indian bor-der (Haridaspur), procedures are the re-verse. From Bangaon (5km) you can take the local train to Kolkata; the trip takes

2½ hours to Sealdah train station and costs Rs 15 (2nd class only).

Places to Stay & Eat

Benapole supports only one small *residential hotel*. Heading towards India, you'll find it on your right along the main drag, not far from the centre of town. This grubby hovel is unmarked and has no name, so you'll have to ask for directions. The single-storey building consists of only several windowless bunk rooms, each with five or six beds crammed one against the other. The cost is about Tk 20 per bed or about Tk 60 for the entire room. The beds are a bit hard but the room has a fan and the common bathroom is reasonably clean, including the shower. A woman travelling with a man can stay here, possibly single women travellers as well. Regardless, you're far better off staying the night in nearby Jessore, where you can still get to the border when it opens at 7 am by taking the first morning bus from Jessore.

There's one decent restaurant in Benapole, a well-marked *Chinese Restaurant* on the same side of the road as the hotel, several hundred metres further east. It has air-con, cold drinks and an extensive menu; a meal costs Tk 80 or so. You'll also find some small ordinary *restaurants* along the road where you can get a meal for Tk 25 or so.

Getting There & Away

Coming from Jessore, ask for both 'Benapole' and 'the border' to avoid any possible confusion. It's worth waiting for one of the minibuses that ply between Benapole and Jessore; the fare is Tk 12 and the trip takes one hour, sometimes 1½ hours. They take the main road, use the main bus station area in Jessore (Moniher Cinema intersection), and pass some old mosques and Hindu temples on the way. Local buses are cheaper (Tk 6), slower and crowded, and they depart and arrive in Jessore on the western edge of town instead of the main bus station area.

KUSHTIA

☎ 071

Kushtia, just south of Rajshahi division, is a poor, neglected town with a long, straight main street, Nawab Sirajuddula Rd. The only 'sights' are a lively Hindu Jagganath temple on Nawab Sirajuddula Rd and Tagore Lodge outside of town. This is one of the poorest areas in the country, and to rub salt into the wounds the deep tube wells in the area are affected by high arsenic levels.

Tagore Lodge

Perched on the south bank of the powerful Padma River, this picturesque bungalow was built in the mid-19th century as an ancestral home of the world-famous Bengali poet, Rabindranath Tagore. From 1880 Tagore lived here for over 10 years, composing some of his immortal poems, songs and short stories. He returned in 1912 for several years, translating his works into English and earning the Nobel Prize (1913) in the process (see the Literature section under Arts in the Facts about Bangladesh chapter).

One of the nicest features of this well-maintained estate is the tranquil rural surrounding. The 15-room two-storey building itself is quite elegant, with open terraces on the ground floor covered partially with a sloping tiled roof, and a central portion covered by a pitched roof with gables.

The estate is located outside Shelaidaha (near the Padma River), 8km east of Kushtia, across the Gorai River.

Shailkupa Mosque

Extensively renovated, this six-domed mosque, which dates from the late 15th or early 16th century, is one of the better preserved examples of architecture from the pre-Mughal period in Bangladesh. The building is largely unadorned, with plain exterior walls and entrances. The main entrance with three arched doorways, now heavily covered with plaster, was originally decorated with terracotta panels.

It's located on the eastern edge of the town of Shailkupa, about 28km south-east of Kushtia and 16km north-east of Jhenaidah.

Places to Stay & Eat

The *Hotel Diamond* has grim doubles with common bathrooms for around Tk 50. The old *Azmiree Hotel* (AJ-mee-ree) (☎ 3012), at

Court Para near Kushtia Halt, is better. It has big, dim, damp-ravaged singles with common bathrooms for about Tk 60, and doubles with attached bathroom for Tk 100. The shutters and bars look as though they could withstand a siege. Another possibility is the *Hotel Jubilee* (☎ *3318)* on the main drag, which has singles/doubles for Tk 60/120.

The best place to stay is unquestionably the large attractive old *Circuit House* in the southern part of town, on the Jessore road. It has spacious well-maintained rooms with twin beds, fans and attached bathrooms for Tk 150. Usually the manager will call the district commissioner and get permission for you to stay, but it's worth making yourself presentable for the district commissioner in case you have to meet him in person. It serves good meals also and, as with most circuit houses, the cost is quite cheap – around Tk 150 per person.

There are the usual local eating places, and two Chinese restaurants. The best of the two is the *Karamai,* on the main street; the *Tai Shun,* in a compound off the main road, is a bit overpriced.

Getting There & Away

Bus Those travelling north must cross the Padma by ferry between Bheramara and Paksey. The ferry takes only 20 minutes and runs next to Harding Bridge, the longest railway bridge in Bangladesh. To Ishurdi, a local bus costs about Tk 15. There are a few direct buses to Jessore but you'll probably have to change at Jhenaidah, which is to the south, about halfway. If you're headed back to Dhaka, you'll pass through Jhenaidah and Faridpur en route to Daulatdia Ghat for the crossing to Aricha. The road between Jhenaidah and Faridpur is one of the most well-maintained roads in the country.

KHULNA
☎ 041
The British used the ancient port of Chittagong and developed Kolkata into a great city port, leaving Khulna to its own devices.

Today, Chittagong port, unable to handle all of the trade that has come its way, and notoriously prone to industrial unrest, has given Khulna and nearby Mongla a considerable amount of business. Modernisation of these ports has attracted industry and commercial development to Khulna, which is now the country's third-largest city. The city council seems to be doing a reasonable job, and the city is quite clean and orderly compared to Dhaka.

Despite the development of Khulna as a port, the Rupsa River is not deep enough to handle ocean-going vessels. Mongla, 40km to the south, has been developed as the modern port for Khulna.

Khulna is the major starting point for trips to the Sundarbans, which starts about 50km to the south. Otherwise the city isn't terribly interesting.

Orientation & Information

Most hotels and restaurants are located in the city's heart. Khan A Sabar Rd, also known as Jessore Rd, is the main drag through the city, and KDA Ave is the major thoroughfare on the western side. The main bus station is 2km north-west of the city centre and the new GPO is similarly a long way north along Khan A Sabar Rd. The old GPO and the telephone and telegraph offices, however, still operate in the city centre, just past Hadis Park. If you take the narrow lane that follows the river south from the BIWTC office (and the train station just opposite) near the city centre, you'll pass through a bustling bazar.

Changing money in Khulna can be a problem. The best place is probably at ANZ Grindlays Bank in KDA Ave, near Shiv Bari Circle, but it charges Tk 300 per transaction. Al Baraka Bank may be better for changing travellers cheques in US dollars; the transaction fee is Tk 110 compared to UK£10 for pound sterling travellers cheques.

For general tourist information and arranging car rentals (and trips to the Sundarbans), the best place is the Hotel Royal International, but only if you have a bit of money to spend because it's likely to try to sell you an expensive package tour. Reception staff speak English well, and the manager is used to dealing with foreign aid-organisation visitors. Travellers on the

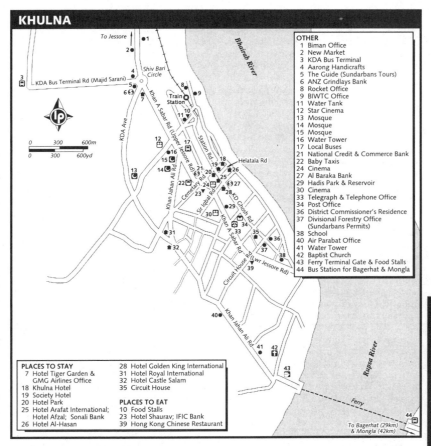

KHULNA

To Jessore

Bhairab River

KDA Bus Terminal Rd (Majid Sarani)

Shiv Bari Circle

Train Station

KDA Ave

Khan A Sabar Rd (Upper Jessore Rd)

Station Rd

Helatala Rd

Khan Jahan Ali Rd

Cemetery Rd

Sir Iqbal Rd

KD Ghosh Rd

Khan A Sabar Rd (Lwr Jessore Rd)

Circuit House Rd

Khan Jahan Ali Rd

Rupsa River

Ferry

To Bagerhat (29km) & Mongla (42km)

0   300   600m
0   300   600yd

OTHER
1 Biman Office
2 New Market
3 KDA Bus Terminal
4 Aarong Handicrafts
5 The Guide (Sundarbans Tours)
6 ANZ Grindlays Bank
8 Rocket Office
9 BIWTC Office
11 Water Tank
12 Star Cinema
13 Mosque
14 Mosque
15 Mosque
16 Water Tower
17 Local Buses
21 National Credit & Commerce Bank
22 Baby Taxis
24 Cinema
27 Al Baraka Bank
29 Hadis Park & Reservoir
30 Cinema
33 Telegraph & Telephone Office
34 Post Office
36 District Commissioner's Residence
37 Divisional Forestry Office
   (Sundarbans Permits)
38 School
40 Air Parabat Office
41 Water Tower
42 Baptist Church
43 Ferry Terminal Gate & Food Stalls
44 Bus Station for Bagerhat & Mongla

PLACES TO STAY
7 Hotel Tiger Garden &
   GMG Airlines Office
18 Khulna Hotel
19 Society Hotel
20 Hotel Park
25 Hotel Arafat International;
   Hotel Afzal; Sonali Bank
26 Hotel Al-Hasan

28 Hotel Golden King International
31 Hotel Royal International
32 Hotel Castle Salam
35 Circuit House

PLACES TO EAT
10 Food Stalls
23 Hotel Shaurav; IFIC Bank
39 Hong Kong Chinese Restaurant

cheap might do better talking with the tour agency at the Hotel Park.

Travel Permits to the Sundarbans
The Divisional Forestry Office (☎ 720665, 721173), which issues permits to the Sundarbans, is on KD Ghosh Rd (on the corner of Circuit House Rd), is open from 10 am to 5 pm Saturday to Thursday. Staff are helpful but have little information about the Sundarbans. Permits are issued on the spot and cost Tk 4 per person per day. The magic words to write on the application are: 'I will avail the Port Authority vessel' (to get to Hiron Point

and back) – you risk not getting a permit otherwise. For overnight trips into the Sundarbans guides are compulsory and cost Tk 50 a day. Budget travellers arranging one-day trips from Mongla might not need a permit, as long as they avoid forestry stations.

For more information on arranging trips to the Sundarbans and accommodation, see the Sundarbans section later in this chapter.

Places to Stay – Budget
Cheap hotels are concentrated in the heart of the city in an area 1km south of the train station. Most are well marked in English.

One of the best places for the price is the *Society Hotel* (☎ 720995) on Helatala Rd; it has singles/doubles with attached bathrooms for Tk 50/80. Singles are tiny, but doubles are a bit more spacious and reasonably clean, with fans and mosquito nets. The hotel is a bit aged but it is well managed.

The *Khulna Hotel* (☎ 724359) is 30m away on the same alley. Fairly clean rooms with attached bathrooms cost Tk 40/80 (slightly less with common bathrooms).

A block south on Sir Iqbal Rd you'll find the friendly *Hotel Afzal* (☎ 720941), which has rooms with common bathrooms for Tk 60/100. The stairs are incredibly narrow and the rooms are rather dark, but the jollity of the staff may help make up for it.

Places to Stay – Mid-Range

One of the best mid-range establishments is the *Hotel Golden King International* (☎ 725917), at 25 Sir Iqbal Rd. It's a well-kept clean place with larger than average rooms and funky 1970s decor. Rooms range from economy rooms for Tk 160/250, to substantially larger rooms for Tk 300/450, and air-con rooms for Tk 500/800.

Close by on Sir Iqbal Rd, down an alley next to the Hotel Afzal is the *Hotel Arafat International* (☎ 725819). It's seen better days; economy rooms with attached bathrooms are Tk 120/200. 'Deluxe' rooms cost Tk 140/250, and there are a couple of air-con doubles for Tk 550. There are pleasant lounge areas on some floors but the beds are lumpy and the carpets are well past their use-by date.

Hotel Park (☎ 720990/725677), which is around the corner at 46 KD Ghosh Rd, is a good option. It has 44 rooms, laundry service, and a small comfortable reception area that features a TV, numerous relaxing chairs and a refrigerator with cold drinks. Rooms cost Tk 110/150 for (Tk 150/220 for deluxe units and Tk 550 with air-con). The standard rooms are a much better buy; the only difference between the two categories being that the deluxe rooms tend to be slightly larger and are equipped with western toilets. The rooftop restaurant also serves decent coffee.

Places to Stay – Top-End

Khulna's best hotel by a mile is the *Hotel Castle Salam* (☎ 720160, 725799, fax 730341, ℮ castle@khulnanet.net), on the intersection of Khan Jahan Ali Rd and KDA Ave. The large, comfortable rooms have all mod cons including international direct dial phones, western bathrooms, air-con, satellite TV and 24 hour room service. Single suites cost Tk 1800, double suites 2400, and deluxe singles/doubles cost Tk 2400/3000; MasterCard and Visa cards are accepted. The hotel has a business centre with Internet connection (Tk 40 per kilobyte), as well as secretarial services. Limo hire is only for guests, and costs from Tk 1200 to Jessore, Mongla and Bagerhat, up to Tk 6000 to Dhaka. The hotel also has the best restaurant in town, offering western and Chinese dishes. Special chow mein costs Tk 90, chicken with almonds costs Tk 115, and a pepper steak costs Tk 135.

Across from the Castle Salam is the *Hotel Royal International* (☎ 721638/9; fax 731803). The hotel was undergoing renovations at the time of research, which is just as well, as it was looking distinctly shabby. 'Tourist' doubles cost Tk 800, 'business' doubles Tk 900, and suites cost between Tk 1200 and Tk 2000. Rooms are reasonably big, with fans and good-sized bathrooms with western toilets and hot water, but in its present form it isn't good value. More useful is the travel agency in the lobby, where you can make arrangements for car rentals and guided trips to the Sundarbans. The restaurant features European and Chinese cuisine, and the menu offers many selections, including sweet and sour fish and chow mein.

The third and last option is the *Hotel Tiger Garden* (☎ 722844, fax 731230) at the northern end of KDA Ave; the lobby is quite grand but the upstairs interior walls look as though they haven't been cleaned since it opened. It's the sort of place where the staff suggestively whisper to single male guests that they can arrange 'anything'. Ordinary rooms cost Tk 180/350, doubles with satellite TV cost Tk 400, and air-con doubles from Tk 750 to Tk 1025.

SALLY DILLON

RICHARD I'ANSON

FELICITY VOLK

RICHARD I'ANSON

FELICITY VOLK

With tourism numbers still relatively low, Bangladeshi curiosity about travellers is high – inquisitive eyes will follow you wherever you go.

RICHARD I'ANSON

SALLY DILLON

SALLY DILLON

CRAIG PERSHOUSE

Whether sailing on the Bay of Bengal or traversing the marshlands, boats are ubiquitous throughout Bangladesh.

Staying at the government *Circuit House* (☎ 20314, 20466), next to the stadium, requires permission from the district commissioner (☎ 25233), across the street. Without some sort of official standing or impressive documentation chances of getting permission are slim. The guest rooms here (Tk 150) are wonderful and spacious, and the two club-like sitting rooms are grand. You can also get meals here.

Places to Eat

For really cheap food, head for the area around the train station; there are several local food stalls nearby. An excellent place in the centre of the city is the well-marked *Hotel Shaurav*, an air-con restaurant just above IFIC Bank on Khan A Sabar Rd. The friendly owner speaks English and is helpful in making selections from the Bangla menu. The place is very neat and prices are quite reasonable.

The city's top restaurants, all expensive in comparison, are the *Chinese restaurant* at the Hotel Castle Salam, *Royal Deck* at Hotel Royal International, the *rooftop restaurant* at Hotel Park, which serves local dishes, and *Hong Kong Chinese Restaurant,* on Khan A Sabar Rd, a block south of the stadium. The latter is poorly lit and nothing special.

Getting There & Away

Air The nearest airport is at Jessore. Biman (☎ 760940/9) and GMG (☎ 732273) provide direct bus services between Jessore airport and their Khulna offices. The Air Parabat office (☎ 724355) is some distance from the centre of town, about halfway between the Hotel Castle Salam and the ferry over the Rupsa on Khan Jahan Ali Rd.

Bus The main bus station is KDA bus terminal (also known as Sonadanga bus terminal), 2km north-west of the city centre on the newer of the two entrance roads north into Khulna. A rickshaw costs about Tk 10 from the city centre and Tk 20 from Rupsa ghat. This station serves all points except Mongla and Bagerhat; buses for those towns leave from south of the city,

just across the river. Inside KDA terminal, each company has its own ticket office, and bus companies with common destinations are grouped in the same area.

Buses to Dhaka leave all day until early evening; companies running air-con coaches include Eagle Paribahan and Shohagh Paribahan. Fares for the best air-con coaches are up to Tk 300, compared to Tk 160 for a chair coach and Tk 100 for an ordinary bus. Buses for Barisal leave mostly in the early morning and again in the early evening. SM Enterprise, for example, has departures for Barisal at 6.30 am (arriving around 2.30 pm), and at 7 and 7.30 pm. Modu Sanda also serves Barisal. The fare to Barisal is Tk 120.

Buses for Jessore leave frequently until the early evening; the fare is Tk 20 for chair coaches and Tk 15 for ordinary buses, and the trip takes 1¾ hours. There is a direct bus to Bogra (Tk 120) at 7.30 am, and possibly one in the late afternoon. It is also possible to find a direct bus or two for Faridpur (Tk 70). In general, however, Bogra and Faridpur are easier to get to from Jessore.

Buses headed south to Mongla and southwest to Bagerhat depart throughout the day from the southern side of the city, across the Rupsa River and just beyond the ferry ghat. Most people take the ferry, which departs about every 20 minutes, but those in a hurry sometimes take one of the smaller boats. The fare for either is only about Tk 1. By direct bus or minibus, Mongla (42km) costs Tk 15 and is just over an hour away. The road is in superb condition. The turn-off east for Bagerhat (29km) is 9km down this same highway; the fare is Tk 10 and the road is also in excellent condition.

Train The main station (☎ 723232) is near the city centre. There are four intercity (IC) expresses a day to Jessore, and two mail trains. The trip takes 1½ hours. The 7 am IC express continues on to Rajshahi, and the 9 pm express goes to Saidpur via Ishurdi. The 1st class/sulob fare is Tk 84/32 to Jessore, Tk 265/130 to Rajshahi and Tk 355/130 to Saidpur. It's far simpler to take the bus to Jessore, but with six trains daily, this would be a good opportunity to ride on a Bangladeshi train.

KHULNA DIVISION

The Bagerhat train terminal is across the Rupsa River, just left (east) of the ferry ghat. Departures are at 7.30 am, 12.15 pm and 4.30 pm, and the fare is just Tk 8 (Tk 12 for the faster 4.30 pm train which doesn't stop at Bagerhat College). It usually takes 1½ hours.

Car If you're driving to Mongla or Bagerhat, you'll have to take the Rupsa ferry (Tk 35), which departs every 20 minutes. The road is excellent.

You can rent a car through the Hotel Royal International or the Hotel Park; the cost is Tk 900 a day, including the driver but not including petrol. It is best to deal directly with the driver when setting the terms.

Boat The BIWTC office (☎ 720423, 721532) is near the city centre, just behind the train station. The house-like office for the Rocket ferries, which opens every day at around 9 am, is just beyond BIWTC. Between Dhaka and Khulna there are four Rockets per week in each direction. These ferries also call at Mongla, Barisal, Chandpur and several smaller ports. The schedules have changed very little over the years. Departures from Khulna are scheduled at 3 am daily, though there can be delays. Fares in 1st/2nd/inter/deck class (see Classes under Boat in the Getting Around chapter) on the *Ghazi* and the *Masood* are Tk 915/555 /139/94 to Dhaka, Tk 479/290/92/61 to Barisal and Tk 126/75/24/16 to Mongla. Fares on the *Moti Moti* and the *Tal* are 15% less. To be assured of a 1st-class cabin, you should reserve at least several days in advance, although it is sometimes possible to get one even on the day of departure.

BAGERHAT

Bagerhat has far more historical monuments in its surrounding area, mostly mosques, than any other town in Bangladesh, except Dhaka, and it also has one of the most famous – Shait Gumbad Mosque. Unfortunately the town lacks any decent hotels, so a day trip from Khulna is a good idea.

Bagerhat was also home to one of the most famous men in Bangladesh history,

Khan Jahan Ali, and is one of the cradles of the Muslim religion in this country.

The principal mosques, all built during the middle of the 15th century, are in one large area about 3km long, starting 4km west of Bagerhat, which nestles tranquilly on the Bhairab River. The beautiful countryside is a joy to walk through. The main Hindu temple, Khodla Math, built roughly 175 years after the mosques, is 12km or so to the north along a twisting road. The equivalent of some six storeys high, it's one of the tallest Hindu structures ever built in Bangladesh, so don't miss it. There's more jungle in this area than paddy and there are lotus-filled ponds, some ancient, which support a variety of bird life. With the Sundarbans so close there are reportedly occasional attacks by crocodiles in the waterways around Bagerhat.

Shait Gumbad Mosque & Surrounding Mosques

Built in 1459, the same year Khan Jahan died, the famous Shait Gumbad Mosque, with its numerous little domes and four short towers at the corners, is the largest and most magnificent traditional mosque in the country. 'Shait Gumbad' means 'the temple with 60 domes' but this is a misnomer because in reality it is roofed with 77 domes. Some 60m long, with 35 arched doorways, countless domes and corner towers topped by cupolas, this single-storey fortress-like structure is quite impressive from a distance. Inside, it's equally fascinating, with a single huge sanctuary dominated by 60 slender stone columns, from which rows of arches spring to support all the domes. The long aisles of pillars and arches emphasise just how big the building is.

Well-maintained and typical of the pre-Mughal 'Khan Jahan style', it's a heavy brick building with two-metre thick walls and a dark veneer of age, and is the more impressive for its rustic surroundings.

Around Shait Gumbad, there are three other mosques worth seeing, all single domed and in reasonably good condition. These are **Bibi Begni's Mosque**, which is about 500m behind Shait Gumbad and

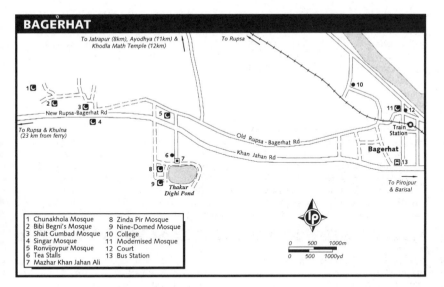

BAGERHAT

1 Chunakhola Mosque
2 Bibi Begni's Mosque
3 Shait Gumbad Mosque
4 Singar Mosque
5 Ronvijoypur Mosque
6 Tea Stalls
7 Mazhar Khan Jahan Ali
8 Zinda Pir Mosque
9 Nine-Domed Mosque
10 College
11 Modernised Mosque
12 Court
13 Bus Station

across a large pond; **Chunakhola Mosque**, which is in a paddy field behind Bibi Begni's also by about 500m; and **Singar Mosque** across the highway from Shait Gumbad.

Mazhar Khan Jahan Ali

About 2km east of Shait Gumbad is Khan Jahan's tomb. Overlooking a pond known as Thakur Dighi, the squat, quadrangular brick structure, which is of the same basic design as all the mosques in this area, has a single dome and 2½ m-thick walls that are relatively unadorned. It's the only monument in Bagerhat that still retains its original cupolas.

The cenotaph, seen right at the entrance, is apparently covered with tiles of various colours and inscribed with Quranic verses, but it is usually covered with a red cloth embroidered with gold threads. The mausoleum and the nearby single-domed Dargah Mosque are enclosed by a massive wall with short towers at each corner and archways on the front and back. There is a tiny bazar with teashops that cater to pilgrims who come to buy rosewater in bottles and joss sticks as offerings at the cenotaph.

As you enter the premises the fakirs will stir on sighting you and commence calling on Allah. They're similar to the spiritual mendicants of all religions you find all over the subcontinent. The main entrance to the shrine faces an archway where stone steps lead down to a fairly large pond in which the faithful bathe before entering. You'll be invited inside for a look and then perhaps asked for a small consideration; a few taka will suffice. The interior at one time was quite beautiful, with multicoloured tiles and moulding around the doorways, but most of that is gone. You'll also probably be implored by the locals to take a walk to the other side of Thakur Dighi to see the crocodiles that inhabit the pond.

Nine-Domed Mosque

This mosque is on the western bank of the Thakur Dighi Pond. Recently repaired, it's an impressive elegant structure of the same period as the other religious buildings in town, with three arched entrances on each side, massive walls and nine low hemispherical domes supported on four slender stone columns. The *mihrabs* are embellished with terracotta floral scrolls and foliage motifs, with a prominent chain-and-bell terracotta motif in the centre.

Khan Jahan Ali

Khan Jahan was a Muslim mystic who settled in Bagerhat in the middle of the 15th century after decades of wandering. Like Sheikh Shah Jalal-ud-din, who immigrated to Sylhet, this Sufi mystic became widely known as a holy man. And like most of the Sufis who settled in the subcontinent in medieval times, he came from Turkey. Sufis are Muslim mystics, the counterparts of the Hindu sadhus or yogis of India.

Upon arriving in Bagerhat with thousands of horsemen, clearing the jungle and founding Khalifatabad (as the town was originally named), this warrior-saint quickly initiated an incredible construction program. He adorned his capital city with an incredible number of mosques, bridges, brick-paved highways to neighbouring regions, palaces and other public buildings in just a decade or two – an astonishingly short span of time. Large ponds of water with staircase landings were built in various parts of the township to provide salt-free drinking water in this predominantly saline belt. No walls were necessary as Khan Jahan would simply retreat into the swamps if attacked.

When he died, a mausoleum was raised to his memory, which you can see, along with some of the major mosques still standing. Today Khan Jahan is the patron saint of the area and his name equates with a major pre-Mughal architectural style in Bangladesh.

You might also check the **Zinda Pir Mosque** just north of the Nine-Domed Mosque.

Ronvijoypur Mosque

Across the main highway from Khan Jahan's tomb is the splendid Ronvijoypur Mosque. It's one of a number of single-domed brick mosques in the area. It is singularly impressive, however, with the largest dome in Bangladesh, spanning some 11m and supported by 3m-thick walls. Each side has three arched doorways, and on each corner is a circular tower which, like most single-domed mosques here, is missing its crowning kiosk.

Khodla Math Temple

This Hindu structure is more remote but well worth the effort of getting to. As you get near the temple, you can't help but spot the 20m-high spire as it rises above the trees. This truly impressive brick tower looks rather like a giant beehive. Built in the early 17th century during Mughal times by a Brahmin, legend has it that it was a memorial to a court adviser. The entrance facade is thought to have been decorated with moulded terracotta art, but it's now badly weathered. The best-preserved side is the one with no entrance; on the false doorway you can still see some delicate terracotta art-

work. The other sides all have entrances with arched doorways, leading through the 3m-thick walls to the square sanctum.

Getting There & Away Khodla Math is just outside the village of Ayodhya, about 11km from Bagerhat. First take a rickshaw or baby taxi on the old road to Khulna to the market town of Jatrapur, a station on the Bagerhat-Rupsa railway line 8km north-west of Bagerhat. During the rainy season, this narrow winding back road is sometimes cut off. In Jatrapur ask for directions to Ayodhya, about 3km east along winding paved paths. Muslims in Jatrapur aren't very knowledgeable about the temple, so you'll do better saying you want to go to Ayodhya.

Places to Stay & Eat

One place to be avoided is the Hotel Khalid, north-west of the railway station, formerly the Hotel Suktara. Somewhat better is the nearby *Hotel Momotaj* on Rail Rd, which is reasonably priced (Tk 50/80 for singles/doubles with attached bathroom). Another possibility is the nearby *Hotel Mohona*, which is cheap and clean and has a friendly manager. Rooms cost Tk 35/70.

There are some basic local *restaurants* around the railway station, and *street stalls* selling samosas and other snacks.

Getting There & Away

Bus Buses from Rupsa (just near Khulna) to Bagerhat cost Tk 12, and the trip takes about 45 minutes. The bus passes Shait Gumbad (6km before town) on the left – this would be a good place to get off, but you might have trouble catching a bus back to Rupsa from here as they're usually very full. The Bagerhat bus station (a stretch of road) is about 1km from the centre of town on the Bagerhat-Khulna Highway (which joins with the Khulna-Mongla highway 9km south of Rupsa). The road is excellent and buses for Khulna leave fairly frequently all day.

If you're headed to Mongla, it may be faster to take a bus to the Khulna-Mongla Rd intersection and hail another there. You may have to stand but the 33km trip from the intersection takes less than an hour. Buses from Khulna headed east to Pirojpur and Barisal also pass through Bagerhat, but finding a seat on one might be very difficult.

Train The train departs from Rupsa, near Khulna, at 7.30 am, 12.45 and 4.30 pm, and from Bagerhat at 10 am, 2.30 and 6 pm. Coming from Rupsa, you could get off at the Shait Gumbad halt (Tk 7), or at Bagerhat, the final stop. Getting off at the former won't save you much time because the road from the halt to Shait Gumbad is so much more inferior.

MONGLA
☎ 4658

Mongla, 42km south of Khulna, is surprisingly small for a major port. Arriving from Khulna, you'll have to catch a tiny sailing boat or public ferry to the other side. Despite being about 80km upriver from the Bay of Bengal, the port on the vast confluence of the Pusur and Mongla Rivers has a string of freighters riding at anchor waiting to be loaded or unloaded at the new dockyards, off limits to the west of town. It's a spectacular sight, especially towards the southern end, where dense jungle lines the banks. The vast Sundarbans national park begins only 5km south.

Despite its small size, there's a hint of city atmosphere about Mongla. Some of the locals have crewed foreign ships, and there are smuggled goods available for sale in the market, sometimes alcohol. If you bring out a bottle of beer or Scotch in at least one hotel restaurant no one will bat an eye, as some of the locals may be doing the same. This is the one place where people won't assume that you work for an aid organisation – if you're a man, they'll assume that you're a crew member from one of the ships in the harbour.

A hospital (☎ 393) is available for medical treatment.

Boat Cruise

The thing to do in Mongla is to hire one of the picturesque boats at the port for a ride out on the river and into the northern stretches of the Sundarbans. Around Tk 80 per hour is a fair rate.

Sagar Enterprise (aka M/s Ahsan & Co) gets bad reports about overcharging and cutting tours short.

Places to Stay

To save money, head north to the market area. Beyond this, along Madrasa Rd, you'll find two more places. The first you'll pass is *Mongla Boarding*, with a Bangla sign, which charges Tk 35/60 for singles/doubles. About 200m beyond is the two-storey *Sundarbans Hotel*, well marked in English. These hotels are pretty similar (not great, but you get what you pay for), but the Sundarbans Hotel is in a quieter area.

The most convenient of the hotels is *Hotel Singapore* (☎ 209), a well-marked two-storey building in the heart of town on the short lane leading to the main ferry ghat. Consequently, getting a room isn't guaranteed. They're reasonably clean but very small, and cost Tk 60/100 with common bathrooms and Tk 80/120 with attached bathrooms.

The city's top establishment is the *Port Authority Guest House* (☎ 399), which is roughly 200m south of the main ferry ghat on the main drag, and can be reserved only through the Mongla Port Authority Chairman in Khulna (☎ 041-762331). It's not marked and is easy to miss. Rooms cost

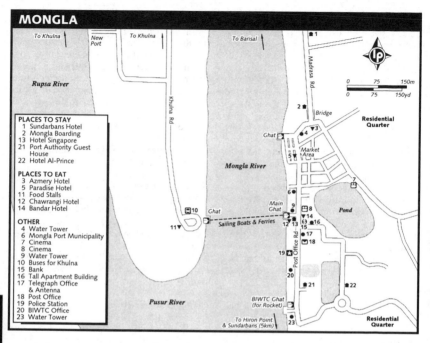

MONGLA

PLACES TO STAY
1 Sundarbans Hotel
2 Mongla Boarding
13 Hotel Singapore
21 Port Authority Guest House
22 Hotel Al-Prince

PLACES TO EAT
3 Azmery Hotel
5 Paradise Hotel
11 Food Stalls
12 Chawrangi Hotel
14 Bandar Hotel

OTHER
4 Water Tower
6 Mongla Port Municipality
7 Cinema
8 Cinema
9 Water Tower
10 Buses for Khulna
15 Bank
16 Tall Apartment Building
17 Telegraph Office & Antenna
18 Post Office
19 Police Station
20 BIWTC Office
23 Water Tower

Tk 120/240 and are unusually large and freshly painted, with nice wooden furnishings, various reading chairs, twin beds with mosquito nets, overhead fans, and large bathrooms with western toilets. Unfortunately, you may be told the rooms are all taken, though that may not be the case.

The popular, well-marked *Hotel Al-Prince* (☎ 454), 150m east as the crow flies, facing another paved street, has a restaurant and lots of rooms. The charge is Tk 70/120 for rooms with attached bathrooms. The units aren't as nice, but they're spacious by Bangladeshi standards, with fresh sheets, fans, mosquito nets, and bathrooms with squat toilets. For lunch or dinner, you could try the fried fish and chips or rice for Tk 60, along with a cold drink, among other choices. You can drink your own alcohol here without problems.

Places to Eat

There's not much choice here. If the *restaurant* at the Hotel Al-Prince is beyond your price range, try one of the eateries near the ferry ghat. The best appears to be *Bandar Hotel*, which is located on the main drag across from Hotel Singapore. There's also *Chawrangi Hotel* at the main ghat. Rice, dhal and curry are the mainstays; Tk 25 will buy you a filling meal at either place. Two similar places in the market area, both on the main drag, are *Paradise Hotel* and *Azmery Hotel*, several blocks further north. The food stalls across the river have basic Bangladeshi food – rice, fish, vegetables and samosas.

Getting There & Away

Bus There is no chair-coach service to Mongla. An express bus from Rupsa, near Khulna, costs Tk 15 and takes a little over an hour. Local buses are cheaper but much slower. Buses and cars do not cross the river. There's a small public barge (50 paisa) but most people take the small Venetian-like boats with sails, which are a lot more fun. The crossing usually takes 10 to 15 minutes and costs Tk 1 (Tk 12 for a boat to yourself).

Boat The BIWTC office is 150m south of the ferry ghat, and the Rocket ghat is 100m further south. You may have difficulty booking 1st- and 2nd-class Rocket tickets here, so if possible you should book in Khulna or Dhaka. Departures for Dhaka are at 6.10 am on Saturday, Monday, Wednesday and Friday. Departures to Khulna are on Saturday, Monday, Wednesday and Thursday at 5.20 pm according to the schedule, but are later in practice.

Fares in 1st/2nd/inter/deck class are: Dhaka Tk 875/540/200/135; Barisal Tk 375/230/100/60; and Khulna Tk 130/80/52/20. By the time Rockets from Dhaka reach Mongla they're often late, so if you think you've missed the boat for Khulna it's worth checking anyway. See the following Sundarbans National Park section for details on travel to Hiron Point.

AROUND MONGLA
Dhangmari Forestry Station

This forestry station, which is on the northern fringes of the Sundarbans and has good maps of the area, is only about 4km southwest of Mongla, across the Pusur River and in an inlet at Dhangmari.

To reach Dhangmari the round trip takes about 2½ hours by row boat (Tk 90 plus tip). The assistant manager at the Hotel Al-Prince can help you make arrangements. Alternatively, try for a boat at one of the little boat builders' yards on the waterfront near the BIWTC office. For a longer motorised excursion into the Sundarbans, expect to pay about Tk 600 plus Tk 50 tip for a five-hour trip.

SUNDARBANS NATIONAL PARK

The Sundarbans is the largest littoral mangrove belt in the world, stretching 80km into the hinterland from the coast. The forests aren't just mangrove swamps, they include some of the last remaining stands of the mighty jungles that once covered the Gangetic plain.

The Sundarbans covers an area of nearly 3600 sq km in Bangladesh and another 2400 sq km in India. Six 'ranges' make up the region. At Partition, Bashirat and Namkhona went to India, while Chandpai, Sharankhola, Khulna and Satkhira went to Bangladesh. About one-third of the total area of this forest is covered in water – basically by river channels, canals and tidal creeks varying in width from a few metres to 5km in some places. Even the land area is subject to tidal inundation during spring tides. The Sundarbans is bound by the Bhaleswari River in the east, the Bay of Bengal to the south, Khulna division to the north, and the Raimangal and Haringhata Rivers to the west. At one time the mangrove forests extended even further.

The impenetrable forests of the Sundarbans begin about 5km south-west of Mongla, along the Pusur River. For about 60km southwards there are no settlements of any kind. There are no permanent settlements within the forest apart from a few government camps housing the labour force for the extraction of timber. These camps are either built on stilts or 'hang' from the trees because of the soft ground and the 2m-high tides that course through the coastal areas. The ground is all mud. The workforce numbers about 20,000, although this more than doubles during April and May.

The ecological balance is extremely delicate and is influenced greatly by tidal shifts that affect the salinity, and hence the growth rates, in the surrounding vegetation. Deer, pigs and even crabs are predators of young trees, and cyclones wreak havoc.

The first historical record of any society inhabiting the region is from the 13th century, when many Hindus, fleeing the Muslim advance, sought refuge among the forests. They settled here, building a number of temples (one of which was memorably fictionalised by Salman Rushdie in *Midnight's Children* – see Literature under Arts in the Facts about Bangladesh chapter). They were later joined by the Khiljis, who were fleeing the Afghans. There are no other signs of early civilisations. In the 17th century the Portuguese-Mogh pirates

Honey & Tigers

The Sundarbans is one of the country's richest sources of honey (madhu or mau), producing over 550,000 pounds annually. About 90% comes from the far western area called Satkhira, where certain flowering trees thrive on the higher salinity.

During the short honey season from April to May, the maualis (honey farmers), mostly destitute day labourers, work in small groups from dawn to dusk, searching for bees. After locating the hive, they smoke out the bees and carry away the honey and beeswax in earthen jars. At night they sleep in their boats, only to be at it again the following day.

Locals say that each season some five to 10 maualis are attacked and eaten by tigers. Indeed, they are far more vulnerable to tiger attack than anybody else. The maualis carry no protection and in the frenzy of following the bees to their hives, they can't possibly keep an eye out for tigers as well. Tigers always attack from the rear, and in a matter of seconds can crush a victim's head or break his neck. On the Indian side of the Sundarbans, the forest department has developed iron head masks for the maualis which have proven quite effective. But in Bangladesh, honey collectors continue to work unprotected.

Most of the honey is sold at Gabura, and it is mostly purchased by pharmaceutical firms. The remainder goes to local merchants, who often adulterate it by adding liquid glucose, making it heavier in the process. In Mongla and Khulna you may see some of this honey for sale. To find out whether or not it's pure, take a thin piece of cotton, dip it in the honey and set fire to it. It'll burn very quickly if it's pure, and much more slowly if it isn't.

KIERAN MANGAN

probably caused the population to leave the area, although the lack of fresh drinking water and the unhealthy climate must have been contributing factors.

Since 1966 the Sundarbans has been a wildlife sanctuary. The government recently set aside three specific areas as tiger reserves. Besides its wildlife, the Sundarbans has great economic potential. The Divisional Forestry Office keeps a close watch on the region and supervises activities to protect the delicate ecological balance. Although hunting is prohibited, in modern-day Bangladesh the people with money and connections can do so without fear of reprisal.

Travel Permits

Officially, permits are required to visit the Sundarbans, and are issued by the Divisional Forestry Office in Khulna. In practice though, a one-day boat trip privately organised in Mongla doesn't require a permit. For overnight trips or longer a permit and guides are required and cost only Tk 50 a day. See Travel Permits to the Sundarbans in the Khulna section earlier in this chapter for further information.

Life in the Sundarbans

From November to mid-February thousands of fishermen from Chittagong converge on the island of Dublar, on the mouth of the Kunga River, a Sundarbans estuary. They come with about 40 trawlers, each with 30 to 40 small boats in tow. During this period fishing is carried on ceaselessly, day and night. They reap the rich harvest of the schooling shrimps that come here to breed, but they also catch fish and sharks.

During the same period, thousands of low-caste Hindus from Khulna, Barisal and Patuakhali come to the island for a three-day festival. They set up statues of deities in makeshift temples, bathe in the holy waters of this distributary of the Ganges, and release or sacrifice goats. During the *mela* (fair), sweetmeats, dried fruits, toys, hookahs, wooden clogs and religious paraphernalia are sold in the market. A few weeks after their departure, the fishermen also head back to Chittagong, and for the next nine months the island is deserted.

Fishing families who live like sea gypsies can also be seen in the Sundarbans. They have large boats with thatched roofs and cabins, and they catch fish using trained otters. Nets are placed at the mouths of streams or creeks, and the otters are released upstream and chase the fish down into the nets. Woodcutters also work in the Sundarbans during much of the year. They build temporary dwellings on the edge of the forest to a height of 3m or so for protection from tigers; others live in boats.

Besides producing fish in great quantities, the region produces the sundari tree, which is in demand for shipbuilding, railway sleepers, lightpoles etc. Other forest products include honey, *gol* leaves (from a local shade tree of that name), reeds, and snails for lime. The people who gather honey, known as *maualis*, occasionally constitute a part of the diet of the royal Bengal tiger. The unfortunate maualis are a particular favourite of the tigers because they're always looking up at the trees (see the Honey and Tigers boxed text in this section).

There are many other animals in the forests, including the beautiful spotted deer. Not surprisingly, bird life matches the lushness of the jungle in its variety and numbers.

Wildlife

The Sundarbans is home to some unique examples of subcontinental wildlife.

Royal Bengal Tigers The royal Bengal tiger is the pride of Bangladesh. It was aptly named by the British as has been known to grow to a body length of more than 2m, has extraordinary strength and agility, and is considered to be the most majestic of tigers. It has a life span of 16 years and preys on deer, boars and fish stranded on riverbeds at low tide. It is only in old age, when it has lost its physical agility and its canine fangs, that it sometimes preys on workers in the area.

There are thought to be roughly 400 tigers remaining in the Sundarbans, but your chances of seeing one are extremely remote. Every year there are reports of people in the area getting eaten by tigers, so the locals are terribly afraid of them and with good reason. Although they may not admit it, most guides, despite carrying rifles, are terrified of the tigers. Consequently, they'll make considerable noise during excursions, scaring them off and virtually ensuring that you won't encounter one. Nevertheless, there are just enough sightings to encourage visitors that they might be lucky. One group reported seeing a tiger swim right by their boat. The pristine environment, rather than the wildlife, is the real attraction of the area.

Other Wildlife Wildlife in the Sundarbans also includes deer, wild boars, clawless otters, monkeys, crocodiles, and some 50 species of reptiles, including snakes and eight species of amphibians, and numerous river dolphins. Spotting animals in these thick mangrove forests is very difficult, however. Most visitors return reporting having seen very little wildlife, but those who enjoy unusual scenery still find the trip interesting. Some elevated viewing towers have been constructed to help visitors spot more wildlife.

There are an estimated 30,000 spotted deer in the Sundarbans; they're among the most beautiful in the world. They are easy to find for they come down to a clearing or to the riverbanks to drink. There are also monkeys. Curiously, they have been observed dropping keora leaves whenever the deer appear on the scene.

Birds Not surprisingly, the Sundarbans is one of the best areas for bird-watching. Over 270 different species have been recorded in this region, including about 95 species of water birds and 35 species of birds of prey. Birdlife found here includes

The spotted deer is easily sighted in the Sundarbans region.

snipes, white and gold herons, woodcocks, coots, yellowlegs sandpipers, common cranes, golden eagles and the madan-tak (adjutant bird), which always looks worried and dejected.

The Sundari Tree

The region derives its name from the sundari trees that grow here to about 25m in height. These trees are very straight, have tiny branches and keep well in water – they become rock hard when submerged for a long time and are thus very suitable for building with. Sundaris are felled mainly for use as shipbuilding materials, electric poles, railway sleepers and house construction. *Gema* wood, also felled in the Sundarbans, is mainly pulped for the Khulna newsprint factory. Timber workers here are called *bawalis*.

Organised Tours

The dry season, November through April, is the most popular season for visiting the Sundarbans.

Another possibility is Unique Tours and Travels in Dhaka (☎ 02-988 5116, fax 818

3392, ✉ unique@bangla.net), at 51/B Kemal Ataturk Ave, Banani. It offers similar four-day tours (including air fares to/from Dhaka) for US$695 (two to three people), US$540 (four to seven people) and US$490 (eight to 10 people).

In Khulna, you can also arrange trips with Mohammed Faruk, the manager of the Hotel Royal International (☎ 041-721638/9). He runs about 20 trips a year, and while most visitors give positive reports there have also been allegations that he runs hunting tours and that garbage from his ships is simply thrown into the rivers. He charges Tk 5000 a person for an all-day excursion from Khulna to the Sundarbans and back by speed boat, and Tk 12,500 a person for a two day trip, staying overnight at Kotka. For 15 people, the price for a four day/three night all-inclusive excursion from Jessore airport is Tk 5500 per person; this price does not include the airfare to Jessore.

The best private tour operator is The Guide, which has offices in Khulna and Dhaka. The Khulna office (☎ 017- 298000, 017- 275506, ☎/fax 731384) is on the ground floor of the KDA building at the northern end of KDA Ave, close to the Hotel Tiger Garden. Their Dhaka office is in Gulshan at DIT II circle (☎ 02-988 6983, fax 988 6984, ✉ theguide@bangla.net), and they also have a desk at the Sheraton Hotel in Dhaka. It's very professionally run and offers similar tours, except guests sleep on board the motor boat and there's no minimum group size requirement; however, the price per person varies considerably. For example, four-day trips cost US$750 (two people), US$625 (three to five people), US$395 (six to nine people) and US$285 (10 to 15 people). Three-day trips cost about 20% less.

Places to Stay

Most tour operators now have guests stay on the boat, as the two places to stay in the Sundarbans have deteriorated in Bangladesh's present malaise. Most visitors stay at the large *Mongla Port Authority Rest House* at Hiron Point (also called Nilkamal). This four-storey hotel-like building is run by the Mongla Port Authority and is principally for their staff. The rooms are pleasant enough, and there's a dining hall, bar and recreation facilities for the staff of about 30, and for visiting pilots. Tourist rates for the rooms are around Tk 500 for a double room with fan (more with air-con), and space is limited. Only the chairman of the Mongla Port Authority, whose office is in Khulna (☎ 762331), can book you a room.

Hiron Point is developing into a small and dirty village. People here don't get sufficiently regular food supplies, so they must resort to illegal hunting to survive. As a result, your chances of seeing wildlife are not great.

The only alternative is the small *Forestry Rest House*, which is at Kotka, about 30km north-east of Hiron Point, just off the Bay of Bengal. It has two bedrooms with four beds each plus common areas, and is not very pleasant. Unless you come on a tour the forestry officials here expect Tk 2500 for a room, plus an extra Tk 500 or so in 'baksheesh'. The staff are apparently not being paid very regularly, so you can understand their predicament. The only person who can give permission to stay here is the Divisional Forestry Office in Khulna (☎ 720665).

Getting There & Away
Hiron Point and Kotka are about 80km south of Mongla with nothing in between. A trip by motor launch takes six to 10 hours from Mongla depending on the tide direction. Getting there and getting around on your own may be more expensive than visiting with a tour. The best place to look for a boat is Mongla, not Khulna. If you don't have much success, try the Port Authority. There is a very slight chance that you might be able to hitch a free ride on one of its boats, but you shouldn't count on it. You could also try to hire a boat from the Dhangmari Forest Station, which is located nearby. See the earlier Mongla and Around Mongla sections for travel to these alternatives.

If you cannot get right down to Hiron Point, you can take local country boats about halfway down. They carry large earthen pots of freshwater for the settlements on the edges of the dense jungle. The boats are pretty fast, speeding down with the ebb-tide current early in the morning and bringing back a load of gol leaves, or bundles of reeds, with the incoming tide in the afternoon. The main problem is communicating with the boatmen, who speak little English.

Getting Around
Once you get to Hiron Point, you still have the problem of getting out into the forest. The only means of transportation inside the forest is boat (usually row boats), because there are no roads and very few forest paths. Walking around is virtually impossible because the ground is so muddy and slippery due to the regular tidal waters. If you want to try, you'll have to wait until the tide goes out. When the tide comes in (at 50 kilometres an hour), the forest almost floats on water.

KHULNA DIVISION

Barisal Division

Of all the divisions of Bangladesh, Barisal is the most marked by the branches of the Padma (Ganges) that braid through it to the Bay of Bengal, creating a maze of waterways. This wide, flat region has little to offer in the way of historical monuments but in many ways Barisal division is the quintessential Bengal. There is hardly any industrial development in this luxuriously deep-green region, fringed by rivers and the sea. The land barely ever seems to be dry, intermingled with ponds, marshes and streams which keep the soft fertile ground moist. A river cruise from Dhaka to Barisal is the main reason visitors come this region, but at the southern tip of the division there is a quiet beach resort. Kuakata boasts a wide sandy beach where it is possible to see the sun rise and set over the Bay of Bengal.

Dhaka division lies north of Barisal division and Khulna division forms its western boundary. To the east flows the silt-laden lower Meghna River, building huge islands in its wide channel as it devours others.

BARISAL
☎ 0431

The capital of the division, Barisal (BORE-ee-shal) is a major port city largely isolated from the rest of Bangladesh. It's one of the more pleasant cities in the country, with only moderate levels of traffic and several large and serene ponds in the city centre. The quiet back streets around the Hotel Paradise have a number of handsome buildings that date from the Raj era. Another interesting area is the busy river port, which is always teeming with activity.

There are a couple of old Hindu temples in the city centre, including a Krishna temple on Chowk Bazar Rd. On the main drag is a Sonali bank that changes travellers cheques.

On the city's western side is a bypass road headed south to Patuakhali. At the intersection on the northern end are lots of baby taxis (fairly rare here) and the main bus station. Near the bus stand, in an idyllic jungle-clad

Highlights

- **Barisal** – riverside town on the Rocket route between Dhaka and Khulna, fine houses on quiet backstreets
- **Kuakata** – quiet beach resort where the sun sets and rises over the Bay of Bengal

surrounding, is the Ramakrishna mission and a large Hindu temple.

Places to Stay – Budget

Quite a few of the cheaper hotels in town, situated around the Hotel Park near BIWTC Ghat Rd, are loath to accept foreigners.

It's fun to stay at the Barisal *YMCA* for Tk 25 for a basic dormitory bed. Unfortunately it doesn't seem to be operating all the time, so you may have to ask the local kids to track down the *chowkidar* (caretaker). It's at the end of a cul-de-sac and is a bit tricky to find. First head down an alley across from the gateway to the Catholic church, then turn left down a lane called Iswar Bose Rd and walk past a large maroon building, then follow the laneway to the right, and at the end you'll find the YMCA.

The *Hotel Melody* (☎ 56538) (no sign in English) is a typical basic hotel. Singles

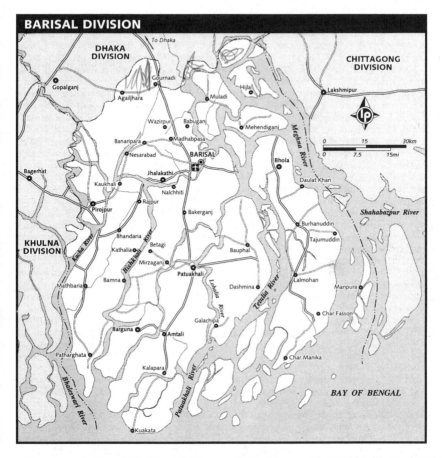

BARISAL DIVISION

with common bath cost Tk 45, while singles/doubles with bathrooms cost Tk 60/90. The rooms are small with concrete floors and the usual stains on the walls, but the bathrooms are not overly slimy, the mattresses are comfortable enough and the hotel is well swept. The hotel is on the right-hand side of a small laneway off Sadar Rd. The laneway is about 100m south of the town hall on the other side of Sadar Rd.

The *Hotel Park* (☎ 52678), on the busy street between BIWTC Ghat Rd and Sadar Rd, is a little overpriced but is otherwise a reasonably good place to stay. Ordinary sin-

gles/doubles are Tk 80/120 with attached bathroom, while somewhat cleaner and larger rooms with better beds and bathrooms are Tk 120/200.

Across the street is the *Hotel Golden Inn International* (☎ 53161). Rooms cost Tk 100/180, which is too high for such small rooms, but they are reasonably clean and have fans, mosquito nets and decent bathrooms.

Places to Stay – Mid-Range & Top End

The *Hotel Hoque International* (one sign in English says Hotel Huq) (☎ 54971) is at

54 Sadar Rd. It charges Tk 130/230 for smallish but pleasant rooms. The beds are very comfortable, the bathrooms are clean and the management is helpful.

The city's best hotel is the *Hotel Ali International (☎ 54122),* in the heart of town on Sadar Rd. It's an orderly, well-managed place with knowledgeable staff on reception and hotel boys who don't try pound the door down. There are some rooms with common bathroom for Tk 150/200. Rooms with attached bath cost Tk 175/250 and are large and spotless, featuring comfortable armchairs, fans, coffee tables, comfortable beds and western bathroom facilities. Deluxe rooms cost Tk 350/400 (Tk 700/900 with air-con and satellite TV) and are even larger, with wide beds. The GMG airlines office is on the first floor of the same building.

The *Paradise Hotel (☎ 52009),* on Hospital Rd, is almost as good as the Hotel Ali International. The exterior looks a bit shabby but there's private parking, a small garden and, besides some musty carpets, it is clean and well furnished. There are ordinary rooms for Tk 125/200 with attached bathroom, larger doubles for Tk 300 (Tk 500 with satellite TV) and air-con doubles with TV for Tk 850.

The *Circuit House (☎ 56464)* is on the main drag on the southern side of town. It is in an attractive old single-storey building and has a relaxing atmosphere, with a large comfortable sitting room. You must first reserve, however, with the district commissioner (☎ 52040), and getting a room could be difficult as it's used by government officials. Doubles cost Tk 150, the usual price for circuit houses.

Places to Eat

For cheap food, try the BIWTC ferry ghat; there's a small *restaurant* just north of this and other small, cheap, not-very-permanent-looking Bangladeshi restaurants in the area. Some of the chai stalls here and elsewhere around town specialise in 'red tea' – cardamom tea without milk. If you head from here towards the centre of town along Faisal Huq Ave you'll come to *Mandiganj Restaurant*, just before Sadar Rd. Its most

popular dish is two slices of good bread and hot milk for Tk 8.

The city's best restaurants are at the *Royal Cinema* on Sadar Rd. The larger restaurant at the end of the hall serves Bangladeshi food, while the smaller one through the door on the right offers Chinese dishes and western snacks. The Chinese restaurant is a pleasant and quiet retreat; the fare and prices are standard, and the quality is pretty good. For ice cream, there's an *Igloo Ice Cream Outlet*, 30m to the north, and for sweets and snacks, try the small clean *Sunda Sweets* half a block further.

Getting There & Away

Air The GMG airlines office (☎ 56510) is in the same building as the Hotel Ali International, and has two morning flights to and from Dhaka for Tk 1470.

The Air Parabat office (☎ 555757) is near the Circuit House on the southern end of Sadar Rd. It also has two flights a day to and from Dhaka, one in the morning and another in the afternoon, for Tk 970.

The airport is a 20-minute ride north of town. Both airlines offer a complimentary minibus service to and from the airport. You can get to the airport by baby taxi for Tk 60.

Bus The principal Dhaka-Barisal overland route now passes via Mawa (the Padma River crossing) and Madaripur. There are three ferry crossings, two just north of Barisal. Day coaches depart from either end, mostly in the morning around 6.30 am, while night buses depart mostly between 6 and 9 pm. The trip takes eight to 10 hours, and costs Tk 110 (Tk 140 by chair coach). Buses depart from the northern entrance to Barisal, 4km from the town centre.

There are also direct connections west to Khulna; the fare is Tk 90 for an ordinary bus and Tk 120 for a chair coach. The trip, which involves two ferry crossings, is via Pirojpur and Bagerhat, and takes at least eight hours.

Buses travelling south to Bakerganj (18km) and Patuakhali (40km) cost Tk 8 and Tk 15 respectively. There are two or three buses each day to Kuakata (5 hours) early in the morning for Tk 45; otherwise you'll have to change in Patuakhali. From Patuakhali there are buses to Barguna, Galachipa and Kalapara. The buses for Patuakhali and Kuakata leave from the southern end of town.

Boat There is a Rocket that goes to Dhaka via Chandpur every day, arriving from Khulna usually between 5.30 and 6.30 pm, and departing from Barisal 45 minutes later. The journey supposedly takes 12 or 13 hours, but 15 or 16 is more typical during the high-water (monsoon) season. Fares to

Dhaka are Tk 435/267/66/45 in 1st/2nd /inter/deck class. To Chandpur it's eight to 10 hours, and it costs Tk 257/156/40/26.

The Rocket from Dhaka arrives here daily, usually between 5 and 6 am, and continues to Khulna, arriving there the same day in the early evening. Fares are Tk 375/ 230/100/60 to Mongla and Tk 479/290/ 125/78 to Khulna.

For information and reservations for the Rocket, see the BIWTC office at the harbour in Barisal. For a 1st-class compartment you must reserve at least one day in advance (preferably earlier), otherwise you

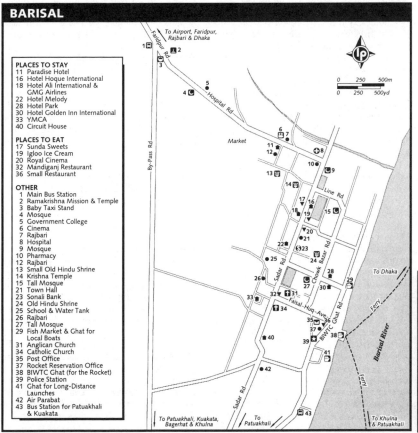

BARISAL

PLACES TO STAY
11 Paradise Hotel
16 Hotel Hoque International
18 Hotel Ali International &
   GMG Airlines
22 Hotel Melody
28 Hotel Park
30 Hotel Golden Inn International
33 YMCA
40 Circuit House

PLACES TO EAT
17 Sunda Sweets
19 Igloo Ice Cream
20 Royal Cinema
32 Mandiganj Restaurant
36 Small Restaurant

OTHER
1 Main Bus Station
2 Ramakrishna Mission & Temple
3 Baby Taxi Stand
4 Mosque
5 Government College
6 Cinema
7 Rajbari
8 Hospital
9 Mosque
10 Pharmacy
12 Rajbari
13 Small Old Hindu Shrine
14 Krishna Temple
15 Tall Mosque
21 Town Hall
23 Sonali Bank
24 Old Hindu Shrine
25 School & Water Tank
26 Rajbari
27 Tall Mosque
29 Fish Market & Ghat for
   Local Boats
31 Anglican Church
34 Catholic Church
35 Post Office
37 Rocket Reservation Office
38 BIWTC Ghat (for the Rocket)
39 Police Station
41 Ghat for Long-Distance
   Launches
42 Air Parabat
43 Bus Station for Patuakhali
   & Kuakata

To Airport, Faridpur, Rajbari & Dhaka

Faridpur Rd

Hospital Rd

By-Pass Rd

Market

Line Rd

Chowk Bazar Rd

Sadar Rd

Faisal-Huq-Ave

BIWTC Ghat Rd

To Dhaka

Barisal River

Ferry

Sadar Rd

To Patuakhali, Kuakata, Bagerhat & Khulna

To Patuakhali

To Khulna & Patuakhali

0   250   500m
0   250   500yd

BARISAL DIVISION

will have to wait until the boat arrives to see whether any of the eight compartments are unoccupied. There is likely to be a vacancy.

There are also a few large launches plying nightly between Barisal and Dhaka, including the *Jalkaporte* and the *MV Sadia*. Their 1st-class compartments are smaller than the Rocket's but they are decent enough, while deck class is just as good. There are four such launches departing every evening at 5.30, 6, 7 and 7.30 pm from either end. The departure points are Sadarghat terminal in Dhaka and the large terminal just south of the BIWTC terminal in Barisal. On the *Jalkaporte*, which departs at 6.30 pm, deck class costs Tk 50 and air-con singles/doubles cost Tk 300/600. On the *MV Sadia* the fares are Tk 60 and Tk 250 respectively. By launch the trip takes the same length of time as the Rocket. There are no launches plying between Barisal and Khulna, only the Rocket.

BIWTC also provides service to/from Chittagong three times a week, departing from Chittagong at 9 am on Monday, Thursday and Saturday, and returning the following day at 8.30 am. The trip takes around 24 hours. The fare is Tk 768/509/ 160/108 (Tk 342/230/81/50 to Hatiya Island). If you want a 1st-class cabin you should reserve at least a day or two in advance, even up to a week to be sure.

There is a ferry every day that makes an overnight trip to Patuakhali, leaving between 5.30 and 6.30 pm. Single/double cabins cost Tk 450/600 and include a TV that plays maddening Hindi movies; deck class costs about Tk 100.

AROUND BARISAL
Madhabpasa

The village of Madhabpasa, about 10km away to the north-west, is where you'll find a lake that is known for attracting birds. There is also said to a medieval Hindu temple close to the village.

KUAKATA
☎ 0441

This isolated beach lies at the southern tip of the delta, about 100km from Barisal. The beach is much quieter and less developed

than Cox's Bazar, at least for now. The name comes from the Kua well, dug by the original Mogh (Rakhine) Buddhist settlers. Don't arrive expecting a turquoise tropical ocean; the river mouths east and west of the beach ensure that the sea is rather murky. The large quantity of sharks drying on racks on the beach doesn't augur well for swimming either. There is a Buddhist temple close to the Parjatan Motel, about 100m from the beach on a slightly raised mound. The tin-walled shrine holds a 100-year-old statue of Buddha, said to be the largest in the country. The nearby forest reserve is pleasant but it is being damaged by illegal logging. Some travellers report that hiring a fisherman to take you across to nearby forested islands is a pleasant excursion.

Places to Stay & Eat

Very basic lodgings are available in a flophouse on the beach. Beds cost Tk 30. There is also a government *Dak Bungalow* here. Several NGOs also have guesthouses in Kuakata. The *BRAC Guesthouse* is open to travellers and charges about Tk 200 for a double room. The *Parjatan Motel* complex (☎ 2751) has a 30-bed dormitory that costs Tk 150 per bed, and ventilated twin-bed rooms for Tk 650 per bed. New hotels are being built and developers have been buying up plots of land.

Bangladeshi tourists often stay with local villagers.

Getting There & Away

The road linking Kuakata with Barisal has been greatly improved in recent years, but with three ferry crossings to make it can still be a slow trip. There are also reportedly launches direct from Barisal to Kuakata, apparently taking around nine hours.

There is an overnight bus from Kuakata to Dhaka that leaves around 7 pm, costing Tk 450. Buses to Patuakhali cost Tk 55, from where you can catch buses on to Barisal. From Patuakhali you could also take the ferry, which leaves between 5.30 and 6.30 pm from the main ghat; single/double cabins cost Tk 450/600, deck class will cost you about Tk 100.

Rajshahi Division

Rajshahi is one of the largest divisions in Bangladesh, with 16 districts and 25% of the country's population. On a clear day the Himalayan peak of Kanchenjunga can be seen from the northernmost district of Tetulia, while the south stretches down to where the waters of the Padma (Ganges) and Jamuna (Brahmaputra) Rivers mingle. The region is less prone to flooding than other parts of the country, but it suffers more from drought and cold snaps during winter. Though the massive Bangabandhu Bridge spanning the Jamuna River now links it to rest of the country, Rajshahi division is still overwhelmingly agricultural, with no large cities and little industrial development. It's the centre of the silk industry and produces more than its share of the wheat grown in Bangladesh. It also grows almost half the country's mangoes, for which the region is famous. As a result it's one of the country's better off areas.

As the north-western division of the country, Rajshahi's borders are, as one would expect, the major rivers. The powerful Jamuna cuts a swathe between it and Dhaka division, while the Padma divides it from Khulna division. The Padma becomes very wide where it enters Bangladesh, stretching almost 20km from bank to bank. The Indian state of Bangla (West Bengal) lies at Rajshahi's jagged western and northern boundaries.

For travellers, the region offers a variety of historical monuments, including numerous mosques, Hindu temples, *rajbaris* (palaces built by the zamindars) and British-era buildings. As with much of Bangladesh, half the fun of visiting these places is seeing rural life on the way there and back. Rajshahi division has a good network of highways and roads, making getting around relatively easy.

HISTORY

With the emergence of the Mauryan empire in the 3rd century BC, and its expansion

Highlights

- **Kantanagar Temple** – the finest Hindu monument in the country, covered in sculptured terracotta plaques
- **Paharpur** – massive ruins of a Buddhist temple, the most impressive archaeological site in Bangladesh
- **Puthia** – quiet country town with several attractive Hindu temples and a rajbari

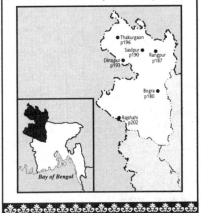

under the Buddhist emperor Ashoka, the region became Buddhist. Brick buildings, mainly a religious character, were introduced, and Pundravardhana (now known as Mahasthangarh) became the capital of Bengal. Pundravardhana was not only a Buddhist centre but also an important commercial entrepot of the silk trade. Chinese visitors in the 5th and 7th centuries were impressed by the large monasteries, the soaring temples and the Ashoka stupas. When the Gupta empire (which emerged in the 4th century) disappeared, the Palas took control, making the region the last stronghold of Buddhism on the subcontinent.

The Pala kingdom eventually fell into poverty and, with the arrival in the 12th century of the Hindu Senas, Pundravardhana

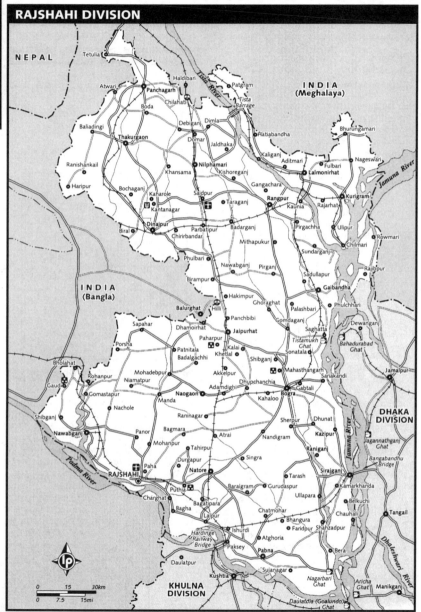

RAJSHAHI DIVISION

declined. The Senas adopted the traditional *bangla* temple design (sloping roof style associated with pre-Mauryan and Mauryan architecture), which the Muslims adopted as a principal feature of their mosques when they came to power a century later.

When the Mughals shifted to Dhaka, the region declined in importance, but with the arrival of the British in the 18th century, Rajshahi was quickly turned into a sugar and cotton-producing region. When the borders came to be drawn during Partition this part of Bengal was untidily divided between Muslim majority and Hindu majority areas, and today many areas near the Indian border of Rajshahi, both on the west and north, have a relatively high proportion of Hindus.

BOGRA
☎ 051

Bustling Bogra (BOGE-rah) lies on a major crossroads and features a compact commercial centre and a vibrant market. The central area seems as busy as parts of Old Dhaka, and at night has a slight air of menace. There are however some outlying residential areas which are pleasant, shady and fairly tranquil.

The heart of town, Sat Mata, is a small traffic circle – it's a good place to begin exploring the central area. The teeming Chandi market is full of life, and this area is so crowded during the day that walking is often faster than taking a rickshaw. To the east lies the Karatuya River, which is mostly blocked from view by numerous multistorey buildings. Walking around, you'll see numerous tea houses; many of them offer *misti doi* (sweet yoghurt) and sweetmeats, which are popular in this area.

A kilometre north of Sat Mata, along busy Kazi Nasrul Islam Rd, off to the east (right) just before the water tower, you'll find an old Hindu quarter including some Hindu ruins. If you're really lucky you might see a ceremony or other activities taking place. In January and early February, for instance, you can watch the mass production of human-size statues of Saraswati for the *puja* (festival) celebrating this goddess.

Bogra is a good base for visiting two of the country's most famous archaeological sites – Mahasthangarh and Paharpur. The former is just 10km north of town, while the latter, which is more impressive, lies 53km to the north-west, over two hours by bus or car.

Information

To change money, head for Janata Bank on Kazi Nasrul Islam Rd, about 600m north of the city centre. Other banks include Rupali, on the same road near Sat Mata, and Shilpa, on Nawab Bari Rd. These banks don't always change money. The Safeway Motel (see Places to Stay later in this section) is one of the few places in Rajshahi division where it is possible to make an international phone call.

Nawab Syed Abus Sobham Chowdhury Memorial Museum

This museum, two blocks east of Sat Mata, is very interesting because it's one of only a handful of rajbaris in Bangladesh that is furnished. Even more remarkable is the fact that the furnishings are original. The elaborately carved wooden chairs and tables, the wall mouldings, the high ceilings and the original glass lighting fixtures combine to give the huge reception room and adjoining dining room a grand and authentic appearance. The rooms have models of the people who used to live there, dressed to impress in both the Bengali and British fashions of their time. You'll also see a portrait of the nawab's heir, Jackie Chowdhury, who still has several rooms at the rear of the building. The caretaker is a very friendly man who'll most likely give you a guided tour of the small but handsome building, and a potted history of the family. One room is a gallery for the talented local painter, Dalal.

The grounds of the museum have been made into a quirky little amusement park, with a miniature railway, rickety fairground rides and charmingly naive statues of peasants, bullock carts and wild animals. Understandably popular with kids, it seems to be more of an attraction than the museum. As one visitor put it, the whole place is so unusual that for once you won't be the sole source of interest to the locals. Just next to the museum's entrance is a 'zoo' of painted cement animals, called a *carnapuli* (car-NA-pou-luu).

The museum is open from 5 to 7.30 pm every day (closed Friday). It costs Tk 3 to enter the grounds, and Tk 5 to see the museum.

Places to Stay – Budget

If price is your only consideration, try the *Hotel Marlin Residential* (☎ 5366), which is at the northern end of Nawab Bari Rd, one block east of the tall landmark mosque, or *Hotel Metro* next door, which is virtually

identical. Only the Metro has a sign in English. Singles/doubles with fans, mosquito nets and common bathrooms cost Tk 40/60. Rooms at both places are dark and tiny, and not particularly clean.

Slightly better is the three-storey *Bogra Boarding* (☎ 5609), nearby on Nawab Bari Rd; there's a sign in English. The rooms are tiny but a bit cleaner, and come with fans and mosquito nets. They all have common bathroom and cost Tk 40/70.

Better still is the *Mandolin Hotel & Chinese Restaurant* (☎ 5176) on the top floor of the Shaptobari market building. It has a

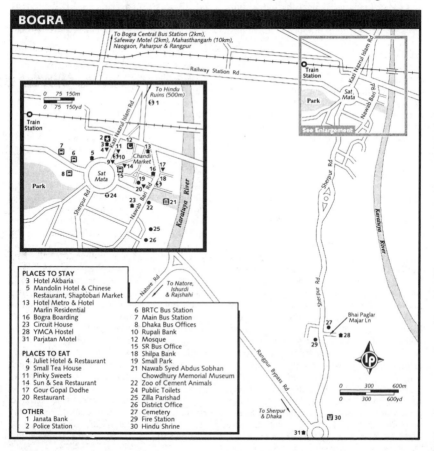

BOGRA

To Bogra Central Bus Station (2km),
Safeway Motel (2km), Mahasthangarh (10km),
Naogaon, Paharpur & Rangpur

Railway Station Rd

Train Station

To Hindu Ruins (500m)

Train Station

Chandi Market

Sat Mata

Park

Karatoya River

See Enlargement

Sat Mata

Park

Sherpur Rd

Kazi Nazrul Islam Rd

Nawab Bari Rd

Karatoya River

Natore Rd

To Natore,
Ishurdi
& Rajshahi

Sherpur Rd

Rangpur Bypass Rd

Bhai Paglar Majar Ln

To Sherpur
& Dhaka

0   300   600m
0   300   600yd

PLACES TO STAY
3 Hotel Akbaria
5 Mandolin Hotel & Chinese
   Restaurant, Shaptobari Market
13 Hotel Metro & Hotel
   Marlin Residential
16 Bogra Boarding
23 Circuit House
28 YMCA Hostel
31 Parjatan Motel

PLACES TO EAT
4 Juliet Hotel & Restaurant
9 Small Tea House
11 Pinky Sweets
14 Sun & Sea Restaurant
17 Gour Gopal Dodhe
20 Restaurant

OTHER
1 Janata Bank
2 Police Station

6 BRTC Bus Station
7 Main Bus Station
8 Dhaka Bus Offices
10 Rupali Bank
12 Mosque
15 SR Bus Office
18 Shilpa Bank
19 Small Park
21 Nawab Syed Abdus Sobhan
   Chowdhury Memorial Museum
22 Zoo of Cement Animals
24 Public Toilets
25 Zilla Parishad
26 District Office
27 Cemetery
29 Fire Station
30 Hindu Shrine

pleasant reception area with comfortable sofas for relaxing on. Rooms with bathroom cost Tk 150/90. Singles with no windows and common bathroom go for only Tk 50. They are basic but clean and roomier than normal, with lots of light, fans and mosquito nets. The staff are friendly too.

The best deal is the **YMCA Hostel** (☎ 5242). To get there from Sat Mata, take Sherpur Rd south and immediately after passing the small Bhai Paglar Majar cemetery on your left (roughly 2km), take the next left (east) down Bhai Paglar Majar Lane. There's a sign on Sherpur Rd at the entrance to the lane. If you pass a fire station on the right, you've gone too far. The 'Y', which runs a primary school and a vocational education program, is in peaceful quiet surroundings, with friendly and helpful staff. The rooms have twin beds, writing tables, fans, balconies, attached bathrooms and clean towels. The price is Tk 80 per person. There's no kitchen, but the staff can arrange for meals to be brought in.

Places to Stay – Mid-Range & Top End

In the centre of town the **Hotel Akbaria** (☎ 5765) is a decent mid-range option. The reception is at the end of an alley just next to the police station. Unfortunately there's no sign in English, so look for the eight-pointed star on the Bangla sign. Rickshaw-wallahs know where the hotel is. Ordinary but clean rooms with fan and mosquito net cost Tk 100/200; larger rooms with small balconies cost from Tk 200 for a single to Tk 600 for an air-con double.

Bogra's top hotel is the three-storey **Safeway Motel** (☎ 6087, ☎/fax 73552, ✉ safeway@bogra.desh.net), on the north-western outskirts of town on the road to Naogaon, a couple of hundred metres west of the junction with the Rangpur bypass road. A garden with chairs and a small pond provides a restful and, for Bangladesh, unusual respite. Rooms with fan cost Tk 460/570, Tk 690/790 with air-con, executive rooms cost Tk 915/1030 and suites cost Tk 2060. All the rooms are spacious and have full carpeting, satellite TV, bureaus

with dressing mirrors, and large bathrooms with hot-water baths. There are also rooms for clients' chauffeurs ranging from Tk 60 to Tk 120. The Safeway also has one of the best restaurants in town, international telephone connections from every room, an email connection (Tk 50 per email), and helpful staff. It's close to the Central Bus Station so you could get off the bus and walk from there, or catch a rickshaw.

Alternatively, try the new **Parjatan Motel** (☎ 6753) at the southern entrance to town, 4km from the town centre. Similar in most respects, it has spacious ventilated rooms with firm stuffed-cotton mattresses and cold-water showers for Tk 400, and air-con rooms with softer mattresses and hot-water showers for Tk 650. It also has Tk 100 rooms for drivers. The government's modern brick **Circuit House**, which is in the heart of town on Nawab Bari Rd, costs far less but with Parjatan here, the district commissioner is unlikely to consent to you staying.

Another possibility is the **Archaeology Department Rest House** at the Mahasthangarh ruins, across from the museum overlooking a winding river. See the Mahasthangarh section later in this chapter.

Places to Eat

A good cheap place to eat in the heart of town is the **Sun & Sea Restaurant**, which is 75m or so north-east of Sat Mata. Marked in English, it's an unusually tidy restaurant with typical Bangladeshi fare at popular prices, and cold soft drinks. Three similar places in the town centre that seem more ordinary are the well-marked **Juliet Hotel & Restaurant**, around the corner on Kazi Nasrul Islam Rd; **Gour Gopal Dodhe** (no English sign), on Nawab Bari Rd a block north of Bogra Boarding; and an unmarked restaurant two blocks south on the same street. At all of these places, two parathas and a small dish of vegetables will cost you about Tk 20.

For Chinese fare, the friendly **Chinese Restaurant** at the Mandolin Hotel is worth a try, despite the fact that it's too dark to properly admire the lurid decor. Still, it's a cosy carpeted restaurant in an unlikely place – the top floor of Shaptobari market. A plate of mixed fried rice costs Tk 80, and 'potatoo cheaps' cost Tk 50.

The city's best **restaurants** by reputation are at the Parjatan Motel and the Safeway Motel. Both are carpeted and have air-con. Mixed chow mein at the Safeway costs Tk 132, chicken tikka Tk 154, and a serving of Bogra's misti doi for dessert is Tk 22. The restaurant at the Parjatan offers a similar variety of Chinese, western and Bangladeshi dishes for less than the Safeway, but the ambience is a bit gloomier.

Getting There & Away
Air The closest airports, both three hours away, are at Rajshahi and Ishurdi. The government plans to develop a nearby airstrip for commercial flights, but this will probably take several years, if it happens at all.

Bus Arriving from Rangpur, Rajshahi or other big towns in the region, buses stop at Bogra's central bus station, 2km north-west of town at the junction of the Rangpur Bypass road and the road to Naogaon (close to the Safeway Motel). From here it's a 25-minute rickshaw ride into town for around Tk 15.

Most offices of buses for Dhaka, including Keya Paribahan, are west of Sat Mata, but the SR bus office is just to the east of Sat Mata. Deluxe air-con buses to Dhaka cost from Tk 250 to Tk 280. Ordinary Dhaka buses charge between Tk 110 and Tk 120. The journey to Dhaka is via the Bangabandhu Bridge and takes around four to five hours.

Buses for the following destinations leave from Bogra central bus station near the Safeway Motel. There are buses throughout the day to Natore (Tk 25) and Rajshahi (Tk 40), but much fewer to Khulna division. There are several around 9 am to Khulna (Tk 120). Northbound buses to Rangpur (Tk 40) depart every 20 minutes from around 6 am, with the last departure around 6 pm; the trip takes 2½ hours. Travellers to Paharpur can take regular buses throughout the day to Jaipurhat; the trip takes 1½ hours and costs Tk 20. From there you can take a tempo to Paharpur.

Train Few people bother to take the lengthy train trip to Dhaka now that the Bangabandhu Bridge is open for business, as the trip entails a lengthy ferry crossing. If and when the rail link over the bridge is finished, this may change. Meanwhile, there's an express every day except Tuesday to Dhaka via Mymensingh, departing from Bogra at 8.35 pm and arriving at Mymensingh at 5 am and Dhaka at 7 am. The 1st/sulob class fares are Tk 455/130 to Dhaka and Tk 280/90 to Mymensingh.

From Dhaka, the Ekota Express departs in the late afternoon and gets into Bogra at around 4.30 am. You won't get much sleep on this trip as there's a three-hour ferry crossing in the middle of it. Still, the train is comfortable and the ferry, which sometimes runs aground, serves meals. If you're coming from Dhaka, when you catch the train waiting at the other side of the river make sure you get into a carriage that goes to Bogra, as the rest of the train goes to Dinajpur.

There are no direct trains from Bogra to Dinajpur or Rajshahi.

AROUND BOGRA
Sariakandi
For a bit of good adventure, consider heading east via Gabtali (General Zia's home town) to Sariakandi (20km) and hiring a motorised boat there to take you out onto the Jamuna River. This is most interesting during flood season as you can see all the broken embankments and people living on the tiny islands created by the massive annual flooding. The banks of the Jamuna are just about the most erosion-prone places in the country, literally forcing farmers off their land. Many dispossessed farmers then try to make do by joining the ranks of the rickshaw-wallahs.

Hat Bazar
Every Friday in a village just south of Bogra there's a *hat bazar*, a market that attracts so many people that they spill onto the highway, often causing a traffic jam. Roaming around these bazars can be interesting and fun. Look for the fish traps; very intriguing, they come in many shapes and styles.

MAHASTHANGARH

The oldest known city in Bangladesh, dating back to at least the 3rd century BC, Mahasthangarh (formerly known as Pundravardhana) is today an archaeological site consisting largely of foundations and hillocks hinting at past riches. There isn't a lot to see, but the scale is impressive and the countryside is good to wander in.

The principal site, called the Citadel, contains traces of the ancient city, but many other sites in the vicinity are usually lumped together under the name Mahasthangarh. This whole area is rich in Hindu, Buddhist and Muslim sites, most of which have all but vanished.

The Buddhists were here until at least the 11th century AD, their most glorious period being from the 8th to the 11th centuries AD, when the Buddhist Pala emperors of North Bengal ruled. It is to this period that most of the visible remains belong. Although there are Hindu and Muslim structures here and there, most are Buddhist.

Mahasthangarh Site Museum

Although quite small, the museum has some interesting Hindu and Buddhist pieces dating from the 6th to 13th century AD. On weekends there are always lots of visitors here, sometimes big groups of school children. During the week it can be very quiet, and the museum may be closed until an official is roused from the office to bring the key. The office is the building on the left side of the gardens as you enter.

Upon entering, to the left you'll find lots of old Buddhist terracotta pieces from the Vasu Bihar excavations, as well as some gold ornaments and coins recovered here that date back to the 3rd century BC. The terracotta pieces were used to decorate Buddhist shrines; some date back to the 2nd century BC. Excellently preserved, many of them depict a female figure with an elaborate headdress and richly bedecked with ornaments. The motifs represent human and semi-divine beings, animals and plants of various kinds, and composite animals or beings. Among the metal objects on display are copper rings, copper medallions, knives and an embossed gold amulet.

There are also some well-preserved bronze images from Vasu Bihar, mostly from the Pala period (8th to 11th century AD), representing Buddha and other Buddhist deities in different forms and sizes. Of the female figures, images of Bodhisattva Tara far outnumber others. Unlike the terracotta pieces, which were all discovered at the shrine area, the Vasu Bihar bronzes were all found in the monasteries, mostly inside the cells, and undoubtedly represent cult images for the private worship and ritual purposes of the resident monks.

Also on display, mostly to the right as you enter, are some large black-stone carvings of various Hindu deities, including Vishnu, Ganesh, Shiva and Saraswati.

From October to March the museum is open 10 am to 1 pm and 2 to 5 pm Sunday to Friday. Opening and closing hours are an hour later from April to September. Admission is Tk 2.

The Citadel

The Citadel, adjacent to the museum, forms a rough rectangle covering more than 2 sq km. More impressive is the fact that the remains of the fortified city rise around 4½m above the surrounding country – in Bangladesh that almost qualifies as a mountain range. It was surrounded by a moat on three sides, with the once mighty Karatuya River guarding the fort.

Probably first constructed under the Mauryan empire in the 3rd century BC, the site shows evidence of various Hindu empires and Buddhist and Muslim occupations. It finally fell into disuse around the time of the Mughal invasions, although Hindus still make an annual pilgrimage to the Karatuya River in mid-April. The site consists mostly of long, partly reconstructed fortifications with indistinct mounds inside. Most of the visible brickwork dates from the 8th century AD, apart from that added in the current restoration program.

Outside the Citadel, opposite the museum, the remains of a 6th century AD Govinda Bhita Hindu temple overlook a picturesque bend in the river.

Lakshindarer Medh

Near Gokul, a couple of kilometres south of the Citadel, this large mound is the partially excavated site of an ancient Shiva temple, over which a Buddhist stupa was constructed in the 7th century AD. Local legend associates it with the snake goddess Manassa or, alternatively, with a dalliance between a wandering prince and a temple dancer.

Vasu Bihar

This Buddhist archaeological site is situated on low hills 7km to the north-west of the village of Mahasthan (MOSH-than). In the 7th century AD, the traveller Xuan Zhang wrote that this site accommodated 700 Buddhist monks in its monasteries, and also noted the gigantic Ashoka stupa. Many of the items on display in the museum came from here. The foundations of two of the monasteries have been partially reconstructed, but the remains mostly consist of low mounds, some of which have yet to be excavated. Unless you have an interest in archaeology, the trip along country tracks to get here will be the highlight of the visit.

Places to Stay & Eat

The *Archaeology Department Rest House* is the bungalow across the road from the museum, overlooking the Karatuya River. There are three good-sized double rooms for Tk 150, with fan, mosquito netting and western bathrooms. There's also a small dining room. Either the caretaker or the attendant at the museum ticket booth can point you to the person you need to pay and fill out any paperwork for. The guesthouse has a garden and a nice view over the river and fields. You can eat here if you order in advance. Otherwise head for Mahasthan, where you'll find a few basic restaurants.

Getting There & Away

Buses run from the Bogra bus station north to Mahasthan, and cost about Tk 5 for the trip (11km, 30 minutes). From here you can take a rickshaw or walk the 1.75km to the Citadel and the nearby museum and guesthouse.

Vasu Bihar is 7km to the west of the museum, and by rickshaw it's a long ride (at least Tk 20 each way) over bumpy little paved and unpaved paths. You might be able to take a tempo most of the way here from Mahasthan. When asking directions use the local name of the site – Narapatir Dhap.

PAHARPUR

The Somapuri Vihara at Paharpur was formerly the biggest Buddhist monastery south of the Himalaya. It dates from the 8th century AD. This is the most impressive archaeological site in Bangladesh, so much so that it was declared a protected archaeological site back in 1919, although the scholar-traveller Dr Buckman Hamilton had shown interest in it as far back as 1807.

Somapuri Vihara

Although in an advanced state of decay, the overall plan of the temple complex is easy to figure out. It is in the shape of a large quadrangle covering 11 hectares, with the monks' cells making up the walls and enclosing a courtyard. From the centre of the courtyard rise the 20m-high remains of a stupa that dominates the countryside. There's a good view from the top. Its cruciform floor plan is topped by a three-tier superstructure with the first tier raised just slightly above ground level. The second level rises almost three times higher, and the third level soars up to be topped by a large, hollow, square cubicle somewhat similar to the hollow tower structure of Mohenjo Daro in Pakistan.

This *mahavihara*, or great monastery, has slightly recessed walls embellished with well-preserved terracotta bas-reliefs of rural folk and wildlife in their local settings. The clay tiles are not sequentially arranged – they were really meant to be admired individually as decorative pieces, not to tell a story. Some of them depict an animal that might be the variety of rhinoceros that is now extinct in Bangladesh.

Lining the outer perimeter are over 170 small monastic cells. There are ornamental pedestals in 72 of them, the purpose of which still eludes archaeologists. It is possible they contained the remains of saintly monks who had resided in these cells.

The cells have a drainage system with 22 outlets to the courtyard, marked by stone gargoyles.

There are points of interest on each side of the courtyard. On the east side you can make out the outline of what was once a miniature model of the temple. On the western wing of the north side are the remains of structures whose purpose continues to baffle archaeologists. On the eastern wing of the south side is an elevated brick base with an eight-pointed, star-shaped structure that must have been a shrine. To the west lie the remains of what appears to have been the monks' refectory and kitchen.

Except for the guardhouse to the north, most of the remains outside the courtyard lie to the south. They include an oblong building, linked to the monastery by a causeway, which may have been the wash house and latrines. In the same area is a bathing ghat, probably of Hindu origin. Only 12m south-west of the ghat is the rectangular Temple of Gondeswari, with an octagonal pillar base in the centre and a circular platform to the front.

The monastery is thought to have been successively occupied by Buddhists, Jains and Hindus. This explains the sometimes curious mixture of artwork, although the basic structure remained unaltered. The Jains must have constructed a *chaturmukhar*, a structure with all four walls decorated with stone bas-reliefs of their deities. The Hindus made alterations to the base walls to replace the Buddhist terracotta artwork with sculptural stonework of their own deities, and with terracotta artwork representing themes from the *Mahabharata* and the *Ramayana*. Artefacts discovered at the site range from bronze statues and bas-reliefs of the elephant-headed Hindu god Ganesh, to statues of the Jain god Manzuri, and from bronze images of the Buddha to statues of the infant Krishna.

Museum

The small museum houses a representative display of the many domestic and religious objects found during excavations. It gives a good idea of the range of cultures that have used this site. Stucco Buddha heads unearthed here are similar to the Gandhara style of Indo-Hellenic sculpture from what is now north-western Pakistan. Sculptural work includes sandstone and basalt sculptures, but the stonework of Hevagara in passionate embrace with Shakti is the collection's finest item. The most important find, a large bronze Buddha, is usually away on tour. The museum is open from 9 am to 1 pm and 2 to 5 pm daily, from 10 am to 5 pm Friday, and closed on Saturday. The museum and rest house are both in the Department of Archaeology compound, which also encloses a well-kept garden.

Satyapir Vita

This complex originally contained the Temple of Tara. Approaching the site on the Jamalganj road, you first come to the ruins 400m east of the Somapuri Vihara. It is trapezoidal in shape, measuring about 75m by 40m by 85m, and was walled up except on the northern side, although the main entrance appears to have been from the south. The main temple is an oblong building, 24m by 12m, composed of three parts – the sanctum in the north, a pillared hall with a circumambulatory passage in the south and a shrine. Today, only scant ruins remain. A square-based stupa, three metres on each side, has a small reliquary that was full of tiny clay stupas when discovered, apparently offerings by pilgrims as tokens of reverence.

Places to Stay

If you plan to spend a day at Paharpur, start early. The place is extensive and fascinating. There is an *Archaeology Department Rest House* and, as at Mahasthan, you can stay here if there's space available, which is likely. The cost is only Tk 150 per double room. Meals are available if you order well in advance, otherwise it's advisable to bring supplies with you.

Getting There & Away

Paharpur is 56km north-west of Bogra. First take a bus to Jaipurhat, 44km away. It is a 90-minute trip costing Tk 20 by direct bus. The bus station in Jaipurhat is on the outskirts of town. From there you have two options. The first is to take a rickshaw from the bus station to a crossroads (Tk 5) and catch a crowded little tempo (Tk 6) from there to Paharpur village (9km). The road is narrow but sealed all the way. Taking this option, you should be able to get from Bogra to Paharpur in 2½ hours.

A slower option is to walk or take a rickshaw the kilometre or so to the Jaipurhat train station. From there, take one of the infrequent trains to Jamalpur that cost Tk 2 and take 15 minutes. This train is often late so see if there's a bus waiting across the tracks; it costs Tk 3 for a bumpy 40 minutes. It's a 45-minute walk to Paharpur from Jamalpur, or a short ride by rickshaw. Either way, when you're heading back to Bogra, don't count on getting a bus from Jaipurhat to Bogra after 6 pm.

NAOGAON

While you're in the area you could also check the old **Dubalhati Palace**, which is about 30km south-west of Paharpur as the crow flies, about 8km south-west of Naogaon. The main building, which has a 65m long facade, features a central block with Corinthian columns. If you look above them you'll see an unusually ornate parapet on top, with highly ornate plaster decorations consisting of floral patterns and sculptures of classical Greek male and female figures, plus an English insignia. The rajbari is now abandoned, so you can wander freely inside, visualising the splendour that the original owners (the Dubalhati Raj family, one of the oldest in the district) lived in.

RANGPUR

☎ 0521

Rangpur is a major transit point for the northern half of Rajshahi division, which is sometimes referred to as North Bengal. The town is home to several historic public buildings of the Raj era, including Carmichael College and Tajhat Palace. The town is also one place you may see members of the Kochi ethnic group, an Indo-Tibetan people related to the plains tribes of Assam who are recognisable by their rounder, more South-East Asian faces.

It's a large spread-out town, although most places of interest to travellers lie between Nawabganj Bazar, the centre of town on the corner of GL Roy and Station Rds; and the train station, 3km south at the end of Station Rd. If you're arriving by bus from Saidpur you can get off at the first circle (Medical Morh) or at the bus station. The first is closer to the central market area and most lower-end hotels, while the latter is closer to the train station.

The Sonali Bank, in an impressive Raj-period building, will change travellers cheques. It's on Station Rd, 500m south of Nawabganj Bazar. Care has an office here but no guesthouse. Its friendly staff may be a good source of information.

Tajhat Palace

Tajhat Palace is one of the finest rajbaris in all of Bangladesh. Indeed, it's so large and impressive that the tendency is to immediately assume that it was always a public building. During the regime of General Ershad (1982–91) it was used by the High Court division of Bangladesh's Supreme Court, but since 1991 it and the modern administrative buildings around it have lain empty.

This magnificent edifice, which is structurally intact but deteriorating fast, is similar to Ahsan Manzil in Dhaka. It has a frontage of about 80m and, like the Pink Palace, is crowned by a ribbed conical dome and features an imposing central staircase made of imported white marble. The balustrade originally featured marble sculptures of classical Roman figures, but these have long since disappeared. The balcony roof is supported by four Corinthian columns, which also feature on the projecting ends of the building.

In the 19th century Manna Lal Ray, a Hindu, was forced to emigrate from the Punjab and found his way to Rangpur. He became a successful jeweller and eventually acquired a lot of land and won the title of raja. His crowning achievement was the construction of this huge mansion

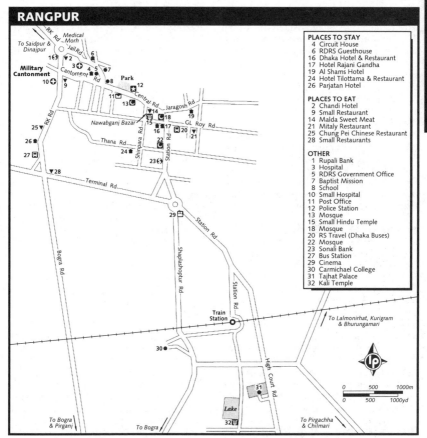

RANGPUR

PLACES TO STAY
4 Circuit House
6 RDRS Guesthouse
16 Dhaka Hotel & Restaurant
17 Hotel Rajani Gandha
19 Al Shams Hotel
24 Hotel Tilottama & Restaurant
26 Parjatan Hotel

PLACES TO EAT
2 Chandi Hotel
9 Small Restaurant
14 Malda Sweet Meat
21 Mitaly Restaurant
25 Chung Pei Chinese Restaurant
28 Small Restaurants

OTHER
1 Rupali Bank
3 Hospital
5 RDRS Government Office
7 Baptist Mission
8 School
10 Small Hospital
11 Post Office
12 Police Station
13 Mosque
15 Small Hindu Temple
18 Mosque
20 RS Travel (Dhaka Buses)
22 Mosque
23 Sonali Bank
27 Bus Station
29 Cinema
30 Carmichael College
31 Tajhat Palace
32 Kali Temple

during the mid-19th century. The last raja fled to India during Partition. Local villagers believe there is treasure hidden in its walls, which doesn't augur well for its long-term survival. It's 5km south of Nawabganj Bazar and 2km south of the train station, outside the de facto city boundaries.

Kali Temple

This delightful architectural folly lies about 1km south of Tajhat Palace, at the southern end of an artificial lake. Few people in Rangpur seems to know about it. Ask around the neighbourhood for the 'Kali mondir'. The temple is modelled on a Florentine dome, or at least a Bengali vision of an English adaptation of a Florentine dome. The dilapidated octagonal building has sculptures of Hindu deities around its upper storey. The Hindu family who live in the compound will no doubt be surprised to see you but are likely to be happy to show you the interior. Inside is a small image of the fearsome Kali, goddess of destruction, with a necklace of human heads and weapons in each of her many arms. Getting there requires taking a rickshaw from High Court Rd.

Carmichael College

This famous old college, which dates from 1916, has a picturesque appearance and is worth checking out in conjunction with the High Court, 2km to the south-east. Similar in inspiration to Curzon Hall in Dhaka, this structure, with a grand frontage of over 100m, represents a splendid fusion of classical British and Mughal architecture. Its mosque-inspired domes rest on slender columns, and a series of arched openings on all sides add to the mosque-like appearance. The campus, which is on the outskirts of town, is spacious and rural, with cows grazing on the main lawn. Coming here might be a good opportunity to meet some students, but you'd have to come on a weekday.

Places to Stay – Budget

Situated in the town centre, a long block east of Nawabganj Bazar, *Al Shams Hotel* (☎ 3768) on Jaragosh Rd has singles /doubles with attached bathroom for Tk 60/90. The mattresses are tough and old, the walls are grubby and the bathrooms smell a bit, but at least they do a good job sweeping the place. The mosquito nets are a bit ratty, though. Rooms are slightly larger here than at the *Dhaka Hotel* on GL Roy Rd, which has rooms with fans, mosquito nets and attached bathrooms for Tk 60/120. The bathrooms are the typical prison-style ablutions chamber, but the Dhaka has one of the better restaurants in this area.

Places to Stay – Mid-Range

Next door to the Dhaka Hotel on busy Station Rd is the six-storey *Hotel Rajani Gandha* (☎ 2669), a well-run establishment with tiled floors and friendly staff. It has clean rooms with attached bathroom for Tk 80/140, and bigger rooms for Tk 120/200 with furniture, rugs and clean pillows and sheets. There is no sign in English.

The beautiful *Circuit House* (☎ 3095), on Cantonment Rd, has lovely gardens in the front and double rooms for Tk 150. The district dommissioner, however, will probably refer you to the Parjatan Motel.

On the quiet Thana Rd you'll find the *Hotel Tilottama* (☎ 3482). It has a small Chinese restaurant, gardens at the front and room to park a vehicle. Singles cost from Tk 115 to Tk 135, doubles from Tk 175 to Tk 195. Rooms come with fan, desk, chair, reasonably comfortable beds and bathrooms with western facilities. Some travellers have complained that management was unwilling to let them stay in the cheaper rooms on the ground floor, so you may have to persist a little. Otherwise the friendly English-speaking manager is very helpful.

Places to Stay – Top End

The top place in town is the *Parjatan Motel* (☎ 3681), on RK Rd, just north of the bus station. It's a modern establishment and features a spacious lobby with comfortable seating and satellite TV. The standard rooms, which cost Tk 575, are ventilated and roomy, and come with carpets, fans, nice furnishings and attached bathrooms with western facilities. Rooms with aircon cost Tk 1050, and VIP suites cost Tk 1600. There is also a restaurant with the usual mix of Chinese, Bangladeshi and western dishes.

You could also try the *RDRS Guesthouse* (☎ 2767) right near the RDRS Government Office, an unmarked three-storey building just north of the Baptist Mission and 100m off Jail Rd. The Rangpur Dinajpur Rural Services Project (RDRS), a local NGO, has very decent and comfortable guest quarters available to all. Rooms are no great bargain at Tk 300/500. Set meals cost Tk 80 except for breakfast, which costs Tk 60. To reserve, you must call here, not its office in Dhaka. On weekends the office is closed, and it also closes on Thursday at noon.

Places to Eat

One of the better places in the centre of town for Bangladeshi food is the *restaurant* in the Dhaka Hotel on GL Roy Rd. It also has Chinese fare, but it's reportedly mediocre. Or check to see if the nearby *Mitaly Restaurant* (no English sign) is still open. It's down an alley off GL Roy Rd near the south-east corner of the intersection with Station Rd. The chicken fry is reportedly good and it serves coffee.

Another place close by is **Malda Sweet Meat**, on Central Rd at the market. You can get a Bengali meal, such as curry and rice, for around Tk 15 to Tk 20.

In the Medical Morh area, try the **Chandi Hotel**, which is just south of the roundabout. It's a friendly and relatively neat place. You can order tasty chicken, dhal and rice for Tk 30.

The **Chung Pei Chinese Restaurant,** about 100m from the Parjatan Motel, is typical of its type; an air-conditioned place for well-to-do locals to be seen spending money. The food isn't bad though, with main dishes such as ginger chicken for around Tk 100. The **restaurant** at the Hotel Tilottama has a similar selection of Chinese dishes in a Bangladeshi context.

Getting There & Away

Air Biman (☎ 3437) flies every morning to Saidpur, which is 40km to the west. Most people take a bus from there to get here, but an expensive taxi from the airport is an option.

Bus The bus station is on RK Rd (Bogra Rd), 3km south-west of the central area (about Tk 12 by rickshaw). Buses for Bogra depart every 20 minutes from 7 am to 5.30 pm, and the fare is Tk 40. There are no direct buses to Dinajpur, Thakurgaon or Chilahati. For these towns you must change at Saidpur. Buses for Saidpur leave every few minutes and charge Tk 14 for the 1¼ hour ride; the last bus departs around 7 pm. Trips to Dinajpur take around 2½ to three hours. Only a few buses make the five-hour Tk 60 journey to Rajshahi, and the last leaves at 3 pm. There are no chair coaches on any of these routes.

Deluxe chair coaches for Dhaka all leave from around 5 to 7 pm; the trip normally takes about 11 hours. Many companies leave from the bus station, but for guaranteed seating you'll do better going to their offices and reserving a seat there. RS Travels is in the town centre on GL Roy Rd, 70m or so east of Station Rd. Its buses all leave between 5.30 and 6.30 pm, and the fare is Tk 300 with air-con, Tk 140 for non-air-con buses and less leg room. Other companies

offering chair-coach services leave from the same area. Some Rajshahi buses apparently leave from there too.

Train Intercity (IC) trains to Dhaka via Mymensingh depart at 8 am and 7.45 pm, and 1st/sulob class fares are Tk 340/165 to Dhaka and Tk 250/140 to Mymensingh. It takes at least 12 hours to get to Dhaka, including a lengthy ferry crossing and a change of trains. Understandably, most people travel by bus.

SAIDPUR
☎ 0552

Saidpur is a quiet little backwater shaded by enormous trees, and the atmosphere of the Raj lingers here. Near the quaint old train station is one of Bangladesh's few surviving English-style churches, and the neat back streets are lined with old cottages. The southern part of the town around Canada House is green and spacious and has some impressively solid red-brick buildings from the latter period of the Raj.

Although Saidpur is fairly small, it has the only airport in northern Bangladesh. Consequently it serves much larger towns, including Rangpur, Dinajpur and Thakurgaon, and is a regional transit point.

The City Bank and Sonali Bank both have branches in the central area and might be persuaded to change cash at bad rates, but you'll have to continue on to Rangpur or Dinajpur to change travellers cheques.

Places to Stay & Eat

The **Hotel Time Star** (☎ 2386) on noisy Station Rd is the usual basic, slightly grubby multistorey concrete place with singles/doubles with bathroom for Tk 50/100.

The **Hotel Prince International** (☎ 2262) is similar but has a wider range of rooms, from singles/doubles with common bath for Tk 40/80, rooms with bathroom for Tk 80/160, and larger doubles rooms with some extra furniture from Tk 200. It's clean and friendly enough, but checkout is by 12 noon precisely.

On another level altogether is **Canada House** (☎ 2580), in the quiet southern part of town just off Airport Rd. This colonial-era

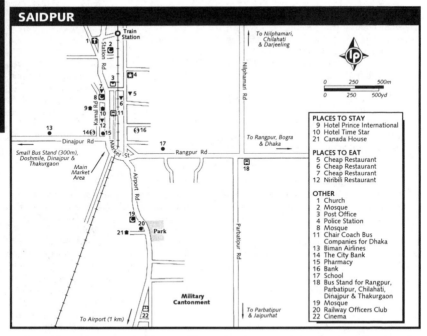

SAIDPUR

To Nilphamari, Chilahati & Darjeeling

Nilphamari Rd

0   250   500m
0   250   500yd

To Rangpur, Bogra & Dhaka

To Parbatipur & Jaipurhat

Rangpur Rd

Parbatipur Rd

Dinajpur Rd

Small Bus Stand (300m), Doshmile, Dinajpur & Thakurgaon

Main Market Area

Market St

Airport Rd

Station Rd

Kamal Rd

Park

Military Cantonment

To Airport (1 km)

Train Station

PLACES TO STAY
9 Hotel Prince International
10 Hotel Time Star
21 Canada House

PLACES TO EAT
5 Cheap Restaurant
6 Cheap Restaurant
7 Cheap Restaurant
12 Niribili Restaurant

OTHER
1 Church
2 Mosque
3 Post Office
4 Police Station
8 Mosque
11 Chair Coach Bus Companies for Dhaka
13 Biman Airlines
14 The City Bank
15 Pharmacy
16 Bank
17 School
18 Bus Stand for Rangpur, Parbatipur, Chilahati, Dinajpur & Thakurgaon
19 Mosque
20 Railway Officers Club
22 Cinema

mansion is surrounded by gardens, with all mod cons including satellite TV and hot water. Each of the 10 rooms costs Tk 500 per person. Three meals a day costs another Tk 350. Canada House is the end of a small lane close to the Railway Officers Club. It's wise to make advance bookings.

Other than Canada House, Saidpur's culinary scene is nothing to get excited about. The *Niribili Restaurant,* next to the Hotel Time Star on Station Rd is larger than most with a slightly broader range of dishes (beef *and* chicken!). Other local eateries include one on Station Rd just before the post office and two others 200m to the east, across the railway tracks. All of them serve typical Bangladeshi meals (curry, bhoona etc) for about Tk 25.

Getting There & Away
Air The airport (☎ 2498) is 2km to the south, beyond the attractive old administrative area and next to the military canton-

ment. The Biman office (☎ 2007) is on the north side of Dinajpur Rd, 300m west of the city's main intersection. There are flights to/from Dhaka every afternoon; the fare is Tk 1325 (including Tk 75 airport tax). Flights go in a triangle between Dhaka, Rajshahi and Saidpur every afternoon, at 1 pm for flights direct to Dhaka and at 3.30 pm for flights via Rajshahi to Dhaka; on Tuesday, Sunday and Friday flights go via Rajshahi and cost Tk 775.

There are lots of rickshaws and a few unmarked taxis for taking travellers into town, but no baby taxis. The rickshaw fare is Tk 10 into town but you'll probably have to bargain hard to get this price. The taxis are impossible to distinguish from private cars so you'll have to ask someone at the airport to point one out.

Bus The main bus station is on the eastern side of town, about 1.5km from the town centre. There are departures every few minutes for Rangpur (1¼ hours), Dinajpur (one hour) and slightly less frequently for Thakurgaon (1½ hours). You can also get buses to Chilahati and Parbatipur. The last buses for all these towns depart around 7 pm. If you're headed south for Jaipurhat (near the Paharpur ruins) you may have to wait so long for a direct bus that you'll be better off taking a series of buses.

You can get buses here for Dhaka, but it's best to go to the offices in the centre of town along Station Rd and reserving a seat there. Chair coaches all leave around 5 to 6.30 pm, and the trip usually takes about 8 hours. For air-con deluxe coaches to Dhaka you'll have to go to Dinajpur or Rangpur.

You'll also find a small bus stand on the western edge of town where some local buses heading for Doshmile, Dinajpur and Thakurgaon leave from. It's about 1km from the town centre, beyond the bridge. Typical fares are Tk 6 to Doshmile, Tk 8 to Dinajpur, Tk 23 to Thakurgaon, Tk 25 to Chilahati, Tk 14 to Rangpur and Tk 140 to Dhaka.

Train Trains to Khulna run via Rajshahi. The IC Rupsa Express departs at 7.45 am and the Shimanto departs at 8 pm. Fares are Tk 525/170 in 1st/sulob class. The fares to Rajshahi are Tk 190/65.

Two express and two local trains a day (including one at 12 noon) make the two-hour trip north to Chilahati. The fare is Tk 70/23 in 1st/2nd class.

DINAJPUR
☎ 0531

Dinajpur, 50km south of Thakurgaon and 70km west of Rangpur, is the largest city in north-western Bangladesh and is famous for its rice. There are some interesting old buildings in town, the most famous being the Dinajpur rajbari. It includes an adjoining Krishna temple. There are also some interesting buildings in the surrounding areas, including the much photographed Kantanagar Temple, which is in all the Bangladesh tourist brochures. In winter the area is slightly cooler than the country's southern regions and there are lots of good back roads for cycling.

Orientation & Information

The train station is in the heart of town. Just north is the market and most hotels and restaurants. South of the train station is the administrative area, including the Circuit House, a large compound of some imposing Raj-era buildings (the GPO, mapping office, etc) and a grass *maidan* (parade ground) that hosts cricket and badminton matches as well as political demonstrations.

Travellers cheques can be exchanged at the Sonali Bank, about a kilometre north of the train station. If you want to check out the Bangladeshi movie scene, try one of the three cinemas along Station Rd.

Dinajpur Rajbari

The Dinajpur rajbari is dilapidated but still one of the country's most picturesque, and it's worth exploring the buildings and grounds. To the left of the entrance is a daintily painted Krishna temple. The rajbari itself lies through a second gate, facing another courtyard. Both structures date from the 1890s when the 18th-century palace was rebuilt after the great earthquake of 1897.

As with many of the magnificent 18th- and 19th-century rajbaris, this one reflects the cosmopolitan tastes of its owners. Florid oriental designs blend with European-inspired proportions and neo-Renaissance features, including ornate gateways and many beautifully carved stone columns. The single-storey flat-roofed Krishna temple, for example, is decorated with attractive stucco floral motifs.

The front verandah is supported on four semi-Corinthian pillars and the main hall is set on another set of similar columns. The main two-storey rajbari has a broad frontage of about 45m, with a series of tall Ionic columns, and on either side of the balcony is a broad spiral masonry staircase leading to the upper storey. Inside, there's a 15m-long, 8m-high hall.

The Krishna temple is open only when the custodian cares to make an appearance, but the friendly Hindu family who have made a home by the side of the main building will send someone to find him. Hindus still worship here, so the cows that wander among the ruins are probably as safe as their ancestors were when the terracotta scenes of Krishna and the *gopis* (milk-maids) were made.

The buildings to the rear of the main building are gradually being chipped away for building material, while trees and vines slowly overrun the substantial structures that remain. On a foggy morning the rajbari has the atmosphere of a Hammer Horror film, and seems to be much older than a little more than 100 years.

The rajbari is about 4km north-east of central Dinajpur. A rickshaw will cost at least Tk 15. Don't bargain a round-trip fare, as it's more expensive to have a rickshaw driver wait for you than it is to simply pick up one of the many rickshaws available nearby.

Places to Stay – Budget

Most of the lower-end hotels are near the train station in the centre of town. One of the cheapest is *Arab Boarding*, just west of the station. Its singles/doubles, which are tiny and dirty with common bathrooms, cost Tk 30/60.

Hotel Rehana, 1½ blocks up Station Rd (no English sign), is next in line, with rooms for Tk 50/80. Avoid rooms at the back which are adjacent to a large cinema.

The *Hotel Nabeena* (☎ 4178) is half a block west and of comparable value. It has ventilated rooms and beds with mosquito nets for Tk 40/50 (Tk 50/70 with attached bathrooms).

A better option is the *New Hotel* (☎ 4155) on Station Road. It's clean, with decent attached tiled bathrooms and rooms with fans, mosquito nets and basic furniture for Tk 50/100. The hotel's restaurant is the best Bangladeshi eatery in the centre of town.

Even better, drop by the office of CDA (☎ 4428), an NGO, on the eastern outskirts of town, just off Fulbari Rd, close to the BRAC and Care offices. The attached *CDA Guesthouse* has 11 double rooms. They are spotless and cost Tk 60 a person; guests can eat here as well. The staff are very kind but you probably shouldn't stay here unless you have a genuine interest in development issues and the sort of work CDA is doing.

Staff can also arrange accommodation at their training centre close to Kantanagar Temple (see the Around Dinajpur section below).

Places to Stay – Mid-Range & Top End

The *Circuit House* (☎ 3122) has eight modern double rooms for Tk 150, if you can get permission from the district commissioner's office, which may direct you to the Parjatan Motel. It overlooks the grassy maidan behind the train station. The District Commissioner's office is on the other side of the maidan.

Hotel Al-Rashid (☎ 4538) is a kilometre north of the train station, a block east of Station Rd. It's a clean, well-run establishment. The small rooms have attached bathrooms and are worth the Tk 80/160. There's a local restaurant nearby.

Another good mid-range establishment is the *Hotel Diamond* (☎ 4629), on a busy commercial street about 200m from the Hotel Al-Rashid. Small singles cost Tk 110, doubles with fan and furnishings cost Tk 300, and air-con doubles with satellite TV cost Tk 750.

The new *Parjatan Motel* (☎ 4718) has clean, modern, furnished rooms with fan for Tk 600, and air-con rooms for Tk 1200. It's on the edge of town, about 3km from the train station on Fulbari Rd, with ample room for parking. There's a restaurant here as well.

Places to Eat

New Hotel has the best *Bangladeshi restaurant* in the town centre. Very popular and open almost to midnight, it's one of the rare places where you can get vegetarian dishes. Two spicy vegetable dishes plus rice costs just Tk 18 and makes a very filling meal.

The small unmarked *Slim Hotel*, just east of the train station, looks grubby but may be cheaper. If you're in the area around the Al-Rashid and Diamond hotels you'll find a few more small *restaurants*, including the unmarked *Dinajpur Brahamian Sweets*, which is two blocks north-east on a corner and better for snacks.

The city's top restaurants, the *Puffin Restaurant*, which faces the train station,

A pot-seller returns home after a successful day at the market.

Imposing walls of books at a second-hand stall

Haggling over the price of spices

Rice merchants inspect the quality of their stock.

From traditional food to local produce, the markets and bazars of Bangladesh are a hive of activity, bursting with colour.

DINAJPUR

To Doshmile,
Thakurgaon, Saidpur &
Kantanagar Temple

To Parbatipur &
bike route to
Saidpur &
Rangpur

To Satagonj

To Satagonj

To Indian Border
(15km)

To Fulbari,
Bogra & Dhaka

To Ramshagar
Lake

OTHER
1 Dinajpur Rajbari
2 Bus Station
3 Cinema
4 Police Station
5 Biman Airlines
7 Small Bus Stand for Parbatipur
9 Cinema
11 Sonali Bank
14 Jail
16 Cinema
23 Telegraph & Telephone Office
24 Hospital
25 Town Hall
26 Fulbaria Bus Stand
27 GPO & Magistrate's Court
28 District Commissioner's Office
30 Eye Hospital
31 BRAC Office
33 CARE Office
34 Water Tower
35 Humanitarian Agency for
     Development Services (HADS) Office
37 Muslim Cemetery

PLACES TO STAY
8 Hotel Diamond
10 Hotel Al-Rashid
17 Hotel Rehana
18 Hotel Nabeena
19 New Hotel
20 Arab Boarding
29 Circuit House
32 CDA Guesthouse & Office
36 Parjatan Motel

PLACES TO EAT
6 Dinajpur Brahamian Sweets
12 Small Restaurant
13 Martin Chinese Restaurant
15 Small Restaurant
21 Puffin Restaurant
22 Slim Hotel

and *Martin Chinese Restaurant* (☎ 4074), which is almost a kilometre to the north along Station Rd, are both Chinese and have air-con. Dishes at both places are mostly in the Tk 80 to Tk 120 range. The Puffin's run-down appearance is misleading because the restaurant inside, on the 3rd floor, is attractive, light and airy, with a menu in English. The well-marked Martin has muzak, but the food isn't as good as at the Puffin.

The *restaurant* at the Parjatan Motel tries its hand at a range of western, Bangladeshi and Chinese dishes. Sweet and sour beef costs Tk 80 and chop suey costs Tk 95.

Getting There & Away

Air The nearest airport is at Saidpur. There's a Biman office (☎ 3340) on Station Rd, about 2km north of the train station.

Bus The station is in the north-east of town, on Rangpur Bypass Rd. The fare is Tk 8 to Saidpur (one hour) and Tk 24 to Thakurgaon (1¾ hours). If you're off to Chilahati you'll have to change in Saidpur as there is no direct service. The trip to Rangpur takes between 2½ and three hours, but you may have to change buses at Saidpur. If you do catch a direct Rangpur bus, the fare is Tk 30.

Buses direct to Dhaka and Bogra cost Tk 65 to Bogra and Tk 140 to Dhaka (Tk 200 by chair coach). Chair coaches all depart between 5 and 7 pm, and some of the companies have offices in town. Buses to Dhaka take 8 or 9 hours.

Train A number of trains serve Dinajpur, although there are better connections available at the nearby junction town of Parbatipur.

IC trains for Khulna (via Ishurdi), Kushtia and Jessore depart from Dinajpur daily at 6.25 am, except Monday. The IC Barendra Express to Rajshahi leaves at 6.25 am daily. The 1st/sulob class fares to Khulna are Tk 400/130; and to Rajshahi they're Tk 213/68.

The *Uttara Express* is a mail train running from Parbatipur to Rajshahi daily at 4 am. Fares are Tk 213/68 in 1st/sulob class. The *Ekota Express* runs from Parbatipur to Bogra; from there you can catch trains to Dhaka. The 1st/sulob fares to Dhaka are Tk 420/135.

If you're headed to the Indian border at Chilahati, you can take the 5 am train east to Parbatipur and connect with trains to Chilahati, arriving there around 1 pm. The total fare comes to Tk 42 in 2nd class. There is also a decrepit 2nd-class train for Thakurgaon and Panchagarh, departing daily around 7 am from Dinajpur. The trip takes about five hours to Panchagarh but delays are common.

AROUND DINAJPUR
Ramshagar Lake
Beyond Pulhat is a large picturesque lake, about 350m long, which is popular with Dinajpur residents as a picnic spot on Fridays. If you're looking for a place to get away from it all, this would be a good spot to come, especially during the week when it's all-but deserted. Some 11km south-east of town, the lake is only about 250m off to the right of the tarred Pulhat Rd, but it's surrounded by paddy fields and not visible from the road. There's an entrance fee of Tk 10 per vehicle. You can get a regular bus here for Tk 5, which leaves from the Fulbari bus stand in Dinajpur. You'll find a guest-house overlooking the lake and possibly several small boats for hire.

The *Ramshagar Lake Guesthouse*, beautifully located on a hill overlooking Ramshagar Lake, is 11km south-east of town on Pulhat Rd. It has two spacious rooms that cost around Tk 120. The rooms have two or three beds, overhead fans, old frayed carpets, mosquito nets and attached bathrooms with western-style toilets. Meals are not available. Not many people stay here overnight, but on weekends the lake attracts numerous residents of Dinajpur.

Kantanagar Temple
One of the most spectacular monuments in Bangladesh, this Hindu temple should not be missed. It is also known as Kantajees Temple. Built in 1752 by Pran Nath, a renowned maharaja from Dinajpur, it is the country's finest existing example of the brick and terracotta style. Its most remarkable feature, typical of late Mughal-era temples, is its superb surface decoration, with endless panels of sculptured terracotta plaques depicting both figural and floral motifs. The interior and exterior walls are simply amazing. Every available space, including the archways, vaults and columns, is profusely decorated with tiny figures and motifs in terracotta. The most prominent panels over the archways depict scenes from the great Hindu epics, particularly battle scenes.

Certainly the folk artists did not lack imagination or a sense of humour. Demons are depicted biting deep into the heads of the faithful (monkeys); one demon can be seen swallowing monkeys whole, which promptly reappear from his ear. Amid this confusion a pair of monkeys are carrying off a demon, like a chicken on a pole. Other scenes are more domestic, such as a wife massaging her husband's legs and a lady combing lice from another's hair. Another portrays a river cruise on a long boat overcrowded with merrymakers and a troupe of dancers, while amorous scenes are often placed in obscure corners. These intricate harmonious scenes are like a richly embroidered carpet.

The temple, a 15 sq metre three-storey edifice, was originally crowned with nine ornamental two-storey towers, giving it a more temple-like appearance. They collapsed during the great earthquake of 1897 and were never replaced. The building sits in a courtyard surrounded by temple offices and pilgrims' quarters, all protected by a stout wall.

Places to Stay & Eat It is possible to stay at the *CDA training centre* at Proshikhan Kendra, 3km from the temple in the village of Mukundupur. It costs Tk 300 for a double room with decent bathrooms and cooking facilities. The staff are friendly and can show you around the green and pleasant complex, which includes trial agricultural plots, a model farmhouse and seminar rooms. The cooks can also prepare food, given enough warning and some money for provisions. Arrange to stay here through the CDA office in Dinajpur (see under Places to Stay in the Dinajpur section).

Getting There & Away The temple is 26km north of Dinajpur on the road to Thakurgaon. Tell the bus driver where you want to go and remind him after about 20km. Get off the bus in Kantanagar village, which is the first village (about 5km) beyond the town of Doshmile; sometimes this is a regular stop, sometimes not. From the highway a dirt track goes left (west) for about 200m through the village and down to the river, from where you can just see the temple's rooftop. A boat will be waiting there to take you across. It's then a 10-minute walk to the temple – up a small hill, then left at the first fork and then along the winding path.

Buddhist Ruins of Sitakot Vihara Monastery

Some 56km south-east of Dinajpur, about 6km north-east of Charkai train station and 3km south-west of Nawabganj, are the Buddhist ruins of Sitakot. Excavations in 1968 exposed a Buddhist monastery dating from the 7th to 8th centuries. There are some 50 similar ancient mounds in the area,

but little remains of them as they have been the target of vandalism by neighbouring villagers searching for building materials.

The Sitakot monastery was built on a square plan and the 40 living spaces for monks overlooked a central courtyard. Unlike the more important Paharpur and Mainimati monasteries, this monastery bears no evidence of having any central temple in the inner courtyard. Instead, there were cell-like shrines in the centre of each courtyard, with deities apparently located inside. Several Bodhisattva images were uncovered during excavations, but nothing remains except for traces of the foundations. The lack of any archaeological finds or objects of daily use, such as coins or icons, suggests that the monastery was abandoned peacefully.

Overall, this small isolated monastery doesn't have enough complexity or archaeological finds to warrant a special trip. If you're in the area, however, it's probably worth a short stop. Buses from Dinajpur to Charkai cost Tk 24. From Charkai, go 6km north-east and look for the low brick structure on the road to Nawabganj. It's about 100m away from the road along dirt paths.

THAKURGAON
☎ 0561
Thakurgaon is one of the more pleasant towns in northern Bangladesh and a good travel destination, especially if you are interested in cycling. There are lots of back roads in the area with relatively few motor vehicles, and the scenery is beautiful. One interesting trip would be north to Panchagarh via Atwari, and then further north to the Indian border at Tetulia (where there's a circuit house available) and Banglabandha. Alternatively, from Atwari you could take a narrow back road south-west to Baliadangi, then either east back to Thakurgaon or further south all the way to Haripur at the Indian border and, from there, south-east to Dinajpur.

It's relatively cool here, so in December and January you will definitely need a jumper (sweater) at night. The town is small enough to cover on foot provided you like to walk, but rickshaws are everywhere and at night you'll be charmed by the tinkling of their lanterns as they run along the dark streets.

If you're interested in seeing what some of the local nongovernment organisations (NGOs) are doing, visit the office of the Humanitarian Agency for Development Services (HADS) in town and its farm on the south-western edge of town. It has a number of small-scale activities in operation, including a small dairy, a biomass generator and Bangladesh's only mozzarella cheese factory. The Swiss-supported Rangpur Dinajpur Rural Services Project (RDRS) is another possibility.

Places to Stay

One cheap option is *Tangon Boarding*, a two-storey structure on the western end of Hospital Rd, one long block west of the heart of town, near the Tangon River. It has small singles/doubles with overhead fans and attached bathrooms for Tk 30/40. It is basic, but adequately clean.

There are several cheap hotels on the Panchagarh Rd, none of which are very nice. The *Hotel Highway (☎ 52519)*, next to a petrol station, is probably the least bad

of the lot, with charmless cell-like rooms with common bathroom for Tk 40/70.

The *Salam International Hotel (☎ 53486)* occupies the upper floors of the Howladar Market shopping centre on Bazar Rd (sign in Bangla only). It's a clean, reasonably well-run hotel with a range of rooms. Rooms with fan cost Tk 80/200, air-con doubles with satellite TV cost Tk 300, and there are a couple of 'family size' rooms that can accommodate five people for Tk 600. There's no hot water, and you'll have to ask for a mosquito net.

The friendly *HADS Guesthouse & Office (☎ 53513)* is on Sirajuddowlah Rd, north of the hospital. There are two triple-bed rooms that cost Tk 300, and three double rooms for Tk 400. The double rooms are spacious and airy, with fans, comfortable twin beds that have mosquito nets, drinking water, and spotless attached bathrooms. Staff can also arrange for meals to be brought to your room. By the time you read this it may also be possible to stay at the HADS demonstration farm just outside town; contact the office in town or call the farm on ☎ 52553.

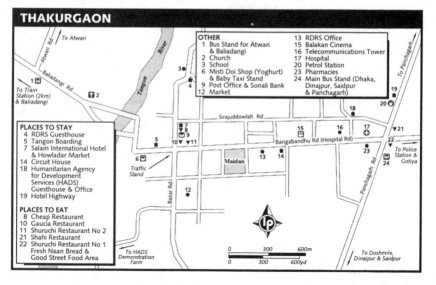

THAKURGAON

PLACES TO STAY
4 RDRS Guesthouse
5 Tangon Boarding
7 Salam International Hotel & Howladar Market
14 Circuit House
18 Humanitarian Agency for Development Services (HADS) Guesthouse & Office
19 Hotel Highway

PLACES TO EAT
8 Cheap Restaurant
10 Gaucia Restaurant
11 Shuruchi Restaurant No 2
21 Shahi Restaurant
22 Shuruchi Restaurant No 1 Fresh Naan Bread & Good Street Food Area

OTHER
1 Bus Stand for Atwari & Baliadangi
2 Church
3 School
6 Misti Doi Shop (Yoghurt) & Baby Taxi Stand
9 Post Office & Sonali Bank
12 Market
13 RDRS Office
15 Balakan Cinema
16 Telecommunications Tower
17 Hospital
20 Petrol Station
23 Pharmacies
24 Main Bus Stand (Dhaka, Dinajpur, Saidpur & Panchagarh)

To Atwari
To Train Station (2km) & Baliadangi
Atwari Rd
Baliadangi Rd
River
Tangon
To Panchagarh
Sirajuddowlah Rd
Bangabandhu Rd (Hospital Rd)
Maidan
Traffic Stand
Bazar Rd
To HADS Demonstration Farm
Panchagarh Rd
To Police Station & Gotiya
To Doshmile, Dinajpur & Saidpur
0   300   600m
0   300   600yd

Another possibility is the **RDRS Guesthouse** (☎ *53670)*, near a school at the northern end of Bazar Rd. The rooms are spacious, with comfortable twin beds, carpets, mosquito nets, emergency lights, drinking water, desks, and clean attached bathrooms that have hot-water showers and western-style toilets. It serves meals as well. Non-air-con singles/doubles cost Tk 300/500, and air-con rooms cost TK 600/1000.

If these guesthouses are full, the chances are good that the district commissioner will allow you to stay at the government *Circuit House*, which is on Hospital Rd and costs Tk 150 for a clean room.

Places to Eat
The best place for a meal is the *RDRS Guesthouse* (Tk 70 for breakfast and Tk 130 for lunch or dinner), but meals are not generally available to non-guests unless you order in advance.

The best local restaurant is *Shuruchi Restaurant No 2* on Hospital Rd; the fare is Bangladeshi, inexpensive and a notch better than at other establishments.

Other places to eat, all similar, are the *Gaucia Restaurant*, around the corner, and several *restaurants* along the Panchagarh Rd at or near the intersection with Hospital Rd, including *Shuruchi Restaurant No 1* and *Shahi Restaurant*. You can get sweet yoghurt at a *misti doi shop* at the western end of Hospital Rd, at the baby taxi stand near Tangon Boarding.

Getting There & Away
Bus Buses for Atwari (Tk 9) and Baliadangi (Tk 8) depart from a small bus station at the western end of town. All other buses depart from the bus station on the Dinajpur-Panchagarh highway, 500m south of Hospital Rd. Buses south to Dinajpur (Tk 24) and north to Panchagarh (Tk 12) depart from around 7 am until 7.30 pm. The trip takes 1¾ hours to Dinajpur and half that to Panchagarh. Buses to Saidpur cost Tk 23 and depart between 6.30 am and 5.30 pm; the trip takes just under two hours. The trip to Bogra via Saidpur takes five hours and costs Tk 75.

If you're headed to Dhaka, you have a choice between a normal bus (Tk 140) and a chair coach (Tk 220); there are about 12 buses per day. The trip takes 8 or 9 hours.

Train The train station is 2km from the western edge of town. The 2nd-class train connecting Dinajpur and Panchagarh departs from either town around 7 am and passes through Thakurgaon several hours later.

AROUND THAKURGAON
Singra Forest Reserve
Just north of town, the 200-hectare Singra (SHENG-grah) Forest Reserve is definitely worth a trip. It is fairly uniformly planted with sal trees, with some areas of mixed woodland on the edge of the reserve. The forestry official here is welcoming. For bird-watching, the best time to come is during the winter months when you'll spot a fair number of winter migrants.

Getting There & Away To get here, starting from the main junction on the Dinajpur-Panchagarh highway, go approximately 1km north where you'll find a driveable dirt track on your left (west) and a small sign in English: 'Singra Picnic Centre'. The gated picnic area is 1.5km down that track and the small reserve is just beyond.

Biganj Forest Reserve
About 23km south of Thakurgaon and 28km north of Dinajpur, just east of the Dinajpur-Thakurgaon Highway near Biganj, is a small forest reserve similar to Singra but more degraded. It attracts basically the same birds as Singra.

PANCHAGARH
☎ 0562
Some 40km north of Thakurgaon, Panchagarh is the site of a mud fort (Bhitar Garh). Built in the 14th century by the Hindus as a defence against the encroaching Mughals, it has since largely disappeared. It's on the main road that heads north to the Indian border crossings at Tetulia and Banglabandha. You cannot cross the border at either town, but the paved route north of

Panchagarh is very scenic and perfect for cycling because few vehicles use it.

Places to Stay & Eat

The best place to stay is the government *Circuit House* (☎ 348), which costs Tk 150 a room (possibly more for foreigners). Located on Tetulia Rd in the northern outskirts of town on the left (west), it's a two-storey building with a front garden. It has six spacious standard rooms that have carpets, fans, attractive furnishings and spotless bathrooms with showers and western-style toilets. To stay here you must get permission from the district commissioner, whose office is a stone's throw away. Guests can also eat here.

If you can't get a room at the Circuit House, try the *Diabetic Association of Bangladesh*, which is a pale yellow two-storey building on the same road closer to the town centre, just north of the bridge. Well-marked, this complex has eight decent guest rooms (about Tk 80) with fans and attached bathrooms.

Much further north, in Tetulia, there's another government *Guesthouse*, which is beautifully located on a hill overlooking a nearby river and India. To stay and eat there, you must reserve a room at the government engineer's office (☎ 223) on Tetulia Rd, just south of the bridge. For food in Panchagarh, look for the stalls near the main intersection and around the market.

Getting There & Away

Buses to Panchagarh cost Tk 12 from Thakurgaon and Tk 32 from Dinajpur. For fun, you could also take the old 2nd-class Dinajpur-Panchagarh train, which leaves daily at 7 am from either town, and stops at Thakurgaon en route; the fare is Tk 20 and the trip takes about five hours.

CHILAHATI

Chilahati is the usual crossing point in northern Bangladesh for India, but it's hardly busy. Before heading from the train station to the last Bangladeshi checkpoint at the border (4km), or when arriving in Chilahati from India, you must pass through immigration and customs at the far end of

the railway platform. All the usual details have to be painstakingly copied into huge ledger books. It is open until 6 pm, and procedures are slow but usually painless. Ask around and it should be possible to change small sums of taka into rupees, but keep enough taka for the rickshaw ride to the border. Bangladeshi time is 30 minutes ahead of Indian time.

Places to Stay & Eat

If you're caught here for the night, you'll find a very basic *guesthouse* that has rooms with attached bathrooms for just Tk 40, and you can eat at one of the incredibly cheap local restaurants.

Getting There & Away

From Bangladesh Travelling north from Bangladesh into India, you can take a local train from Saidpur to Chilahati. There are two trains daily, the last departing at 3 pm and arriving at 6.15 pm. By bus it costs about Tk 25, but it may include a long break at Domar to collect more passengers.

Procedures at the last Bangladeshi checkpoint at the border (a hut with two soldiers), about 4km from Chilahati, are usually straightforward. It's a long walk from Chilahati, but if you take a rickshaw be sure to agree on the price first. It's then a short walk through the fields, through a gap in the fence and on to the first Indian border post – another hut. From here it's a 30-minute rickshaw ride to Haldibari, where you pass through the customs and immigration formalities again. There's nowhere to change money until you get to Haldibari. From Haldibari you have the option of a bus or train. The train to New Jaipalguri costs about Rs 8 and departs at 7.30 am; the last train leaves at 4.30 pm. Change trains at New Jaipalguri for most destinations in north India, including Kolkata, Varanasi, Delhi, Guwahati.

From India Travelling from Darjeeling to Shiliguri takes 3 hours by bus. A train from Shiliguri to Haldibari is a two-hour trip and costs about Rs 15 in 2nd class. It is advisable to take the early train as Haldibari is not a great place to stay. If you do have to stay, the only place is a Dak Bungalow (a guesthouse for government officials). Ask around the market to change rupees into taka, but you're not going to get a great rate so keep it to a small amount.

From Haldibari to the border is a 30-minute rickshaw ride. With luck there'll be a rickshaw on the Bangladeshi side, otherwise it's a 4km hike along a dirt road to Chilahati, where you'll find immigration.

RAJSHAHI
☎ 0721

Built on the northern bank of the Padma River, Rajshahi is a big university town, laid-back and relatively prosperous.

Unlike most riverbanks in Bangladesh, the levee by the Padma River is somewhat elevated (partly natural and partly as a dike for flood control) and thus affords one of the best river views in the country. Sunsets here are particularly worth seeing. The thing to do in Rajshahi in the late afternoon is to walk south from the Parjatan Hotel towards the river and then stroll along the river. It's almost carnival-like, with people strolling and chatting, children playing, and vendors selling ice cream and other snack food.

Looking across the vast flood plain to the opposite bank you'll see India, where the river is called the Ganges. In the dry season it is sometimes possible to walk across the empty riverbed, which aids the thriving smuggling trade along the border.

The presence of Rajshahi University (RU), which also has a large campus on the north-eastern outskirts of town, a medical college, an engineering college, a zoo, a sericulture institute, a Christian mission hospital, a Parjatan Motel, an airport, and two museums, adds to the relatively sophisticated atmosphere of this town. If you come during the first half of the year through early July, you'll get to sample some of the area's famous mangoes.

Orientation & Information
The Parjatan Motel has the usual brochures but no tourist information. The Sonali Bank will reluctantly change money, but you'll get better rates and service at the nearby Agrani Bank in Saheb Bazar. The post office is on Greater Rd on the western side of town.

Being a university town, there are quite a few bookshops in New Market and to the north of Saheb Bazar. They sell mainly academic texts, but the odd novel is available.

With the Indian border so close, there is a huge local trade in smuggled goods, most evident in Saheb Bazar. Indian beer can sometimes be found at very high prices.

Varendra Research Museum
Founded in 1910 with the support of the maharaja of Dighapatia, who donated the land to the government, the Varendra Research Museum is the oldest museum in the country and is definitely worth visiting. It is managed by Rajshahi University. The building, which is predominantly British in style, has some interesting Hindu-Buddhist features, including a trefoil arch over the doorways and windows, and small *rekha* temple forms on the roof.

Inside, artefacts from all over the subcontinent are on display, including some rare examples from the ancient city of Mohenjo-daro in Pakistan. Other displays include a superb collection of local Hindu sculpture (in stone imported from Bihar). Tantric motifs are evident, and the figures are relaxed, giving them a more natural appearance.

The museum is open daily from 10 am to 4.30 pm, except Friday when it's only open from 2.30 to 5 pm, and Thursday when it's closed. Admission is free.

Martyrs' Memorial Museum
The collection of Liberation War mementos at the Shaheed Smriti Sangrahashala (Martyrs' Memorial Museum) at Rajshahi University (RU) is a good reminder of the dreadful days of the 1971 war. Unfortunately, the dilapidated state of the museum, with its dusty collection of war artefacts, is more likely to make one feel that the country has forgotten its heroes. Among the exhibits are blood-stained uniforms, a pen used by a fighter to write his last love letter, the deed papers of surrender by the Pakistani

forces, remnants recovered from a mass grave of victims, among whom were intellectuals from RU, and weapons used by the freedom fighters. Photographs serve as testimonials to the Pakistani army's torture, murder and rape, and the burning of thousands of homes.

Buildings of the British Raj

Near the centre of Rajshahi are some Raj-era buildings. Rajshahi Government College, which dates from 1873 when several maharajas donated money for its establishment, is an elegant two-storey edifice with beautiful semi-circular arched windows. Others nearby include Collegiate School (1836), which consists of two single-storey structures east of the college, with verandahs along the facades, and Fuller House (1909), a large two-storey red-brick building which is similar in appearance to the college.

Baro Kuthi

A block south-east of Rajshahi Government College on a high bank of the Padma River is a historic structure known as Baro Kuthi. Reasonably intact, it's one of the last remaining examples of the indigo *kuthi* (factories) that once flourished in the region. They were simple buildings and are of no architectural interest except for their defensive arrangements. The history of the kuthis is fascinating, however.

In the early 19th century Baro Kuthi was built by the Dutch for the silk trade. Serving as a fort in times of emergency, this massive building had about 12 rooms. Those on the ground floor, comparatively unventilated and dark, were probably used as a prison and for mounting cannons. After 1833, when Baro Kuthi was taken over by the British East India Company, it was used for the infamous indigo trade, which lasted for about 25 years. It is reputed to have been the scene of countless crimes, including murder and torture, during that period.

Sericulture Centre

Rajshahi is at the heart of Bangladesh's silk-producing area, and the Sericulture Centre has a showroom of silk fabrics

The Infamous Indigo Kuthis

In the 18th and early 19th centuries the indigo trade was highly profitable. By the mid-1800s the Rajshahi region alone had more than 150 indigo factories or *kuthis*. The local zamindar owners even loaned money to the peasants so that they would plant more indigo. Indeed, trade was so lucrative and the kuthis so numerous that factory labourers had to be imported.

The farmers, however, didn't profit at all and began changing crops. Using oppression and torture to keep the peasants growing indigo, angry zamindars sometimes went as far as to commit murder and burn whole villages. An adage at the time held that 'no indigo box was despatched to England without being smeared in human blood'.

In 1859 the peasants revolted against the brutal repression. The Indigo Revolt, which lasted two years, brought the cultivation of indigo to a halt. Eventually the government had no choice but to decree that the peasants could no longer be forced to plant indigo. As a result, by the end of the century the indigo trade had completely disappeared. Some of the kuthis were converted into silk factories but most simply fell into ruin.

where you can pick up some fair bargains, or order lengths and colours to your specifications. If you aren't interested in buying, there isn't much else to see here. The small showroom is in a walled garden of mulberry trees, south-west of the train station on Railway Station Rd.

Zoo

Just west of the Parjatan Hotel is a zoo, which has entrances on both the northern and eastern sides. It's small but there are enough animals in reasonably humane conditions to entertain for a while.

Places to Stay – Budget

The very cheapest hotels in town are pretty awful. One that isn't too bad is the *Hotel Parijat* (☎ 773434), a poorly marked two-storey building facing the police station on

Emaduddin Rd. Small, reasonably clean and well-ventilated singles with common bathrooms cost Tk 40; doubles with attached bathrooms cost Tk 80.

The well-marked *Rajshahi Metropolitan Hotel* (☎ 772861), on New Market Rd, slightly closer to the town centre, has singles/doubles with fans, mosquito nets and attached bathrooms for Tk 60 to Tk 80/110. The rooms are not cramped and the hotel features a 2nd-floor reception area that is breezy and has lots of comfortable chairs – good for relaxing.

A decent budget hotel close to the train and bus stations is the multistorey *Hotel Heaven* (☎ 775054). Look for the red sign with yellow Bangla script. There are a couple of cramped singles with common bathroom for Tk 65. Rooms with attached bathroom and comfortable beds cost Tk 85/165; larger doubles with couch, table and western toilet cost Tk 250.

Places to Stay – Mid-Range
Three good mid-range hotels in the Saheb Bazar area in the centre of town are the Hotel Nice, Hotel Rajmahal and Hotel Sky.

The *Hotel Nice* (☎ 776188, fax 775625) is the pick of the bunch. It is large, airy, tastefully decorated and has balconies decorated with pot plants. The hotel is on a side street off Saheb Bazar Rd. Singles with common bathroom cost Tk 50, singles/doubles with fan and attached bathroom cost Tk 125/250, and air-con rooms cost from Tk 450/650.

Hotel Rajmahal (☎ 774399), just east of New Market Rd, has rooms with carpets, fans, mosquito nets and attached bathrooms for Tk 80/140. There are also larger doubles for Tk 180, which have sofas, and Tk 280 rooms with satellite TV that are almost like suites. Air-con rooms with TV cost Tk 400/550.

The five-storey *Hotel Sky* (☎ 772026), 1½ blocks to the west of the Rajmahal has rooms from Tk 100/250 and air-con rooms with satellite TV for Tk 400/500. The hotel has unusually spacious open hallways that give the place a very breezy atmosphere. Rooms are bright and fairly large by local standards, and the doubles have mirrors and comfortable reading chairs.

Places to Stay – Top End
The large *Parjatan Motel* (☎ 775492), just south of the Rajshahi City Church at the western end of town, has big rooms with twin beds for Tk 350/450 with fans and Tk 600/800 with air-con. All rooms have hot water. The motel features a carpeted reception area with comfortable cane furnishings and a carpeted dark restaurant. The surrounding area is quiet and there is ample room for parking. The Biman office is here as well.

Places to Eat
The *Khan Hotel & Restaurant* is at the intersection of Airport and Railway Station Rds. A typical Bangladeshi meal will cost you around Tk 20. Before ordering, you could check to see if the restaurant next door has anything different to offer.

In the heart of town around Saheb Bazar you'll find similar places. For snacks, sweets and tea, try *Roochita Confectionery* on New Market Rd.

For better Chinese food, head for the *Nanking Chinese Restaurant* at Monibazar crafts centre, at the intersection of Nawabganj and Greater Rds; it's one of the city's best eateries. Another good Chinese restaurant is the *Shan Dong,* on Saheb Bazar Rd, which has fried rice for Tk 40 and chicken dishes for Tk 80.

The *Mahananda Restaurant* at the Parjatan Motel is expensive for what you get, but it has an extensive selection of Bangladeshi, Chinese and Continental cuisine. Choices include fish curry (Tk 80), chicken biryani (Tk 120) and roast chicken with vegetables (Tk 100).

Another possibility would be to take a picnic out to the well-marked Simla Park and picnic spot, which is just beyond the Circuit House on C & B Rd, overlooking the Padma River.

Getting There & Away
Air The airport is 10km from the centre of town. To get to and from the airport, hail

RAJSHAHI

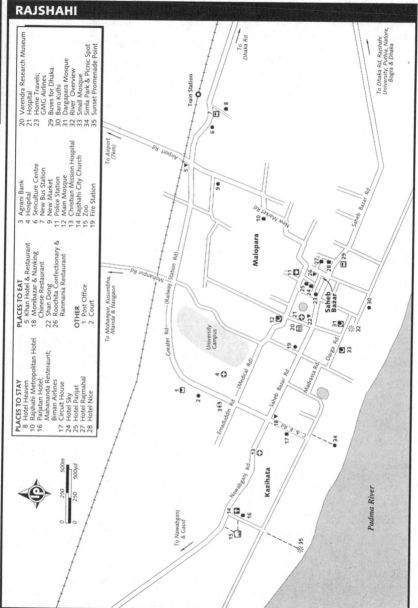

PLACES TO STAY
8 Hotel Heaven
10 Rajshahi Metropolitan Hotel
16 Parjatan Hotel;
    Mahananda Resteraunt;
    Biman Airlines
17 Circuit House
24 Hotel Sky
25 Hotel Parjat
27 Hotel Rajmahal
28 Hotel Nice

PLACES TO EAT
5 Khan Hotel & Restaurant
18 Monibazar & Nanking
    Chinese Restaurant
22 Shan Dong
26 Roochita Confectionary &
    Ranmania Restaurant

OTHER
1 Post Office
2 Court
3 Agrani Bank
4 Hospital
7 Sericulture Centre
7 New Bus Station
9 New Market
11 Police Station
12 Main Mosque
13 Christian Mission Hospital
14 Rajshahi City Church
15 Zoo
19 Fire Station
20 Varendra Research Museum
21 Hospital
23 Home Travels;
    GMG Airlines
29 Buses for Dhaka
30 Baro Kuthi
31 Dargapara Mosque
32 River Overview
33 Small Mosque
34 Simla Park & Picnic Spot
35 Sunset Promenade Point

To Dhaka Rd

To Dhaka Rd, Rajshahi
University, Puthia, Natore,
Bogra & Dhaka

Train Station

To Airport
(7km)

Airport Rd

New Market Rd

Malopara

Saheb Bazar Rd

To Mohanpur, Kusumbha,
Manda & Naogaon

(Railway Station Rd)

Mohanpur Rd

Greater Rd

University
Campus

(Medical Rd)

Emadduddin Rd

Saheb Bazar Rd

Madrassa Rd

Saheb
Bazar

Darga Rd

Nawabganj Rd

Kazihata

To Nawabganj
& Gaud

B B Rd

Padma River

0   250   500m
0   250   500yd

a baby taxi (Tk 30). Biman (☎ 774373) has daily flights between Dhaka and Rajshahi (Tk 1125). Four days a week Biman flies via Saidpur (Tk 775). Its offices are in the Parjatan Hotel.

GMG also flies daily between Rajshahi and Dhaka (Tk 1470); its office is at Home Travels (☎ 773050) on Saheb Bazar Road, in the centre of town.

Bus Most buses, except those to Dhaka, depart from New Bus Station, across from the train station. You can get ordinary buses here to Bogra (Tk 35) from 6.30 am to 3 pm; Jessore (Tk 90) from 6.30 am to 5.45 pm; and to Rangpur (Tk 80), Pabna (Tk 40) and Nawabganj (Tk 20). Buses for Dhaka leave from the town centre on Saheb Bazar Rd, a block east of the intersection with New Market Rd. Ordinary buses will cost you between Tk 150 and Tk 170, and it costs Tk 260 to Tk 300 for air-con coaches. The trip normally takes somewhere in the vicinity of 7 hours.

Train IC trains depart from the train station (☎ 774060) for Dhaka daily at 7.15 am and 6 pm, and cost Tk 385/130 in 1st class/sulob. The journey takes about 11 hours. To Jessore and Khulna, an express runs every day at 2.45 pm; the fare is Tk 215/75 and Tk 265/90 respectively for 1st/sulob class.

Rail connections with the north are more frequent from Natore, which is on the main north-south line and only an hour's bus ride away. From Rajshahi, there's an express daily to Saidpur, except on Friday; it departs at 2.15 pm and costs Tk 190/65 in 1st/sulob class (Tk 200/65 to Dinajpur). There's also a daily mail train to Saidpur at 10.45 am.

Car Hire cars can be arranged through the Parjatan, Nice and Sky hotels. Parjatan is likely to be the most expensive company to use. The cost for one day's drive to Gaud, Puthia and Natore (about 10-12 hours) should be Tk 800 a day. You'll have to pay for fuel as well, which costs between Tk 800 and Tk 1000. The vehicle is usually a minivan.

AROUND RAJSHAHI
Kusumbha Mosque
This mosque, 42km due north of Rajshahi by tarred road, was built in 1558, just prior to the Mughal era. Attractive, well maintained and nicely located, this very traditional structure features black-stone walls, three arched mihrabs at the front, six domes and, somewhat unusually, a women's gallery on the upper storey.

Buses from Rajshahi depart for Kusumbha and Manda (15km further north) from the bus station across from the railway terminal. The fare is Tk 20.

PUTHIA
Puthia (POU-tee-ah) has the largest number of historically important Hindu structures in Bangladesh. It's a very scenic little town. It also has one of the country's finest old rajbaris, although it's in such poor condition it's positively picturesque. Only 23km east of Rajshahi (16km west of Natore) and 1km south of the highway, it's also very accessible. Coming from the highway, you'll pass a tall Hindu shrine to your left. Continue past it to the heart of the village, which is a large grassy field, with the rajbari just beyond. You can start your tour from here. As you walk around, ask for the *mandir* (temple), which may lead you to the discovery of some lesser Hindu structures in the area besides the ones mentioned here.

Puthia Palace
This two-storey stately edifice was built in 1895 by Rani Hemanta Kumari Devi in honour of his illustrious mother-in-law, Maharani Sharat Sundari Devi. She was a major benefactor in the Rajshahi region, having built a boarding house for college students and a Sanskrit college, for which she was given the title maharani in 1877. Very imposing, the building is in just good enough condition to serve as a college today.

Its grand appearance is due to the 13 huge round columns lining the 60m-long facade, with symmetrical projections on either end of the facade. The central part has an imposing portal at the front, capped by a triangular pediment with a parapet tastefully decorated with floral plasterwork. Inside, there are 16 rooms, including two fairly large halls. Most of the walls have political slogans scrawled over them.

Govinda Temple

The most amazing of the village's monuments is the Govinda Temple, which is on the left-hand side of the rajbari's inner courtyard. Erected between 1823 and 1895 by one of the maharanis of the Puthia estate, it's a large square structure with incredibly intricate designs in terracotta embellishing the entire surface. In this sense, it's very similar in inspiration to the Kantanagar Temple north of Dinajpur, which is about a century older. Both have the appearance of being covered with red oriental carpets. Most of the terracotta panels depict scenes from the love affair between Radha and Krishna as told in the Hindu epics. The building's structure is also interesting, rising in two storeys and crowned by a set of miniature ornamental towers.

Shiva Temple

Built in 1823, this photogenic Shiva temple at the entrance to Puthia, overlooking a pond, is an imposing square structure and an excellent example of the *pancha-ratna* (five-spire) Hindu style of temple common in northern India. It's very ornate, with three gradually tapering tiers, and is topped by four spires plus a much larger central one. Unfortunately, many of the stone carvings and sculptures were disfigured during the 1971 Liberation War. There's still an impressive intact *lingam* (a phallic image of Shiva) of black stone, however, which the cheerful and informative caretaker will undoubtedly show you.

Jagannath Temple

One of the finest examples in the country of the hut-shaped temple is the Jagannath Temple, which is about 150m to the right (west) of the rajbari. Dating from the 16th century and nicely restored, this elegant little temple, measuring only about 5m on each side, features a single tapering tower

that rises to a height of about 10m. The temple's western facade is finely adorned with terracotta panels of mostly geometric design.

Tahirpur Palace

If you're really into exploring old rajbaris, you could also check Tahirpur Palace, which is in Tahirpur, 18km due north of Puthia up a back road, along the Baralai River. Rebuilt after the great earthquake of 1897, it's an imposing two-storey structure that, despite the collapse of its roof, remains largely intact. There are 16 rooms, including a large central hall, and chances are good that you can roam freely inside.

Getting There & Away

There are numerous buses between Rajshahi and Natore throughout the day, which pass through Puthia. The 23km trip from Rajshahi only takes about half an hour (Tk 15). Upon leaving Puthia, you can easily hail one of the buses traveling between Rajshahi and Natore on the main highway.

NATORE
☎ 0771

Located on the Rajshahi-Dhaka highway, some 40km east of Rajshahi and 75km south-west of Bogra, Natore (NUT-or) is most noted for having two of the most outstanding rajbaris in the country. There's also a regional Care office here, and if you need any information you can count on the staff to be friendly and receptive.

Otherwise, there's not much reason to stop in this busy crossroads town, the main drag of which runs east to west. A bus station, Care and several cheap hotels are at the eastern end of town, at a three-way intersection, with major highways heading east to Pabna and Dhaka and north to Bogra. The train station is at the city's opposite end, on the road west to Rajshahi.

Uttara Gano-Ghaban (Dighapatia Palace)

The building that was once the palace of the Dighapatia Maharaja, the region's governor, is now a government building called Uttara Gano-Ghaban. It serves as one of the president's official residences. Situated 3km north of town off the road to Bogra, this beautifully maintained complex, occupying about 15 hectares of land and enclosed within a moat and a high boundary wall, is approached from the east through an imposing four-storey arched gateway. The main single-storey palace presents a beautiful 50m-long frontage, relieved with plaster floral decorations and a series of pointed arches. The incongruous mosque-like dome covering the central hall was added in 1967.

Inside you'll find a huge domed reception hall, a large dining room, a conference room and nine bedrooms. Furnishings include marble-top tables, life-size bronze figures, chandeliers, carved wooden chairs, tables and beds. Visiting hours are Saturday to Thursday from 10 am to 4 pm.

Natore Rajbari

One of the oldest rajbaris in Bangladesh, dating from the mid 1700s, the magnificent but dilapidated Natore rajbari is actually a series of seven rajbaris, four of which are notable and remain largely intact. The main block, called Baro Taraf, consists of three separate palaces and is approached by a long avenue lined with impressively tall imported bottle palms, the white trunks of which resemble temple columns.

The very classical looking principal rajbari has a frontage of about 35m, with an elegant central porch supported by a series of Corinthian columns and semi-circular arches. Inside you'll find a large reception hall that rises to a height of 10m and is lit by 18 clerestory windows, originally fitted with coloured glass panes. At the back there's a verandah supported on 20 pairs of Corinthian columns. You'll find some stairs there leading to the roof, from which you can get a fairly good view of the entire 15-hectare complex.

Also facing the main block are a palace lined with columns and a smaller rajbari lined with a series of paired Doric columns. Next to the latter, which is inhabited, you'll see the family's shrine, a small Krishna temple whose deity has been destroyed.

To the rear of the main block is a second block called Chhota-Taraf, consisting of two rajbaris. The principal one faces a pond and is unquestionably one of the most beautifully proportioned buildings in Bangladesh. Entering through the front triple-arched portico, you'll find a reception hall with a lofty ceiling crowned by a pyramidal roof with clerestory windows. Much of the palace's black and white marble floor has been ripped up, but this imposing 15-room structure is otherwise largely intact. There are stairs out the back leading to the roof, where you can peek down into the main hall.

Getting There & Away Natore rajbari is at the northern edge of town. To get here, you can head northward from the heart of town, but to avoid getting lost it's easier to take the Natore-Bogra road and, 1km before the turn-off for Dighapatia Palace, take a left on an unmarked paved road that leads westward towards the complex. It's 1.5km down that road, just beyond a school on your right. You can wander around as you will.

Rani Bhawani Gardens

For over half a century until she died in 1791, Rani Bhawani, wife of the owner of the Natore rajbari, managed the huge estate after her husband's death. She became a legendary figure because of her boundless charity. Many organisations were the recipients of her largesse, and even today her name is recognised by many Bangladeshis. A garden bearing her name is now a popular picnic spot. To get there, take a right (north) at the thana office on the main east-west drag through town and begin asking directions.

Places to Stay & Eat

One of cheapest places to stay is the *Hotel Raj* (☎ 6660), at the eastern end of town, 200m north of the three-way intersection. Unmarked in English, it has a small lobby with TV. Tiny singles/doubles with fans, mosquito nets and common bathroom are Tk 40/75, rooms with attached bathroom are Tk 75/130.

The **Uttara Motel** (☎ 2519), on the 3rd floor of a building overlooking the intersection, is better value. Rooms cost Tk 60/80. Doubles are spacious with lots of light, and have tables, mosquito nets, fans and attached bathrooms. The inviting reception is a spacious airy balcony, with a TV viewing area and a fridge with cold drinks, and just below is the Care office.

In the centre of town another option is the **Hotel Rukshana**, with rooms for Tk 50/80 with attached bath.

The main drag is the best place for finding street food and perhaps a restaurant or two.

Getting There & Away
Bus Buses headed north and east leave from the intersection at the eastern end of town, while those headed for Rajshahi leave from the west. Buses for Rajshahi cost Tk 15 and take about an hour, while those to Pabna cost Tk 20 and take about 1½ hours. To get to the gardens, catch a bus from Rajshahi's New Bus Station, or one from Pabna.

Train The train station is on the western side of town. Trains from the nearby junction of Ishurdi run through Natore northward to Jamalpur (stop for the Paharpur ruins), Saidpur, Dinajpur and Chilahati at the Indian border.

PABNA
Located between Rajshahi and Dhaka, Pabna, which dates from medieval times, features some fine old buildings, including a superb Hindu temple, as well as two well-known rajbaris. Outside of Pabna there's also the Shahzadpur Mosque (1528), which is a splendid 15-dome pre-Mughal mosque in traditional bangla style, with thick walls and various arched entrances.

Jor Bangla Temple
Built in the 18th century in the form of two traditional village huts intertwined and standing on a platform, this temple, 2km east of the town centre, is the best remaining example of the *jor bangla* (twin-hut) style. Before construction was completed something sacrilegious occurred on the site, so the temple was never used. While the building is not large or imposing, it is extremely elegant and has been beautifully restored. Like all hut-style temples, it features an exaggerated arched roof, and the entrance's facade is enriched with intricate terracotta panels depicting several scenes from Hindu mythology.

Taras Rajbari
The Taras rajbari, viewed from the street through an unusually impressive archway flanked by huge Doric columns, is a few hundred metres south of the town centre on the main road. Dating from the late 19th century, it was evidently once an elegant palace, but it's now all too obviously the drab home to government offices. The building's most prominent feature is its two-storey front portico supported by four tall columns, resembling that of a pre-civil war *Gone with the Wind* mansion in the southern USA.

Sitlai Palace
Picturesquely situated on the banks of the Padma River, to the east of town, Sitlai Palace, dating from 1900, is a grand imposing rajbari that's still fairly well preserved. Today, it's occupied by a drug company, EDRUC, so you can't see the 30-room interior. The exterior is interesting, however, with a broad staircase flagged with white marble, leading to a 2nd-storey arched portico. Like so many zamindars, the Maitra family received extensive properties in the area and were successful in business, eventually becoming philanthropic as well and thus acquiring the title raja.

Places to Stay
In the town centre, on Hamid Rd, the **Hotel Prince** (☎ 5451) has fair singles/doubles with common bathroom for Tk 40/60.

Towards the northern edge of town at Radhanagar, on the main road, **Hotel Tripti Niloy** is good value with rooms, including attached bathrooms, for Tk 75/100.

Back on Hamid Rd, the large **Hotel Park** (☎ 4096) is a slightly more comfortable option, with clean rooms for Tk 80/120 and a couple of air-con rooms for Tk 300/400.

Places to Eat
The *Midnight Moon* is a tiny, basic restaurant serving expensive and unappetising Chinese food. It's in the Huq Supermarket Arcade off Hamid Rd. Your only other choices include the restaurant at the *Hotel Tripti Niloy* and a few reasonable local restaurants.

Getting There & Away
Most buses leave from the main road just south of the town centre. There are buses to Dhaka via Aricha, although the expresses that originate in Rajshahi will probably be full.

Buses run west to Natore (Tk 20, 1½ hours) and Rajshahi (Tk 30, 2½ hours), and north-west to Ishurdi (Tk 7, 45 minutes), which has better bus and train connections. You have to go to Ishurdi to get to Kushtia in Khulna division; all buses leave from the town centre.

GAUD
A site of great historical importance, Gaud (or Gaur) has more historic mosques than any area in Bangladesh, except for Bagerhat. It's over 100km west of Rajshahi, right on Bangladesh's western border – some of the sites are in India, and the rest are in Bangladesh. An old solid brick-built gate in a long embankment is now being utilised as the Indian border checkpost.

The Hindu Senas established their capital here and called it Lakhnauti, after which the Khiljis from Turkistan took control for three centuries, to be followed in the late 15th century by the Afghans. Under the Afghans, Gaud became a prosperous city surrounded by fortified ramparts and a moat, and spread over 32 sq km. Replete with temples, mosques and palaces, the city was visited by traders and merchants from all over central Asia, Arabia, Persia and China. A number of mosques are still standing today, and some have been restored, but none of the buildings from the earlier Hindu kingdoms remain.

On arrival in Gaud it is a good idea to call in on the friendly soldiers at the border post. They can advise you where not to go; the strip of no man's land between the two countries is just as intensively farmed as surrounding areas, so it's easy to make a mistake.

Chhota Sona Masjid
Built between 1493 and 1526, the well-preserved Chhota Sona Masjid (Small Golden Mosque) is the most impressive structure in the area and a fine specimen of pre-Mughal architecture. Rectangular in plan, it originally had 15 *sona* (gilded) domes, hence its name. The mosque's chief attraction, however, is the superb decoration carved on its black-stone walls. On both the inner and outer walls, ornate stonework in shallow relief covers the surface. It also features an ornate women's gallery, arched gateways and lavishly decorated mihrabs.

Khania Dighi Mosque
Also known as Rajbibi Mosque, this single-domed mosque, built in 1490, is in Chapara village and is in reasonably good condition. It also has some ornately decorated walls, but here they are embellished primarily with terracotta floral designs. As at Chhota Sona, it also features some highly ornate stonework, primarily on the three arched entrances on the western wall.

Darasbari Mosque
Built around 1470, Darasbari Mosque is not in as good condition as Khania Dighi Mosque and is missing some of its original domes. It has two sections: a long oblong prayer hall measuring 30m; and a wide verandah on the east. The walls are 2m thick, and on the interior western wall of the prayer hall you'll see nine doorways relieved with some superb terracotta ornamentation of various floral and geometric patterns.

Monuments in Firozpur
Nearby, at Firozpur, you'll find several interesting structures that are all fairly well preserved and close to one another. One is the picturesque **Shah Niamatullah Mosque**, or Three-Domed Mosque, which

was built in 1560 and is beautifully located overlooking a large pond. About 100m away is the **Mausoleum of Shah Niamatul-lah Wali**; it has three domes and four squat towers. The third structure, a bit north of the mausoleum, is **Tahkhana Palace**, which was built by Shah Shuja in the early 17th century and is the area's major Mughal-era building. A large two-storey brick edifice, it has a flat roof, which in those times was virtually unheard of in Bangladesh.

Places to Stay
The *Archaeology Department Rest House* in Gaud is fairly basic but decent, and the cost is only Tk 150 a room. If you just show up, chances are excellent that you'll be allowed to stay here because there is no other accommodation in Gaud, barring some extremely basic rooms above an equally basic restaurant where the bus stops near the Bangladeshi border post.

Getting There & Away
Getting to Gaud involves taking two buses. The route is via Nawabganj, 48km northwest of Rajshahi, which costs Tk 20. From Nawabganj to Gaud you must take another bus, which also costs Tk 20. If you don't have to wait too long in Nawabganj the total trip takes three hours, although it could easily stretch to four or five with delays.

Chittagong Division

Stretching down to the south-eastern corner of the country, Chittagong division shares borders with Sylhet division to the north, India and Myanmar (Burma) to the east, and Dhaka division along the Meghna River. Around Chittagong, particularly in the Chittagong Hill Tracts and south to the Myanmar border, hills are the dominant feature. The Pathua Hill Chain averages heights of 650m, with 1230m Keokradang the highest peak in the country.

The coastal strip in Chittagong is very narrow, crowded in to the sea by the hills to the east. This is the only coastal region of Bangladesh where the land is not fragmented by river deltas. The beaches are long and broad, and extend from Sitakunda to Patenga, where the estuary of the Karnaphuli River cuts them off, then they continue to Teknaf. This last uninterrupted stretch (120km) is said to be the world's longest beach.

The peace settlement between the government and tribal rebels in the Chittagong Hill Tracts in 1997 has meant that travel restrictions to the area have recently been dropped.

HISTORY

Comilla, particularly the Mainimati archaeological site, is probably the oldest inhabited area. In the 7th century the area was a small part of the kingdom of Samatata, ruled by a line of Buddhist kings known as the Khadgas, who were eventually overthrown by a new Buddhist dynasty, the Devas. According to the famous Chinese traveller Xuan Zhang, Buddhism flourished during this period. From his visit during 637–639 AD, he reported 30 monasteries with a total population of 2000 monks.

The history of the area is most notable as a centre of Buddhist resistance to Hinduism and Islam. The southern half of the division is home to Bangladesh's small Buddhist community. It wasn't until the latter part of the 17th century that the Mughals extended their empire this far and superseded the

Highlights

- **Rangamati** – scenic town scattered along islands in Kaptai Lake; boat rides to nearby Chakma villages are a highlight
- **Chittagong Hill Tracts** – predominantly tribal area only recently accessible to foreigners, with some of the country's best remaining forests
- **Ethnological Museum** – located in Chittagong, this interesting museum features displays on the people of the hill tribes and their culture
- **Cox's Bazar** – the country's main holiday destination, gateway to an enormous expanse of beach
- **Lamapara** – the distinct appearance of Burmese-Buddhist monasteries are a highlight in themselves, but even more so for being in Bangladesh

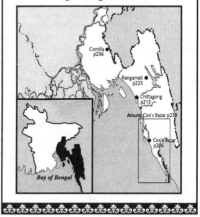

Buddhist Arakanese kingdom of Burma (now Myanmar) in Chittagong. With the collapse of Mughal power it was the British who finally overran the various local rulers, although prior to this, Portuguese pirates had long preyed upon the rich maritime trade of the region.

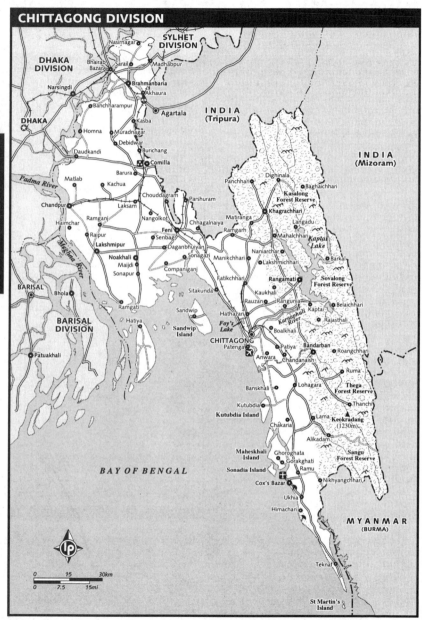

CHITTAGONG DIVISION

The two main racial types in the Chittagong area are the Tibeto-Burmese tribal people and the more numerous Dravido-Aryan Bengalis. For centuries the tribal people have lived in the hills, attempting to maintain their religious and cultural identity.

There are 14 tribal groups, with a total estimated population of around 600,000. Most are Buddhist. Their *khyangs* (temples) and stupas date mostly from the 18th and 19th centuries. The atmosphere as you move south is quite different – quieter, gentler, and more languid – more like Myanmar (Burma) or Nepal than the subcontinent.

CHITTAGONG

Chittagong city, the second largest in Bangladesh, has a population of around 3 million. The climate is pleasant year-round – it becomes cool in winter and only slightly humid in summer, and the annual rainfall is 2400mm (twice that of Dhaka).

The city, 264km south-east of Dhaka, is on the north bank of the Karnaphuli River and its port is the country's busiest. Chittagong is the initial jumping-off point for the Chittagong Hill Tracts to the east and for Cox's Bazar to the south.

This strategic port and industrial city is notoriously prone to demonstrations, hartals and industrial strikes (see Hartals under Dangers & Annoyances in the Facts for the Visitor chapter). Despite this the urban environment is noticeably less chaotic than Dhaka, and a strong local civic movement works hard to keep the streets reasonably clean and unclogged by traffic. The central bazar is fascinating.

The Chittagong dialect of Bangla is somewhat different than in other parts of the country, incorporating words from Arabic, Portuguese, Arakanese and tribal languages.

History

Locals will say the word Chittagong originated from 'chattagram', meaning 'small village', though it more likely comes from the Arakanese phrase *tsi-tsi-gong* inscribed on a tablet brought here by an invading Buddhist army. It means 'that war should never be fought'. Chittagong appears to have been thriving as a port as early as Ptolemy's era (2nd century AD). He described it as one of the finest ports in the east. Xuan Zhang, the Chinese traveller, records the city as a 'sleeping beauty emerging out of the misty water'.

Despite its name, Chittagong has been fought over in a fairly consistent fashion. In 1299 Muslims occupied the city, until the Arakanese retook it and retained it until 1660. The Mughals took possession next, only to be expelled by the Arakanese in 1715. Finally, in 1766 the British raised their flag.

By this time the Burmese had subdued the hill area of Arakan (now known as Rakhine), and many Arakanese fled into the British-occupied territory south of Chittagong. Continuing friction between the British and the Burmese led to the first Anglo-Burmese war in 1824, and resulted in the British annexing Arakan. The Burmese thus were forced to give up any claims they previously had to the region around Chittagong.

The evolution of the city followed a similar pattern to Dhaka, except that the oldest parts, where the city of Sadarghat now stands, were wiped out during the British and post-independence periods. The Pakistani navy shelled the city during the Liberation War.

Orientation

Station Rd is more or less the centre of town and it forms a good reference point. Towards its eastern end, on the corner of Jubilee Rd, is the large New Market building (Riponi Bitan). Jubilee Rd continues south over Station Rd to merge with Sadarghat Rd, the main artery of the Old City. Sadarghat Rd officially begins on an offshoot near the GPO, rather than at its apparent beginning at the intersection near New Market.

The central bazar is a warren of lanes between the lower ends of Jubilee and Station Rds. It's almost impossible not to lose your way among the densely packed rows of shops, which sell mostly garments (including every possible variety of *lungi*).

The more upmarket shopping area is along CDA Ave, in the vicinity of the

CHITTAGONG DIVISION

Meridian Hotel. Aarong has a large outlet here, offering a wide range of handicrafts along with books, postcards and ethnic clothing, such as *salwar kameez* and punjabi suits. There are more upmarket stores in this area.

Chittagong's business district is the Agrabad Commercial Area, the grid of streets between Sheikh Mujibur Rahman Rd and the Hotel Agrabad. Besides the Ethnological Museum, a couple of hotels and a large number of banks, this part of town is of little interest.

Maps The best map available is the Chittagong City Guide Map published by The Mappa. It's available from the bookshop near the Meridian Hotel on CDA Ave, and from the Hotel Agrabad's bookshop.

Information

The Tourist Information Centre is at Parjatan's Shaikat Hotel on Station Rd, and as usual the snooty staff hand out brochures and deny any further knowledge. Worse than that, they may try and convince you that a permit is necessary to visit the Chittagong Hill Tracts (available for a price, of course). Don't believe them – permits are not required.

Money Most convenient to the Station Rd area is ANZ Grindlays, just down a small street running north off Station Rd, west of the intersection with Jubilee Rd. There's another ANZ Grindlays branch on CDA Ave, near Sarina's restaurant, which has a 24-hour ATM. Chittagong's other ATM is at the HSBC branch near the Ethnological Museum in the Agrabad Commercial Area; there are many other banks in this area.

Standard Chartered Bank, right across from New Market, charges Tk 65/90 for travellers cheques of US$50/100 denominations. Most banks want to see proof of purchase in addition to a passport.

Post & Communications The GPO is just behind the New Market on Suhrawardi Rd (the continuation of Station Rd). It is open from 8 am to 8.30 pm except Friday,

when it is open from 3 to 9 pm. There are numerous telephone offices around town with direct international connections.

As yet there is no Internet cafe in Chittagong, but you could try some of the computer businesses along Station Rd. Aztech Computers, upstairs at 92 Station Rd, has two computers with Internet connections and charges Tk 5 per minute.

Old City

As in Dhaka, the city's oldest area is the waterfront area called Sadarghat. The early arrival of the Portuguese is evinced by the proximity of the Paterghatta district, just next to Sadarghat. The Portuguese had their enclave here, and it remains a Christian area. There isn't much to see in Paterghatta, but it's a quiet, clean place to walk around – until you get into the slums of the prawn-shellers near the waterfront near Feringhee Bazar, which will leave a stench on your shoes that will take days to wear off. A rowing boat back to Sadarghat costs anything from Tk 5.

Across the river is the fish harbour and market. You can hire a local boat from the boat terminal to go across (10 minutes, Tk 20) and wander around the fish market. There's a big fish processing plant, and 50m from the fish market is the Marine Fisheries Academy housed in a new building with a small museum. It has a few fish specimens to look at, if you need to add a little excitement to your day and think this will do it.

Shahi Jama-e-Masjid The mosque in Anderkilla (inner fort) was built in 1670 on a hillock and hence looks a bit like a fort. It has a tall minaret, Saracenic or Turkish in design, which looms up out of the press of shops that have since surrounded it. In the early 1950s it was greatly enlarged and most of its original features altered, though a number of original inscriptions are still embedded in the thick walls.

Chilla of Badar Shah West of Bakshirhat, is this *chilla*, or place of meditation, that derives its name from a Sufi who came to Chittagong in 1336. It is a modest-sized place with a courtyard and worship area

CHITTAGONG

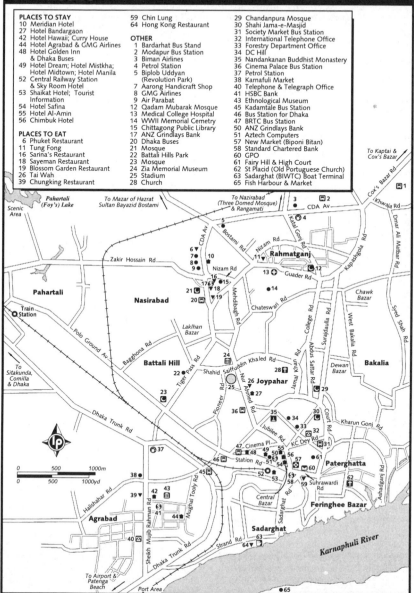

PLACES TO STAY
10 Meridian Hotel
27 Hotel Bandargaon
42 Hotel Hawaii; Curry House
44 Hotel Agrabad & GMG Airlines
48 Hotel Golden Inn
   & Dhaka Buses
49 Hotel Dream; Hotel Mistkha;
   Hotel Midtown; Hotel Manila
52 Central Railway Station
   & Sky Room Hotel
53 Shaikat Hotel; Tourist
   Information
54 Hotel Safina
55 Hotel Al-Amin
56 Chimbuk Hotel

PLACES TO EAT
6 Phuket Restaurant
11 Tung Fong
16 Sarina's Restaurant
18 Sayeman Restaurant
19 Blossom Garden Restaurant
26 Tai Wah
39 Chungking Restaurant

59 Chin Lung
64 Hong Kong Restaurant

OTHER
1 Bardarhat Bus Stand
2 Modapur Bus Station
3 Biman Airlines
4 Petrol Station
5 Biplob Uddyan
   (Revolution Park)
7 Aarong Handicraft Shop
8 GMG Airlines
9 Air Parabat
12 Qadam Mubarak Mosque
13 Medical College Hospital
14 WWII Memorial Cemetry
15 Chittagong Public Library
17 ANZ Grindlays Bank
20 Dhaka Buses
21 Mosque
22 Battali Hills Park
23 Mosque
24 Zia Memorial Museum
25 Stadium
28 Church

29 Chandanpura Mosque
30 Shahi Jama-e-Masjid
31 Society Market Bus Station
32 International Telephone Office
33 Forestry Department Office
34 DC Hill
35 Nandankanan Buddhist Monastery
36 Cinema Palace Bus Station
37 Petrol Station
38 Karnafuli Market
40 Telephone & Telegraph Office
41 HSBC Bank
43 Ethnological Museum
45 Kadamtale Bus Station
46 Bus Station for Dhaka
47 BRTC Bus Station
50 ANZ Grindlays Bank
51 Aztech Computers
57 New Market (Biponi Bitan)
58 Standard Chartered Bank
60 GPO
61 Fairy Hill & High Court
62 St Placid (Old Portuguese Church)
63 Sadarghat (BIWTC) Boat Terminal
65 Fish Harbour & Market

CHITTAGONG DIVISION

built around the grave of Badar Shah, and it is walking distance from the Shahi-Jama-e-Masjid, though with several *mazars* (graves) in the same area check to be sure you're directed to the right one – ask for 'Badar Shah Chilla'. On the same road are several interesting shops that make traditional tablas.

British City

The British originally occupied the area just north-west of Sadarghat, a slightly hilly section where they built their usual collection of administrative and cultural edifices: a hospital, the Secretariat, and the High Court. Station Rd, with its brightly lit stalls, forms the boundary with the Old City.

The British City has become the central business district of the city. The area retains its colonial air and comparative sense of order and cleanliness.

Zia Memorial Museum On a knoll on Shahid Saiffuddin Khaled Rd, one of the most attractive structures left by the British, the massive Chittagong Circuit House, was where President Zia Rahman was machine-gunned by a group of soldiers in May 1980. Built in 1913 in the style of a Tudor manor house, it originally stood amid 35 acres of landscaped gardens and lawns. It is one of the few remaining timber structures in the country, and is constructed predominantly of wood with a brick masonry foundation. Part of the building is now a museum commemorating the death of President Zia; opening hours are completely flaky though. Things might improve if the BNP, the political party of Zia's widow Begum Khaleda, gets back into power.

Chandanpura Mosque This mosque is north of the city centre on the road to Kaptai, near Dewan Bazar. It has no historical importance but is an attractive sight with its delicate design.

Fairy Hill This area is said to be named for the fairies and genies that were believed to occupy this hill when the Sufi saint Badar Shah first came to Chittagong. Legend says

that he had to make a number of requests to the fairies before they would allow him to build a place of worship. Views from the top are good, especially at sunset, when you might catch a cooling breeze as well. It's behind the GPO and New Market – climb the path leading off Jubilee Rd just north of the pedestrian bridge near New Market. Ask directions for the High Court, the building on top of the hill – Fairy Hill was the common name during the Raj era and is rapidly being forgotten.

DC Hill Atop this hill is the district commissioner's residence, but the surrounding area is open to the public. A neglected helicopter pad sits at the top and from here there is a commanding view of Chittagong. It is a pleasant place with many old trees. The views are just as good as from Fairy Hill.

WWII Memorial Cemetery This peaceful well-maintained cemetery on Fazul Rd contains the graves of soldiers from both the Allied and Japanese forces who died on the Burma front.

Modern City

Agrabad, the modern commercial section, with its banks, large hotels and corporate offices, is quite in keeping with the trends of a 20th-century city. The outer reaches of the city have become industrialised; the only steel mill and oil refinery in Bangladesh are in Chittagong.

Ethnological Museum Around the corner from the Hotel Agrabad, this interesting museum has displays on Bangladesh's tribal people and is well worth visiting. Unfortunately it isn't always open when it should be. Some of the exhibits are looking a bit tattered, but it covers all the major tribal groups of the nearby Chittagong Hill Tracts. The museum's assumption that these cultures are doomed is depressing. It's open during the winter from 9 am to 5 pm Saturday to Thursday and is closed on Friday. In summer it opens and closes 30 minutes later. There is a 30-minute break for lunch at 1 pm year-round.

Qadam Mubarak Mosque

Built in 1719 in the Rahmatganj area, the late-Mughal Qadam Mubarak ('footprint') mosque derives its name from a slab that bears an impression of the Prophet's foot.

Chittagong Port

The port of Chittagong is on the west bank of the Karnaphuli River south-west of the city centre. It has 20 berths and handles bulk cargoes and container ships – up to 900 vessels and 5.5 million tonnes annually. The port has made Chittagong the commercial centre of Bangladesh, but the rail, road and river transportation facilities from Chittagong are barely able to cope with the port's cargo-handling facilities. The port area is closed to all but permit-holders due to strict security measures.

Mazar of Hazrat Sultan Bayazid Bostami

This gaudily painted shrine is in the Nasirabad area, 5km north-west of the city centre. A great *mela* is held here during the Muslim festival of Shab-e-Barat.

The shrine isn't especially impressive, and women are not allowed to enter. It may be worth visiting to see the dirty pond full of turtles; legend says they are evil spirits that were turned into turtles by the curse of a saint over 1000 years ago. Judging by their size they could well be that old. They like to be fed bread, which you can buy at the stalls near the entrance.

The easiest way to get there is to take a rickshaw or tempo to the corner of CDA Ave and Bostami Rd. From there you can take any bus or tempo (Tk 3) heading along Bostami Rd; they all stop near the shrine. The key word to emphasise is 'Sultan' – 'Bostami' gets you directed to a post office. If you see a sign saying 'Chittagong Cantonment' on the left, you've just passed the mazar. Tempos run between here and Station Rd for Tk 6.

Pahartali Lake

More often known as Foy's Lake, this area has boating facilities and is a popular picnic spot; things get hectic on weekends. Earlier in the morning is a nice time to visit. On a cool day, walking is pleasant in the denuded hills around the lake. There is a zoo here too but it's a wretched place. A high hill near the lake's edge affords some grand views of Chittagong and the Bay of Bengal. You can get there by rickshaw (Tk 10) or tempo (Tk 3) from the junction of CDA Ave and Zakir Hossain Rd.

Places to Stay – Budget

The cheapest deal in the city is the series of 'boarding shacks' across from the central train station on Station Rd. These are basically covered shop-fronts with rows of beds crammed together. Out the back are common toilets and bathrooms. There are no mosquito nets, but they do have fans. All this costs only Tk 16, though there is absolutely no privacy and you could end up knowing your neighbour more intimately than you might like. For more 'worldly' lodgings, read on.

One of the best budget hotels is the *Chimbuk Hotel (☎ 619028)*, on Jubilee Rd about 50m from the corner with Station Rd. Singles with common bathrooms are small but adequate for Tk 50, while singles /doubles with bath are Tk 70/140. The staff are friendly, there's a TV in the pleasant reception area and there's a balcony overlooking the city's busiest intersection.

Further up Jubilee Rd is the *Hotel Safina (☎ 614317)*. It's a labyrinthine place from the British period, but the staff are friendly and knowledgeable about local sights, and some of the rooms are quite OK. Rooms with short beds and common bathrooms cost Tk 70/130 (Tk 100/185 with attached bathrooms).

The central train station is unusual for having its own hotel, the *Sky Room*. It's decent and convenient. Double rooms only cost Tk 300.

Places to Stay – Mid-Range

There are quite a few mid-range hotels bunched together on Station Rd, all large and reasonably run if a little overpriced.

At No 91, *Hotel Dream (☎ 619401)* is cleaner than many and is one of the best bets in this category. The staff are accustomed to foreign travellers. Although the stairs aren't for the weak of knee, the high building allows for airy rooms; best are the corner doubles. Rooms with attached bathrooms cost Tk 165/260. Air-con rooms cost Tk 375/600. There's also a restaurant.

Hotel Mishtka (☎ *610923),* at No 95, next to Hotel Dream, charges Tk 175/250 for rooms with attached bathrooms, but no mosquito nets (Tk 300 for doubles with TV). Its older than the Hotel Dream but the rooms are bigger. There's a good restaurant here.

At No 85, *Hotel Midtown* (☎ *617236)* has not-so-clean singles/doubles/triples with attached bathrooms for Tk 100/150/200, but no mosquito netting. A few doors away the *Hotel Manila* (☎ *614098)* is expensive for what you get, with rooms with attached bathrooms for Tk 150/200. Some rooms are much better than others so it pays to see a few before you decide.

Also on Station Rd, about 300m west of the station, the multistorey *Hotel Golden Inn* (☎ *610683)* is clean with friendly staff. Its glossy brochure describes the 'modern, mini shopping corner' as a place 'for meeting your petty needs.' Economy rooms cost from Tk 325/525, and doubles with air-con and TV are Tk 950. It has a restaurant, and there's a travel agency at the front of the building, which is convenient for buying domestic tickets on Biman Airlines.

Hotel Bandargaon (☎ *228811),* at No 875 Nur Ahmed Rd (the northern extension of Jubilee Rd), in an area called Enayet Bazar, has clean, larger-than-average rooms with attached bathrooms for Tk 125/160 and a helpful manager.

Hotel Hawaii (☎ *724057),* on the same road as the Ethnological Museum, has larger versions of the standard hotel room from Tk 300/375 with attached bathrooms (including a bath). Service is lackadaisical and the place looks a bit run-down, but the price is right.

Places to Stay – Top End
The *Meridian Hotel* (☎ *652050, fax 650124),* at 1367 CDA Ave, is the best value top-end hotel in town. It's conveniently lo-

cated near the city's better restaurants and shops. Economy rooms are US$30, deluxe rooms US$35 and suites US$35; all are air-con, with carpeted, modern bathrooms and satellite TV. There's a restaurant and coffee shop here, and the hotel is secure.

Parjatan's *Shaikat Hotel* (☎ *619514),* on Station Rd east of the train station, is centrally located but there's little to recommend it. Hardly anyone seems to stay here. Doubles cost from Tk 650/500 with/without air-con.

Hotel Agrabad (☎ *501199, fax 710572),* in the Agrabad Commercial Area, is a mammoth luxury hotel with rooms that cost from US$120/135. It has a couple of restaurants, a swimming pool, and one of the few bars in the city. The rooms are looking quite dated, but the 1960s decor adds some charm to the Trishita Bar. Rickshaws from here are very expensive – rickshaw-wallahs will charge more if they think you're staying here. Walk up the street away from the hotel to catch a cheaper ride.

Places to Eat
Jubilee Rd is one of the best restaurant areas. Even the cheap eateries are pretty good by Bangladeshi standards. There are a number of good local places just north of the Hotel Al-Amin. The *Mitan Biriani Restaurant* to the right as you leave the Hotel Al-Amin has excellent kebabs.

Eating places in the bazar near the Hotel Al-Amin are good value, especially for the popular Chittagong beef.

Many of the upmarket restaurants cater to East Asian businesspeople. The *Chin Lung* Chinese restaurant, opposite the GPO on Suhrawardi Rd, is just above average in quality and prices. The *Tai Wah* restaurant on Nur Ahmed Rd is popular with Korean businessmen and has tasty Chinese and Korean fare, if a little expensive; main courses cost around Tk 120.

There are expensive *restaurants* at Hotel Agrabad. Nearby, the *Curry House* at Hotel Hawaii has reasonably priced Bangladeshi food, and there's also a Chinese restaurant. *Chungking Restaurant*, in the same area on Sheikh Mujibur Rahman Rd, is one of the oldest Chinese establishments and is reputed to have the best Chinese food in town.

The best, more expensive restaurants are on CDA Ave around the Zakir Hossain Rd junction. Locals consider the *restaurant* at the Meridian Hotel to be the city's finest; it serves Bengali and Chinese food. On the same street, *Sarina's* serves Indonesian, Thai, Chinese, Mughlai and Bengali dishes for reasonable prices while Indian rock videos pulse enticingly on the TV. Next door, the *Sayeman* is Chittagong's best known Mughal restaurant. Meals range from Tk 150 to Tk 250 per person.

South of these restaurants, the similarly priced *Blossom Garden* sits on the edge of a hill and offers outside garden dining complete with a small waterfall, with the option of indoor dining. It serves Mughlai, Chinese and Bengali dishes.

The *Tung Fong* is another decent Chinese place, on the corner of Nizam and Guader Rds. It's a little dark but the air-conditioning is sweet relief on a hot day. Chicken with cashew nuts costs Tk 150.

On Strand Rd, down from the BIWTC terminal, *Hong Kong Restaurant* has a limited Chinese menu, but is one of the last surviving bars in the city. Housed in a bright, tomato-red, fort-like building from the Raj era, it is hard to miss. Upstairs it is dark and shady, but you can buy beer (Tk 150) and hard drinks, except on Friday.

Getting There & Away

The Dhaka-Chittagong highway is probably the busiest in the country and prone to bumper-to-bumper traffic jams. Travelling to Dhaka by train is far less nerve-wracking.

Air Chittagong has the busiest regional airport in the country, and Biman, GMG and Air Parabat all have frequent flights between Dhaka and Chittagong.

The Biman office (☎ 650 7671) is on CDA Ave, near Bardarhat Bus Station. Biman has three to four flights daily to Dhaka (Tk 1865), the last one departing at 7.15 pm. Morning flights on Biman to Cox's Bazar depart on Sunday and Thursday for Tk 500. Biman also flies twice a

week to Kolkata (Calcutta) for US$86. Indian Airlines also used to fly this route, and may recommence in the future.

GMG has six flights a day to/from Dhaka for Tk 1870. There's a GMG office at the Hotel Agrabad (☎ 503147) and another on CDA Ave (☎ 655659), near the Aarong store.

Air Parabat has two flights a day for Tk 1870; their office is also on CDA Avenue (☎ 654320).

Bus The largest bus station is Bardarhat, 4km north of the city centre. To get there, take a local bus (Tk 2) from Nur Ahmed Rd. Most buses for Cox's Bazar and Kaptai leave from there. Soudia is one of the better companies serving Cox's Bazar (four hours); the standard fare is Tk 65. Buses for Rangamati (three hours) leave from Modapur bus station on CDA Ave.

Most Dhaka-bound private bus companies operate out of the old BRTC bus station on Station Rd. An air-con chair coach to Dhaka takes five to six hours, depending on traffic congestion in Dhaka, and costs between Tk 230 and Tk 300. Bus companies with ticket offices around the Hotel Golden Inn include Green Line, Greyline, Borak and Soudia. Several other companies, including Neptune, have offices on CDA Ave, across from the Blossom Garden restaurant. Chair coaches without air-con cost Tk 130.

Another departure point is Cinema Palace bus station on Nur Ahmed Rd, next to Cinema Palace; it has a few Dhaka-bound buses. Buses returning from Cox's Bazar usually continue on to this more convenient station after stopping briefly at Bardarhat.

For express buses to Comilla (Tk 55) and Chandpur (Tk 55), head for Kadamtale bus station, just over the railway lines at the west end of Station Rd. There are no direct buses to Sylhet; you must change in Comilla.

Train There are three intercity (IC) trains a day to Dhaka, and the trip takes around six hours. Snacks and soft drinks are available during the journey. Fares to Dhaka are Tk 320/160 for 1st class/sulob and Tk 510 for a sleeper (night train only). According to the schedule, trains depart at 7 am, 3.25 pm and 11.30 pm for Dhaka, and arrive at 12.25 pm, 8.55 pm and 6 am respectively. The morning train is supposedly slightly nicer. Tickets on Dhaka trains should be booked at least two or three days in advance. The fare to Comilla is Tk 55 in sulob class.

IC trains also run to Sylhet via Comilla in the morning, departing at 10.30 am, and cost Tk 280/150 in 1st class/sulob. Daily Noakhali trains go via Laksham and to Chandpur as well.

Boat There are no direct launches to Dhaka from Chittagong. Some large launches ply between Chittagong and Barisal via Hatiya Island. If you want a 1st-class cabin you should buy your ticket a day or two in advance. For Barisal, purchasing tickets even a week in advance is recommended.

The BIWTC terminal is at the end of Sadarghat Rd, a few hundred metres to the west along the riverbank. The administration office is clearly marked in English, but the tickets are sold from a nondescript building just before the office. Launches leave for Barisal on Saturday, Monday and Thursday at 9 am, and the 24-hour trip costs Tk 768/509/160/108 in 1st/2nd/inter/deck class. These boats also travel to Hatiya, which is an 11-hour trip. The fare is Tk 430/286/83/62.

There are daily private launches for Kutubdia Island, a six- to seven-hour trip, plus a BIWTC ferry on Wednesday at 9 am. The BIWTC fare is Tk 221/149/36 in 1st/2nd/deck class. There's a government rest house on Kutubdia Island, which you might be able to use. You can continue on to Cox's Bazar by private launch (at least one a day).

Getting Around
To/From the Airport There isn't always a bus to meet incoming flights and the airport is a long way out from town – baby taxis cost around Tk 80. At the T-junction, 500m from the airport, you can catch a bus (Tk 5) to New Market.

Local Transport Rickshaws and baby taxis are plentiful, and cost about the same as in

Dhaka. Tempos and buses are cheaper, but they are cramped and crowded and can be quite frustrating if you don't speak Bangla. The routes are also not well established.

AROUND CHITTAGONG
A couple of sites are difficult to get to but are worth making the effort.

Shakpura
This small village, 24km south of the city, has Buddhist and Hindu temples. The Nindam Kanon Temple is a meditation centre. Buses leave from Bardarhat bus station in Chittagong (the same bus station as for Cox's Bazar). There are about 8 buses going there each day, which cost Tk 20.

Patenga Beach
This public beach, 24km south of Chittagong via the airport road, is adjacent to an industrial area and there is quite a lot of construction going on, so it's hard to recommend. The fare to get here is over Tk 100 by baby taxi. You might try finding a public bus (BIWTC Bus No 1, available from the BIWTC boat terminal, reportedly travels there).

Bird-watching enthusiasts will find the mudflats near Patenga Beach an excellent high-tide roost for waders, the occasional spoon-billed sandpiper, Nordman's greenshank, and good numbers of great knot and grey-rumped tattlers. The best time of year is winter, but bird-watching is good from August to May. A mid/late morning high tide is the best time of day; you'll need tide tables to figure out when to go. Look for a schedule at the BIWTC terminal in Chittagong.

Getting to the mudflats is not much easier. Take a baby taxi to the Steel Mill Colony (housing development) on the way to Patenga. From there walk to the beach and head north a short distance to the mudflats.

SHIPBREAKING YARDS
On the seashore north of Chittagong every kind of ocean-going vessel from supertankers to container ships and tugboats are dismantled, and it's all done with manual labour. At any one time there can be 30

ships beached on the shoreline between the towns of Bhatiara and Sitakunda. Armies of workers use blow torches, sledge hammers and plain brute force to tear them apart. Supervisors don't seem to mind visitors, but it's best to ask permission first. Once you've received permission and there is a high tide, you can get out on top of the ships, some of which are five to seven storeys high. Be advised, however, that this is not an entirely safe undertaking and can be a dirty process. It is impressive, not just for the sheer size of the ships, but for the scenes of hundreds of men struggling across the mudflats hauling huge plates of steel. It's such a bizarre sight that the shipbreaking yards have become a popular setting in Bangladeshi movies; typically as where bad guys have their base.

After a series of critical media reports the managers at the shipbreaking yards have become nervous of anyone they suspect of being a journalist. If you approach a work crew, don't openly wave a camera around.

This section of the Dhaka-Chittagong highway is lined with businesses selling every salvageable part of the ships; from brass taps, mirrors and foam cushions to enormous turbines, cables and plates of steel. The metal inner partitions of the ships are used to build the hulls of river boats; most of the steel is sold on to scrap merchants overseas.

Getting There & Away
The yards are easy enough to get to; take any bus north along the Dhaka road and get off when you see a supertanker (or part thereof) looming over the palm trees. From the highway it is between 1km and 2km to the seashore, either walking or by rickshaw along the many tracks. There are frequent buses back into Chittagong for Tk 6 or so.

SITAKUNDA
Some 36km north of Chittagong, this sleepy little town has one attraction – the historic Hindu **Chandranath Temple**, 6km away on top of a hill, an hour's hard climb. There are great views from the top, which can be a real treat in flat Bangladesh. Unless you

have a particular interest in Hindu temples, however, the only time it's really worth visiting is during the Shiva Chaturdasi Festival, held here for 10 days in February. It attracts thousands of Hindu pilgrims. Sitakunda's Buddhist temple is just a ramshackle wooden building, not worth the effort.

Getting There & Away
Take a bus for Feni from the Kadamtale bus station in Chittagong; the trip takes 45 minutes and costs around Tk 12.

RAMGARH
It's a little-known fact that there are tea estates in the Chittagong area that are as large as those in Sylhet. One of the best places to see them is north-east of Ramgarh. Two of the country's largest tea estates are located here, and you can walk around them at your leisure. Ramgarh is only easily accessible by bicycle or private vehicle. You could take a bus to Feni and get a Ramgarh-bound local bus from there.

RAUZAN
The area around the town of Rauzan, about halfway along the road from Chittagong to Rangamati, is the centre of the Bengali Buddhist community. Nearly all of them share the surname Barua, and the community is often known by this name. There are many Buddhist temples in this area. The most famous is Mahamuni, a huge cement replica of the original Mahamuni image, which was taken to Mandalay in Myanmar (Burma) as booty in the 19th century.

CHITTAGONG HILL TRACTS
Decidedly untypical of Bangladesh in topography and culture, with steep, jungled hills, Buddhist, Christian and animist tribal people, and a relatively low population density, the 13,180 sq km of the Hill Tracts are an idyllic place to visit. The region comprises a mass of hills, ravines and cliffs covered with dense jungle, bamboo, creepers and shrubs.

From 1973 until 1997 the hill tracts area was the scene of a guerilla war between the

Bangladeshi army and the Shanti Bahini rebels. The troubles stemmed from the cultural clash between the tribal groups, the original inhabitants of this region; and the plains people, who are desperate for land. Centuries ago, the tribal ancestors wandered into the teak forests of the Chittagong Hills, mostly from the Arakan hills in Myanmar. Predominantly Buddhist, they are Sino-Tibetan in origin and appearance.

About half the tribal population are Chakma, and most of the remainder are either Marma, who represent about a third, or Tripura. Among the 11 much smaller groups (Mru, Tengchangya, Bohmong, Khumi, Mizo, Pankhu, Sak, Bawm, Mogh, Kuki and Reang), the Mru (called the Murung by Bangladeshis) stand out as being the most ancient inhabitants of the area.

Like the general population, most tribal people are poor and illiterate, but their culture and way of life are very different from those of the Bengali farmers of the plains. Some of the tribes are matriarchal and all have similar housing – made entirely of bamboo, raised on a bamboo platform about 2m to 5m high and covered by thatched roofs of dried leaves.

In most other respects, the tribes are quite different. Each tribe, for instance, has its own distinctive rites, rituals and dress; the Chakma women, for example, all wear indigo and red-striped sarongs. Each tribe also has its own dialect.

The women, who are known to be hard workers, are particularly skilled in making beautiful handicrafts, while some of the men still take pride in hunting with bows and arrows. Both women and men love music and dancing.

Under the British, the Hill Tracts had special status and only tribal people could own land there, but the Pakistani government abolished the special status of the Hill Tracts as a 'tribal area' in 1964. The construction of the Kaptai Lake for hydroelectricity in 1960 was another blow, submerging 40% of the land used by the tribal people for cultivation and displacing 100,000 people. The land provided for resettlement was not sufficient and many

Chakma women are known for their handicraft skills, such as weaving.

tribespeople became refugees in neighbouring north-east India.

During the Liberation War, the then Chakma king sided with the Pakistanis, so when independence came the tribal people's plea for special status fell on deaf ears. The Chakma king left for Pakistan and later became that country's ambassador to Argentina.

Meanwhile, more and more Bengalis were migrating into the area, usurping the land. The tribal people, with no legal recourse, did not take this lying down. In 1973 they initiated an insurgency. To counter it, the government started in 1979 to issue permits to landless Bengalis to settle there, with title to tribal land. This practice continued for six years and resulted in the mass migration of approximately 400,000 people into the area – almost as many as all the tribal groups combined. Countless human rights abuses occurred as the army tried to put down the revolt.

Sheikh Hasina's government cemented an internationally acclaimed peace accord in December 1997 with tribal leader Jyotirindriyo Bodhipriya (Shantu) Larma. Rebel fighters were given land, Tk 50,000 and a range of other benefits in return for handing in their weapons. The peace deal handed over much of the administration of Khagrachhari, Rangamati and Bandarban districts to a Regional Council.

Rangamati
☎ 0351

Rangamati, 77km east of Chittagong, is beautifully sited on a series of ridges and islands in the midst of Kaptai Lake. The town was laid out as an administrative centre and modern-day hill station in the 1960s, after the damming of the Karnaphuli River. Most of the town is spacious but the poorer parts of town around the main bazar are as crammed with houses as any slum in Dhaka. The town's fleet of noisy, smoky baby taxis detracts from the charm as well.

The outlying islands and lakeshore around Rangamati belong to the Chakma people, much of whose ancestral land was flooded by the lake. The countryside is lush, undulating and verdant. Virtually all of the tribal people you meet here are Chakma. The population of the town is overwhelmingly Bengali, however, and tourists from the cities descend on the town en masse on weekends.

Orientation & Information Rangamati extends for about 7km from the army checkpoint to the Parjatan Motel. The Tribal Cultural Institute and Sabarang Restaurant are about 1.5km past the checkpoint. A couple of hundred metres further on is a concrete market complex and the Agrani and Sonali banks. The main road passes the fish market and then crosses a long causeway, at the end of which is a traffic circle. The road to the right leads to the Parjatan Motel (crossing a steel bridge), while the road to the left leads to the main bazar and the main port, Tobolchuri Ghat.

The best place to see and buy tribal textiles is at the collection of handicraft shops between the steel bridge and the Parjatan Hotel. The display is quite good and prices are fair, and, strangely, finding these textiles in Dhaka is extremely difficult.

Tribal Cultural Institute This small museum has displays on the tribes of the Hill Tracts, including costumes, bamboo flutes, coins and silver and ivory necklaces. There is also a map showing where in the region the different tribes live. It is open Sunday to Thursday from 10 am to 4 pm.

Buddhist Temples There are several modern Buddhist *viharas* in and around the town. The biggest is the **Bana Vihara**, a monastery located on a headland at the northern end of town. In one open-walled hall there are several elaborate thrones for the head abbot, made in the form of a *naga* serpent.

The Chakma king, a barrister in Dhaka, has his rajbari on a neighbouring island. The rajbari is not open to visitors but the **Raja Vihara** on the same island has a large bronze statue of Shakyamuni (the historical Buddha) overseen by a small and friendly monastic community. The island is reached by small launches at the end of the lane that runs between the Tribal Cultural Institute and the Sabarang Restaurant; the boat also paddles across to the Bana Vihara.

Kaptai Lake A boat trip on Kaptai Lake, the country's largest artificial lake, with stops at tribal villages along the way, is the highlight of a trip here. The lake is ringed with banana plantations and thinning patches of thick tropical and semi-evergreen forests dominated by tall teak trees. The level of the lake varies quite considerably throughout the year. When it starts to fall in March the emerging land is farmed before the lake rises again in the monsoon season.

Tribal Agriculture

Most tribal people are farmers, practising shifting cultivation called *jhum*. They slash and burn the slopes between January and April, then sow the seeds with the first rains. While the hill people's staple is rice, from which their favourite intoxicant beverage is prepared, they also plant other crops, including cotton, maize, sesamum, pumpkin, yam and melon. By tradition, the jhumias, as the farmers are called, often plant various seeds together. The following year they plant elsewhere, allowing the land to recover for a year or two. By lowland standards this seems wasteful, but the lands here lack the constant replenishment of rich nutrients from the rivers.

While the lake itself is beautiful, the villages you'll see around the lake really make the trip special. Bring your binoculars for bird-watching and better viewing of some of the thatched villages and fishing boats you'll see along the way. The tourist boats usually stop at Chakma villages, allowing you to see traditional bamboo houses and small Buddhist shrines made of bamboo.

Hiring a boat is cheaper the further away you are from the Parjatan Motel. Tourist boats from the Parjatan Hotel charge Tk 300 per hour for the boat and take up to about 10 passengers. The Parjatan also has smaller, faster speedboats for Tk 800 an hour. Motorboats at the Aranjak Cafe cost around Tk 200 per hour, while in the vicinity of the steel bridge boats cost around Tk 100 per hour. Tobolchuri Ghat is another option. You can go anywhere around the lake but there are plenty of interesting villages within a half-hour's distance. Villagers generally don't crowd around you or ask for baksheesh – a welcome relief.

A good place to visit is the Buddhist monastery, **Jawnasouk Mountain Vihara**, across the lake from Rangamati. Another interesting boat trip is to go through the narrow, steep-sided waterway that leads into the lake's upper basin. You can take a plunge anywhere, so bring your swimming gear.

There are also two public launches a day leaving Rangamati for the town of Kaptai; they depart at 8.30 am and 3.30 pm but verify the schedule beforehand to be sure. The trip takes 1½ hours (four hours round trip). There is also a speedboat that does the round trip in two hours. These boats leave from Tobolchuri Ghat.

Places to Stay & Eat Rangamati has only several budget hotels, in the Tk 50 to Tk 120 range. Some may insist that foreigners can only stay in the Parjatan Motel, which isn't true. There are cheap hotels at the town's main port, Tobolchuri Ghat, including the *Boarding House* (Tk 40 per person). There are several cheap *restaurants* here, often serving curries made of fish and shrimp harvested from the lake. Some other budget hotels that have been recommended include

the *Hotel Anika, Hotel Lake View, Hotel Hiramon* and *Hotel Dreamland.* They are all close to the main launch ghat, where the bus stops.

Most of the guesthouses here are geared towards weekend Bengali tourists, many touring around in buses fitted with loudspeakers blaring movie soundtracks. Those on economical organised tours often stay at the *Hotel Shapla* in town, where ordinary singles/doubles cost Tk 100/150.

The best place to stay is the *Hotel Sufia* (☎ 2145), on the main road close to the Town Hall. It's a new concrete building with clean white rooms and modern bathrooms. Rooms with fan are Tk 200/300, air-con rooms are Tk 500/600. Next to the modern building there is a wooden building with simpler rooms for around Tk 50, but you'll have difficulty convincing the manager to let you stay in them. There's a restaurant on the top floor but it's nicer to eat on the surrounding balcony overlooking the lake.

The *Parjatan Motel* (☎ 3126) is in a choice location at the southern point of the town, offering beautiful views of Kaptai Lake from rooms with balconies. Unfortunately it hasn't been particularly well looked after and the management is brusque, even by Parjatan standards. The charge is Tk 550 for ventilated double rooms (Tk 750 with air-con). It also has three cottages for families (Tk 700), with three to four beds each. The restaurant here serves particularly greasy food. Travel between the Parjatan and Rangamati is either by foot (about an hour) or baby taxi. There's also a *Circuit House*, but with the Parjatan Motel available, you're likely just to be told to stay there.

Not far from the Parjatan Motel is the pleasant *Aranjak Cafe* overlooking a branch of the lake, where you can sit outside at tables or eat indoors in a small western-style restaurant.

The *Sabarang Restaurant,* next to the Tribal Cultural Institute, across from the open grassy 'stadium', is an initiative of the Chakma raja. Local specialities include *sumaat gudeya kurahera* (chicken cooked

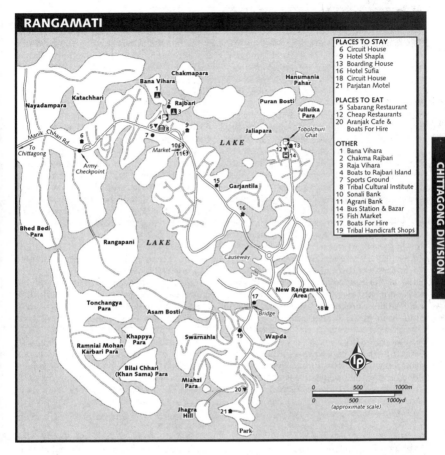

RANGAMATI

PLACES TO STAY
6 Circuit House
9 Hotel Shapla
13 Boarding House
16 Hotel Sufia
18 Circuit House
21 Parjatan Motel

PLACES TO EAT
5 Sabarang Restaurant
12 Cheap Restaurants
20 Aranjak Cafe &
   Boats For Hire

OTHER
1 Bana Vihara
2 Chakma Rajbari
3 Raja Vihara
4 Boats to Rajbari Island
7 Sports Ground
8 Tribal Cultural Institute
10 Sonali Bank
11 Agrani Bank
14 Bus Station & Bazar
15 Fish Market
17 Boats For Hire
19 Tribal Handicraft Shops

CHITTAGONG DIVISION

in bamboo) for Tk 180 and *kuchya maach ranya* (curried eel) for Tk 190. For an appetiser you could try *sok sok samuk* (snails with shell) for Tk 60 or *kilatthur vaza* (banana flowers with dried shrimp) for Tk 50. The choice of spices is not dissimilar to Thai food. The waiters speak English and can acquire some Chakma liquor if you ask. There is also a Chinese and Bangladeshi menu; main dishes cost around Tk 150.

Getting There & Away Chittagong to Rangamati buses (three hours, Tk 35) depart, periodically, from Modapur bus station on

CDA Ave. You'll pass two security checkpoints en route, the second on the edge of town. Normally the authorities ask your nationality and your destination, and that's it. If you arrive in your own vehicle you may have to fill out a detailed form; this seems to depend on whether the officer wants to break the monotony of his day.

Getting Around Due to its hilly topography Rangamati is a rare example of a Bangladeshi town without rickshaws. Baby taxis operating as share taxis (five or six passengers is normal) putter along the main roads; it costs about Tk 5 to go from the Circuit House to Tobolchuri Ghat. Hiring a baby taxi can be expensive. The other option is to jump on a passing bus. There is no direct route to Kaptai; you'll have to go back to Chittagong to catch a bus from there.

Kaptai

Once a hunting ground for wild animals, Kaptai is 60km east of Chittagong and at the southern end of Kaptai Lake, 1½ hours by boat from Rangamati. Today it's the site for a 50m dam wall and a hydroelectric plant, and the atmosphere is rather oppressive (signs say there should be no photography or 'unauthorised movement'). The Kaptai ghat looks quite picturesque at night, however.

Kaptai is a flat town with one main street consisting of a long row of low structures; this is the bazar where you'll find all the eating places, hotels and boarding houses, tea houses and general stores. There is a crane at the dam wall that lifts stacks of bamboo ferried in rafts across the lake over and into the Karnaphuli River, from where it floats down to Chittagong.

Places to Stay There's a government *Circuit House*; as always you'll need to seek permission from the district commissioner to stay here. His office is nearby. The *Kamal Boarding House* is clean and cheap. Other places to stay, such as *Sat Khana Boarding House*, are very basic.

Getting There & Away Direct buses from Chittagong's Modapur bus station leave throughout the day and cost Tk 24. Unless you have a private vehicle, you cannot travel here straight from Rangamati; instead you'll have head back to Chittagong for the bus.

Chitmorong

This is a Buddhist village of the Marma tribe, 5km from Kaptai on the road to Chandraghona, 26km further west.

Part of the attraction of Chitmorong is the languid, serene atmosphere. Amongst the bamboo and thatched village huts you can purchase a cup of the local palm wine, *tari*. The village contains some richly adorned

Buddhist sculptures, and the monastery is presided over by an English-speaking head monk. On the hilltop is a huge stupa with a temple to one side. Here you may come across the head monk, who will chat with you over a cup of tea, which is your donation. A Buddhist festival is held here every Bengali New Year, around mid-April.

Getting There & Away The bus from Chittagong will drop you off at a bus stop with a milestone; there is no village in sight, but the rooftop of the stupa-like monastery can be seen above the trees. There is a footpath on the left that ends at the top of a rather steep, concrete stairway; at the bottom, you hope, waits a boat to ferry you across to the village. If not, you'll just have to wait.

Bandarban

The market town of Bandarban lies on the Sangu River, 92km from Chittagong. The river is the centre of local life, with bamboo crafts carrying goods downstream while country boats make leisurely trips to neighbouring villages. Most of the inhabitants belong to the Buddhist Marma tribe.

The small *Tribal Cultural Institute* has a museum and library. Opening hours are vague but if you can locate the curator he is very knowledgeable about the different tribes. The *Bohmong Rajbari* is the residence of the Bohmong king, an amiable elderly man whom you may have the good fortune to meet.

There is a tribal bazar on Sunday and Wednesday, where trading is conducted in Marma rather than Bangla.

Officially no permits are required to visit Bandarban but you should call on the district commissioner and tell him your plans, especially if you intend to visit some of the outlying towns such as Ruma (where there is a tribal market on Monday and Thursday).

Places to Stay & Eat The *Green Hill Hotel* on the main intersection has singles/doubles for Tk 80/100. The *Purabi Hotel* nearby has a floor of cheap singles with shared bathrooms for Tk 40, and doubles/triples on the upper floor with attached bathrooms for

CHRISTINE OSBORNE

In the scorching sun, bricks are broken by hand to make aggregate for road-building.

RICHARD I'ANSON

Catching a quick nap in the back of a rickshaw

RICHARD I'ANSON

Just a little bit off the side...

TONY WHEELER

Loading timber on the Buriganga River

Jute and rice farming are perfectly suited to the watery conditions in Bangladesh. Both young and old work hard to ensure the success of each year's crop.

Tk 150/200. At the bus station the *Hotel Hillbird* costs the same as the Purabi but the location isn't as good. Around the launch ghat there are a clutch of anonymous little places used by poor locals.

Eating options are limited; there are some basic *restaurants* and *tea houses* on the main street.

Getting There & Away During the day small coaches leave every 30 minutes or so between Chittagong's Bardarhat bus station and Bandarban for Tk 30. The trip takes about three hours.

Another option is to take a bus on the Chittagong-Cox's Bazar Highway and get off at the junction settlement of Kerani Hath. From here there are buses, jeeps, tempos and microbuses to Bandarban. Buses cost about Tk 10.

Organised Tours
Bangladesh Ecotours (☎ 018-318345, ✆ bangladeshecotours@yahoo.com; in USA fax 01-987-285 6214) offers tailor-made tours of up to seven days in the Hill Tracts, including Chittagong, Rangamati, Kaptai Lake boat cruise, Bandarban, Alikadam, hiking up Keokradang and visiting Mru villages. Cost per person per day ranges from US$100 (two people) to US$65 (six people), excluding domestic airfares.

The Guide tour company in Dhaka (☎ 02-988 6983, fax 988 6984, ✆ theguide @bangla.net), at Rob Super Market, DIT II Circle, Gulshan, takes groups of two or more. A four day/three night tour includes all the sights of Rangamati and its environs, a boat trip on Kaptai Lake, swimming, hiking, Bandarban, Chimbuk and visits to tribal villages. The Guide's cost per person, including airfare from Dhaka, for a four-day/three-night trip is US$425 (two people), US$355 (three to five people), US$320 (six to nine people) or US$300 (10 to 15 people). Three day/two night tours costs 20% less.

Unique Tours and Travels in Dhaka (☎ 02-988 5116, fax 818 3392, ✆ unique @bangla.net), at 51/B Kemal Ataturk Ave, Banani, is another option. Four-day Hill Tract tours to/from Dhaka include Mainimati and Sonargaon in the schedule. The cost is US$750 (two to three people), US$620 (four to seven people) or US$580 (eight to 10 people).

COX'S BAZAR
☎ 0341
The country's biggest beach resort is disappointing if you're expecting another Goa. The centre of town is a grubby mess, the area is being carelessly overdeveloped, the sea is murky, there are criminal elements to watch out for and even the vast and magnificent beach can become crowded. On the other hand, there's no better way to escape the crowds than taking a swim, there's a good range of hotels, alcohol is available (both legal and smuggled – but always expensive). Welcome to beach life, Bangladeshi style. At least the usual question, 'Why have you come here?' doesn't get asked because the answer is obvious – you've come to the seaside. During the winter, from November through March, Cox's Bazar gets crowded (especially on weekends) and accommodation can be scarce. During the low season, most hotels will reduce their prices by as much as 40% if asked.

The surrounding area, adjacent to the Chittagong Hill Tracts, runs south down the coastline to the Myanmar border. This is still a relatively sparsely populated part of the country. The population of the region is about one million and is a mix of Muslims, Hindus and Buddhists. The culture here is less overtly Muslim, or even Hindu for that matter, having a more Burmese-Buddhist atmosphere.

This region was a favourite of the Mogh pirates and brigands who, with the Portuguese, used to ravage the Bay of Bengal in the 17th century. The Moghs have remained, maintaining their tribal ways through handicrafts and cottage industries, such as the manufacture of cheroots and hand-woven fabrics. To some degree the Moghs, who have a sizeable population here, have assimilated into the ways of the dominant Muslim culture more than other tribes.

When the area was taken over by the British in 1760, Captain Hiram Cox founded the town as a refuge for the Arakanese fugitives who were fleeing their homeland after being conquered by the Burmese. These new refugee Mogh settlers erected quite a number of the stupas found today on the low hills around town. In recent years there has been a new influx from Arakan, now known as Rakhine state in Myanmar (Burma). In the early 1990s at least 250,000 Rohingyas (Muslims from Rakhine) fled to Bangladesh to escape persecution by Myanmar's military regime. Today most of the refugees have returned although there are still several refugee camps between Cox's Bazar and the border. There has also been an influx of migrant workers from Rakhine, attracted by the relatively better wages and more secure environment. Many of them work as labourers and rickshaw drivers.

Information

The Uttara Bank on Ramu Rd across from Laldeghi Lake, accepts foreign currencies and cashes travellers cheques (US dollars and UK pounds). There's an Agrani Bank branch close by that is reportedly an easier place to change money. The tourist office in Parjatan's Upal Motel is more useful than

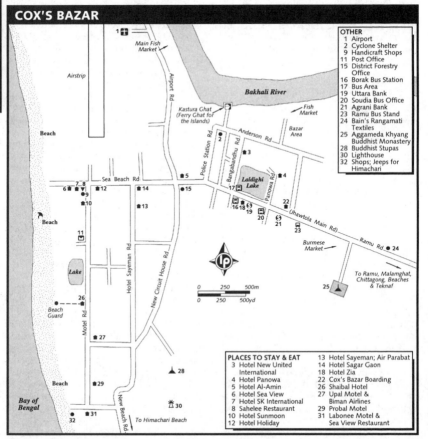

COX'S BAZAR

Main Fish Market

Airstrip

Bakhali River

Airport Rd

Kastura Ghat
(Ferry Ghat for the Islands)

Fish Market

Beach

Police Station Rd

Bangabandhu Rd

Anderson Rd

Bazar Area

Sea Beach Rd

Laldighi Lake

Panowa Rd

Beach

Hotel Sayeman Rd

New Circuit House Rd

Lake

(Jhawtola Main Rd)

Burmese Market

Ramu Rd

Beach Guard

Motel Rd

0   250   500m
0   250   500yd

To Ramu, Malamghat, Chittagong, Beaches & Teknaf

Beach

New Beach Rd

To Himachari Beach

Bay of Bengal

OTHER
1 Airport
2 Cyclone Shelter
9 Handicraft Shops
11 Post Office
15 District Forestry Office
16 Borak Bus Station
17 Bus Area
19 Uttara Bank
20 Soudia Bus Office
21 Agrani Bank
23 Ramu Bus Stand
24 Bain's Rangamati Textiles
25 Aggameda Khyang Buddhist Monastery
28 Buddhist Stupas
30 Lighthouse
32 Shops; Jeeps for Himachari

PLACES TO STAY & EAT
3 Hotel New United International
4 Hotel Panowa
5 Hotel Al-Amin
6 Hotel Sea View
7 Hotel SK International
8 Sahelee Restaurant
10 Hotel Sunmoon
12 Hotel Holiday
13 Hotel Sayeman; Air Parabat
14 Hotel Sagar Gaon
18 Hotel Zia
22 Cox's Bazar Boarding
26 Shaibal Hotel
27 Upal Motel & Biman Airlines
29 Probal Motel
31 Labonee Motel & Sea View Restaurant

CHITTAGONG DIVISION

most. There's a poorly marked post office on Motel Rd on the edge of the grounds of the Shaibal Hotel; look for the letterbox outside.

Though a 'tourist' town, Cox's Bazar has little directed specifically to tourists. Stalls next to the Hotel Sea View sell an amazing array of trinkets made from seashells, from tiny bracelets to finely made chandeliers. There are other handicraft and Burmese shops near the Buddhist monastery in town. Here you will find hand-woven fabrics, saris, cheroots, jewellery and conch-shell bangles.

Police noticeboards at the beach warn you not to stay in isolated places without informing the police, not to go too far out in the water (there are no lifeguards), and that swimming at low tide is risky. The northern end of the beach next to the airport may be temptingly quiet, but armed robberies have occurred here, even in daytime. The beach is not safe at night either.

The colourful Buddhist Water Festival takes place from 13 to 18 April each year.

Things to See & Do

The main reason to come to Cox's Bazar is the beach. The route to the beach along Sea Beach Rd is quite filthy; buses dump litter here and at night it serves as a public toilet.

The nicest place is in front of the Shaibal Hotel, where there is a friendly uniformed guard and umbrellas and sun lounges for hire. There is a path leading from the Shaibal through the 'golf course' to this area. A hawker with a cartload of snacks, soft drinks and even beer works here too. The guards will watch over your gear if you go swimming and shoo away the kids selling shell necklaces. They will also deal with the crowds of gawkers if they get too intrusive.

Foreign women in swimsuits are the subject of an awful lot of interest from Bangladeshis, and may be hassled by men. Even the Bangladeshi upper-class are not accustomed to seeing women in swimsuits, so they will gawk. Some will even want to take a few photographs. It's a switch being at the other end of the lens. Bangladeshi women who swim (a very rare breed) do so in their flowing salwar kameez.

Bangladeshi holidaymakers congregate at the southern end of the beach near the Labonee Motel to watch the sunset, and there are some simple beachside cafes here selling drinks and snack food. A concrete path runs beside the beach between Sea Beach Rd and this area.

If you're intrigued by the high-prowed wooden fishing boats chugging along the sea shore, head to the Bakhali River on the north side of town. The river port positively teems with different types of craft. There are several boatyards on the shore, where ships are built using methods that haven't changed much in centuries. Some of the boats are decorated with numerous ragged flags and look uncannily like pirate ships from an old movie. Given that piracy is on the rise in the Bay of Bengal there's the possibility that some might be the real thing.

Aggameda Khyang

This 19th-century Buddhist monastery at the east end of town is representative of the Burmese style of architecture. Its distinct appearance would stand out anywhere, but nestled among trees in the middle of Cox's Bazar it's all the more fascinating. The main sanctuary is built around massive timber columns, and the teak flooring throughout adds an air of timelessness to the place. The temple houses a number of small bronze Buddhas, mostly Burmese in origin, and a few old manuscripts. The main temple has modern Buddhas made of concrete with a backdrop of flashing lights. Expect to be approached for a donation – Tk 10 is a reasonable amount to give.

Places to Stay – Budget

There are some cheap dives in the town centre around Laldeghi Lake, but it's a very noisy and congested area. If that's no deterrent, options include *Cox's Bazar Boarding* (☎ 3565), a shack with singles/doubles with common bathrooms for Tk 40/60.

The *Hotel Al-Amin* (☎ 3420), on Sea Beach Rd (no English sign), quite a way from the beach, charges Tk 50/100 for rooms with attached bathrooms. It's opposite the District Forestry Office.

Hotel New United International (☎ 4489), on Bangabandhu Rd, is decent value. Rooms with attached bathrooms are Tk 80/100. Cheaper singles with common bathrooms are Tk 40.

Hotel Zia (☎ 4497), right across from the bus station, is ageing badly but has rooms for Tk 70/130 with attached bathrooms.

The *Hotel Holiday* has a pink bungalow next to the main building with cell-like rooms with common bathroom for Tk 50.

Places to Stay – Mid-Range

The *Hotel Sagar Gaon* (☎ 3445), on Sea Beach Rd, is a large multistorey edifice with friendly management. Economy rooms with attached bathrooms cost Tk 70/150, and from Tk 100/200 for deluxe.

Toward the beach end of Sea Beach Rd, *Hotel SK International* (☎ 3830) is away from the hustle and bustle of the town. Singles with common bathrooms are Tk 100, and singles/doubles with attached bathrooms are Tk 150/200.

Next to the Hotel SK International, the *Hotel Sea View* (☎ 3515) genuinely does have sea views and is clean and professionally run. All the rooms have balconies facing the sea, and there is a rooftop garden. Double rooms cost Tk 395, Tk 495 with TV and large bed, and Tk 795 with air-con.

Hotel Sunmoon (☎ 3231), on Motel Rd, near the corner with Sea Beach Rd, is a cheerful place, smaller than most, with rooms for Tk 150/200, and doubles facing the balcony for Tk 300.

There are more hotels in the centre of town but most of them are run-down. One exception is the *Hotel Panowa* (☎ 3282). It's down a lane to the east of Laldeghi Lake, across the road from the bus station. Small but clean singles/doubles/deluxe rooms with attached bathrooms cost from Tk 90/120/350. A TV costs an extra Tk 50. Singles with common bathrooms are Tk 70.

Places to Stay – Top End

Hotel Sayeman (☎ 3900, fax 4231) is the town's best hotel, with doubles from Tk 350 and four-bed suites from Tk 650. The rooms are airy, clean and well-furnished – this place gets positive reports. The Sayeman also has air-con doubles from Tk 850. All rooms, except economy, have satellite TV. There are two restaurants and a dark bar with a loud TV where you can actually order a beer. There's a swimming pool here, a bakery that makes tasty biscuits, and the offices of Air Parabat are here too.

Hotel Holiday (☎ 3892) on the corner of Motel Rd and Sea Beach Rd is overpriced, with doubles from Tk 300 and air-con rooms from Tk 600.

Parjatan has three mid-range motels, all rather expensive, but they are set on large blocks of land with ample space for parking. The *Probal Motel* (☎ 3211), on Motel Rd, is similar to the Upal but is slightly more shabby. It has a small restaurant, shabby economy doubles for Tk 250 and better doubles from Tk 500. Rooms with hot water cost an extra Tk 100.

The *Labonee Motel* (☎ 4703), at the southern end of Motel Rd, is newer than the Probal or Upal but doesn't have much open space. Doubles on the lower floors (no sea view) cost Tk 550, doubles on the upper floors cost Tk 600 (an extra Tk 100 for a TV).

The *Upal Motel* (☎ 4258) has large clean doubles for Tk 500, Tk 800 with air-con. All rooms have balconies. The Biman office is located here.

If you'd prefer a hotel to a motel, rooms at Parjatan's flagship *Shaibal Hotel* (☎ 3275) run from Tk 1200 to Tk 2000, and suites are Tk 3000. It has a good restaurant that is not too expensive. There is also a discreetly positioned bar in a separate building nearby. Other facilities include a tennis court, barbecue and a small lake which some complain breeds hordes of mosquitos. There's also a swimming pool but it isn't cleaned very often. The expanse of parkland around the hotel is actually an old and overgrown golf course.

Places to Eat

There are, miraculously, no Chinese restaurants in Cox's Bazar, though many hotel restaurants have Chinese dishes. There are many good local restaurants, mainly around the west end of Sea Beach Rd.

The **Sahelee Restaurant**, upstairs on the building next to the Hotel Sunmoon, is clean and spacious. Its motto is 'economy food with aristocracy'. A big plate of tasty mixed chow mein costs Tk 60.

Two of the best hotel restaurants are the inexpensive and relaxed **restaurant** at the Hotel Panowa (try the delicious, but bony Hilsa curry cooked in traditional mustard oil, or the abundant biryani) and the more expensive **restaurant** at Hotel Sayeman, which has excellent seafood.

Parjatan's **Sea View Restaurant**, in the octagonal building near the Labonee, serves Bengali, Chinese and American food (fried chicken and burgers). Prices tend to be on the high side, but it's recommended, for both food and service. The Shaibal has a good **restaurant**, but it's more expensive (although cheaper than the room prices would suggest), with a mixture of Bengali and western dishes. There is an economical **restaurant** at the Probal.

The **Alpha Restaurant** at the Hotel SK International is popular with the locals, and the Hotel Sagar Gaon also has a **restaurant**. Prices are around Tk 50 for a fish curry, and around Tk 30 for a vegetable curry.

Getting There & Away

Air Biman (☎ 4019) is at the Upal Motel. It operates afternoon flights between Cox's Bazar and Dhaka (Tk 2365) via Chittagong (Tk 550) on Sunday and Thursday. Once you're in the air, it's less than 20 minutes to Chittagong; the plane flies at only 1000m, so the views are good – try for a seat on the right-hand side.

Air Parabat (☎ 3900) is at the Hotel Sayeman, and has flights to/from Dhaka every day except Friday (Tk 1770).

GMG currently has no office in Cox's Bazar, though it apparently plans to open one at the Hotel Sayeman. Tickets are available at the airport. It flies between Dhaka and Cox's Bazar on Saturday and Thursday for Tk 2395.

Bus Express buses to Dhaka leave throughout the day and take eight or nine hours. The fare is Tk 160. Chair coaches without air-con cost around Tk 200. The last one

leaves around 7 pm. For the four-hour trip to Chittagong, the last bus leaves at 4.30 pm and the fare is Tk 70. There are express buses to Teknaf (three hours) that depart until 6 pm; the fare is Tk 45.

For an air-con chair coach check the offices of Soudia, Borak or Green Line, which are all close by on the main drag, Sea Beach Rd. Green Line has several departures a day to Chittagong (Tk 130); the last one at 4 pm goes directly to Dhaka (Tk 315).

Getting Around

Most places are within walking distance, even the airport. There are plenty of rickshaws. For trips further afield you can hire jeeps for rides along the beach, although they aren't cheap. A ride just to Himachari costs Tk 700, while Parjatan's shiny models cost Tk 2500 per day from the Shaibal Hotel!

The Hotel SK International can arrange motorbike hire for around Tk 1500 per day; the person you need to ask for is Mohammed Shahjahan.

AROUND COX'S BAZAR

A new road is slowly being built from Cox's Bazar south along the seashore to Teknaf. The project is particularly controversial because of the deforestation caused along the way. In the process, a bridge has been constructed over the Rezu River, making it possible for the first time to drive entirely on the beach from Cox's Bazar to Teknaf. A 4WD vehicle is required if you want to try this.

The evergreen and semi-evergreen tropical rainforest bordering this stretch of beach is still some of the best in the country, despite the recent heavy pressure from the Rohingya refugees and others who have settled in the area.

This forest is home to a wealth of plant and animal life. Bird-watching, especially in the patches of forest on the low hills running off the beach just south of Cox's Bazar and around Teknaf, should reveal quite a number of interesting species. The staff at the District Forestry Office in Cox's Bazar are happy to give more information about local species to watch out for.

CHITTAGONG DIVISION

Malamghat

An hour north of Cox's Bazar on the Chittagong road is more of the same exemplary forest that is found south of Cox's Bazar. Bird-watching is also very good in this area. The village of Malamghat is well known for its excellent Baptist missionary hospital. It has a Guest House that charges Tk 1000 per person for non-missionaries. Arrangements should be made before arrival with the Association of Baptists (AOB) office in Chittagong (☎ 031-65 1935) or Dhaka (☎ 02-882 4699).

Himachari Beach

By reputation, Himachari is the nicest beach near Cox's Bazar, though many travellers feel that it's a bit overrated and not exceptionally beautiful. You'll find a shack where tea, soft drinks and some basic Bengali food are sold.

Just before the beach are some low cliffs and gorges; this area is very quiet. Cattle and water buffalo appear at sunset, their bells tinkling on their way to the nearby village. There is a waterfall here, though it's not very impressive. It sometimes dries up in late winter. If you walk a little higher you'll find forests which, sadly, are slowly being cut down.

To get here, take a public bus from Cox's Bazar to Himachari village and walk across the village to the beach. You can also take a jeep. In Cox's Bazar, jeeps leave from the shops on the southern end of the beach by the Labonee Motel Youth Inn. The fare is Tk 60, but it takes a lot of bargaining. If you have time (about two hours) you could walk back to Cox's Bazar.

Inani Beach

Inani Beach, one of Bangladesh's claims to fame, is considered the world's longest and broadest beach: 180m at its narrowest at high tide and 300m at low tide. Even here, some 30km south of Cox's Bazar, it's not completely deserted, so don't be surprised if you attract a small audience.

There's a *Forestry Department Guest House* right on the beach, just south of Inani Beach, with fine views of the sea. It

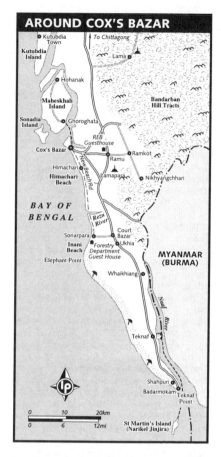

AROUND COX'S BAZAR

has three guest rooms with common facilities; the cost is Tk 300 a room or Tk 1500 for the entire guesthouse. You have to take your own food and the facilities are limited, but it is furnished. Get permission from the District Forestry Office (☎ 3409) in Cox's Bazar, west of the bus stand area just off Sea Beach Rd.

To get here, take a bus to Teknaf and get off at Court Bazar (30km), a tiny village 2km before Ukhia. From there you can find rickshaws or maybe a tempo to take you west to the beach, which is 10km away. If you're headed for the guesthouse, ask the rickshaw driver to let you off at the tiny village of Sonarpara, which is on the beach and halfway to Inani. From there you must walk south until you reach the guesthouse. Transportation between Court Bazar and Sonarpara – tempos and rickshaws – should not be difficult to find since locals use this route to get to nearby villages.

Alternatively, hire a jeep from Cox's Bazar to take you directly to Inani using the scenic beach route (see Himachari Beach, earlier in this section).

Ramu & Lamapara

Ramu and Lamapara are noted for their Buddhist khyangs and are worth visiting for that purpose. Ramu is an undistinguished market town 14km east of Cox's Bazar just off the Chittagong road. Some of the hills in this area are topped with pagodas.

In addition to its khyangs, Ramu, a subsidiary capital of the Arakan kingdom for nearly three centuries, is noted for a beautiful **monastery** containing images of Buddha in bronze, silver and gold inlaid with precious and semiprecious stones. Start at the far end of the street of Buddhist buildings at the lovely U Chitsan Rakhina Temple, and work your way back towards the town centre.

The beautiful Burmese **Bara Khyang** at Lamapara has the country's largest bronze statue of the Buddha, and its three wooden buildings house a number of relics – precious Buddhist images in silver and gold, set with gems. The temple lies in a quiet, palm-shaded village about 5km from Ramu, accessible only by zigzagging paved village paths. It would be almost impossible to find it on your own, so the only options are taking a rickshaw or chartering a baby taxi for around Tk 100 to Tk 150 for a return trip.

About 2km away from Lamapara, at the village of Ramkot, there are Buddhist and Hindu temples perched on adjacent forested hills. The monks at the Buddhist temple are Bengali rather than tribal, and the modern building resembles a Hindu temple rather than a Burmese khyang. Between the two temples is a modern boarding school for tribal children from the Hill Tracts, the Jagatjyoti Children's Welfare Home. The

director is friendly and may be able to give directions to tribal villages about a 6km walk away. There is a metalled road from Ramkot back to Ramu.

Buses and tempos to Ramu leave Cox's Bazar from a stand a few blocks east of the bus stand on Sea Beach Rd. The trip takes about 30 minutes by tempo and costs Tk 8.

Sonadia Island

According to legend, centuries ago a ship laden with gold sunk here during an attack by Portuguese pirates and an island eventually formed around the shipwreck. However it formed, this tiny, 4.63 sq km island is barely 7km (10 minutes by speedboat) from Cox's Bazar. It was once a place renowned for growing pink pearls, but the economic benefits from more profitable commercial fishing have seen this tradition slowly fade away. Fishermen set up camp here in winter, and Bangladeshi tourists make the trip here to buy dried pomfret fish from them.

Sonadia, with a variety of mangroves, is noted for its bird life and, in particular, acts as a temporary sanctuary for migrating birds – petrels, geese, curlews, ducks and other waterfowl. The western side of the island is a beach known for its interesting seashells. There is a small bazar here with seashell crafts. Quite a few visitors come here during the winter season for beach picnics and to hunt for pink pearls. Unfortunately, there are no public launches, so you'll have to hire a boat (Tk 700 or more for a day trip) at Kastura Ghat or ask around the port if any fishermen are heading that way.

Maheskhali Island

Some 6km north-west of Cox's Bazar, Maheskhali (mosh-KHAL-ee) Island makes a pleasant day trip. It's a large island, mostly flat and barren but with a pleasant hilly area on its eastern side. Arriving by ferry from Cox's Bazar, you must pass along an impressively long high jetty for about 500m until you reach the town of Maheskhali, also known as Ghoroghata. If there are any festivals underway among its mixed population of Buddhists, Hindus and Muslims you might be invited to stay and watch.

Betel Nuts

On Maheskhali, you'll see betel trees everywhere. This island is one of the major sources of the nuts, which are sold at street stands all over the country. Taken as a digestive stimulant and mild narcotic, the betel nut is broken into tiny pieces and chewed with leaves and lime paste. There are two kinds, one with a hint of sweetness from additives, and one with a raw, bitter taste. Try some – you'll see people everywhere chewing and spitting red juice. Chances are you'll find them unbearably bitter, but the locals will get a big kick out of seeing you indulge in their habit.

Regardless, you'll find rickshaws to take you wherever you want.

Walking along the jetty into town, you'll see a hill to the north, about a 20-minute rickshaw ride away. This holy spot is the principal tourist attraction, with a famous stupa on top. The climb takes only five minutes. From the top you can get a good view of most of the island.

A few hundred metres away is the sole remaining wooded area on the island. Somewhat hidden therein is **Adinath**, a Shiv Mandir (ashram) dedicated to Shiva. It's a delightfully serene place set in a beautiful garden, and the priest is very friendly. It's definitely worth the effort.

If it's the dry season and you have the time you might consider some hiking. There are paths along the top of the cliff that lines the eastern side of the island. Almost no-one stays overnight on the island, which is perhaps a mistake as there are lots of paths to explore besides those along the cliff. Swimming is also an option, but the sandy beaches on the island's western side are better for this.

When you return to town, ask to be pointed towards the small fishing settlement nearby, where you can watch the boat-building activity. During the dry season (which is also the fishing season) you can see people fishing, setting up temporary camps and drying their catches.

The area is famous for its large prawns. In inlets along the coast you'll see people fishing with their nets, hauling in the catch. Fishing for other species is supposed to be good, and during the festive season of Falgoon (March to April), a visit here can be most interesting.

In the north of the island the little town of Hohanak has a betel bazar on Monday and Thursday evenings. Baby taxis run between Ghoroghata and Hohanak for Tk 25 and take about 45 minutes to make the 26km trip.

Places to Stay & Eat The *Hotel Bhai Bhai* and the *Hotel Sea Guard*, facing each other on the main road near the bazar, are the only hotels in Ghoroghata. They both offer very basic accommodation, with singles/doubles with common bathroom for Tk 50/100. The usual bazar food is available and there are a few reasonable restaurants including the *Mishtimuk*.

Getting There & Away The public ferry departing from Kastura Ghat in Cox's Bazar costs Tk 20 and takes an hour. Check to see what other passengers are paying, however, as one traveller reports that the locals told him the fare is normally Tk 7 and Tk 20 only when there's foul weather. There are also faster speedboats that depart from Kastura Ghat and take only 15 minutes. They depart when full (about 10 passengers) and cost Tk 45. Market days are Tuesday and Saturday, when more ferries are available. The main town has an impressive jetty, but if you want to continue around the coast, which is possible, disembarking will involve balancing on ladders and wading through mud.

TEKNAF

This bustling smugglers' town is on the southern tip of the narrow strip of land adjoining Myanmar, 92km south of Cox's

Bazar. The Bangladesh-Myanmar border is formed here by the Naaf River, and a branch of the Naaf divides the town, separating the flat and elevated portions. Most of the town is a crowded area of narrow alleys. From the main road where the bus stops, a narrow street runs eastward, downhill and across the creek. Over the bridge, a left turn leads up to the marketplace, where you'll find lots of smuggled Burmese merchandise and a few food stalls. Some travellers report a slightly menacing atmosphere in this town, but as long as you don't stick your nose into the local import-export business it's safe enough. It is not legally possible to cross into Myanmar from here, and since the Myanmarese army has planted minefields along the border to deter illegal immigrants and smugglers it wouldn't be wise to try.

Things to See & Do

The main reason for visiting Teknaf is to reach St Martin's Island, which lies 38km south. Other possibilities include a walk west to Teknaf Beach and a ride south to Badarmokam at the tip of the peninsula. Particularly nice at sunset, the white sandy beach at Badarmokam is quite deserted, except for people fishing, bringing in their catch and working on their boats and nets at various times of the day.

Back in Teknaf, just south of the market and police station you'll find jeeps that provide transport to surrounding villages. For Tk 20, a jeep will take you over a bumpy brick road to the very last village on the mainland, **Shahpuri**, a half-hour ride. You'll be let off at a cafe. The left fork here leads down to the seafront and mangrove swamps. Its main attractions are the beautiful view from the embankment through the mangrove swamps across to the Myanmar coast, and the village's peaceful atmosphere, as people mend their fishing boats and nets.

In 1994, some non-locals walked from Teknaf all the way to Cox's Bazar, a trip that took three days but is better done in four. Finding a place to sleep was apparently not a major problem. On one or two nights, villagers reportedly welcomed them into their homes, offering board and lodging. A hike similar to this might be worth considering, except during the rainy season.

Places to Stay & Eat

The *Niribili Hotel* is a block north of the market. Singles/doubles with fans and attached bathrooms cost Tk 60/100. It's not great but it's about as good as it gets.

Other establishments of slightly lower quality and price around the St Martin's launch ghat are the *Hotel Naf International* and *Hotel Samrat*.

Finding cheap food is no problem, but don't expect it to be very tasty. There are some basic restaurants near the market, and some cafes on the main highway, just west of the bridge over the creek.

Getting There & Away

Between Cox's Bazar and Teknaf (70km) there are buses departing every hour in either direction until around 4.15 pm.

ST MARTIN'S ISLAND

Barely 13km south-west of Badarmokam and 25km from Teknaf, St Martin's is the country's only coral island. Named after a British provincial governor and called Narikel Jinjira (Coconut Island) by the locals, the dumbbell-shaped island has an area of only about 8 sq km, which reduces to about 5 sq km – and from one to four islands – during high tide. The main island to the north, Uttar Para, gradually narrows several kilometres southward, to a point where its width is roughly 100m. Three smaller islands – Zinjira, Galachira and Ciradia – are located just south of the main island. At low tide they're essentially one body of land, and a narrow strip of land connects them with the main island. The western side of the island is very tranquil, and while the sand and surf are nice the water is too murky for snorkelling.

Most of the island's 5500 inhabitants live on Uttar Para. The majority are Muslims and live primarily off fishing, although some plant rice and vegetables. During the peak fishing season, October to April, fishermen from neighbouring areas bring their catch to

Hiking St Martin's Island

St Martin's Island is one of the best places in Bangladesh, especially in winter, to get away from it all. You can walk around the main island in a day. The island has two lagoons that support thick mangrove forests, though without the plant diversity of the Sundarbans. You'll also see numerous sand dunes, typically covered by screw pine and beach creeper. A rocky platform surrounds the island and extends into the sea, but the sand is excellent almost all the way around and is ideal for sunbathing. You may, however, encounter an oily patch here and there. If you are bothered by mosquitoes you'll love this place because there are very few in winter.

St Martin's Island, where wholesale buyers with temporary stalls stand ready to purchase their catch. It's fascinating to see so many different types of fish drying in the sun on endless bamboo racks along the beach.

Information
Finding your way around Uttar Para is simple as there's only one tarred street, opposite the landing point on the beach, where the island's shops and restaurants are located. Uttar Para boasts a primary and high school, as well as a post office, police station and border patrol, a barber and tailor, a generator, and a cyclone warning centre and shelter. For information on the island, try the post office. The people there are very friendly, and will most likely invite you for a cup of tea.

Places to Stay
One of the island's two cyclone shelters serves as a *rest house*. From the landing, you'll find it about 300m south down the beach. It's a concrete building on stilts overlooking the sea. It has only one room with two beds, mosquito nets and a bathroom that doesn't work. The cost is Tk 100 a night. The location overlooking the water is marvellous, and every morning you'll wake up to a view of the sun rising over the mountains of Myanmar.

A better choice is the *Bay of Bengal Lodge*, a family home. The cost is Tk 100 a person including two meals a day. The lodge is on the main street on your right, a few minutes' walk from the beach.

One of the new hotels opening on the island is the *Green Abakash Hotel*, which has eight double rooms with attached bathroom for Tk 700. The hotel also has a restaurant.

Places to Eat
There is no dearth of grocery shops and tea houses. Shops sell biscuits and bananas among other things. The tea houses serve rice with fish, lentils, roti, local vegetables, and coconuts from the island. Even though limited food is available, it's probably a good idea to bring some tinned food and other goodies as gifts for your hosts.

Getting There & Away
Between Teknaf and St Martin's Island there are apparently two ferries in operation, one leaving every morning and returning the next day. The ferry departs from Teknaf around 9 am, give or take an hour, depending on the tides. To confirm the exact departure time beforehand, check at one of the hotels or the post office. Information on the boat departure is often conflicting so check a couple of sources and arrive at least half an hour early. Ignore the fishing boat owners who will probably tell you there is no ferry – they want you to use their private boats at a cost of Tk 1200 for the one way trip.

The ferry, in comparison, costs only Tk 50 (three hours). On market days (Sunday and Thursday) you might find two trawlers making the trip, and on stormy days during the monsoon season there is sometimes no service at all. The high seats on the stern are the best as they give good views and catch the breeze. There's no shade on the boat, so bring a hat and water.

There is no landing, so when the ferry arrives, passengers must roll up their clothing and walk through knee-deep water. There is no such thing as a timetable, but the boat back to Teknaf usually leaves around 9 am, or whenever there are enough passengers.

COMILLA
☎ 081

Some 90km south-east of Dhaka, on the highway to Chittagong and just a few kilometres west of the Indian state of Tripura, Comilla is an important regional centre. During WWII, Japanese troops penetrated the area, and the graves of some 40 Japanese soldiers are among the hundreds on the manicured grounds of the Maynamati War Cemetery.

Comilla is easy to miss because the bypass road on the western outskirts of town has few signs suggesting that a large urban area is only several kilometres away. There is a major military base in the huge cantonment west of this road. Just south of the cantonment in Kotbari is the Bangladesh Academy for Rural Development (BARD), a major training institute; a cadet college; and the city's major tourist attraction – the 6th to 13th century Buddhist ruins of Mainimati, some mounds of which are in the cantonment itself. Comilla is also the home of the Bangladesh Rice Research Institute.

Orientation & Information
The centre of Comilla is the Kandirpar district, the heart of which is Kandirpar Circle, from where four major arteries extend. Fazlul Haque Rd, heading eastward and eventually becoming Chowk Bazar Rd and the road to Chittagong, is lined with shops of all sorts and is the centre of the commercial district. Heading east along this street you'll come to Rajshinda Market, one of the city's major landmarks, and Chowk Bazar, which is another major commercial area and the location of the Chittagong bus station. Just past Chowk Bazar, on the outskirts of town, are some impressive Hindu temples.

About 500m north of Kandirpar Circle you'll find a small well-maintained park, with lots of shade trees, benches and a lake nearby. This is definitely the best place for escaping the crowds. There are several hotels in the Kandirpar district, but most hotels and restaurants are well west of the Circle along Station Rd, near the train station.

If you're an architecture buff, head for Nazrul Ave, which runs parallel with Station Rd two blocks to the south. A number of early-20th-century mansions line this street. Although dilapidated, their original architectural features are largely intact.

Maynamati War Cemetery
On the north-western outskirts of town on the road north to Sylhet, 1km off the Dhaka road, this beautifully maintained cemetery is one of the city's principal tourist attractions. British, African, Indian, Australian and Japanese troops from WWII are all buried here. Coming from Dhaka, you'll arrive at the left turn-off for the cemetery 2km before the left turn-off for Comilla.

Places to Stay – Budget
There are a couple of cheap hotels on Station Rd, just north of the train station. Coming from Dhaka, just before the railway crossing, you'll pass *Hotel Peoples (☎ 5103)*, a clearly marked five-storey structure. It's a bit dumpy but the cramped, single-bed rooms with overhead fans and attached bathrooms (Tk 60) are tolerable, and there's a decent restaurant across the street.

A better deal is the poorly marked three-storey *Hotel Abedin (☎ 6014)*, another 70m further, on the corner. The exterior is dilapidated but inside it's OK. If you can afford Tk 120, take the double on the top floor; it's spacious, bright and has reading chairs, a fan, mosquito nets, common bathrooms and great views of the city from the porch. A small single on the same floor costs Tk 60, while tolerable singles/doubles on the lower floors cost Tk 50/80 (Tk 40 for a single with common bathrooms).

In Kandirpar, check the *Nirapad Guest House*, across from the military hospital, or *Lilufa Rest House* across from the Comilla Zila School, just south of the stadium. Nirapad is a dumpy two storey structure that has tiny rooms with fans and common bathrooms for Tk 45/90, while Lilufa has ventilated rooms with attached bathrooms for Tk 40/80.

Hotel Meraj, just a block east of the busy Circle, has singles/doubles with attached bathrooms for Tk 50/70 and is noisy. Much better is the new *Hotel Al-Rafique* almost

COMILLA

PLACES TO STAY
15 Hotel Abedin &
    Sonali Bank
22 Nirapad Guest House
23 Hotel Peoples
29 Lilufa Rest House
33 Hotel Al-Rafique &
    Hotel Meraj
35 Ashique Residencial
    Rest House
42 BARD Training Institute &
    Rest House
47 Salban Vihara Rest House &
    Archaeological Museum
50 Hotel Dreamland

PLACES TO EAT
2 Kakoli Restaurant
6 Biroti Restaurant
14 Albarakat Restaurant
24 Restaurant Jolin &
   Restaurant Al-Amin

OTHER
1 Maynamati War Cemetery
3 Military Checkpoint
4 Charpatra Mura
5 Petrol Station
7 Coca Cola Plant
8 Kotila Mura
9 Military Checkpoint
10 Bangladesh Rice
    Research Institute
11 Petrol Station
12 Main Bus Station
    (for Dhaka & Sylhet)
13 Baby Taxi Stand
16 Pharmacies
17 Military Hospital
18 Civic Court
19 Our Lady of Fatima
    Catholic Church
20 Sonali Bank
21 Cinema
25 Colonial-Era Mansions

26 Comilla Law College
27 Comilla Zilla School
28 Stadium
30 Post Office
31 Rajshinda Market
32 Sonali Bank
34 Medical Centre
36 Telecommunications Antenna
37 Sign for BARD Training Institute
38 Ananda Vihara
39 Itakhola Mura
40 Military Checkpoint
41 College
43 Rupban Mura
44 Hitigara Mura
45 Cadet College
46 Salban Vihara
48 Local Buses
49 Mosque
51 Bus Station (For Chittagong)
    & Chowk Bazar
52 Hindu Temples

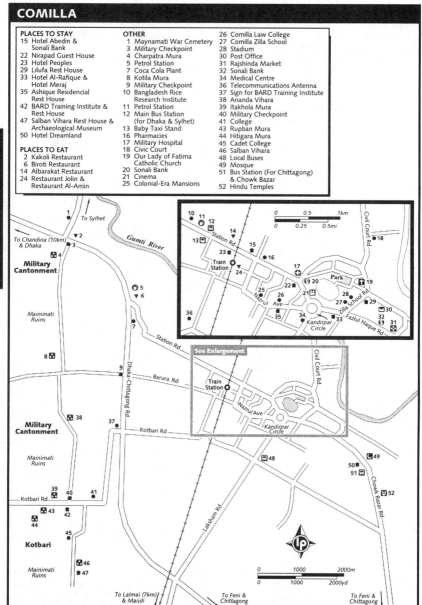

next door. It has fresh-looking rooms with fans and attached bathrooms for Tk 60/100. Another possibility is *Hotel Dreamland*, 2km south-east of the Circle off Chowk Bazar Rd and down a lane opposite the flowery minaret. At Tk 80/125, rooms with attached bathroom are no bargain, but it's handy for the Chittagong bus.

Places to Stay – Mid-Range & Top End

Ashique Residencial Rest House (☎ 8781), a modern four-storey structure on Nazrul Ave, 50m west of Comilla Law College, has no competition in the central area. It has clean and unusually spacious rooms, with twin single beds, mosquito nets, rugs, reading chairs and attached bathrooms. Rooms cost Tk 250.

There are at least two guesthouses in the Mainimati area, but they're rather remotely located. The best is the modern *BARD Training Institute (☎ 6428)*, a large and attractive campus. From the entrance follow the road to the left around to a car park; the office is at the end of the nearest building. Rooms cost Tk 80/120 (economy), Tk 150/200 (standard), Tk 300/350 (air-con) and Tk 500 (family). Cheap meals are available in the large dining hall, or there's a market across the road from the entrance. BARD is 8km west of town; finding a baby taxi or rickshaw is no problem. If you're driving, you'll find a large sign (in English) for BARD on the Dhaka-Chittagong highway.

The *Salban Vihara Archaeological Rest House and Museum (☎ 6905)*, 2km south of BARD, has two rooms plus a common dining area. The charge is Tk 100/150 for one/two people.

Places to Eat

For cheap Bangladeshi food, the area around the train station has several good restaurants, including *Restaurant Jolin* and *Restaurant Al-Amin* next door. Both places serve naan, curries, and rice dishes for around Tk 15 to Tk 20. You will also find a restaurant or two in the area around Kandirpar Circle.

Across from the Chowk Bazar bus station you'll find a cafe (no English sign) that serves excellent chicken with rice and tea (Tk 44), and ice-cold drinks.

Try *Albarakat Restaurant,* on Station Rd, just west of the railway line. The most popular dish is meat with sauce accompanied by rice or naan. It's a good-sized establishment, with overhead fans.

The city has two upmarket restaurants, both of which are on Dhaka-Chittagong Rd on the north-western outskirts of town: the *Biroti Restaurant*, just north of the turn-off for Comilla, and *Kakoli Restaurant*, 2.5km further out of town in the cantonment, at the turn-off for the WWII memorial cemetery in a row of shops marked with Coca-Cola signs. Both places, which cater to individuals and families, are carpeted and have air-con. Both offer Bangladeshi and Chinese menus.

Getting There & Away

Bus Buses for Dhaka (two hours), Sylhet (six hours) and other cities to the north leave from a bus station on Station Rd just west of the railway line. Chair coach/bus fares are Tk 125/100 to Sylhet and Tk 50/35 to Dhaka. If you're planning on heading to Mymensingh and don't want to go via Dhaka, go north to Bhairab Bazar, in Dhaka division, and pick up connections there.

Buses for Chittagong and other towns to the south leave from Chowk Bazar bus station, about 2km east of Kandirpar Circle on Chowk Bazar Rd. Buses for Chittagong leave throughout the day and early evening. The trip takes 3½ hours and costs Tk 60/45 for chair coach/bus.

Train Comilla is on the Dhaka-Chittagong line. There are three IC trains daily in both directions; the morning trains are best. The 1st class/sulob fare is Tk 170/55 to Chittagong and Tk 160/52 to Dhaka; the sulob fare is about 50% more on the 'best' trains. There's one train a day to Sylhet. The six-hour journey will cost you Tk 180/95 in 1st class/sulob.

MAINIMATI RUINS

The Mainimati-Lalmai ridge is a 20km-long range of low hills 8km west of Comilla. Famous as an important centre of Buddhist

CHITTAGONG DIVISION

culture from the 6th to 13th centuries, the buildings excavated were wholly made of baked bricks. There are more than 50 scattered Buddhist sites, but the three most important are Salban Vihara, Kotila Mura and Charpatra Mura.

A large section of Mainimati is a military cantonment, and it was while the army was clearing the area with bulldozers that the archaeological site in the Kotbari area was discovered. This was a centre for Buddhism and was visited by Xuan Zhang in the 7th century AD, who found 70 monasteries, about 2000 Buddhist monks and an Ashoka stupa from the 2nd century BC.

Some of the major ruins are within the cantonment, and cannot be visited without permission from military officers. For this reason, most visitors see only the museum and the ruins outside the cantonment. You could try asking to speak to an officer at one of the checkpoints, but your chances aren't good.

Salban Vihara

This 170 sq m monastery has 115 cells for the monks, which face a temple in the centre of the courtyard. While it lacks Paharpur's imposing stupa, the remains give a better idea of the extent of the structure, as they were rebuilt more recently.

The royal copper plates of the Deva kings and a terracotta seal bearing a royal inscription found here indicate that the monastery was built by Sri Bhava Deva in the first half of the 8th century. The original cruciform plan of the central temple was changed and reduced in scale during subsequent rebuilding. The entire basement wall was heavily embellished with decorative elements such as terracotta plaques and ornamental bricks.

Site Museum

A museum just beyond Salban Vihara houses the finds excavated there, most of which cover the 6th to 13th century AD period. The collection includes terracotta plaques, bronze statues, a bronze casket, silver and gold coins dating from the 4th century AD, jewellery, kitchen utensils including old grinding stones, pottery, and votive stupas embossed with Buddhist inscriptions. The marvellous terracotta plaques, richly detailed with a bewildering variety of subjects, including all kinds of animals, birds, flowers, and men and women in various poses, reveal a rural Buddhist art alive with animation, vivid natural realism and simple expressions of emotionalism.

Also on display is a collection of tiny dark Buddhist bronzes that the monks kept in their cells and used for praying, an unusually large bronze bell from one of the Buddhist temples, and instructive plans of some of the major shrines and monasteries, including a model of Kotila Mura. You'll also find some Hindu art, including large black-stone carvings of gods and goddesses including Vishnu, Ganesh and Parvati.

The museum, which is free, is open from 10 am to 5 pm daily (10.30 am to 5.30 pm from April to September), and from 2.30 to 5.30 pm (3 to 6 pm April to September) on Friday. It is closed Saturday.

Kotila Mura

Like all the ruins in the cantonment, this one cannot be visited without permission from the military. Situated 5km north of Salban Vihara, it comprises three large stupas representing Buddha, Dharma and Sangha, the 'Three Jewels of Buddhism', plus some secondary stupas, all enclosed by a massive boundary wall. The ground plan of the central stupa is in the shape of a *dharma chakra*, or the 'wheel of the law'. The hub of the wheel is represented by a deep shaft in the centre, and the spokes by eight relic cells. The two stupas on either side each contain a sealed central relic-chamber that has yielded hundreds of miniature clay stupas.

Charpatra Mura

Situated 2km north of Kotila Mura, not far from the Dhaka-Chittagong highway, this is another oblong Buddhist shrine perched on a hilltop in the cantonment. The main prayer chamber of the shrine is to the west, and is approached from a spacious hall to the east through a covered passage. The roof was originally supported on four thick brick columns, and a covered entrance led to the prayer chamber.

Ananda Vihara

Also in the cantonment, 1.5km south of Kotila Mura, this mound is the largest of the ancient sites on the ridge, occupying an area of over 100 sq m. Similar in plan to Salban Vihara, it was badly damaged and plundered by contractors during WWII, and consequently there's not much to see. Since you'll pass this monastery on the way to Kotila Mura, however, it may be worth checking very briefly.

Getting There & Away

From Kandirpar Circle, you can get a tempo to Kotbari for Tk 7. Most rickshaw drivers aren't interested in the long trip to Mainimati, but if you go down Laksham Rd to the intersection with Kotbari Rd (where there's a petrol station), you'll find lots of drivers willing to do the trip (about 5km). If you bargain really hard you can get a ride for as little as Tk 15; otherwise expect to pay about Tk 30.

AROUND COMILLA

One interesting excursion is to the **Chandina Aat-Chala Temple**, in Chandina, about 10km north-west of town. This 19th-century Shiva temple, constructed in the popular hut design, is probably the best example of the 'aat-chala' variation in Bangladesh, which is a hut-style structure with a second smaller hut repeated on top to gain height. It's a small square temple but very well proportioned. The terracotta artwork on the facade and ornate entrance combine to give this building a lovely appearance.

If you happen to pass through Lalmai, a small town 7km south of Comilla on the road to Maijdi, check out the **Lalmai Temple**, 1km west of town. It's small and nothing special, except for its location on top of a hill – an unusual feature in most of Bangladesh.

MAIJDI
☎ 0321

Four hours south of Dhaka by bus or car and 46km west of Feni, Maijdi, together with Sonapur just to the south, is often labelled 'Noakhali' on maps and timetables. It's one of the principal towns in the district of Noakhali, the site of much bloodshed between Hindus and Muslims at the time of Partition. Mahatma Gandhi visited the area for several months in 1947, shortly before his death, to pacify the rioting communities. The people here have the reputation of being as fiery as the chillies grown in the district, and are also more conservative than elsewhere in the country. Many families have relatives working in the Middle East, so don't be surprised if you occasionally see Bangladeshi men wearing clothes from that region.

Orientation & Information

There is one long main drag running north-south through town, and virtually all the shops and offices are here. The post office is reliable should you want to mail something. You'll find plenty of baby taxis, including a stand for them on the main drag near the post office.

Places to Stay

The well-marked *Mobaraka Hotel (☎ 6266)* on the main drag in the heart of town, has singles with common bathrooms for Tk 40 and singles/doubles with attached bathrooms for Tk 50/100. The dingy rooms have fans but no mosquito nets.

The smaller *Royal Hotel (☎ 5075),* on the same block, is clean and presentable, and charges Tk 120 for rooms with mosquito nets, fans, a sitting area with a TV, and decent attached bathrooms.

You might also try the *Circuit House (☎ 6151),* on the road to the train station. There's a chance the district commissioner (who has a separate office nearby) will give the required permission. The rooms are spacious, with carpet, overhead fans and clean attached bathrooms, and meals are available for guests. There's even a tennis and squash court.

Another place to visit is the *Gandhi Ashram*, 30km to the north in Joyag. See the following Around Maijdi section in this chapter for more information.

Places to Eat

If you're not staying at a guesthouse your best bet for meals is the *Kiron Hotel* (Bangla sign only), a small restaurant on the main drag on the northern side of town next to the Bilash bus station. It offers decent Bengali meals at standard prices.

You'll find the *Farid Bakery* a block to the south. It is good for sweets and biscuits, and there is a *shop* around the corner that serves the best ice cream in town. There are also several *tea houses* a block further south.

At any of these places you may find some sweets, including *rashmelai* (RASH-mah-lie) and *misti doi* (or bogra doy), a sweet yoghurt served in a small bowl.

Getting There & Away

Bus The bus station is on the northern side of town, 1km north of the market. The trip from Dhaka takes five to six hours and costs Tk 70. For a more comfortable chair coach try Bilash, two blocks closer to the centre of town. The fare is Tk 120 and there are several departures a day. From Dhaka buses depart from the Fakirapur area near the Green Line office at 9 and 11 am, and 3 pm.

Train There are two daily trains between Dhaka and Maijdi, departing from Dhaka at 7.30 am and 10.30 pm, and from Maijdi at 9 am and 8.30 pm. The six-hour trip costs Tk 240/82 in 1st/2nd class.

AROUND MAIJDI
Bajra Shahi Mosque

The area's most notable historical monument is the Bajra Shahi Mosque, which dates from 1741 and is in a rural setting overlooking a pond. It's a well-maintained building and is completely covered in bits of broken china; the total effect is beautiful. Both men and women are allowed to enter; inside you'll find a small prayer hall pleasingly painted in bold red, blue, green and yellow.

The mosque is 15km north of Maijdi, just off the Maijdi-Comilla road. Head north from Maijdi, pass through Begamganj (9km) and onto Bajra (5km further). The mosque is 1km further north on your left, 200m down a dirt road just south and behind a hospital.

Gandhi Ashram

The Gandhi Ashram (☎ 6017) dates from 1947, when Gandhi undertook a series of 'peace walks' through the area for several months. When a group of local Hindus presented Gandhi with a gift of about 10 hectares of land in the area, he shrugged it off, saying it would be of no use to him, and suggested that it be used to help the poor. Gandhi promised to return but his assassination prevented him from fulfilling his word. Charu Chowdhury, who accompanied him on his trip here, began running the place, using it to help the local people as Gandhi had requested. In 1953, the Pakistanis confiscated the property and put Chowdhury in jail, where he remained until 1971. Chowdhury was released at independence, the property was returned, and the ashram resumed its activities under his leadership until he died in 1990.

Today, the ashram is essentially a development organisation, helping both Hindus and Muslims in nearby villages. If you come here, you'll see some of the interesting projects: a school covering grades one to eight; three fish ponds plus a fascinating fish-hatchery machine donated by an international aid agency; a jute-weaving training program for women; and, most fascinating, a bio-gas generator that uses dung from the ashram's six cows to produce enough fuel to run the kitchen's stove for four hours a day. They'll also be delighted to show you a prayer room dedicated to the memory of Gandhi, with photographs dating from 1947 and one of Gandhi's spinning wheels. They'll probably offer you some tea heated by the cow-manure gas and show you some of the women's weavings, which you may purchase.

The ashram has two guest rooms; the staff are extremely friendly and staying here should not be a problem if they have beds available. Calling in advance might be wise.

To get here from Bajra Shahi Mosque, proceed 15km further north, stay on this paved highway (rather than turning right for Laksham) and you'll come to the tiny village of Joyag (JOY-ah). Turn right through the village and after 400m or so you'll come to the ashram.

Ramthakur Ashram

The Ramthakur (ram-TAH-gore) Ashram is in Chomahani, the neighbouring city to the east of Begamganj, 9km north of Maijdi. Just south of the station, this ashram, dating from 1949, is far less interesting than the Gandhi Ashram, but it's worth a visit if you're in Chomahani.

HATIYA ISLAND

To get off the beaten track, take a ferry to Hatiya (HAT-tee-ah) Island. There are many people on this fertile *char* (silt) island, so don't expect to be on your own, but they are friendly. A paved road runs through the centre of the island, from the northern tip where the boats stop (there's no dock here) to the south-western end. From the fishing villages on the south coast you may be able to hire a boat to some of the forested parts of the shoreline.

Places to Stay & Eat

In the centre of the island on the west side of the road you'll find an *NGO Guest House*, which is the best place to stay. Meals are available here. The offices are across the road in a cyclone shelter; the NGOs run many programs here including a demonstration farm. There is also a

Government Rest House a couple of kilometres to the north in the island's district headquarters, but it's more likely to be full. Otherwise there are some very basic *hotels* in Chowmuhani Bazar, about 2km south of the NGO Guest House. You'll also be able to find a few small *tea houses* that serve very basic spicy meals at standard prices here.

Getting There & Away

From Maijdi, take a bus headed south-west for the tiny port of Steamerghat (35km), also known as Hatiyaghat and close to Ramgati (ram-GOH-tee), a much larger town. The route passes through Sonapur (5km south of Maijdi). Be sure to get a bus to Steamerghat, not to Ramgati. Bus connections between Maijdi and Steamerghat are frequent and good, and you'll be able to find several restaurants at Steamerghat that serve very spicy food. There is one ferry per day, which departs the island at around 2 pm. The trip takes 1½ to three hours, depending on the condition of the tides. There are also thrice-weekly boats travelling from Barisal and Chittagong to Hatiya; see Getting There & Away in the Chittagong section of this chapter for details.

CHITTAGONG DIVISION

Sylhet Division

Fringed by the Khasi and Jaintia hills to the north and the hills of Tripura to the south, Sylhet division is essentially one broad valley. The countryside is covered mostly with terraced tea estates, small patches of tropical forests, and large pineapple plantations and orange groves.

This area has an annual rainfall of 5000mm – the highest in the country. Just north across the border in the Indian state of Meghalaya is Mawsynram, the wettest place on earth. On the whole, however, the area has the best climate in the country – it is temperate and cool with clean, crisp, fresh air in winter, and is moderately warm in summer.

This is a tea-growing region with more than 150 tea estates spread over 40,000 hectares, producing over 30 million kilograms of tea annually, mostly for export. Sylhet is considered the richest region of the country, with its agricultural produce including oranges and pineapples, and its mineral resources including gas reserves and possibly oil deposits. The region has also been a disproportionately large source of migrants, and remittances are a significant source of income.

The valley is fed by two rivers, the Kusiyara and the Surma. The Surma River passes through the city of Sylhet and eventually joins with the mighty Meghna further south. The valley is dotted with broad shallow natural depressions known as *haors* (HOW-ar). These low-lying marshy areas are permanent wetlands and provide verdant sanctuaries for migratory birds from places as far away as Siberia. These haors and Sylhet's subtropical forests combine to make this region one of the best in the country for bird-watching. An incredible variety of ducks, other wetland birds that are scarce elsewhere in Bangladesh, Pallas' fishing eagles and other migratory birds, such as geese and snipe, abound. There are also reportedly a few jungle cats and wild boars roaming in the small patches of forests, but travellers are very unlikely to see any of them.

Highlights

- **Tea Estates** – the rolling hills are pleasant and fun to explore, especially by bike
- **Madhabkunda Waterfalls** – this famous, remote waterfall is a popular sightseeing destination where you may see some of the few remaining elephants in Bangladesh
- **Shrine of Hazrat Shah Jalal** – this shrine in Sylhet city to the early 14th century Sufi mystic Shah Jalal attracts more than 2000 pilgrims a day

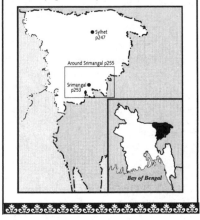

The hilly area along the northern border at the foot of the Khasi-Jaintia hills is tribal land. There are also tribal communities scattered through the southern hills. The Khashia (or Khasi), Pangou, Tripura and Monipuri people who live here are all easily distinguishable from the Bengali population by their slightly slanted eyes, a reflection of their oriental heritage, and their shorter stature. They tend to shun regular contact with the outside world, venturing only occasionally from their settlements. The Monipuri (Manipuri) are the exception to this; they have become artisans, jewellers

SYLHET DIVISION

and businesspeople, and have entered into the general Bangladeshi community. Monipuri classical dance, seen only during Hindu festivals dedicated to the worship of Radha-Krishna, is the best known feature of Manipuri culture. The Radha-Krishna cult is distinctive to eastern Indian and Bangladeshi Hinduism. It is centred on the tale of Krishna's love affair with the female cowherd Radha. She symbolises human spirituality, while Krishna is the embodiment of divine love.

The Khashia people are noted horticulturalists, and grow most of the nation's betel nut crop, which is the prime ingredient in paan.

The Sylhet region lacks the magnificent mountainous backdrops and much cooler climate of Darjeeling, but the rolling scenery is nevertheless quite pleasant and fun to explore, especially by bike. The tea estates here are every bit as interesting to see, though the terrain is not so steep and the tea itself is of lesser quality.

HISTORY

The history of the Sylhet division was principally tribal until its conquest by the great

Sufi mystic, the Muslim Shah Jalal-ud-din from Konya (Turkey), in the early 14th century. Upon arriving from Delhi, the war-like saint defeated the ruling Hindu raja, Gour Govinda, creating Shah Jalal's legendary stature among Muslims.

Ibn Battuta, a noted Moroccan traveller from Tangier, visited Sylhet to see the Sufi – and also picked up a slave for only Rs 7 while he was there. At about the same time as the Shah's arrival in Sylhet, Marco Polo spoke of the Sylhet region as a recruiting centre for eunuchs for the Kingdom of Kamrup.

In the 17th century, during the reign of Emperor Jahangir, the Mughal empire over-ran the region. The Mughals, who apparently considered the area of little importance, gave way in the 18th century to the British East India Company, which developed it as part of its Assam tea-growing region. Though Sylhet was a centre for Muslim pilgrimage during the era of the Tuglaq dynasty, the town itself was most influenced by the British occupation. They gave it a unique style of architecture: tall windows shaded by large, curved awnings, and roofs topped by several enclosed glass cubicles to provide light and ventilation.

Leading up to Partition in 1947 Sylhet division was part of Assam Province, which gave that region a Muslim majority. Fearing that the whole of what is now north-eastern India would become part of Pakistan, Hindu politicians connived to jettison Sylhet, which then joined East Bengal.

In the 1950s and 1960s the area was targeted by British officials looking for workers in the UK's postwar boom, and they and their descendants now form the core of Britain's 500,000-strong Bangladeshi community.

SYLHET
☎ 0821

The town of Sylhet has a faintly British atmosphere and, while hardly charming overall, does have a few interesting sights. Apart from the usual administrative buildings, the former residences and social structures seem to have weathered the transition from independence better than many other pieces of British Raj flotsam. Colonnaded residences are still fronted by neatly trimmed lawns, and verandahs still have leather armchairs and sofas arranged for delicate tastes. Most wealthy Bangladeshis and expatriates, however, now live in the more modern eastern quarter of town, Upashahar.

Compared to most Bangladeshi cities Sylhet seems to be quite prosperous, with smart new shops, airline offices, large homes and cars. However, this prosperity is concentrated in the hands of Sylheti emigres and their relatives. There is some resentment in the wider community that money received from overseas goes towards mosques, shrines and shopping centres rather than into developing local industry.

Sylhet has various religious festivals – Muslim, Hindu and Buddhist. The Hindu *melas* (fairs), the Laspurnima, Jolung Jatra, and Rota Jatra, are the most colourful, all dedicated to Radha-Krishna. During these Hindu melas the Manipuri dances are held.

Orientation
Across the Surma River to the south is where you'll find the train and bus stations. This section of town, which is newer, but hardly modern, has little of interest other than the vegetable market and river life. The river is traversed by two bridges. The older, more central one, Kean Bridge, is a narrow steel structure that is continually congested with rickshaws, usually pushed by 'assistants' who get paid Tk 1 for the crossing. The bridge was repaired after being damaged by Pakistani bombers during the Liberation War. If you walk across, (often faster than taking a rickshaw), watch out for rickshaws hurtling down the steep slope whenever the way is clear. Just east of that bridge, on the northern side, is a dock with some speed boats. If you'd like to rent one for a trip on the river, ask here or at the nearby Circuit House, which has friendly helpful staff. See Places to Stay later in this section for more information.

Information
Money The Sonali Bank in the heart of town on Shah Jalal Rd exchanges foreign

currency. ANZ Grindlays, in the same building as the Surma Valley Rest House on Shah Jalal Road, also changes foreign currency and travellers cheques. You can also make withdrawals on a Visa card here.

Shrine of Hazrat Shah Jalal
In the north of the city, off Airport Rd, lies the region's holiest place, the **Shrine of Hazrat Shah Jalal**. The 14th-century Sufi saint Shah Jalal is buried here, and this is a major pilgrimage place for Bangladeshi Muslims. Shah Jalal's sword and robes are preserved within the large new mosque, but they are not on display. The tomb itself is covered with rich brocade, and at night the space around the tomb is illuminated with candles – it is quite magical. There is a small cemetery at the rear of the tomb chamber; being buried in close proximity to the saint is considered a great honour. It is not entirely clear whether non-Muslims can always visit the shrine; outside of holy days it is usually possible if you are suitably dressed, but the final decision lies with the shrine guardians. Of course if you are invited to see the tomb, behave with appropriate solemnity.

The pond in front of the shrine complex is filled with huge sacred catfish that are fed by the pilgrims and are, according to legend, the metamorphosised black magicians of the Hindu raja Gour Govinda, who was defeated by Shah Jalal in 1303. There is also a tiny tank around the back with ordinary goldfish that are also apparently considered sacred.

Nearby, on a hillock named **Rama Raja's Tilla**, where the ruins of Gour Govinda's palace were once visible, you can get some partially blocked views of the city. Legend has it that a Hindu temple that once stood here was destroyed by an earthquake instigated by Shah Jalal.

Osmani Museum & Ramakrishna Mission
The Osmani Museum is a small, plain colonial-era house in Nur Manzil, near the centre of town, east of Noya Sarok Rd and on the same block as the jail. It's open Satur-

day to Wednesday from 10.30 am to 4.30 pm and Friday from 3.30 to 7.30 pm. A block to the north-east is the Ramakrishna Mission, which is worth checking out. Hindu melas are often held here.

Monipuri Village
East of the Shah Jalal Bridge is a pleasant village inhabited mainly by people of the Monipuri tribe. Their houses are decorated with carved awnings, and there are several small Hindu shrines nearby. Many of the friendly locals wear traditional costume, and you can purchase handicrafts from them, though there is no pressure put upon you to do so.

Organised Tours
Sylhet Tourism Agency (☎ 712995) at Hotel Polash offers two standard one-day tours. One covers the scenic area of Tamabil, Jaflang and Sripur, with a visit to the stone megaliths in Jaintiapur and several tea estates en route (Tk 500 per person). Another heads south-east to Madhabkunda Waterfall (another scenic area), also with a visit to a tea estate en route (Tk 600 per person).

Places to Stay – Budget & Mid-Range
There is a good range of hotels in Sylhet. A number of the lower-end choices are in the centre of town in Taltala, along Taltala Rd and the adjoining Telihaor area, west of Kean Bridge. Unless otherwise stated, rooms at all of these places have overhead fans and attached bathrooms.

The cheapest in this area is *Rahmania Boarding (☎ 714939)*. It's a friendly place with tolerably clean singles/doubles for Tk 40 to Tk 50/Tk 80 to Tk 90.

A block further west is the large *Hotel Sufia (☎ 714697)*. Rooms here cost Tk 50 to Tk 60/Tk 100 to Tk 120. The Tk 120 rooms are a bit grubby, but they're fairly spacious, with one large bed and a large bathroom. The cheaper rooms are smaller. The hotel is on the 2nd floor, with a TV viewing area that's large, if not attractive.

A little further on Telihaor Rd, next to the Nanditha Cinema, is the four-storey *Hotel*

Belash (☎ 4659), which has a Bangla sign and offers better value. It has standard rooms for Tk 50/90 and more deluxe rooms for Tk 135/250. The economical units are reasonably clean and not too cramped, while the deluxe rooms have carpets, comfortable armchairs and large bathrooms with western facilities.

Better, but more expensive, is the four-storey *Hotel Gulshan* (☎ 716437), across from the Hotel Sufia. It's well-managed, with rooms for Tk 70/100, deluxe rooms with satellite TV for Tk 250/300, and air-con doubles with TV, carpeting and western-style bathrooms for Tk 850. The standard rooms are spacious, with mirrors, desks and mosquito nets.

The *Modern Rest House* (☎ 717713), a modern five-storey building in Bandar Bazar, is much more presentable and features a small reception area with TV. The rooms cost Tk 75 to Tk 100 for singles, and Tk 150 for doubles. They are clean with wide and relatively soft beds.

Another possibility is *Hotel Cassana* near the train station. Rooms with shared bathroom cost only Tk 30/60, but the rooms are small and not terribly clean.

One mid-range option is the *Hotel Shahban* (☎ 718040) off Taltala Rd. It has four categories of rooms, two with fans (Tk 75/130 and Tk 150/250) and two with air-con (Tk 500 and Tk 700).

Places to Stay – Top End
The small *Surma Valley Rest House* (☎ 712670) in the town centre on Shah Jalal Rd, above a modern department store, has 12 units with rooms for Tk 1200/1100 with air-con (Tk 900/800 with fans). Rooms, which are modern, large and truly first-rate, have satellite TVs, telephones, minibars, comfortable chairs, big beds and tile bathrooms.

The modern *Hotel Polash* (☎ 718811, 718309), on Airport Rd, has a travel agency and one of the city's best restaurants. The hotel is well-run and comfortable, with large airy rooms. It has air-con rooms with TV for Tk 650 to Tk 750/Tk 850 to Tk 1000, including breakfast, plus 15% Value Added Tax (VAT). It also has rooms with

fans for Tk 400/550, and more economical units for Tk 200/300 and Tk 300/400.

The *Hotel Holy Side* (☎ 722278, fax 722279), close to Shah Jalal's shrine, is a new multistorey hotel; all rooms have air-con, hot water and satellite TV. Singles cost Tk 650 and Tk 850 while doubles range from Tk 800 to Tk 1700. There's also a restaurant here.

The *Parjatan Motel* (☎ 712426) is spacious and modern, but it's well out of town on a hill just south of the airport and is thus quite isolated. It has rooms with fan for Tk 500, rooms with air-con and TV for Tk 1000 and a decent but unatmospheric restaurant. It can also arrange car rentals.

Best of all is the lovely *Laakatoorah Tea Gardens Guest House* (☎ 712600). Located just north of town in the Laakatoorah tea estate, it has two large nicely furnished guest rooms with air-con (Tk 450 a room). You can reserve by calling the manager's office (☎ 716016). It features a front porch with wicker furnishings, a comfortable living room with sofas, TV and library, and a dining room where you can eat fairly cheaply.

Places to Eat – Budget
If you're staying in the Telihaor area, you'll have lots of choices, including the friendly *New Green Restaurant*, *Banani Restaurant* (no English sign) and the well-marked *Jamania Restaurant*, all on Telihaor Rd. You can get delicious hot puris at the Banani and good vegetable kebabs at the New Green, plus full meals for Tk 20 to Tk 25 at both. The similarly priced Jamania has received even better reviews from travellers. There are lots of similar places closer to Kean Bridge at Surma Market, including the popular *Suruli Restaurant* (no English sign) on Taltala Rd.

Similar places in Bandar Bazar include the *Oriental Restaurant* across the street. The *Ponchokhana Restaurant,* up on Zinda Bazar Rd is a bit more upmarket, with areas curtained off for women (local women are never seen at the preceding restaurants).

If you're further north on the same road, which becomes Airport Rd, you could try

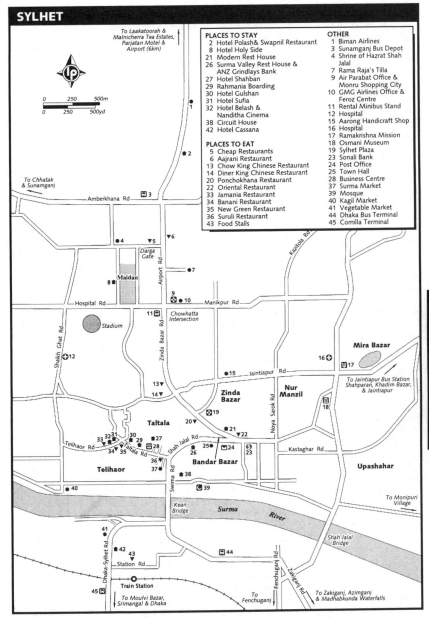

SYLHET

To Laakatoorah &
Malnicherra Tea Estates,
Parjatan Motel &
Airport (6km)

0   250   500m
0   250   500yd

PLACES TO STAY
2 Hotel Polash& Swapnil Restaurant
8 Hotel Holy Side
21 Modern Rest House
26 Surma Valley Rest House &
    ANZ Grindlays Bank
27 Hotel Shahban
29 Rahmania Boarding
30 Hotel Gulshan
31 Hotel Sufia
32 Hotel Belash &
    Nanditha Cinema
38 Circuit House
42 Hotel Cassana

PLACES TO EAT
5 Cheap Restaurants
6 Aajrani Restaurant
13 Chow King Chinese Restaurant
14 Diner King Chinese Restaurant
20 Ponchokhana Restaurant
22 Oriental Restaurant
33 Jamania Restaurant
34 Banani Restaurant
35 New Green Restaurant
36 Suruli Restaurant
43 Food Stalls

OTHER
1 Biman Airlines
3 Sunamganj Bus Depot
4 Shrine of Hazrat Shah
    Jalal
7 Rama Raja's Tilla
9 Air Parabat Office &
    Monru Shopping City
10 GMG Airlines Office &
    Feroz Centre
11 Rental Minibus Stand
12 Hospital
15 Aarong Handicraft Shop
16 Hospital
17 Ramakrishna Mission
18 Osmani Museum
19 Sylhet Plaza
23 Sonali Bank
24 Post Office
25 Town Hall
28 Business Centre
37 Surma Market
39 Mosque
40 Kagil Market
41 Vegetable Market
44 Dhaka Bus Terminal
45 Comilla Terminal

To Chhatak
& Sunamganj

Amberkhana Rd

Darga
Gate

Maidan

Airport Rd

Hospital Rd

Manikpur Rd

Chowhatta
Intersection

Kazitola Rd

Mira Bazar

To Jaintiapur Bus Station
Shahparan, Khadim Bazar,
& Jaintiapur

Shaikh Ghat Rd

Zinda Bazar Rd

Stadium

Jaintiapur Rd

Zinda
Bazar

Nur
Manzil

Taltala

Telihaor Rd

Taltala Rd

Shah Jalal Rd

Noya Sarok Rd

Bandar Bazar

Kastaghar Rd

Upashahar

Telihaor

Swima Rd

Kean
Bridge

Surma   River

To Monipuri
Village

Shah Jalal
Bridge

Dhaka-Sylhet Rd

Station Rd

To Moulvi Bazar,
Srimangal & Dhaka

Train Station

To
Fenchuganj

Fenchuganj Rd

Zakiganj Rd

To Zakiganj, Azimganj
& Madhabkunda Waterfalls

SYLHET DIVISION

the similar, well-marked *Aajrani Restaurant* or the establishments along the Darga Gate road to the Shrine of Shah Jalal.

Places to Eat – Top End

Two of the city's very best restaurants, both near the town centre, are the *Chow King Chinese Restaurant* (☎ 713651), on Zinda Bazar Rd, and *Diner King Chinese Restaurant* (☎ 718647), around the corner to the south. Both are nicely decorated and the food is excellent – good places to splurge if you've been eating meals for Tk 20 for too long. Dishes served at the Chow King include beef and onions, Thai prawns and Thai chicken, all for around Tk 100. It also has non-oriental selections. The Diner King is similar but cheaper, serving dishes such as sweet and sour chicken (Tk 80), Mandarin steamed fish (Tk 70) and fish with mushrooms (Tk 45).

The *Swapnil Restaurant* at Hotel Polash features mostly Bangladeshi food (eg, chicken tikka for Tk 95 and fish curry for Tk 55), but it also serves a number of Chinese selections. Some other hotel restaurant possibilities are the *restaurant* at the Parjatan Motel and the *Jharna Restaurant* at the Hotel Holy Side. *Hotel Shahban* has a TV and a restaurant with a wide selection of Bangladeshi dishes for around Tk 40 for a main course.

Shopping

The city's liveliest area is Bandar Bazar, which is in the heart of town and is bustling until midnight. You'll find just about anything and everything here. Smuggling goods from India is widespread, and around this bazar products from India such as cosmetics, confectionery and saris are widely available. The city also has some modern shopping establishments, in particular the ultra-modern three-storey Sylhet Plaza on Zinda Bazar Rd and the Feroz Centre near the Chowhatta.

Sylhet has a variety of handicrafts, including chairs, baskets, handbags, trays and lampshades made from locally grown cane. Floor mats called 'sital patis' are a speciality, and the exquisite home-spun fabrics of the Monipuri make colourful souvenirs. The best selection of such handicrafts and textiles is available at the Aarong outlet on Jaintiapur Rd, just over a block east of Zinda Bazar Rd.

Getting There & Away

It's worth taking a day trip by bus or train between Dhaka and Sylhet, as it's an interesting journey through varied countryside, with bits of seemingly wild jungle in the hills. Day buses sometimes make a brief stop in Brahmanbaria, although many do not stop at all.

Air GMG, Biman and Air Parabat all have frequent flights between Dhaka and Sylhet. GMG charges Tk 1770.

The Biman office (☎ 717076) is about 1km north of Amberkhana Rd on Airport Rd. The GMG office (☎ 711225) is in the Feroz Centre just to the east of Chowhatta intersection on Manikpur Rd. Air Parabat (☎ 715999) is in the Monru Shopping City building, next to the Feroz Centre.

Bus Buses for Dhaka, Zakiganj and Fenchuganj leave from the large bus station south of the river, most often referred to as Dhaka terminal, even though there are actually several separate terminals. Non-stop air-con chair coaches to Dhaka cost Tk 250, Tk 140 for an ordinary chair coach, and Tk 110 for an ordinary bus. The last bus departs around 11.30 pm. The trip takes about 6 hours (7 hours by ordinary bus). Buses to Fenchuganj cost Tk 10 and take about one hour, with the last bus departing from Sylhet around 8 pm. Buses to Zakiganj (Tk 35) take two hours, departing between 6 am and 7 pm.

In Dhaka, buses for Sylhet leave from Sayedabad bus station. There are lots of bus companies; one of the better ones is SylCom.

There are no direct buses to Chittagong. Those to Comilla leave from Comilla terminal on Dhaka-Sylhet Rd, south of the railway station. Fares are Tk 100 for ordinary buses and Tk 125 for a chair coach.

Buses north-east to Tamabil, Jaintiapur and the Indian border leave from the small Jaintiapur bus station on Jaintiapur Rd, several kilometres east of the centre of town, just beyond a UCB bank branch. They depart between 6.45 am and 5.35 pm. The trip to Jaintiapur (Tk 22) takes just under three hours; the Indian border is 8km further.

If you're headed west for Chhatak or Sunamganj, you'll find the bus station for these towns on Amberkhana Rd. It's possible to travel from Sunamganj to Mymensingh via Mohanganj, which involves a seven-hour boat ride from Sunamganj to Jaysiri and hiking or taking rickshaws from there to Mohanganj (see under Bicycle later in this section).

Train The train station (☎ 717036 for reservations) is on the south side of town. There are three express trains a day for Dhaka, departing at 7.30 am, 2.30 and 10 pm (winter hours). The trip normally takes about seven hours. There are also two daily trains to Chittagong, departing from Sylhet at 11.30 am and 10.30 pm and taking about 9½ hours. Only the night train to Dhaka has a sleeper car (Tk 470/650 fan/air-con). Fares are Tk 270/135 to Dhaka, Tk 180/95 to Comilla and Tk 320/170 to Chittagong in 1st class/sulob. Departures are reasonably punctual, so don't arrive late.

Car If you rent a vehicle at the Parjatan or Polash hotels, it'll cost you between Tk 1500 and Tk 2000, with petrol and driver. You can save money by negotiating with one of the taxi or minibus drivers at the airport, or in town on Airport Rd at the Chowhatta intersection, where they all hang out. A fair price would be Tk 1000 a day plus petrol. The easiest way to calculate petrol usage (vehicle petrol indicators rarely work) is to agree to pay for one litre for every eight to 10km travelled in the van (slightly more kilometres in a car).

Bicycle If you want to cycle in Sylhet, consider coming here by train from Dhaka with your bike, cycling around the Sylhet region and then cycling back to Dhaka via Mymensingh. The best route for this is the less-travelled route to Mymensingh via Chhatak, Sunamganj and Mohanganj. The trip takes

three or four days to Mymensingh, depending on whether you stop the first day in Chhatak. There are hotels in all of these towns.

The really fun section is between Sunamganj and Mohanganj, where the route virtually disappears from the maps. At Sunamganj you can take back roads and dirt tracks south-west to Mohanganj (you'll have to ask directions every few kilometres) or, much easier, you can catch a launch on the Surma River all the way to Jaysiri (an interesting and fun seven-hour trip), which is 15km or so from Mohanganj. Along the short route between Jaysiri and Mohanganj, you'll pass through Chandrabara and some very pleasant countryside.

From Mohanganj, which is a major town, and the halfway point between Sunamganj and Mymensingh, you can continue cycling south-west to Mymensingh (about 60km) or catch a train if you'd prefer.

To/From India It takes 2½ hours to get to Tamabil from Sylhet by bus, and a 15-minute hike to the border. It is then a further 1.5km walk to Dawki in India, from where buses run to Shillong, a 3½-hour trip. From Cherrapunji, 58km south of Shillong on a different road, the views over Bangladesh are superb.

Getting Around

The Airport Located 7km north of town, the airport has a post office, snack bar, and numerous taxis and baby taxis waiting outside. If you wish to rent a car or van by the day, do it here and save yourself the extra cost of a taxi into town (see under Car earlier in this section). For a vehicle into town, expect to pay about Tk 200 for a taxi, Tk 100 for a baby taxi and Tk 10 for a seat in a 10-seat tempo.

AROUND SYLHET
Tea Estates & Jaflang Area

To see the process of tea manufacturing, try the Laakatoorah Tea Estate, where the manager may lecture you on the history and production of this beverage in exchange for a tour of the factory. Malnicherra Tea Estate, which was the first tea estate in Bangladesh, dating back to 1857, offers tours as well. The Laakatoorah and Malnicherra tea estates are just beyond the city's northern outskirts on Airport Rd.

Just east of Sylhet are the Khadim Tea Gardens. From Khadim Bazar, which is 10km east of town, you can take a tempo there as they transport estate workers to and from their villages. Some 23km further east, 7km before Jaintiapur, you'll pass Lalakal Tea Estates on the right side of the road; its staff are accustomed to receiving visitors and they will gladly show you around.

The largest number of tea estates in the northern half of Sylhet Division are further on, around **Jaflang**, just beyond Tamabil and near the Indian border. This is one of the most scenic areas in the division, so definitely try to get here. It is also a major tribal area, where many Khasi are found. The bus from Sylhet takes 2½ hours to Tamabil and another half hour to Jaflang. You must constantly ask to be let off in Jaflang, as there are no signs and you can easily pass by it, causing much lost time.

There's a Bangladesh Tea Board guesthouse in nearby Sripur where you may be able to stay. There's more basic accommodation in Tamabil. If you tour Laakatoorah Tea Estate, the manager there (☎ 716016) may be able to help you make a reservation.

Shrine of Shah Paran
Some 8km east of Sylhet, just off the highway to Jaintiapur, is the Shrine of Shah Paran in Shahparan, a tiny village. It's a single-domed mosque that attracts some 2000 pilgrims a day; you'll see charter buses from Dhaka all around the place.

Jaintiapur
The town of Jaintiapur (JOINT-tah-poor) is two hours by bus (40km) north-east of Sylhet, on the road to Tamabil. Until the annexation of Sylhet by the British in 1835, it was the capital of the Jaintia kingdom of Jaintiapur, which included the Khasi and Jaintia Hills (modern-day Meghalaya) and the Plains of Jaintia.

Today, nothing remains of the old splendour of the Jaintia kingdom except a **rajbari**

in town and the **Temple of Kali** on its grounds. The rajbari is now in an extremely ruinous state and hardly worth seeing. It once had outer wall reliefs representing, among other things, horses and lions prancing in a tree. It formerly consisted of two grandiose palaces, one of which contained the Kali temple. This temple was widely feared in the district due to the frequent human sacrifices that took place upon its altars, and which ultimately led to the downfall of the Jaintia royal family.

Even more unusual and unexpected are a small group of striking **stone megaliths** nearby, which are a prominent landmark in the countryside. They're about 2½ metres high and grouped in odd numbers of three, five, seven or nine. There are around 20 such monuments in the vicinity of the rajbari, scattered over an area of about 1km. Unfortunately the monoliths are a popular local picnic spot and the area around them is filthy.

Also found in Meghalaya in neighbouring India, and very similar in shape to the menhirs found in England, Brittany, Ireland, Denmark and Scandinavia, these megaliths, blackened with age, bear historical and social significance, and are believed to be memorials to the chiefs of the Khashia tribe.

Madhabkunda Waterfall
A three-hour drive south-east of Sylhet (and equally accessible from Srimangal by road and rail), and 3km from Dakshinbagh train station, is the famous remote waterfall of Madhabkunda, which is pictured in many tourist brochures and attracts a good number of sightseers. Again, it is popular with busloads of Bangladeshi tourists and the area around is often covered with litter. This general area is also where you may be able to find some of the few elephants in Bangladesh, which are still being used as work animals, hauling huge logs.

Fenchuganj & Chhatak
Fenchuganj, a 45-minute bus ride south of Sylhet, is a fairly scenic town despite the huge fertiliser factory that operates on natural gas and produces half of the country's

Bird-Watching in the Sunamganj Haors

For a worthwhile tour of the Sunamganj haors, you'll need at least four days to find some exciting bird species. Baer's pochard is probably the rarest bird, and not difficult to spot if you're there at the right time; other pochards include the white-eyed and red-crested varieties. The baikal teal and the falcated teal are both impressive winterers, along with an assortment of crakes, including the ruddy crake and the little crake. You'll also see the spotted redshank and the blue-bearded bee-eater (pictured), and the assortment continues with various sandpipers and lapwings. A number of raptors are here as well, including several fishing eagles, such as the Pallas', grey-headed and spotted eagles. So little has been done to record species here, that it's not unreasonable to expect to see new, previously unrecorded birds during each trip.

The trip begins at Aila Haor, four hours upriver. A knowledgeable boatman will know exactly where to go. It's another two hours on foot into the haor area, but it's worth it for the rich birdlife awaiting. It may be dark by the time you return to the boat, so carry a torch (flashlight). You'll sleep on the boat and continue to Pasua early next morning.

Pasua Haor, four hours upriver, lies just over an embankment from the river. You can sit and watch the wildlife or walk for a couple of kilometres on the fringes of the marshy basin. After another four hours' travel the next morning, you'll arrive at Tangua Haor, bordering India and the furthest point of the trip. In this area, scrub and grassland are a bonus, and you'll see some interesting grassland species of birds.

On the return to Sunamganj, river travel is spartan yet peaceful, and it is an exceptional way to experience rural life in Bangladesh, where so much of it takes place on or near a river's edge.

Dave Johnson

total requirement of synthetic urea. The Halaluki haors about 12km west of town are a fine place for bird-watching.

Some 38km north-west of Sylhet, Chhatak has orange groves and cement and pulp factories, plus a sky ropeline used to transport lime from the hills. The cement factory, which is the largest of its kind in the country, has a *guesthouse* with four air-con rooms.

SUNAMGANJ

Approximately 70km west of Sylhet, this small town offers little for tourists. However, the local haors (wetlands) are rife with bird life, especially during mid-winter through to the end of March, and sometimes until the end of April. At this time, migrants, winterers and residents all get together for one big bird party. Varieties of rails, raptors, ducks, sandpipers and more congregate here. The three haors that seem to be the best for bird-watching are several hours upriver from the Sunamganj River. It's too far for a day trip, but overnight excursions and longer can be arranged in town.

Organised Tours

The best trip, which includes visiting all three haors, is a four-day affair. Except for true bird enthusiasts, this is probably more than most travellers want. Nevertheless, an overnight trip would get you out into some of the most fascinating rural areas in Bangladesh.

To arrange a trip into the haor area, the best person to see is Mr Shokat, master of two boats, the *Rubaia* and *Al-Amin*. He has considerable experience with bird-watchers and the haors, and has worked for ornithology survey teams. Ask for Mr Shokat, or mention either of his two boats by name, at Sachna Ghat, the boat dock area, (the entrance into Sunamganj). Smack in the middle of a line of food/tea/dry goods stalls is an 'office' with a desk and a few chairs, and, more than likely, several men sitting around. This is the Sunamganj Boat Owner's Association. If he's not there, someone will fetch him.

You can contact him during the day or evening before you want to go to set up a departure time (6 to 7 am is recommended) and decide on the length of the trip. His rate is Tk 1200 per day, but if there is a group (four sleep comfortably on the boat; if there are more than six, someone may have to curl up on the outside deck) it's not a bad deal. The boatmen cook the meals, you provide the food, or the money for food, and Mr Shokat will buy all supplies that evening. He'll need a cash advance to buy fuel and a few other necessities.

For the trip you'll need water, a mat, a sleeping bag of some sort and a torch (flashlight). A mosquito net would also be a good idea. Bird-watchers will want a scope; binoculars will suffice for the less serious.

Places to Stay

In the Sachna Ghat area there are two basic *hotels* that are spartan but not bad. In town, the best accommodation is at the *Circuit House*.

Getting There & Away

From Sylhet, there are regular buses to Sunamganj, leaving from the local bus depot on Amberkhana Road, soon to be renamed Sunamganj Bus Station. The trip takes about two hours.

SRIMANGAL
☎ 08626

Some 75km south of Sylhet, Srimangal (or Sreemongal) is the tea centre of Bangladesh. This hilly area, with tea estates, shade trees, lemon orchards and pineapple plantations everywhere, is one of the most picturesque parts of the country. For miles around you can see tea estates forming a perennially green carpet on the sloping hills. It's the one area besides the Sundarbans where in certain parts you can look

around and not see a single human being. This is particularly true of the dense Lowacherra Forest Reserve, 8km east of town. In short, if you're feeling overwhelmed by people everywhere, spend a few days in Srimangal. Visits to the rainforest and several of the tea estates, plus the slightly cooler climate, are the main attractions, although getting here by train from Dhaka is often half the fun.

The town itself is quite small. A single road, the Dhaka-Sylhet Rd, passes from one end to the other, with a four-way intersection in the middle. While Srimangal is of no particular interest, it has the bare essentials, including several banks, a restaurant or two, a tourist information agency that rents out bikes and a handful of hotels. Also, the locals are quite friendly.

If you're lucky you might get to stay in a guesthouse. A number of companies and organisations have them, but you'll have no chance unless you book in advance, usually by contacting the company's head office in Dhaka or Chittagong. The luckiest ones are those who get invited to stay for free at one of the private tea estates, virtually all of which have tiny guesthouses.

Information

There is no government tourist office, but there is one very enthusiastic amateur tour guide. If you don't seek out the ebullient local tailor Mr Razu, chances are better than even that he'll find you. His Classic Tourism and Media Centre (☎ 169), on the 2nd floor of a building right on the main intersection, is currently a tailor's and fabrics shop, but he has grand plans to turn it into a tourist office. He can help with finding hotels and restaurants and with planning excursions to tribal villages, tea estates and haors. He also rents out ordinary one-speed bicycles for Tk 100 per day, and better bikes for Tk 200 per day.

Places to Stay

There are several near-identical lower-end hotels, all well-marked establishments on the main drag, as well as two hotels with air-con rooms. One place worth avoiding is the Hotel

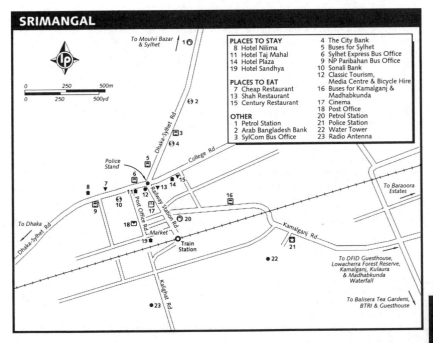

SRIMANGAL

To Moulvi Bazar & Sylhet

Police Stand

To Dhaka

To Baraoora Estates

To Dhaka

Market

Train Station

To Kamalganj Rd

To DFID Guesthouse, Lowacherra Forest Reserve, Kamalganj, Kulaura & Madhabkunda Waterfall

To Balisera Tea Gardens, BTRI & Guesthouse

PLACES TO STAY
8   Hotel Nilima
11 Hotel Taj Mahal
14 Hotel Plaza
19 Hotel Sandhya

PLACES TO EAT
7   Cheap Restaurant
13 Shah Restaurant
15 Century Restaurant

OTHER
1   Petrol Station
2   Arab Bangladesh Bank
3   SylCom Bus Office

4   The City Bank
5   Buses for Sylhet
6   Sylhet Express Bus Office
9   NP Paribahan Bus Office
10 Sonali Bank
12 Classic Tourism,
    Media Centre & Bicycle Hire
16 Buses for Kamalganj &
    Madhabkunda
17 Cinema
18 Post Office
20 Petrol Station
21 Police Station
22 Water Tower
23 Radio Antenna

Mukta, as we've received several letters about thefts from this place.

Coming from Dhaka, the first hotel you'll pass is the *Hotel Nilima*, a typical country hotel with singles/doubles for Tk 60/120 with attached bathrooms, fan and mosquito net.

About 250m away on the other side of the road is the *Hotel Taj Mahal*, a newish establishment with rooms for Tk 60/100. The rooms are small and the beds are rather hard, but at least it's clean.

Hotel Plaza (☎ 525), on College Rd, has room for private parking. Ordinary singles/doubles cost Tk 100/150, while larger air-con rooms are Tk 400/500. The hotel entrance is through a small shopping centre.

The only mid-range establishment in town is the *Hotel Sandhya* (☎ 243, 439), on the south side of the large concrete market building. Furnished air-con rooms cost Tk 300/600 with comfortable beds and decent bathrooms. Unfortunately the carpets tend to give off a musty odour that can't be dispelled by spraying sickly sweet air freshener, as much as the staff may try. There are also some cheaper single rooms that don't have air-con. They will cost you between Tk 60 and Tk 200.

Places to Eat

The *Shah Restaurant* in the heart of town, a few doors south of the main intersection, has good Bangladeshi food. You can get a filling meal for around Tk 25.

The *Century Restaurant* is the closest thing in town to a western restaurant, with snacks such as fried chicken rolls and hamburgers on the menu. It also serves a range of Bangladeshi food. It's located on the first floor just along from the Hotel Plaza on College Rd.

There's a *restaurant* on the main drag close to Hotel Mukta, and you may find *tea stalls* around the market near the railway station.

Getting There & Away

Bus Buses for Sylhet, including Sylhet Express, all have their offices on the main drag near the town's main intersection. Those headed east towards Kamalganj (Tk 10) and Madhabkunda leave from Kamalganj Rd. If you're headed to Dhaka or Comilla you can catch buses en route from Sylhet on the main drag in the centre of town. They stop along this route and hail passengers. Expect to pay about Tk 70 for the cheapest Dhaka buses, Tk 150 for a chair coach and Tk 250 for an air-con bus to Dhaka. Two bus companies running air-con and ordinary chair coaches with offices on the main road are SylCom and NP Paribahan.

Buses to Comilla cost about Tk 60 (Tk 110 for a chair coach), and to Sylhet Tk 30.

Train There are three trains a day in either direction to and from Dhaka. At the time of writing, departure times from Dhaka station were 7 am, 3.30 pm and 10 pm. According to the schedule, the trip takes five hours, but in reality it normally takes 5½ hours. These trains continue on to Sylhet. The summer and winter train schedules vary slightly, so it's best to check.

Fares vary per train. It costs Tk 200/110 for 1st class/sulob on the morning train; Tk 200/110 for 1st class/sulob on the afternoon train (Tk 300 for air-con); and Tk 350/110 for 1st class (sleeper)/sulob (Tk 500 for an air-con sleeper) on the evening train. Only the evening train has sleepers. Air-con compartments and sleepers must normally be booked at least several days in advance, and in practice you must book them to Sylhet, which costs about 20% more.

Heading back to Dhaka, you can take trains at 9 am, 4 pm and 11.30 pm. Only the afternoon and evening trains have air-con compartments and only the evening train has sleepers.

You can also travel from Chittagong to Sylhet via Comilla and Srimangal twice a day by express train; the trip takes about eight hours to Srimangal and 9½ hours to Sylhet. One train departs from Chittagong at around 10.30 am, arriving in Srimangal in the late afternoon, the other leaves Chittagong at 9 pm, arriving in Srimangal around 5 am. Trains to Chittagong depart from Sylhet at 11.30 am and 10.30 pm, arriving in Srimangal about 90 minutes later. The fare to Chittagong is Tk 260/150 1st class/sulob. Only the night train has air-con sleepers (Tk 395).

AROUND SRIMANGAL
Cycling

The area around Srimangal is one of the best in Bangladesh for cycling. Despite the rolling terrain, the roads are reasonably level, so even the ubiquitous one-speed Chinese bike can be used. Certainly the Bangladeshis find the hills no trouble for cycling.

There's an intricate network of roads connecting all the tea estates to the main highways. Only the major routes are tarred or bricked, but even the numerous dirt roads are, by necessity, in good condition so that the tea can be easily transported to market.

Most tea estates have guest lodges for friends, relatives and visitors from Dhaka. If you show up at a tea estate in the afternoon, you'll be such a novelty that if you ask for a room for the night, chances are they may be only too happy to oblige. If not, you can try the next tea estate down the road. There are so many tea estates all over the area that your chances of getting a room for the night are good. Cycling around here could well be your most enjoyable time spent in Bangladesh.

Tea Estates

There are so many tea estates that it's not easy to determine which are the best for visiting. Some are more receptive to showing visitors around than others. One of the most frequently visited gardens is Madabpore Tea Gardens, which has a lake on its premises. The turn-off for the gardens is about 1.75km beyond the DFID compound.

Two of the largest estates are Deanston and Rajghat, which are close to one another and well south of Srimangal, many kilometres past the BTRI complex and the Balisera Tea Gardens, managed by Finlays. Other tea estates that are good for viewing are scattered far and wide in the greater

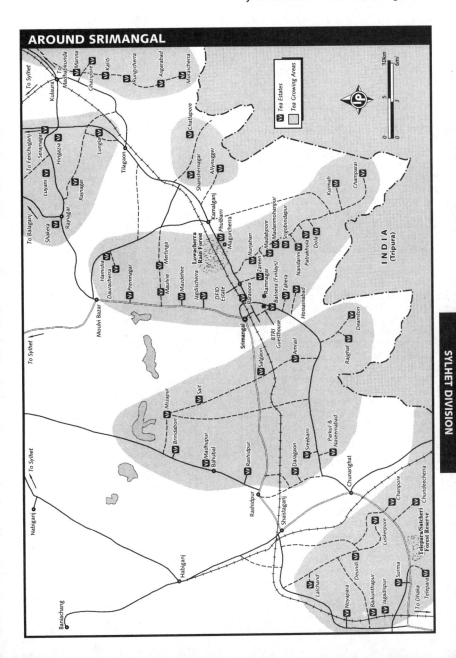

Srimangal area, and are shown on the regional map, Around Srimangal.

Places to Stay It is possible to stay at the *Bangladesh Tea Research Institute Guesthouse (☎ 225)* as long as it isn't full. There are only three double rooms, costing Tk 300 per person, so it's best to try and book in advance if possible. Meals are available for about Tk 200 per day. The guesthouse is charming, with a verandah to relax on in the evenings. One week each month it is possible to stay at the BTRI Management Training Centre Guesthouse in the same compound, where there are four air-con double rooms for Tk 400.

Staying at the wonderful *DFID Estate (☎ 207),* which is run by the Department for International Development and can be found about 3km from Srimangal, is highly recommended if you can afford it. Lawns surround the main building and guest bungalows, and there is a swimming pool, tennis and badminton courts, satellite TV and bar. There are eight double rooms here, with all mod cons; four in the annexe attached to the main building (Tk 1400) and four in two bungalows (Tk 1600). There is also a VIP annexe, which costs Tk 1700 per night if it is available. Three meals a day cost an additional Tk 750. Bills must be paid for in cash (taka).

It is necessary to have permission from the estate manager, Mr MH Choudhury, to stay here, so try to make an advance booking. Priority is given to official British aid workers.

Lowacherra Forest Reserve

Some 8km east of Srimangal on the road to Kamalganj, Lowacherra Forest is not to be missed, especially if you're a birdwatcher. The local name for the forest is Shaymoli. It extends for only a few kilometres, but the terrain is hilly and the vegetation is fairly thick, thus slowing your walk. Fortunately, this forest is in an area that's not so heavily populated. Consequently it's less threatened than Madhupur Forest in Dhaka division.

There are unmarked trails to follow, but you can wander off without fear of getting lost. Look for wild orchids growing in the upper branches of trees, and keep an eye out for gibbons that make lots of noise as their troupe swings through the branches in the upper canopy. The blue-bearded bee-eater and the red-breasted trogon are a couple of interesting birds to watch for in addition to the variety of forest birds that show up. Take care during the wet season, as leeches are not unheard of here.

Getting There & Away From Srimangal, take the paved road east towards Kamalganj. The poorly marked turn-off to your left (north), which is easy to miss, is about 4.75km past the ODA compound and another 2.75km beyond the well-marked turn-off for the Nurjahan and Madabpore tea estates. The dirt road into the forests, which crosses the railroad tracks, is less than a kilometre long and thus an easy walk.

Tribal Villages

There are 11 Khashia villages and several Monipuri villages in the Srimangal area, scattered among the tea plantations. Khashia villages (called *punji*) are usually on hilltops surrounded by betel nut trees, their cash crop. When visiting a Khashia village you should first call in on the local chief, as the community will not extend full hospitality without his permission. The Magurcherra Khashia punji is on the edge of the ruined Magurcherra gas field, 8km from Srimangal on the road to Kamalganj. The gas field caught fire in 1997 and was ablaze for three months, laying waste to betel nut plantations and tea estates in the vicinity.

There is a Monipuri village called Ramnagar very close to the Bangladesh Tea Research Institute; if you call in on the institute they will be able to give you directions. A Monipuri village is usually called a *para*.

Telepara/Satcheri Forest Reserve

About 60km south-west from Srimangal on the Dhaka-Sylhet highway is the small Telepara/Satcheri Forest Reserve. Similar to the Lowacherra Forest Reserve, this reserve provides a good habitat for quite a number of forest birds and small animals. There is a track heading into the forest from

Tea Gardens & Tea Estates

Tea production in Bangladesh dates from 1857, when Malnicherra Tea Estate, just north of Sylhet, was set up by the British. The tea grew well here and by the end of the century there were some 150 tea estates, almost all under British ownership. Approximately the same number exists today, but since independence, only 48% are British-owned. The rest mainly belong to wealthy Bangladeshis and, to a lesser extent, the government's Tea Board. In some cases, British companies, most notably Finlays and Duncan, manage the estates but are not themselves the owners.

When the British began growing tea in Sylhet, they didn't bother training the indigenous people. Rather, they brought over experienced Indian labourers, mainly from tea estates in Bihar, Orissa and Bangla (West Bengal). Today, virtually all of the labourers, or 'coolies', are descendants of these original Hindus, living in colonies established by those first brought here. Small Hindu shrines are a common feature of tea estates with worker colonies.

Each estate provides an elementary school (and a doctor). Since many of the estates are in remote locations, few of the workers' children are able to go beyond the primary grades. However, the tea workers have the only trade union in Bangladesh that effectively bargains with management, so their contracts often include special privileges, such as a festival allowance. New Year's Eve is one of the most festive times, in part because the tea season is over. The Hindu religion does not ban alcohol and many workers get a bit tipsy at festival time. Several private 'clubs' outside Srimangal cater to the owners and managers year round. Faced with these long-standing traditions, the government looks the other way.

Generally even the smallest estates are at least a thousand hectares. Because each requires its own processing plant, a sizeable production is necessary to be profitable. Most estates have excess land from which timber can be sold in bad years to generate a profit.

The trees can last for 80 years, but they are usually replaced after 50. Since the mid-1980s, production has increased significantly with a new dwarf variety of tea plant that allows the trees to be planted much closer together. Bangladeshi tea is a black variety of ordinary quality and is mainly combined with teas that must be blended, such as Kenyan tea. Virtually all of it is sold by auction companies in Chittagong and shipped to Europe to be mixed. It ends up mostly in lower-end markets, typically Eastern Europe, Russia and parts of the Middle East.

If you come to Srimangal or Sylhet, visiting a tea estate is a must. The colourfully dressed female pickers are a picturesque sight, and a tour of the factory can be fascinating. The equipment in some of these factories is very old. Some of it is even the original machinery. However, don't make the mistake of touring on a Friday, the day of rest, or visiting between mid-December and the 1st of March, as everything will be at a standstill. The picking season is during the rainier months from early March to early December and the factories are in full operation.

the main road, which eventually leads to a sandy ravine and an old, grown-over logging road/path. Follow this path and you'll come to a tea plantation at the edge of the forest and will be able to loop back (left) across the ravine and follow the continuation of the path through the forest. Though this 'logging' path is the best one, there are other ill-defined tracks throughout the forest.

Getting There & Away The forest is on the south side of the main road, about 1km east of the Satcheri bus stop/Telepara Tea Estate, just where the highway takes a sharp left (hairpin) bend. You could get the driver of the Dhaka-Sylhet bus to drop you here if you don't mind missing the early hours when bird-watching is best. Alternatively, you could get a bus from Srimangal to Telepara, which is well marked, and walk to the trailhead a kilometre away. To return to Srimangal you could try flagging one of the Dhaka-Sylhet buses, which tend to be full, or walk back to Telepara and catch one there.

Language

Bangla is the national language of Bangladesh and the official language of the state of Bangla (West Bengal) in India. Bangla is the easternmost of the Indo-European languages and finds its roots in Pali, the local speech of Bengal, which is a *prokrit* or vernacular language. In addition to Arabic, Urdu and Persian words, the Sanskrit of Brahmin Hindus was assimilated into the local speech, giving Bengali a strong resemblance to Hindi, with some variation in pronunciation. The vocabulary was further expanded through contact with European traders and merchants. Today, Bangla has a number of regional variations but remains essentially the same throughout Bangladesh.

History

The modern development of Bangla as a symbol of the cultural separateness of Bangladesh began under the British. In keeping with the Raj's policy of working within local cultures, Bangla was taught to officers, who used it in their dealings with locals. This resulted in the fusion of the vernacular of the peasants with high-caste literary Bangla, which had fallen into disuse under Muslim rulers who favoured Urdu. The Hindus took enthusiastically to Bangla, seeing it as a way of reasserting their cultural heritage, and the 19th century saw a renaissance in Bangla literature. Rabindranath Tagore gave Bangla literature kudos when he won the Nobel Prize for literature (see Literature in the Facts about Bangladesh chapter for more information).

It wasn't until partition, and the departure of most of the Hindu ruling class, that Bangladeshi intellectuals felt the need for Bangla as a means of defining their culture and nationalism.

There is a much lower proportion of English speakers in Bangladesh than in India. It's surprising how many conversations you can have in which you *think* that you're being understood. English has lapsed for three main reasons: there aren't distinct regional languages which make a lingua franca necessary; the symbolic importance of Bangla in the independence movement; and the many weaknesses in the public education system. In recent years, however, the value of English has risen considerably, especially if the number of colleges and schools advertising tuition is anything to go by.

Making the effort to learn some Bangla will not only be appreciated, at times it's your only hope. You'll find that most billboards and street signs are written in Bangla script only.

Lonely Planet's *Bengali phrasebook*, if you'll allow us to boast a bit, is extremely useful. There are a few Bangla phrasebooks available in Dhaka in the New Market bookshops, though the standard of English in some isn't very good. The Heed Language Centre in Dhaka produces a useful Bangla-English/English-Bangla dictionary and a basic course instruction booklet. See Language Courses in the Facts for the Visitor chapter for more information.

Pronunciation

Pronunciation of Bangla is made difficult by the fact that the language includes a variety of subtle sounds with no equivalents in English. To make this language guide easier to use for basic communication we haven't tried to cover all the sounds, instead using nearest English equivalents – you should have no trouble making yourself understood.

With regard to word stress, a good rule of thumb is to place the emphasis on the first and last syllables of words.

a	as in 'cat'
ā	as in 'father'
b	as in the English 'b' but often as 'v'
ch	as in 'chant'

e	as in 'bet'
i	as in 'police'
j	as in 'jet'
o	as in 'hot'
ō	as in 'hold'
u	as in 'put'
v	a cross between 'v' and 'w'
w	a cross between 'v' and 'w'
y	as in 'boy'

Useful Verbs

Two useful verbs are *āchhe* (there is, has), and *lāgbe* (need). You can ask *khānā āche?* (Is there food?) or *bāngti āche?* (Do you have change?) The negative form of *āche* is simply *nāi*. Saying *bāksheesh nāi* means you don't have any *bāksheesh* to give. You can say *pāni lāgbe* (lit: water is needed), or say *lāgbe nā* (lit: don't need) to turn down any unwanted offer.

Āchā

Āchā, the subcontinent's ambiguous 'OK/ Yes/I see' is used widely, but the local slang equivalent is *tik āssāy* or just *tik*. *Ji* or *hā* is more positive – if the rickshaw-wallah answers *āchā* to your offered price, expect problems at the other end; if it's *tik* or *ji* he won't demand more money. Well, not much more, anyway.

Greetings & Civilities

Men might hear people greet them with *bāhādur*, an honorific implying that you're wise and wealthy and should pay top price. Married or otherwise 'respectable' women might be addressed as *begum*, roughly the equivalent of 'Madam'. However, most often you'll be referred to as *bondhu* (friend).

'Please' and 'Thank you' are rarely used in Bangla. Instead, these sentiments are expressed indirectly in polite conversation. The absence of these should not be misread as rudeness. If you want to thank someone, you may use the equivalent Bangla phrase for 'Thank you (very much)', *(onek) donyobād*, or alternatively, pay them a compliment.

Bangla Greetings

Greetings vary in Bangla according to religion and custom. The Muslims greeting is *āsālām wālekum* (peace be on you). The response is *wālekum āsālām* (unto you, also peace). Hindus say *nomashkār* when greeting and saying goodbye. This is accompanied by the gesture of joining the open palms of both hands and bringing them close to the chest.

Hello. (Muslim greeting)	*āsālām wālekum*
(response)	*wālekum āsālām*
Hello. (Hindu greeting)	*nomāshkār*
Goodbye.	*khudā hāfiz*
See you later.	*pore dakhā hobe*
See you again.	*ābār dekā hobe*
Excuse me/ Forgive me.	*māf korun*
Yes.	*ji*
No.	*nā*
Not any/None.	*nāi*
It's all right/ No problem.	*tik āche*

Small Talk

How are you?	*(āpni) kāmon āchen?*
I'm well.	*bhālo āchi*
What's your name?	*āpnār nām ki?*
My name is ...	*āmār nām ...*
Where are you from?	*āpnār desh ki?*
My country is ...	*āmār desh ...*
How old are you?	*kotō boyosh?*
Do you like ...?	*āpnār ... bhālo lāgge?*
I like it very much.	*āmār khub bhālo lāgge*
I don't like ...	*āmār ... bhālo lāgge nā*
What do you want?	*ki lāgbe?*
Do you smoke?	*cigarette khāben?*
It's available.	*pāwā jāi*
It's not available.	*pāwā jāi nā*

Language Difficulties

I understand.	*āmi bujhi*
I don't understand.	*āmi bujhi nā*
Do you speak English?	*āpni english/ingreji bōlte pāren?*
I speak a little Bangla.	*āmi ektu bānglā bōlte pāri*

Please write it down.	*likhte pāren*
How do you say ... in Bangla?	*bānglāi ... ki bole?*

Getting Around

I want to go to ...	*āmi ... jābo*
Where is this bus going?	*ey bās kotāi jābe?*
When does the ... leave/arrive?	*kokhōn ... chārbe/ pōchābeh?*
boat	*nōukā/launch*
bus	*bās*
train	*tren*
car	*gāri*
rickshaw	*richkshā*

Where is ...?	*... kotāi?*
How far is ...?	*... kōto dur?*
I want to go to Dhaka.	*āmi dhākā jābo*
I'm going to Chittagong.	*chittāgong jāchi*
Go straight ahead.	*shojā jan*

left	*bāme*
right	*dāne*
here	*ekhāne*
there	*okhāne*
before	*āge*
after	*pore*
above	*upore*
below	*niche*
north	*uttor*
south	*dokkin*
east	*purbodik*
west	*pōsh-chim*

Around Town

For many words, such as 'station', 'hotel' and 'post office', the English word will be understood.

Where is the ...?	*... kotāi?*
bank	*bank*
change (money)	*bhāngti*
embassy	*embassy*
hospital	*hāshpātāl*
market	*bājār*

Signs

ভিতর	Enter
বাহির	Exit
ধুমপান নিষেদ	No Smoking
হোটেল	Hotel
বাস	Bus
শৌচাগার	Toilets
মহিলা	Ladies (also bus seats reserved for women)
পুরুষ	Men

Cities

ঢাকা	Dhaka
খুলনা	Khulna
রাজশাহি	Rajshahi
সিলেট	Sylhet
চট্গ্রাম	Chittagong
বরিশাল	Barisal

mosque	*moshjid*
palace	*rājbāri*
post office	*pōst offish*
temple (Hindu)	*mondir*
town	*tāun*
village	*grām*

What time does it open/close?	*kokhōn khole/ bondo-hoy?*
Where is the toilet?	*pāikhānā kotāi?*
What is this?	*etā ki?*
When?	*kokhōn?*
How much?	*kōto?*

Accommodation

Is there a hotel/ guesthouse nearby?	*kāche kōno hōtel/ guesthouse āche ki?*
Do you have a room?	*rum āche?*
I'd like to book a room ...	*āmi ektā rum buk ... korbo*
for one person	*ekjon thākbe*
for two people	*duijon thākbe*
How much is it ...?	*... tākte kōto tākā lāgbe?*
per night	*ek dine*
per person	*ek jon*

May I see the room?	*rum dekte pāri?*
Is there a toilet?	*pāikānā āche?*

Shopping

How much does it cost?	*dām kōto?*
It's too expensive.	*etā ōnek beshi dām*
bookshop	*boyer dokān*
chemist/pharmacy	*oshuder dokān*
clothing store	*kāporer dokān*
laundry	*kāpor dhobār dokān*

Food

I'm a vegetarian.	*āmi shudhu shobji khāi*
breakfast	*nāshtā*
lunch	*dupurer khābār*
dinner	*rāter khābār*
restaurant	*resturent*
beef	*gorur māngshō*
bread	*ruti/nān*
chicken	*murgi*
chilli	*morich*
egg	*dim*
fish	*māch*
food	*kābhār*
fruit	*p'hol*
meat	*māngshō*
milk	*dudh*
mutton	*khāsir māngshō*
rice	*bhāt*
salt	*lobon*
sugar	*chini*
tea	*bhāt*
vegetable	*shobji*
water	*pāni*
(sweetened) yoghurt	*(mishti) doy*
apple	*āpel*
banana	*kolā*
coconut	*nārikel*
jackfruit	*kātāl*
mango	*ām*
pineapple	*ānārosh*
orange	*komlā*

Health

I need/(My friend needs) a doctor.	*āmār/(āmār bondhur) dāktār lāgbe*

Emergencies

Please help me!	*āmāke shāhājjo koren!*
Go away!	*jāo!*
Call a doctor/the police!	*dāktār/pulish lāgbe!*
I've been robbed. (of things)	*āmār jinnish churi hoyecheh*
I've been robbed. (of money)	*āmār tākā churi hoyecheh*
I'm lost.	*āmi hāriye ghechi*
Where is the toilet?	*pāikhānā kōtāi?*

I'm a (diabetic/epileptic).	*āmār (diābetes/mirghi rog) āche*
I'm allergic to antibiotics/penicillin.	*āmār (āntibiotikeh/penisillineh) āllergy āche*
I'm pregnant.	*āmi pregnant*
antiseptic	*savlon*
aspirin	*aspirin*
condom	*kondom*
nausea	*bomi-bhāb*
sanitary napkins	*softex/modess* (brand names)

Time & Dates

What is the time?	*kōto bāje?*
2.45	*pōne tin tā* (quarter to three)
1.30	*der tā* (one thirty)
4.15	*shōā chār tā* (quarter past four)
hour	*ghontā*
day	*din*
week	*shoptā*
month	*māsh*
year	*bochor*
date (calendar)	*tārikh*
today	*āj*
tonight	*āj rāte*
tomorrow	*āgāmikāl*
yesterday	*gotokāl*
in the morning	*shokāle*
in the afternoon	*bikāle*
night	*rāt*
every day	*prōti din*
always	*shob shomoy*

now	*ekhon*		11	*egārō*
later	*pore*		12	*bārō*
			13	*terō*
Monday	*shombār*		14	*chod-dō*
Tuesday	*mongolbār*		15	*ponerō*
Wednesday	*budhbār*		16	*shōlō*
Thursday	*brihoshpotibār*		17	*shoterō*
Friday	*shukrobār*		18	*āt-hārō*
Saturday	*shonibār*		19	*unish*
Sunday	*robibār*		20	*bish*
			30	*tirish*

Numbers

Counting up to 20 is easy, but after that it becomes complicated, as the terms do not follow sequentially. In Bangla 21 is not *bish-ek* or *ek-bish* but *ekush*; 45 is actually *poy-chollish* but the simpler *pāch-chollish* is understood.

			40	*chollish*
			50	*ponchāsh*
			60	*shātt*
			70	*shottur*
			80	*āshi*
1	*ek*		90	*nobboy*
2	*dui*		100	*ekshō*
3	*tin*		1000	*ek hājār*
4	*chār*		100,000	*ek lākh*
5	*pāch*			
6	*ch-hoy*		ten million	*ek koti*
7	*shāt*			
8	*āt*		1/2	*shāre*
9	*noy*		1/4	*shoā*
10	*dosh*		3/4	*pōne*
			1-1/2	*der*
			2-1/2	*ārāi*

Glossary

The following is a list of unfamiliar words and acronyms that you may come across in this book or on your travels through Bangladesh.

animism – the belief that natural objects, phenomena, and the universe itself have desires and intentions

baby taxis – mini auto-rickshaws with three wheels
baksheesh – donation, tip or bribe, depending on the context
Bangla – *see* Bengali; also the new name for the Indian state of West Bengal
bangla – architectural style associated with the Pre-Mauryan and Mauryan period (312–232 BC); exemplified by a bamboo-thatched hut with a distinctively curved roof
baras – old houseboats
bawalis – timber workers in the Sundarbans
bazar – market
Bengali – the national language of Bangladesh, where it is known as Bangla, and the official language of the state of Bangla (formerly West Bengal) in India
bhang – powdered marijuana extract
bhikkus – Buddhist monks
BIWTC – Bangladesh Inland Waterway Transport Corporation
BNP – Bangladesh Nationalist Party
BRAC – Bangladesh Rural Advancement Committee
BRTC – Bangladesh Road Transport Corporation
buraq – winged creature that carried Mohammed from Jerusalem to heaven and back

cantonment – administrative and military area
caravanserai – traditional accommodation for camel caravans
carnapuli – a zoo of painted cement animals
chai – milky sweet tea
chair coach buses – modern buses with adjustable seats and lots of leg room

chan-chala – type of hut design
char – a river or delta island made of silt, highly fertile but highly susceptible to flooding and erosion
chaturmukhar – a structure with all four walls decorated with stone images of gods
chilla – place of meditation
coasters – minivans
crore – 10 million
cupola – domed roof or ceiling

dachala – gatehouse
dacoity – armed robbery
Dak Bungalow – a guesthouse for government officials
do-chala – a hut-shaped pavilion
dupatta – a long scarf worn by Bangladeshi women, draped over the shoulders to cover the chest; also called *orna*

eid – Muslim holiday
encaustic – ceramics decorated by burning in colours, especially by inlaying coloured clays

fakir – a Muslim who has taken a vow of poverty, but also applied to Hindu ascetics

ganja – marijuana
gema – type of wood that is felled in the Sundarbans
ghat – steps or landing on a river
guarni jaur–cyclone

hammam – a sort of bathroom
haors – wetlands
hartals – strikes, ranging from local to national
hazrat – Muslim saint

jamdani – ornamental loom-embroidered muslin or silk
Jamuna River – the name for the Brahmaputra River when it flows into Bangladesh
jatra – folk theatre
jhum – slash-and-burn agriculture
jor bangla – twin hut architectural style

kabigan – debate conducted in verse
kantha – embroidered, quilted patchwork cloth, often with folk motifs
khyang – Buddhist temple
kuthi – factories

lakh – one hundred thousand (100,000)
lingam – phallic symbol of *Shiva* the Creator

mahavihara – large monastery
maidan – open grassed area in a town or city, used as a parade ground during the *Raj*
mandir – temple
mau – honey; *also* madhu
maualis – honey gatherers in the Sundarbans
mazars – graves
mela – festival
mihrab – niche in Mosque positioned to face Mecca; Muslims face in this direction when they pray
mishuk – smaller, less colourful version of a *baby taxi*
mohajons – rickshaw or taxi fleet owners
Mughal – the Muslim dynasty of Indian emperors from Babur to Aurangzeb (16th-18th century)
Mukti Bahini – the Bangladesh Freedom Fighters, led by Ziaur Rahman during the Liberation War
mullah – Muslim scholar, teacher or cleric
mustan – mafia-style bosses who demand, and receive, payment from baby taxi drivers, roadside vendors, or people living on public land

naan – Indian flat bread
nava-ratna – nine towered; used to describe certain mosques
nawab – Muslim prince
NGO – non-government organisation, a catch-all phrase for a variety of non-profit aid and development agencies

orna – *see* dupatta
oshok – banyan tree

paan – a mild intoxicant made from betel nut, lime and some spices wrapped in an edible leaf; sold from stalls across the country, paan is responsible for the red spit blotches seen just about everywhere

Padma River – the name for the Ganges River as it flows through Bangladesh
pagoda – *see* stupa
paisa – unit of currency; there are 100 paisa in a taka
pancha-ratna – five-spice powder
Parjatan – the official Bangladesh government tourist organisation
pashi – a blistering wind that blows through the day in April
pir – a Sufi religious leader
polligiti – village songs
pukka – genuine; permanent

qawwali – Islamic devotional song

Radhna-Krishna – a cult distinctive to eastern Indian and Bangladeshi Hinduism, centred on the tale of Krishna's love affair with the female cowherd Radha
Raj – also called the British Raj; the period of British government in the Indian Subcontinent, roughly from the mid-18th century to the mid-20th century
raj – rule or sovereignty
raja – ruler, landlord or king
rajbari – Raj-era palace built by a *zamindar*
REB – Rural Electrification Board
rekha – buildings with a square sanctum on a raised platform
rest house – government-owned guesthouse
rickshaw – small, two-wheeled bicycle-driven passenger vehicle
rickshaw-wallah – rickshaw driver

sadar – the central section of a city
sadhus – spiritual men
sal – hardwood tree
salwar kameez – women's outfit, comprising a long, dress-like tunic (the kameez) and a pair of baggy trousers (the salwar)
sari – traditional women's clothing; a six foot length of material wrapped in a complicated fashion around the body
shankhari – Hindu artisan
Shia – Islamic sect that sees the authority of Mohammed as continuing through 'Ali, his son-in-law
shishu park – children's park
Shiva – Hindu god; the destroyer, the creator
slash-and-burn – a form of agriculture

sona – gilded dome
stupa – Buddhist religious monument
Subedhar – provincial governor
Sufi – ascetic Muslim mystic
sulob – upper 2nd class on a train (with reserved seating)
Sunni – school of Islamic thought that sees the authority of Mohammed as continuing through Abu Bakr, the former governor of Syria

tea estate – terraced hillside where tea is grown; *also* tea garden
tempo – auto-rickshaw
thana – the lowest political administrative division in Bangladesh; divisions (like a state or a province) are divided into districts, and districts are divided into thanas

tik-tiki – gecko
tolars – motorised passenger boats

UBINIG – the acronym for the organisation Unnayan Bikalper Nitinirdharoni Gobeshona, which stands for 'Policy Research for Development Alternatives'
uchango – classical music
upazila – local-level government

veena – Indian stringed instrument

WAPDA – Water and Power Development Authority

zamindar – landlord; also the name of the feudal landowner system itself
zila – district

LONELY PLANET

You already know that Lonely Planet produces more than this one guidebook, but you might not be aware of the other products we have on this region. Here is a selection of titles which you may want to check out as well:

Read this first Asia & India
ISBN 1 86450 049 2
US$14.99 • UK£8.99 • 99FF

Healthy Travel Asia & India
ISBN 1 86450 051 4
US$5.95 • UK£3.99 • 39FF

India
ISBN 0 86442 687 9
US$25.95 • UK£15.99 • 190FF

Indian Himalaya
ISBN 0 86442 688 7
US$19.95 • UK£12.99 • 160FF

Bengali phrasebook
ISBN 0 86442 312 8
US$5.95 • UK£3.50 • 45FF

Trekking in the Indian Himalaya
ISBN 0 86442 357 8
US$17.95 • UK£11.99 • 140FF

Trekking in the Nepal Himalaya
ISBN 0 86442 511 2
US$17.95 • UK£10.99 • 140FF

Nepal
ISBN 0 86442 704 2
US$19.95 • UK£12.99 • 160FF

Bhutan
ISBN 0 86442 483 3
US$19.95 • UK£12.99 • 160FF

Available wherever books are sold.

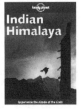

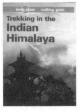
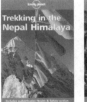

Index

Text

Bold indicates maps.